Lecture Notes in Artificial Intelligence 7670

Subseries of Lecture Notes in Computer Science

Fabio Massimo Zanzotto   Shusaku Tsumoto
Niels Taatgen   Yiyu Yao (Eds.)

Brain Informatics

International Conference, BI 2012
Macau, China, December 4-7, 2012
Proceedings

 Springer

Series Editors

Randy Goebel, University of Alberta, Edmonton, Canada
Jörg Siekmann, University of Saarland, Saarbrücken, Germany
Wolfgang Wahlster, DFKI and University of Saarland, Saarbrücken, Germany

Volume Editors

Fabio Massimo Zanzotto
University of Rome "Tor Vergata", 00133 Roma, Italy
E-mail: fabio.massimo.zanzotto@uniroma2.it

Shusaku Tsumoto
Shimane University, Shimane 693-8501, Japan
E-mail: tsumoto@computer.org

Niels Taatgen
University of Groningen, 9747 AG Groningen, The Netherlands
E-mail: niels@ai.rug.nl

Yiyu Yao
University of Regina, SK, Canada S4S 0A2
E-mail: yyao@cs.uregina.ca

ISSN 0302-9743   e-ISSN 1611-3349
ISBN 978-3-642-35138-9   e-ISBN 978-3-642-35139-6
DOI 10.1007/978-3-642-35139-6
Springer Heidelberg Dordrecht London New York

Library of Congress Control Number: 2012952029

CR Subject Classification (1998): I.2, H.3-5, F.1-2, H.2.8, I.4-5

LNCS Sublibrary: SL 7 – Artificial Intelligence

Typesetting: Camera-ready by author, data conversion by Scientific Publishing Services, Chennai, India

Printed on acid-free paper

Springer is part of Springer Science+Business Media (www.springer.com)

Preface

This volume contains the papers selected for presentation of the technical sessions and invited special session of the 2012 International Conference on Brain Informatics (BI 2012) organized by the Web Intelligence Consortium (WIC), IEEE Computational Intelligence Society Task Force on Brain Informatics (IEEE-CIS TF-BI), and University of Macau.

Brain Informatics 2012 was organized under the umbrella of the 2012 World Intelligence Congress (WIC 2012) in Macau, a special event of the Alan Turing Year (centenary of Alan Turing's birth), and it was held jointly with other four international conferences: Active Media Technology 2012 (AMT 2012), Methodologies for Intelligent Systems 2012 (ISMIS 2012), IEEE/WIC/ACM Web Intelligence 2012 (WI 2012), and IEEE/WIC/ACM Intelligent Agent Technology 2012 (IAT 2012). The WIC aims to facilitate interactions and exchange of ideas among researchers working on a variety of focused themes under intelligent informatics.

Brain informatics (BI) is an emerging interdisciplinary and multi-disciplinary research field that focuses on studying the mechanisms underlying the human information processing system (HIPS). BI investigates the essential functions of the brain, ranging from perception to thinking, and encompassing such areas as multi-perception, attention, memory, language, computation, heuristic search, reasoning, planning, decision making, problem solving, learning, discovery, and creativity.

This field goes along with the mainstreams of both medical science and information science. Medical research aims at the understanding of the structure and function of the human body: anatomy looks for structure behind a given function, and physiology studies a function achieved by interaction between components, which are analogous with geometry and algebra in mathematics. Brain research can be understood in the same framework, although methods for research were very much limited, compared with other medical fields. In the end of the last century, rapid progress in brain image and electrophysiological measurements changed such research environments and we can easily measure brain functions by combinations of imaging and signal processing. For example, functional MRI depicts the temporal change of activities in brains, which gives insights into cognitive function from the information on structure, and EEG topography gives information about brain structure from the measurements of brain signals. However, all the technologies introduced have limitations for understanding brain functions, due to one important missing point: the introduction of informatics. Since a brain is a highly advanced information processing device, higher brain function should be studied from the viewpoint of informatics. Brain informatics will give new insights into the deep understanding of the brain as an information processor. As computer science enriches geometry and algebra in mathematics, brain informatics is expected to enrich studies on neuroanatomy and neurophysiology, which is the basis of brain research. We believe that the person who introduced this perspective is Alan Turing, who proposed the Turing test as an examination of the intelligence of computing machinery.

One goal of BI research is to develop and demonstrate a systematic approach to an integrated understanding of the macroscopic- and microscopic-level working principles of the brain, by means of experimental, computational, and cognitive neuroscience studies, as well as by utilizing advanced Web intelligence (WI)-centric information technologies. Another goal is to promote new forms of collaborative and interdisciplinary work. New kinds of BI methods and global research communities will emerge, through infrastructure on the wisdom Web and knowledge grids that enable high-speed and distributed large-scale analysis and computations as well as radically new ways of data/knowledge sharing.

The series of Brain Informatics Conferences started with the First WICI International Workshop on Web Intelligence Meets Brain Informatics (WImBI 2006), held at Beijing, China, in 2006. The second, third, and fourth conferences, Brain Informatics 2009, 2010, and 2011 were held jointly with the International Conferences on Active Media Technology (AMT 2009, AMT 2010, and AMT 2011), respectively, in Beijing, China, Toronto, Canada, and Lanzhou, China.

The conferences provide a leading international forum to bring together researchers and practitioners who explore the interplay between studies of the human brain and research in computer science. On the one hand, studies of human brain models characterize the functions of the human brain based on the notions of information processing systems. WI-centric information technologies are applied to support brain science studies. For instance, the wisdom Web and knowledge grids enable high-speed, large-scale analysis, simulation, and computation as well as new ways of sharing research data and scientific discoveries. On the other hand, informatics-enabled brain studies, e.g., based on fMRI, EEG, and MEG, significantly broaden the spectrum of theories and models of brain science and offer new insights into the development of human-level intelligence on the wisdom Web and knowledge grids. Different fields are involved in this challenge: computer science, information technology, artificial intelligence, Web intelligence, cognitive science, neuroscience, medical science, life science, economics, data mining, data and knowledge engineering, intelligent agent technology, human–computer interaction, complex systems, and system science.

Here we would like to express our gratitude to all members of the Conference Committee for their support. BI 2012 had a very exciting program including keynote talks shared with the other four conference of the WIC 2012, technical sessions, special sessions, workshops, tutorials, and social programs. This would not have been possible without the generous dedication of the Program Committee members and the external reviewers who reviewed the papers submitted to BI 2012, our keynote speakers, Edward Feigenbaum of Stanford University, USA (1994 Turing Award Winner) and Jianhua Ma of Hosei University, Japan, and without the enthusiasm of the organizers of our two special sessions with invited papers: (1) Granular Computing for Brain Informatics organized by Duoqian Miao, Andrzej Skowron, Dominik Slezak, Guoyin Wang, JingTao Yao, and

Yiyu Yao; (2) Cognitive Architectures Meets Brain Informatics organized by Jian Yang and Peipeng Liang.

BI 2012 could not have taken place without the great team effort of the Organizing Committee, the support of the University of Macau, Hong Kong Baptist University, the International WIC Institute, Beijing University of Technology, China. Special thanks to Gong Zhiguo, Ryan Leang Hou U, Feng Wan, Juzhen Dong, Qin (Christine) Lv, Lars Schwabe, Daniel Tao, Jian Yang, and Shinichi Motomura for their supportive work. We are grateful to Springer *Lecture Notes in Computer Science* (LNCS/LNAI) for their generous support. We thank Alfred Hofmann and Anna Kramer of Springer for their help in coordinating the publication of this special volume in an emerging and interdisciplinary research field.

September 2012   Fabio Massimo Zanzotto
                                                            Shusaku Tsumoto
                                                             Niels Taatgen
                                                               Yiyu Yao

Conference Organization

Conference General Chairs

Niels Taatgen	University of Groningen, The Netherlands
Yiyu Yao	University of Regina, Canada

Program Chairs

Fabio Massimo Zanzotto	University of Rome "Tor Vergata", Italy
Shusaku Tsumoto	Shimane University, Japan

Local Organizing Chairs

Ryan Leang Hou U	University of Macau, Macau SAR
Feng Wan	University of Macau, Macau SAR

Publicity Chairs

Qin (Christine) Lv	University of Colorado Boulder, USA
Lars Schwabe	University of Rostock, Germany
Daniel Tao	Queensland University of Technology, Australia
Jian Yang	Beijing University of Technology, China
Shinichi Motomura	Maebashi Institute of Technology, Japan

WIC Co-Chairs/Directors

Ning Zhong	Maebashi Institute of Technology, Japan
Jiming Liu	Hong Kong Baptist University, Hong Kong

IEEE-CIS TF-BI Chair

Ning Zhong	Maebashi Institute of Technology, Japan

WIC Advisory Board

Edward A. Feigenbaum	Stanford University, USA
Setsuo Ohsuga	University of Tokyo, Japan
Benjamin Wah	The Chinese University of Hong Kong, Hong Kong
Philip Yu	University of Illinois, Chicago, USA
L.A. Zadeh	University of California, Berkeley, USA

WIC Technical Committee

Jeffrey Bradshaw	UWF/Institute for Human and Machine Cognition, USA
Nick Cercone	York University, Canada
Dieter Fensel	University of Innsbruck, Austria
Georg Gottlob	Oxford University, UK
Lakhmi Jain	University of South Australia, Australia
Jianhua Ma	Hosei University, Japan
Jianchang Mao	Yahoo! Inc., USA
Pierre Morizet-Mahoudeaux	Compiegne University of Technology, France
Hiroshi Motoda	Osaka University, Japan
Toyoaki Nishida	Kyoto University, Japan
Andrzej Skowron	Warsaw University, Poland
Jinglong Wu	Okayama University, Japan
Xindong Wu	University of Vermont, USA
Yiyu Yao	University of Regina, Canada

Program Committee

Laura Astolfi	Sapienza University of Rome, Italy
Quan Bai	Auckland University of Technology, New Zealand
Marco Baroni	University of Trento, Italy
W. Art Chaovalitwongse	University of Washington, USA
Xiaocong Fan	The Pennsylvania State University, USA
Philippe Fournier-Viger	University of Moncton, Canada
Yike Guo	Imperial College London, UK
Huiguang He	Chinese Academy of Sciences, China
Frank D. Hsu	Fordham University, USA
Bin Hu	Lianzhou University, China
Kazuyuki Imamura	Maebashi Institute of Technology, Japan
Hanmin Jung	Korea Institute of Science and Technology Information, Republic of Korea
Renaud Lambiotte	University of Namur, Belgium
Peipeng Liang	Xuanwu Hospital, Capital Medical University, China
Xiaohui Liu	Brunel University, UK
Duoqian Miao	Tongji University, China
Mariofanna Milanova	University of Arkansas at Little Rock, USA
Brian Murphy	Carnegie Mellon University, USA
Kazumi Nakamatsu	University of Hyogo, Japan
Valentina Poggioni	University of Perugia, Italy
Zhihai Rong	Donghua University, China
Hideyuki Sawada	Kagawa University, Japan
Lars Schwabe	Universität Rostock, Germany

Andrzej Skowron	Warsaw University, Poland
Dominik Slezak	University of Warsaw and Infobright Inc., Poland
Diego Sona	Italian Institute of Technology, Italy
Andrea Stocco	University of Washington, USA
Piotr S. Szczepaniak	Technical University of Lodz, Poland
Sunil Vadera	University of Salford, UK
Frank van der Velde	Leiden University, The Netherlands
Feng Wan	University of Macau, Macau
Guoyin Wang	Chongqing University of Posts and Telecommunications, China
Jinglong Wu	Okayama University, Japan
Qi Yanbing	Lanzhou University, China
Jian Yang	International WIC Institute, Beijing University of Technology, China
Yiyu Yao	University of Regina, Canada
Haiyan Zhou	International WIC Institute, Beijing University of Technology, China

Additional Reviewers

Nouman Azam
Fabrizio De Vico Fallani
Usef Faghihi
Xiuqin Jia
Othalia Larue
Chin Ian Lou
Fan Min

Linchan Qin
Jlenia Toppi
Giovanni Vecchiato
Yan Zhang
Bing Zhou

Table of Contents

Thinking and Perception-Centric Investigations of Human Information Processing System

Information Technologies for theManagement, Use, and Simulatiton of Brain Data

Applications

Special Session on Granular Computing and Brain Informatics

Associative Information Processing in Parahippocampal Place Area (PPA): An fMRI Study

Mi Li[1,2,6], Dongning Han[3], Shengfu Lu[2,6], Zheng Liu[4], and Ning Zhong[2,5,6]

[1] The School of Computer and Communication Engineering
Liaoning ShiHua University, Liaoning 113001, China
[2] International WIC Institute, Beijing University of Technology
Beijing 100024, China
[3] College of Optical and Electronical Information
Changchun University of Science and Technology, Jilin 130022, China
[4] Dept. of Biomedical Engineering, Tianjing University
Tianjing 300072, China
[5] Dept. of Life Science and Informatics, Maebashi Institute of Technology
Maebashi-City 371-0816, Japan
[6] Beijing Key Laboratory of MRI and Brain Informatics, China
limi135@gmail.com, lusf@bjut.edu.cn, zhong@maebashi-it.ac.jp

Abstract. The function of the parahippocampal place area (PPA) is a matter of debate. We investigated this issue in fMRI experiment by 36 normal subjects using two types of tasks: figure and text. Furthermore, the figure tasks contain two kinds of contextual associations: one is among items; the other is among items and their locations which refers to the spatial contextual associations. In contrast, the text tasks contain only item contextual associations - they do not have any spatial information. The results showed that the right PPA located at anterior lingual gyrus and left anterior parahippocampal gyrus nearby amygdala were significantly activated during both figure and text tasks, which indicate that the PPA is more involved in associative information processing.

1 Introduction

A variety of previous studies have consistently implicated that the parahippocampal cortex (PHC) is crucial for several cognitive processes such as episodic memory [1–6] and spatial analysis [7–12]. The parahippocampal place area (PPA) is a subregion of the PHC, which locates at the boundary between the posterior PHC and the anterior lingual cortex. This region is firstly named by Epstein and Kanwisher and is considered to respond preferentially to scenes with spatial layout [13]. Numerous observations have reported that the PPA is strongly activated during encoding local scenes and spatial navigation [14–16] as well as mental imagery of place [17]. Consistent with these findings, neurophysiology studies also showed that damage to this region often leads to the cognitive impairment in

F.M. Zanzotto et al. (Eds.): BI 2012, LNCS 7670, pp. 1–9, 2012.

spatial processing [18–20]. All these results support the PPA is special for processing spatial-related information. However, recent studies by Bar and his colleagues proposed the contextual hypothesis that the PHC including PPA only mediates the contextual associative information. Their experiments compared strong-context with weak-context among the individual objects, showing that the contextual associations activated a network including the PHC, retrosplenial complex, and parts of the medial prefrontal cortex [21]. They also found a segregation network in the PHC that spatial contextual associations activated more posterior PHC including PPA and nonspatial contextual associations activated more anterior PHC [21, 22]. Another study about the associative and item recognition memory also found the PPA was necessary for recollection of associative information [23]. These studies indicate that whether the PPA mediates associative information processing is still a matter of debate [24, 25].

To elucidate the function of the PPA, we designed the experimental materials as two types of task-figure and text, which can describe the same event using the associations among items. For example, an event in 2007 with items "the GDP (Gross Domestic Product) per head and country" can be described by the bargraph shown in Fig. 1(a). The bar and its location describe the spatial contextual associations, whilst the relations between a country and the GDP per head, as well as its ranking of countries, describe the item contextual associations. These event item associations can also be expressed in the form of written text as shown in Fig.1(b). Thus, the tasks illustrated by figures are related to the processing of both item contextual associations and spatial contextual associations, whereas written text is only related to item contextual associations but not particularly spatial information. To determine the association-specific activations, two types of tasks were used to test the hypothesis that if the activated regions (including PPA) are involved in processing the associative information, these activations would response to both figure and text tasks. In addition, two baseline type tasks corresponding to the stimuli tasks were designed: a figure-baseline and a text-baseline task. The figure-baseline task consisted of a blank background of the same size as the figure task(see Fig. 1(c)); the text-baseline task is a string of stars (*)s which are of similar length as the words used in the text task(see Fig. 1(d)).

2   Methods

2.1   Participants

Thirty-six volunteers (eighteen female and eighteen male; mean age ± standard deviation (S.D.) = 22.5 ± 1.7) participated in this study. All of the subjects were right-handed and native-Chinese speaker. The subjects had no history of neurological or psychiatric illness, and no developmental disorders, including reading disablities. All of the participants gave their written informed consent, and the protocol was approved by the Ethical Committee of Xuanwu Hospital of Capital Medical University and the institutional Review Board of the Beijing University of Technology.

2.2 Stimuli and Procedure

In the experiment, 20 text and figure stimuli, as well as 8 text-baseline and figure-baseline stimuli were used. Each text stimulus was presented for a period of 16 seconds, the figure was presented for 14 s, and both text-baseline and figure-baseline were presented for 8 s. The presentation time was set according to the behavioral experiment, in which participants can fully understand the information of text or figure presented to them. The text and figure tasks describing the same event were counterbalanced across subjects; no individual read the same event twice [26].

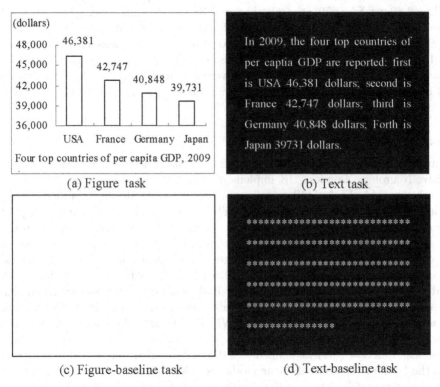

(a) Figure task   (b) Text task

(c) Figure-baseline task   (d) Text-baseline task

Fig. 1. Examples of four types of stimuli (two tasks and two baselines) used in the experiment. (a) A figure task is an example of statistical graphs including bar and line-graphs. (b) A text task is a paragraph ranging between 20 and 30 (mean 25) Chinese characters in length (here translated into English). (c) A figure-baseline task consists of a blank background of the same size as that used in the figure task. (d) A text-baseline task is a string of *s of similar length to the words used in the text task.

The experiment consists of 4 sessions. The order of the text and figure stimuli was pseudo-randomized in each session. All stimuli were presented on a blank background screen. The participants were instructed to read text and figure information attentively. Four sessions were collected per each participant. The images for the initial 10 s were discarded because of unsteady magnetization; the remaining images in the session were used in the analysis.

2.3   Image Acquisition

Blood oxygenation level-dependent fMRI signal data were collected from each participant using a Siemens 3-T Trio scanner (Trio system; Siemens Magnetom scanner, Erlangen, Germany). Functional data were acquired using a gradient-echo echo-planar pulse sequence (TR = 2000 ms, TE = 31 ms, FA = 90°,the matrix size = 64× 64 mm, Voxel = 4 × 4 × 4 mm, 30 slices, slice thickness = 4 mm, inter-slice interval = 0.8 mm, FOV = 240 × 240 mm). High-resolution T1-weighted anatomical images were collected in the same plane as the functional image using a spin echo sequence with the following parameters (TR = 130 ms, TE = 2.89 ms, FA = 70°, the matrix size = 320 × 320 mm, Voxel = 0.8 × 0.8 × 4 mm, 30 slices, slice thickness = 4 mm, inter-slice interval = 0.8 mm, FOV = 240 × 240 mm). Stimulus presentation and data synchronization were conducted using E-Prime 2.0 (Psychology Software Tools, Pittsburgh, USA). Prior to each run, the first two (10 s) discarded volumes were acquired to enable the stabilization of magnetization. The scanner was synchronized with the presentation of every trial in each run.

2.4   Data Analysis

Data analysis was performed with SPM2 from the Welcome Department of Cognitive Neurology, London, UK implemented in Matlab 7.0 from the Mathworks, Sherborne, MA, USA. MNI coordinates were transferred into Talairach coordinates (Talairach and Tournoux, 1988). The functional images of each participant were corrected for slice timing, and all volumes were spatially realigned to the first volume (head movement was < 2 mm in all cases). A mean image created from the realigned volumes was coregistered with the structural T1 volume and the structural volumes spatially normalized to the Montreal Neurological Institute (MNI) EPI temple using nonlinear basis functions. Images were resampled into 2-mm cubic voxels and then spatially smoothed with a Gaussian kernel of 8 mm full-width at half-maximum (FWHM). The stimulus onsets of the trials for each condition were convolved with the canonical form of the hemodynamic response function (hrf) as defined in SPM 2. Statistical inferences were drawn on the basis of the general linear modal as it is implemented in SPM 2. Linear contrasts were calculated for the comparisons between conditions. The contrast images were then entered into a second level analysis (random effects model) to extend statistical inference about activity differences to the population from which the participants were drawn. Activations are reported for clusters of 10 contiguous voxels (80 mm^3) that surpassed a corrected threshold of $p < .05$ on the cluster level.

3   Results

3.1   Behavioral Results of the fMRI Study

Behavioral accuracy was larger than 0.75 in each of the memory retrieval tasks under scanning, indicating that the brain activity being measured was associated with successful memory encoding and retrieval in all tasks (Table 1). The accuracy from the fMRI experiment showed that there was no significant difference among the three forms (Analysis of variance between the forms showed that: Text vs. Figure $[F(1, 71) = 0.03, p = 0.87]$). These results suggest that the three forms of social statistical information have no significant effect on the comprehension of the content of social statistical information.

Table 1. Behavioral results during the fMRI experiment

	Accuracy (%correct)	Reaction time (s)
Text	78.62 ± 8.76	3.88 ± 0.57
Figure	78.96 ± 9.29	4.17 ± 0.61

3.2 fMRI Results

During two conditions of experimental stimuli, the text tasks more significantly activated the anterior portion of PHC than text-baseline. In contrast, the figure tasks more significantly activated the posterior portion of PHC (Table 2). In PHC, the results were consistent with that nonspatial contexts activated the anterior PHC, whereas spatial contexts activated the posterior PHC [22]. In addition, both text and figure tasks commonly showed two greater activated regions that the anterior tip PHC (Talairach: -30, -1, -20, BA34, L > R) nearby the amygdala (see Fig. 2(a)) and the posterior tip PHC (Talairach: 22, -45, 4, BA30, R > L) adjacent to the anterior lingual gyrus, namely PPA [13, 14] (see Fig. 2(b)). The results indicated that the two activations commonly contribute to the item associations. Bar et al. found that the left region of PPA was greater activated than the right region during contextual associative processing [21, 22]. However, we found that the activation in the right PPA was greater than that in the left PPA, which may be relevant to the tasks involving the complex information integration [26]. Taken together, the PPA mediates the associative information processing.

4 Discussion

The parahippocampal place area (PPA) was so named because it is more involved in perceiving and encoding local visual scenes [13]. However, recent studies have reported that this region responds particularly to contextual associations processing [21, 22]. The function of PPA, therefore, is still a matter of debate [24, 25]. To examine this issue two types of task were used: written text tasks which are only related to the associative information, not particularly spatial information; figure tasks which are related to both associative information and spatial information.

The hypothesis put forward in this paper is that (1) if the PPA is only involved in the spatial information processing, this region would not be activated in text

Table 2. Brain activations within PHC related to different contrasts

Anatomical regions	Coordinates[a]			t	Cluster size (mm^3)
	x	y	z		
TR vs. Text-baseline					
Lt.PHC (amygdala)	-30	-1	-20	7.76	2048
Lt.PHC (BA34)	-18	-1	-18	5.90	152
Lt.PHC (BA34)	-16	1	-15	5.87	80
Rt.PHC (BA34)	16	3	-15	6.54	176
Rt.PHC (BA30)	20	-46	4	6.44	2040
FR vs. Figure-baseline					
Lt.PHC (amygdala)	-30	-1	-20	8.94	1992
Lt.PHC (BA37)	-30	-41	-10	8.92	1808
Lt.PHC (BA36)	-20	-41	-10	8.43	648
Lt.PHC (Hippocampus)	-24	-9	-21	5.95	256
Rt.PHC (BA36)	22	-37	-8	8.47	1920
Rt.PHC (BA36)	32	-22	-21	6.82	800
Rt.PHC (BA30)	22	-45	2	7.49	1808
Conjunction analysis					
Lt.PHC (amygdala)	-30	-1	-20	7.76	2024
Rt.PHC (BA30)	20	-45	4	6.44	2008

[a] The Talairach coordinates of the centroid and associated maximum t within contiguous regions are reported. BA, Brodmann area; TR, text reading; FR, figure reading; Lt, left hemisphere; Rt, right hemisphere; PHC, parahippocampal cortex.

tasks; (2) if the PPA is only related to the text processing, this region would not be activated in figure tasks; (3) if the PPA is involved in item associations processing, this region would be activated in both text and figure tasks which are commonly associated with the items associations. The results show that the PPA was significantly more activated during both text and figure tasks, which indicates that the PPA mediates the item associations processing. It was also found that left anterior tip PHC nearby amygdala was significantly more activated during both text and figure tasks. The results suggest that these two activations commonly contribute to the item associative information processing.

Our finding, the PPA is more activated in associative information processing, is supported by the study of the associative and recognition memory, in which object-color associations elicited more activation than old/new recognition in the posterior PHC overlapping the PPA [23]. Recent studies using various stimuli with contextual associations have also found that the PPA plays a key role in processing the contextual associative information [21, 22]. Several previous imaging studies [1–12] have indicated that spatial processing and episodic memory are distributed overlapping on the PHC along an anterior-posterior hierarchic, and do not show any tasks-related spatial specificity, which indicates that there may be a relationship between spatial processing and episodic memory. Spatially-related processing is associated with processing the relations among various components of spatial information. The episodic memory includes the item memory and source memory, and the source memory is also involved in the related associative information. Thus, we considered that, local visual scenes in PPA [13] may be mediate associative information processing materially. Moreover, the function of spatial navigation in this area [14] requires mental image of places [17] to link landmarks to places regardless of allocentric frames reference [27] or egocentric frames reference [28].

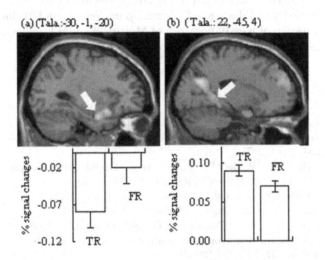

Fig. 2. Statistical parametric map (SPM) through the subjects normalized averaged brains of interesting regions for conjunction of text and figure. (a) Left anterior parahippocampal (BA34) nearby amygdala was more activated in both figure and text tasks. (b) Right posterior parahippocampal (BA30) (PPA) was more activated in both figure and text tasks. The bar graph below shows the BOLD signal change percentages to the two kinds of visual stimulus tasks. TR, text reading; FR, Figure reading.

In addition, it was found that another region in left anterior PHC serves to process the item associative information. This region is adjacent to the perirhinal cortex which is often perceived as processing "what" information [29]. Previous studies have also suggested that the anterior medial temporal lobe is involved in the relational processing of nonspatial stimulus such as associating abstract nouns [2], or face-name pairs [30]. Furthermore, recent contextual associations studies have also found that a similar region was recruited by the nonspatial associations [21]. In this study, the anterior PHC showed significantly greater activated in both text (nonspatial) and figure (spatial) tasks. Therefore, the activation may be more involved in the item identification of associative information processing.

Therefore, linking the present findings with previous reports, it seems reasonable to propose that the PHC, in particular PPA, may mediate associative information processing.

Acknowledgements. This work is partially supported by the National Natural Science Foundation of China (No. 60905027), the Beijing Natural Science Foundation (No. 4102007), the China Postdoctoral Science Foundation Funded Project (2012M510298), Projected by Beijing Postdoctoral Research Foundation (2012ZZ-04), the Science Foundation of Liaoning Shihua University (No. 2012XJJ-003), and the grant-in-aid for scientific research (No. 18300053) from the Japanese Ministry of Education, Culture, Sport, Science and Technology, and the Open Foundation of Key Laboratory of Multimedia and Intelligent Software Technology (Beijing University of Technology) Beijing.

References

1. Gabrieli, J., Brewer, J.B., Desmond, J.E., Glover, G.H.: Separate neural bases of two fundamental memory processes in the human medial temporal lobe. Science 276, 264–266 (1997)
2. Henke, K., Buck, A., Weber, B., Wieser, H.G.: Human hippocampus establishes associations in memory. Hippocampus 7, 249–256 (1997)
3. Henke, K., Weber, B., Kneifel, S., Wieser, H.G., Buck, A.: Human hippocampus associates information in memory. PNAS 96, 5884–5889 (1999)
4. Dobbins, I.G., Rice, H.J., Wagner, A.D., Schacter, D.L.: Memory orientation and success: separable neurocognitive components underlying episodic recognition. Neuropsychologia 41, 318–333 (2003)
5. Sommer, T., Rose, M., Weiller, C., Buchel, C.: Contributions of occipital, parietal and parahippocampal cortex to encoding of object-location associations. Neuropsychologia 43, 732–743 (2005)
6. Bird, C.M., Burgess, N.: The hippocampus and memory: insights from spatial processing. Nat. Rev. Neurosci. 9, 182–194 (2008)
7. Aguirre, G.K., Detre, J.A., Alsop, D.C., DEsposito, M.: The parahippocampus subserves topographical learning in man. Cereb. Cortex 6, 823–829 (1996)
8. Maguire, E.A., Frackowiak, R., Frith, C.D.: Recalling routes around London: Activation of the right hippocampus in taxi drivers. J. Neurosci. 17, 7103–7110 (1997)
9. Mellet, E., Bricogne, S., Tzourio-Mazoyer, N., Ghaem, O., Petit, L., Zago, L., et al.: Neural correlates of topographic mental exploration: The impact of route versus survey perspective learning. Neuroimage 12, 588–600 (2000)
10. Levy, I., Hasson, U., Avidan, G., Hendler, T., Malach, R.: Center-periphery organization of human object areas. Nat. Neurosci. 4, 533–539 (2000)
11. Goh, J.O., Siong, S.C., Park, D., Gutchess, A., Hebrank, A., Chee, M.W.: Cortical areas involved in object, background, and object-background processing revealed with functional magnetic resonance adaptation. J. Neurosci. 24, 10223–10228 (2004)
12. Yi, D.J., Chun, M.M.: Attentional modulation of learning-related repetition attenuation effects in human parahippocampal cortex. J. Neurosci. 25, 3593–3600 (2005)

13. Epstein, R., Kanwisher, N.: A cortical representation of the local visual environment. Nature 392, 598–601 (1998)
14. Epstein, R., Harris, A., Stanley, D., Kanwisher, N.: The parahippocampal place area: Recognition, navigation, or encoding? Neuron 23, 115–125 (1999)
15. Ghaem, O., Mellet, E., Crivello, F., Tzourio, N., Mazoyer, B., Berthoz, A., et al.: Mental navigation along memorized routes activates the hippocampus, precuneus, and insula. Neuroreport 8, 739–744 (1997)
16. Rosenbaum, R.S., Ziegler, M., Winocur, G., Grady, C.L., Moscovitch, M.: I have often walked down this street before: fMRI studies on the hippocampus and other structures during mental navigation of an old environment. Hippocampus 14, 826–835 (2004)
17. O'Craven, K.M., Kanwisher, N.: Mental imagery of faces and places activates corresponding stimulus-specific brain regions. J. Cognitive Neurosci. 12, 1013–1023 (2000)
18. Aguirre, G.K., D'Esposito, M.: Topographical disorientation: a synthesis and taxonomy. Brain 122, 1613–1628 (1999)
19. Epstein, R., DeYoe, E.A., Press, D.Z., Rosen, A.C., Kanwisher, N.: Neuropsychological evidence for a topographical learning mechanism in parahippocampal cortex. Cogn. Neuropsychol. 18, 481–508 (2001)
20. Mendez, M.F., Cherrier, M.M.: Agnosia for scenes in topographagnosia. Neuropsychologia 41, 1387–1395 (2003)
21. Bar, M., Aminoff, E.: Cortical analysis of visual context. Neuron 38, 347–358 (2003)
22. Aminoff, E., Gronau, N., Bar, M.: The parahippocampal cortex mediates spatial and nonspatial associations. Cereb Cortex 17, 1493–1503 (2007)
23. Yonelinas, A.P., Hopfinger, J.B., Buonocore, M.H., Kroll, N., Baynes, K.: Hippocampal, parahippocampal and occipital-temporal contributions to associative and item recognition memory: an fMRI study. Neuroreport 12, 359–363 (2001)
24. Epstein, R.A., Ward, E.J.: How Reliable Are Visual Context Effects in the Parahippocampal Place Area? Cereb Cortex 20, 294–303 (2010)
25. Bar, M., Aminoff, E., Schacter, D.L.: Scenes unseen: The parahippocampal cortex intrinsically subserves contextual associations, not scenes or places per se. J. Neurosci. 28, 8539–8544 (2008)
26. St George, M., Kutas, M., Martinez, A., Sereno, M.I.: Semantic integration in reading: engagement of the right hemisphere during discourse processing. Brain 122, 1317–1325 (1999)
27. Mou, W.M., McNamara, T.P.: Intrinsic frames of reference in spatial memory. J. Exp. Psychol. Learn. 28, 162–170 (2002)
28. Wang, R.F., Spelke, E.S.: Human spatial representation: Insights from animals - Ranxiao Frances Wang and Elizabeth S. Spelke. Trends Cogn. Sci. 6, 376–382 (2002)
29. Murray, E.A., Bussey, T.J.: Perceptual-mnemonic functions of the perirhinal cortex. Trends Cogn. Sci. 3, 142–151 (1999)
30. Sperling, R., Chua, E., Cocchiarella, A., Rand-Giovannetti, E., Poldrack, R., Schacter, D.L., et al.: Putting names to faces: Successful encoding of associative memories activates the anterior hippocampal formation. Neuroimage 20, 1400–1410 (2003)

Language Acquisition Is an Optimized Process Balanced between Holistic and Compositive

Qingyuan Tian

Beijing Language and Culture University, Beijing, China
tianqy@tsinghua.org.cn

Abstract. From the viewpoints of information theory and system theory, this paper proposes that language is an optimal encoding system to communicate in the most efficient way. An Information Optimizing Model of language acquisition is proposed. It proposes that the precondition of language acquisition is that human has the ability of holistic cognition on systems, the ability of categorizing, the ability of voice meaning recognition; and the ability of level-2 perspective-taking. It proposes that binding speeches holistically into basic concepts they present is the key process of language acquisition. When the basic concept is accessed, it is accessed directly as a sentence. According human's cognitive ability and communication requirement, load balance is achieved between the direct accessing process and the generating/analyzing process based on syntax and lexical structure. By this way, the communication optimization is achieved as a whole system.

1   Introduction

By studying the origin and the evolution of language, from the view points of information theory and system theory, we had proposed an Information Optimizing Model of language. In that model, we define language as a communication system, which can maximize information exchange ability while minimizing information exchange cost [1]. In this paper, we study the process of language acquisition and propose an Information Optimizing Model of language acquisition.

This paper has five sections: Section 2 introduces the Information Optimizing Model of language we proposed. Section 3 analyzes the optimizing of cognitive abilities of human, which are prerequisites of language acquisition. Section 4 proposes our Information Optimizing Model of language acquisition. Section 5 analyzes the language acquisition as a lifelong learning process. Section 6 concludes this paper.

2   The Information Optimizing Model of Language

The basic function of language is communication. Its basic characteristic is the ability of real-time interaction. Voice is chosen as the media of language because it has following characteristics: high coding efficiency; no special transmission condition requirement; long distance transmission; robust to interference; parallel interaction ability.

F.M. Zanzotto et al. (Eds.): BI 2012, LNCS 7670, pp. 10–17, 2012.

The basic law of natural selection favors the more optimized life system. Evolution makes humans optimize their action by instinct, including communication. Minimizing the cost while maximizing the information exchange ability is the evolutionary result selected by nature. For this reason, language must following rules of efficiency, cooperation, distinction, evolution, and reliability. Information Optimizing Model of language is proposed that language is the coding system which minimizes the cost in the unit amount of information exchange, and it can be expressed using equation 1 [1].

$$L = arg\ min_{coding}((\sum_t \frac{\sum_{i=1}^{n_t} C_{t\,i}}{n_t} \alpha^t) f_{env} f_{task})$$ (1)

L represents language; t is the length of time. $C_{t\,i}$ is the cost of the ith person in the past time t to exchange a unit amount of information; n_t is the population size of the people who use this language in time t; α is aging factor; f_{env} and f_{task} are increasing functions respective to the environment harshness and criticalness of the communication task; and C is the cost, which is calculated by the amount of consumed energy as equation 2.

$$C = \frac{E_{lea} + E_{sto} + \sum_{\substack{all \\ speeches}} (E_{enc} + E_{art} + E_{hea} + E_{dec})}{\sum_{all\ speeches} I}$$ (2)

E is energy, and the subscripts of E respectively represent *lea*rning and *sto*ring of language rules, and using these rules to *enc*ode, *art*iculate, *hea*r, and *dec*ode language. I is information. Summation operation is calculated based on all the speech utterances that a human will use in his life.

Phonetic statistic data done for Mandarin Chinese agrees with the efficiency rule and reliability rule, and supports the Information Optimizing Model of language we proposed [2,3].

3   The Optimizing of Cognitive Abilities

As the prerequisites of language acquisition, following human cognitive abilities have been optimized.

3.1   Perceiving the World Holistically and Systemically

Human receives huge amount of information from all his senses. Paying same attention to all the information is inefficient, if not impossible. Human optimizes his information processing in such a way: perceiving the world holistically, and perceiving things in the world as systems. Just like the lenses of a camera zooms in and zooms out, when human needs the information in some detail, he focuses in the specified detail, and ignores other information. When human does not need the detail information, he ignores the detail. In this way, human focuses his attention only on the level that he want to perceive, and uses his limited information processing and storing abilities to process all the received information.

3.2   Cognizing the World Using Categories

Human perceives things as systems, and extracts the common features from similar systems and marks them as the fundamental set of features of a category. Categories have levels that are pertinent to the levels of systems respectively. Only when the features on one category level cannot fulfill the request of human's cognition, the focus of human attention moves up to broader features to get more general information, or moves down to more detailed features to get information in detail. Abstracting the systems to be perceived into conceptual categories, human furthers his optimizing ability on information processing.

3.3   Inherent Ability to Perceive the Meaning of Human Voice

Different voices will cause different psychological feelings on the hearer. For example, some voices will cause human to feel as if touching something thick or thin, and some voices will cause human feel as if something being moving from far away to nearby or vise versa. This kind of information is used in language encoding.

A 6-month's fetus has a hearing sense close to that of an adult. The voices heard by mother (including the voices of her own) are heard by fetus too, and mother's psychological feelings transmit to fetus directly by the changes of heartbeat rate, body temperature, blood pressure, and blood compositions (such as hormones). In this way, from the time he was inside his mother's body, human begins to get an inherent ability to perceive the meaning of voices.

3.4   Level-2 Perspective-Taking

The three abilities mentioned before are not unique to human, though they might be more optimized than other primates. The ability unique to human is that he can perceive others' perception, it is called "level-2 perspective-taking". It means not only can human know what others are seeing, but also can he construct in his own mind what others really look on the things which they are seeing. This ability is unique to human [4-6]. It is important for humans when using language to exchange information, because only with this ability can humans put the information they want to exchange into an agreed context, which defines the objective of a discourse to the same system or category. For example, if I pointed to an ordinary dog and said, "I like it," the hearer will have no difficult to know that I like the "dog", but not the place where I actually pointed to, it might be the "back", or the "tail", or the "nose" of that dog. In another condition, if pointed to a puppy with a butterfly knotted braid and said "I like it", hearer is likely to think that I like the braid or the knot, even my finger was not accurately pointing to that braid or that knot. Using this ability, humans establish a shared knowledge platform when communicate with each other.

4   The Information Optimizing Model of Language Acquisition

From late 1950s, language acquisition theory develops with the controversies between the behaviorism and constructivism [7-8]. Thinking that language is an optimal encoding system to communicate in the most efficient way, we proposed new viewpoints about language acquisition as following.

4.1   Language Is Acquired Holistically with Concepts

The native language acquisition is a process simultaneous with the construction of basic concepts. In the language environment of an infant, the speech voices and their meanings, or the concepts that the speech represents, are embracing the infant simultaneously, so that human constructs the earliest and the most basic concepts bound together with the language representing them. The critical period of language development is the period in which the basic concepts are constructed bound directly with the pertinent speeches.

After critical period, basic concepts are constructed. Confined by the storage limitation, new concepts are not directly bound with their pertinent language, but are extended and constructed using basic concepts. If human has not constructed the basic concepts bound directly with a language after the critical period, it will be difficult for him to acquire that language.

4.2   Sentence Is the Basic Encoding and Decoding Unit of a Language

Because the basic concepts of human are holistically bound with language, the basic encoding and decoding unit of language should represent a concept completely. This unit should be sentence.

We observed how an infant acquired his native language at the beginning, whose native language is Japanese, a language with morphological transformation. He can use some words' past form to describe a state, and some word's imperative form to express a command, without knowing their original forms. For example, when he was 16-month-old, he spoke following sentences using morphological transformation of verbs accurately before he started to use (or known) the original forms of these verbs:

- *"Papa   i-   ta."*

"Papa be past-form-suffix". It means "Papa is here". The word "*i-ta*" is the past form of the verb "*i-ru*", which means that human or animal to "be" in some place. Japanese uses past form of this verb to describe this kind of state.

- *"ati   i-   ke."*

"There go imperative-form-suffix". It means "go away". The word "*i-ke*" is the imperative form of the verb "*i-ku*", which means "go".

These examples show us that at the beginning of language acquisition, infant does not care whether there is morphological transformation, or what the word's original form is, he simply stores and accesses that sentence as it was when he need the concept it represents.

4.3   The Feedback of the Context

Language communication occurs in a certain context, which provides a basic platform to share information between the speaker and the hearer as a prerequisite for a successful information exchange.

Any language communication has its result: success or failure of the information exchange, and this result is the most basic form of the feedback. In detail, it could be an answer, or an action pertinent to the requirement of the speaker. Once the communication is successful, both the encoding method of the speaker and the decoding method of the hearer are encouraged. Otherwise, they must adjust themselves to smooth the information exchange process. This adjustment is triggered by feedback information.

In our observation of that Japanese native speaker infant, the effect of feedback was obviously. When he was 20 month-old, he misused intransitive verb *"aku"* (similar as intransitive English verb "open") as the transitive verb *"akeru"* (similar as transitive "open"). Every time he asked the adults to help him to open something (for example, a biscuit box), he said *"aku, aku!"* (similar as English: "It open, it open!"). According the three different feedbacks from adults, the infant adjusted his words as following:

- The adults understood what he meant, and opened the box for him without saying anything. In this condition, the infant is encouraged and would speak *"aku"* ("It open") again next time he want adults to help him to open the box.
- The adults were not sure what he meant, and asked back using a rising tone: *"akeru?"* ("Open it?") In this condition, the infant would reply: *"akeru!"* ("Open it!")
- The adults had not heard or understood his request, and had given back neither a reply, nor an action. In this condition, the infant would try to adjust himself to the right words: *"aku, aku!... akeru, akeru!"* ("It open, It open! ...Open it, open it!")

It is the feedback that helps infant gradually adjust inaccurate words to accurate words.

4.4   The Interaction between Syntactic/Lexical Structure and the Basic Concepts

Language is an optimized information exchange system. Grammar rules are constructed by the laws only based on which can language achieve the optimization, and this kind of grammar rules are acquired unconsciously. Nevertheless, this optimization of language is for all the people who use this language, so that the optimization is not for a specific individual, but for all the language users as a whole. Because differences exist between individuals, language is only a suboptimal system for a specific individual. To fill the gap caused by interpersonal differences, more rules are adopted as grammar rules. This kind of grammar rules must be learned consciously.

Human infant uses sentence as the basic encoding/decoding unit, and stores language bound with the concepts holistically. These concepts build up human's basic concept database. Confined by the storage capacity, when this database grows into a certain size, human instinctively uses acquired grammar rules to parse sentences into words, and begins the building up of syntactic/lexical structure databases. When syntactic/lexical structure databases are built up, sentence processing is optimized into to paths: on one path, human directly accesses the sentences stored in the basic concept database; on the other path, human uses syntactic/lexical structure to generate and parse sentences. The direct access is fast, but it is confined by the size of basic concept database. The generating/parsing is comparative computing intensive and slow, but the sentences it can process are almost not limited. Human adjusts the capacity of these three databases in real time to achieve a dynamic balance between the two processing paths and to make his language system optimal. Figure 1 depicts the relationship between them.

There is a common phenomenon in languages which have morphological transformation: most of commonly used words are irregular transforming words, and less commonly used words are most likely to be regular transforming words. Less commonly used words are transformed based on general rules in real time, while commonly used words, as well as their morphological transformations, are directly stored and accessed, no need to comply with the general rules because they present the most basic concepts of human. By treating words differently according their using frequencies, the language system achieves its optimization.

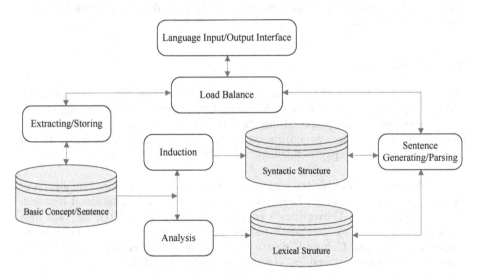

Fig. 1. The relationship between the Basic Concept/Sentence and the Syntax/Lexical structures

5   The Language Acquisition in Different Stages

Generally, 0-6 years of age is considered the first critical period of language development, and 7-12 years of age is considered the second one. The above descriptions mainly studied the first critical period.

7-12 years of age is the period that child accepts primary school education, so that in this period, language acquisition has the characteristics of consciously learning:

- Studying grammars and vocabularies purposely. By this method, child expands and reorganizes his syntactic and lexical structures acquired unconsciously in his first critical period (0-6 years of age).
- Expanding the basic concept database. In school study, new concepts are introduced, described, and explained using language. Furthermore, concepts are used in reasoning and deduction, and this reasoning and deduction must use language as the media. By this way, concepts bind with language again, and child's basic concept database expands.

The basic concept database and the syntactic/lexical structure databases keep on expanding, and are automatically adjusted to achieve an overall optimal dynamic balance. After 12 years of age, the basic concept database has been constructed and fixed, so that the language development mainly depends on the increasing of the syntactic/lexical structure databases, and the improving of the parsing and generating abilities. Confined by the basic concept database storage capacity, new concepts are stored into the extended concept database, where concepts are not bound with their pertinent speeches directly, but using sentence parsing/generating process as an agent to relate them to syntactic/lexical structure databases.

Because base concept database is constructed and fixed before 12 years of age, if human has not started to learn a language before 12, he is difficult to reach the native level on this language.

6 Conclusion

In this paper, we introduced our proposition that language is an optimized information exchange system, and proposed an Information Optimizing Model of language acquisition. In this model, we proposed that the key point of language acquisition is that human's basic concepts are constructed bound with language holistically. In our future work, we will use psycholinguistic approaches to verify this model.

Acknowledgment. This research was financially supported by Science Foundation of Beijing Language and Culture University (supported by "the Fundamental Research Funds for the Central Universities") (Approval number: 12YBT01), and was also financially supported by the Youth Independent Research Supporting Program of Beijing Language and Culture University (supported by "the Fundamental Research Funds for the Central Universities") (Approval number: 10JBG05).

References

1. Tian, Q.: The Information Optimizing Model of the Origin and Evolution of Language. IEICE Technical Report 110, 7–12 (2011)
2. Tian, Q.: The Information Optimizing Model of Language and its Verification by Mandarin Phonetic Statistics. In: 2011 International Conference of Information Technology, Computer Engineering and Management Sciences, pp. 7–10. IEEE Computer Society, Los Alamitos (2011)

3. Tian, Q.: The Phonetic Information Redundancy in Mandarin: a Support for Information Optimizing Model of Language. In: 2011 International Conference of Information Technology, Computer Engineering and Management Sciences, pp. 271–274. IEEE Computer Society, Los Alamitos (2011)
4. Flavell, J.H.: Perspectives on perspective-taking. In: Beilin, H., Pufall, P. (eds.) Piaget's theory: prospects and possibilities, pp. 107–139. Erlbaum, Hillsdale (1992)
5. Perner, J., et al.: Theory of mind finds its Piagetian perspective: Why alternative naming comes with understanding belief. Cognitive Development 17, 1451–1472 (2002)
6. Tomasello, M.: The cultural origins of human cognition. Harvard University Press, Cambridge (1999)
7. Skinner, B.F.: Verbal behavior. Prentice-Hall, NJ (1957)
8. Piaget, J.: The Principles of Genetic Epistemology. Rourledge & Kegan Paul Ltd. (1972)

Object Recognition Test in Peripheral Vision: A Study on the Influence of Object Color, Pattern and Shape

Chin Ian Lou[1], Daria Migotina[2], Joao P. Rodrigues[2], Joao Semedo[2],
Feng Wan[1], Peng Un Mak[1], Pui In Mak[1], Mang I. Vai[1], Fernando Melicio[2],
J. Gomes Pereira[2], and Agostinho Rosa[2]

[1] University of Macau, Macau, China
[2] Technical University of Lisbon, Lisbon, Portugal

Abstract. As an important factor for central vision preview, peripheral vision is a crucial ability for most ball game players in motion detection. A critical problem with peripheral vision is object recognition which has not yet been given much attention. This paper presents an experimental study to evaluate the influence on object recognition in peripheral vision due to different patterns, colors and shapes of the objects. More specifically, four types of shapes (including circles, triangles, horizontal stripes and vertical stripes) with various colors presented in different patterns were applied during the peripheral vision test. The results show that different patterns and colors indeed affect object recognition in peripheral vision in terms of accuracy and response time, while different types of shapes do not vary the performance significantly.

1 Introduction

Human vision system is composed of not only central vision but also peripheral vision. According to the constitution of human eye, retina is made up of two types of photoreceptor cells which are rod cells and cone cells. Cone cells are mostly concentrated in the central area of the retina, while rod cells are distributed in the outer edges of the retina and peripheral vision employs mainly rod cells. Due to the higher density of cone cells at fovea and less density populated at periphery, peripheral vision is characterized as poor spatial resolution [2]. Owing to the feature of rod cells, in peripheral vision humans are good at detecting motion but weak in distinguishing colors and shapes.

As a part of vision, peripheral vision provides a rich source of visual information outside the central field. While perceiving an object in periphery, people make the direction and span of leading eye movements by using visual information from peripheral vision. Thus, peripheral vision has been suggested important in the feature recognition and object identification as it directs the eye movements of neutral search tasks in real world sense [1]. In particular, peripheral vision is important for many people, especially for most of ball games players. For instance, in a football game, if a player wants to pass the ball to his teammate, he should not look at his teammate

F.M. Zanzotto et al. (Eds.): BI 2012, LNCS 7670, pp. 18–26, 2012.

directly and make a heel-dragging decision, otherwise he may lose the control of the ball as defenders will identify and prevent the passing through the detection of opponent's eye gaze. Therefore, the player has to use his peripheral vision to gather information from the environment (goal, teammates, etc.) and keep focused without revealing his intention, to avoid defending actions by his opponents.

Previously, a number of studies have examined why the performance of peripheral vision is weaker than that of central vision. Several factors (including age, distance, form and condition) have been found affecting the identification of a stimulus in peripheral vision without the usage of eye movements [3]. In addition, perceptual research also provides strong evidences that young children have poor peripheral vision ability compared to the adults [4], but it can be improved along with the growth of age [5]. Furthermore, it is observed that peripheral sensitivity will decrease along with enlarging of eccentricity [6], while forms and conditions of stimuli also affect the performance of peripheral vision (for instance, the size of stimuli target).

A recent study [11] has proposed a suprathreshold discrimination method to investigate natural-scene information processed in central and peripheral vision, using a set of stimulus images made from colored photographs of neutral scenes and their variants (in different colors, shape orientations). The method requires subjects to give a magnitude estimate rating of the perceived target and the changes. The results show that observers' rating of color changes in periphery is higher than that of peripheral orientation changes, implying that human's peripheral vision is indeed more sensitive to specific types of stimuli targets.

To the best of our knowledge, there is no study on the impact of football players' peripheral vision performance in relation to different patterns, colors and shapes. Because of the poor ability of peripheral vision, it is necessary and meaningful to further investigate the mechanism of peripheral vision or more precisely in this work, human's peripheral vision is more sensitive to which types of stimuli targets, this may help ball game players identify their teammate in periphery easily.

In our recent study [12], we have proposed a new peripheral vision evaluation index which can reveal the underlying correlation between global peripheral vision performance and personal sports ability, but the number of subjects is limited and no analysis is provided about the influence on colors, shapes and patterns. Therefore, in this study, the pattern recognition in peripheral vision based on the aforementioned work will be studied to evaluate the influence on peripheral vision performance in football players due to different patterns, different colors and different shapes.

2   Methods

2.1   Participants

A total of 62 football players (aged 14-19 years: mean=16.44, SD=1.5) with normal or corrected-to-normal vision participated in this experiment and all the subjects have reported no color blindness history. The protocol was in accordance with the declaration of Helsinki (World Medical Association. 1996) and approved by the Research Board of "Academia do Sporting Club de Portugal".

2.2   Experiment Set Up and Peripheral Vision Measurement

A resolution of 1920x1080 dots with diagonal size of 102 cm LCD display was used to present the stimuli objects. Subjects were seated in front of the screen with away from 53 cm. The distance of 53 cm ensured that the horizontal vision angle and vertical vision angle was 60° and 33.75° respectively. Fig. 1 shows the test screen of the experiment, the background color simulated the football field environment and five objects were presented at the central and four corners of the screen. Experiment was conducted in a comfortable room and illuminated by incandescent lights. A comfortable chair with adjustable height was used to keep subjects' eyes leveled with the screen.

Fig. 1. Test screen

Four types of shapes (including circles, horizontal stripes, triangles and vertical stripes) in seven different colors (including black, blue, brown, green, red, white and yellow) was used as stimuli objects in the experiment and each displayed objects were framed in a square with diagonal of 6.5 cm. The combinations of all the different stimuli objects composed the two types of object sets which were the targets and non-targets. In the target sets, three of the five objects must equal in color and shape, otherwise it was considered as non-target sets. The target sets could be produced by ten different types of target patterns (see Fig. 2 where a dot represented an object) which cover different visual fields. The whole experiment was divided into two parts: the first part, Test 1, included 56 different patterns with 13 target patterns and 43 non-target patterns, and this part was designed for the impact due to different colors and patterns (all the objects were circles with different colors); the second part, Test 2, included also 56 different patterns but with 14 target patterns and 42 non-target patterns, this part was designed to cover all situations with different colors, shapes and patterns. In both tests, target patterns appeared in a predefined order as shown in Fig. 3 (the horizontal axes).

When the experiment started, subjects were required to track with a mouse pointer on the central object binocularly and use peripheral vision to perceive the changed objects in the periphery. During the experiment, the central object first moved slowly and then faster while different types of stimuli objects were presented in periphery, thereby different patterns could be shown in the test screen. The sequence and exposure time of the stimuli objects were determined by a script file which was programmed and loaded into the system before the experiment. If the subjects noticed that any three equal objects (including the central one) were the same, they were required to click as fast as possible on the central object to identify it as a target. Subjects were instructed to avoid the usage of eye scanning and concentrate on the central object tracking its movements with the mouse pointer.

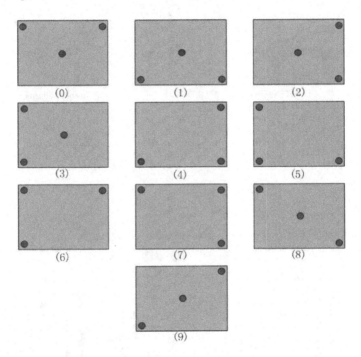

Fig. 2. All of the target patterns used in the tests

2.3 Peripheral Vision Performance Evaluation

To evaluate the performance in the peripheral vision test, true positive (stands for clicking a target) and false positive (accounts whenever a non-target is hit) associated with the reaction time was recorded over each pattern. To detect eye movements, combined horizontal and vertical electrooculogram (EOG) was recorded at the outer canthi of eyes [12], one above an eye and one below another. The EOG measurement was used to distinguish whether the subjects were using pure peripheral vision instead of eye scanning to perceive the changes. There were totally four types of responses which were "target clicked" (subjects identified the pattern as target in peripheral vision), "target non-clicked" (subjects did not identify the pattern as target in peripheral vision), "non-target clicked" (subjects confused with the pattern as target in peripheral vision) and "non-target non-clicked" (subjects identified the pattern as non-target in peripheral vision). Moreover, the reaction times corresponding to four types of responses were distinguished in the session reports.

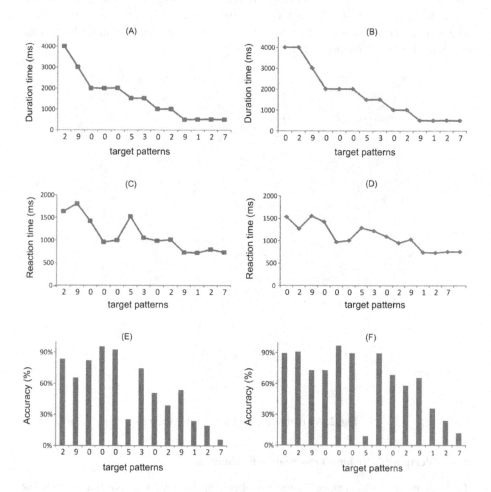

Fig. 3. Performance in accuracy, duration time and reaction time for each target pattern. (A), (C) and (E) show the results from Test 1 while (B), (D) and (F) show the results from Test 2. (A) and (B) present the performance of each target pattern which identified by the subjects. (C) and (D) show the duration time while (E) and (F) show the reaction time for each target pattern.

3   Results and Discussions

3.1   Influence Due to Patterns

Fig. 3 presents the accuracy, duration time and reaction time over each target pattern. The peripheral vision test did not cover all the target patterns in order to reduce the test duration. More specifically, target pattern types 4, 6, 8 (see Fig. 2) were not used in this test, since they were symmetrical to patterns 5, 7 and 9 respectively. Some of patterns had been tested many times (with different shapes and colors of objects), for instance, target pattern type 0. Fig. 3A and Fig. 3B show that different target patterns resulted in significant differences in performance. The easiest target patterns were types 0 and 3, for which 80.22% and 80.09% subjects had successfully recognized them in peripheral vision respectively. Type 9 was relatively easy to identify, 64.55% subjects had recognized it correctly. However, some target patterns had shown a greater difficulty than the others for all the subjects to identify, for example only 17.16% and 8.96% subjects were able to recognize the target pattern type 5 and type 7 correctly. For target pattern type 9, the poor performance may be due to the short duration presentation time of this pattern. Even subjects had recognized the target pattern in peripheral vision, they probably did not have enough time to react and click on the central object (time allowed to respond is the pattern duration plus 300ms). But for the target pattern type 5, even with the same duration time (compared with type 3), the accuracy of target pattern type 5 was still 64.93% lower than that of target pattern type 3. It was probably due to the larger visual-span [14] required for target pattern type 5 as subjects needed to cover the upper and lower visual field at the same time (target pattern type 6 may have the same results). These findings confirm that the ability of peripheral vision of human is weak, and if the stimuli objects cover a larger visual span, the performance of peripheral vision would get worse. To summarize, different patterns do affect objects recognition in peripheral vision.

In addition, a correlation was observed between the duration time and reaction time: the Pearson correlation coefficient is 0.81, which implies a significant correlation ($p<0.01$). As shown in Fig. 3E and Fig. 3F, a shorter duration time can produce a faster reaction time, subjects needed to react fast during a short presentation time. The fastest reaction time was obtained from target pattern type 1, which was 724.95ms including 510.03ms of stimuli presentation time. The slowest response time was observed in target pattern type 9, which was 1805.68ms with 3011.17ms of stimuli presentation time (if subjects click on the central object before the completion of duration time, reaction time will shorter than duration time). The results seem consistent with the habit of human's behavior: when the test is more demanding, subjects need more concentration on the peripheral changes to respond more quickly. The accuracy for targets with duration below the vicinity of 2 seconds also follow the inverse trend (with respect to duration) as response time, that is, the shorter the duration the lower the accuracy.

3.2   Influence Due to Colors and Shapes

In Test 1, the same kind of shapes (all objects are circle) with seven different colors were used to present in the central and peripheral vision. As shown in Fig. 4, different color objects resulted in significantly different performances in the peripheral vision test. Green and brown showed a higher accuracy than the other colors in the test. The highest accuracy was obtained from the objects in green, for which 83.58% subjects had identified it in peripheral vision correctly. However, red had caused a great difficulty for all the subjects, that only 15.67% subjects had successfully identified the stimuli objects in red. It seems that object identification in peripheral vision did not benefit from a high contrast color (red). By comparison with red, low contrast or similarity to the background color (green) has a positive contribution to object recognition in peripheral vision. The results prove that human's peripheral vision is indeed more sensitive to some specific colors. More importantly, the objects with these specific features may be easier to attract subject's interest in terms of human's peripheral vision.

In Test 2, different types of shapes were used in the peripheral vision test. Based on the independent-samples t test, there are no significant difference between the results of Test 1 and Test 2 (p=0.51). It shows that circles, triangles, horizontal stripes and vertical stripes had not much influence on identifying the target patterns in peripheral vision. It suggests that the subjects were able to distinguish different types of objects in peripheral vision.

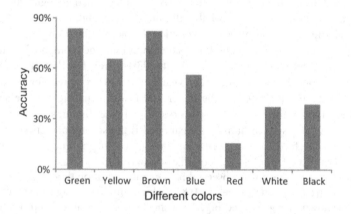

Fig. 4. Performance in accuracy of different colors

3.3   Difficult Situations

Interestingly, there were some object color combinations of non-target patterns which can confuse the subjects. Ten of the most confusing color combinations of non-target patterns are presented in Fig. 5. As shown in Fig. 5, the combinations of red and brown of non-target patterns had presented a great difficulty to identify as non-target during the test, for which 61.19% subjects were confused by this type of non-target. Also, the combinations of green and red confused many subjects, more than 55% subjects had misperceived them as target patterns. This result confirms the lack of color discrimination in the peripheral vision due to the low density of cones cells. Colors with the same grey level contribute greatly for this confusion.

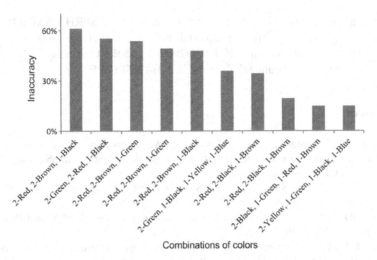

Fig. 5. Top 10 confusing color combinations. The horizontal axes represent the color combination of the non-target patterns, for instance "2-Red, 2-Brown, 1-Black" means that the non-target pattern is composed of two red objects, two brown objects and one black object.

4   Conclusions

This paper presents an object recognition experiment for the impact of peripheral vision due to different patterns, different colors and different shapes. Four types of objects (including circles, horizontal stripes, triangles and vertical stripes) with seven different colors (including black, blue, brown, green, red, white and yellow) presented in different patterns were applied in the experiment. The results show that target pattern types 0 and 3 were easiest to be recognized in peripheral vision, for which 80.22% and 80.09% subjects had recognized them respectively. In addition, different colors led to significant different performances in peripheral vision, but different shapes of objects do not. For instance, green was the easiest color as 83.58% subjects had identified the objects with green in peripheral vision while no significant difference was observed between Test 1 and Test 2 which implies no influence due to object shapes.

These findings provide an evidence for instructing how to design a compelling and recognizing symbol. For instance, the team jersey is better in green or brown instead of red which is the lowest sensitive color, so that football players can easily identify their team members during games. Furthermore, the traffic signs should be placed on the same side, because drivers have difficulty to recognize the traffic signs which are placed on both sides (the performance of peripheral vision get worse when the objects cover a large visual span). On the other hand, a comprehensive study would be desired, to cover all types of target pattern with different colors and shapes, which can provide us a better understanding of the visual ability on peripheral vision and help us enhance our perception and improve ergonomic design of products.

Acknowledgement. This work is supported in part by FCT SFRH/BSAB/1101/2010 and PEst-OE/EEI/LA0009/2011 grants and the Macau Science and Technology Development Fund under Grant FDCT 036/2009/A and the University of Macau Research Committee under Grant MYRG139(Y1-L2)-FST11-WF.

References

1. Torralba, A.O., Castelhano, M.S., Henderson, J.M.: Contextual guidance of eye movements and attention in real-world scenes: the role of global features in object search. Psychol. Rev. 113(4), 766–786 (2006)
2. Yeotikar, N.S., Khuu, S.K., Asper, L.J., Suttle, C.M.: Configuration specificity of crowding in peripheral vision. Vision Res. 51(11), 1239–1248 (2011)
3. Holmes, D.L., Cohen, K.M., Haith, M.M., Morrison, F.J.: Peripheral Visual Processing. Perception & Psychophysics 22(6), 571–577 (1977)
4. Miller, L.K.: Eye-movement latency as a function of age, stimulus uncertainty, and position in the visual field. Percept. Mot. Skills 28(2), 631–636 (1969)
5. Lakowski, R., Aspinall, P.A.: Static perimetry in young children. Vision Res. 9(2), 305–311 (1969)
6. Chung, S.T., Mansfield, J.S., Legge, G.E.: Psychophysics of reading. XVIII. The effect of print size on reading speed in normal peripheral vision. Vision Res. 38(19), 2949–2962 (1998)
7. Chung, S.T.: Reading speed benefits from increased vertical word spacing in normal peripheral vision. Optom. Vis. Sci. 81(7), 525–535 (2004)
8. Gurnsey, R., Roddy, G., Chanab, W.: Crowding is size and eccentricity dependent. J. Vis. 11(7), 15 (2011)
9. Pelli, D.G., Tillman, K.A., Freeman, J., Su, M., Berger, T.D., Majaj, N.J.: Crowding and eccentricity determine reading rate. J. Vis. 7(2), 20–36 (2007)
10. Brown, L.E., Halpert, B.A., Goodale, M.A.: Peripheral vision for perception and action. Exp. Brain Res. 165(1), 97–106 (2005)
11. To, M.P., Gilchrist, I.D., Troscianko, T., Tolhurst, D.J.: Discrimination of natural scenes in central and peripheral vision. Vision Res. 51(14), 1686–1698 (2011)
12. Rodrigues, J.P., Semedo, J.D., Migotina, D.G., Melicio, F.M., Pereira, J.G., da Rosa, A.C.: Peripheral vision dynamic test for athletes. ACTA Press (in press, 2012)
13. Legge, G.E., Mansfield, J.S., Chung, S.T.: Psychophysics of reading. XX. Linking letter recognition to reading speed in central and peripheral vision. Vision Res. 41(6), 725–743 (2001)

Basic Level Advantage
during Information Retrieval: An ERP Study

Sanxia Fan[1,2], Xuyan Wang[1,2], Zhizhou Liao[1,2],
Zhoujun Long[1,2], Haiyan Zhou[1,2], and Yulin Qin[1,2,3]

[1] International WIC Institute, Beijing University of Technology, China
[2] Beijing Key Laboratory of MRI and Brain Informatics, China
[3] Dept. of Psychology, Carnegie Mellon University, USA
zhouhaiyan@bjut.edu.cn, yulinq12@gmail.com

Abstract. Categorization concept could be divided into three levels according to the degree of generalization: superordinate, basic and the subordinate levels. To investigate the neural mechanism of concept information retrieval from the different levels, animals and vehicles were chosen as materials and a picture-word matching task was used in this study with the technique of ERP. The behavioral results showed basic concepts were retrieved most quickly and much faster than retrieving those concepts in superordinate and subordinate levels. The ERP results showed that there was an enhanced ERP signals in the early stage for the condition of superordinate level, including the time windows of N1 and $300-500$ ms, suggesting a superordinate level advantage; but in the late stage (time window $500-600$ ms), a basic-level advantage was observed. These results indicated the retrieving advantage of concept level appeared from superordinate back to basic.

1 Introduction

Human being has an amazing ability to retrieve information from the semantic memory system quite quickly and efficiently according to the external environment's demands. For example, the basic level advantage effect and its reversal to superordinate level founded in cognitive psychology. An object could be named in three levels based on the degree of generalization. In the most general level (superordinate), a particular object could be classified as an "animal"; in the intermediate level (basic), an object could be classified as a "dog" and in the specific level (subordinate) as a "beagle". Basic level was first found by Rosch. She found that children tended to use the basic level concept (such as "dog","cat") to name a picture. Many other researchers also found this kind of phenomenon in adult people in picture naming and other picture-word matching tasks [10] [11], and the response to this level was more correctly and faster than others. In their seminal paper on object categorization, Rosch et al. [9] argued that basic level categorizations are privileged because they include an optimal combination of distinctiveness between classes of objects and information within a class. For instance, "dog" and "cat" are clearly distinguished from each other

F.M. Zanzotto et al. (Eds.): BI 2012, LNCS 7670, pp. 27–37, 2012.

and provide specific information comparing with superordinate class "animal". Behavioral research had shown that the semantic and visual processing requirements involved in the differences when comparing superordinate and subordinate categorizations to basic categorizations [3,7,8,14].

Jolicoeur and Gluck put forward the entry-level theory, the theory holds that people are fastest to name and verify category membership at the basic level because basic category representations are the first to be activated by a visual stimulus, so participants should always be most accurate to verify category membership at the basic level, no matter how quickly they are required to respond. Murphy proposed the differentiation theory, this theory states that different levels of processing are carried out in parallel, why people are often fastest to categorize at the basic level is mainly due to the basic level of abstraction taxonomy is the level at which categories carry the most information, possess the highest cue validity, and are, thus, the most differentiated from one another. Although subordinate level categorizations provide more information than the basic level, there is too much overlap property under the concept, so its distinguish is smaller than the basic level. Similarly, although there is a good distinction for the superordinate level categorizations, it provides little information.

But some other researches found that the basic level advantage would disappear in some constraints and the processing advantage level switched to other levels [1]. In VanRullen and Thorpe's [14] study, participants indicated whether an animal or a vehicle was present in various scenes. They found that these superordinate categorizations took place within a time window of 150 ms poststimulus. They argued that it was extremely unlikely that a basic level categorization could produce shorter latencies. VanRullen [14] also used a rapid visual categorization of objects task in their study, and found categorizations in superordinate level took place before that in basic level. Large [4] manipulated the similarity between target and nontarget, they found the response time was shortest when matching word and picture in the superordinate level, Tanaka et al. also found the superordinate level advantage.

For the unconsistent findings about the advantage effect in basic or superordinate level, a possible explanation might be related to the external task demands. So some studies used ERP technology and tried to understand more about the mechanism of advantage effect. In Tanaka et al.'s study (1999) [13], object categorization processes were investigated by measuring ERP while subjects categorized objects at the superordinate (e.g. animal), basic (e.g. dog) and subordinate (e.g. beagle) level. An enhanced negative waveform (N1)was found for subordinate level categorizations comparing with basic level categorizations and was interpreted as a marker of increased visual analysis. In contrast, superordinate level categorizations produced a larger negativity relative to basic level categorizations and was interpreted as a marker of increased semantic processing. These results suggested a neurophysiological basis for the separate cognitive processes for subordinate and superordinate object categorizations respectively. In Large et al.'s study (2004), category level was manipulated by sequentially presenting subordinate, basic or superordinate target objects among a variety of non-target objects. It was found that superordinate categorizations were performed more quickly and differentiated from basic level categorizations in amplitude early in visual processing (320−420 ms). In contrast, subordinate categorizations took longer to perform and differentiated from basic level categorizations in amplitude and latency at later stages (450−550 ms). Notably, these effects were observed using the same objects categorized at different levels suggesting that visually categorizing objects at varying levels of abstraction engaged specific cognitive processes. These results were consistent with research on rapid visual categorization and it challenges the generality of basic category level superiority effects.

In both Tanaka and Larges research the word-picture matching task was used, but there were no basice level advantage founded in behavioral performance. In the early stage, there was a superordinate level advantage. According to Rogers and Pattersons view (2007), information in the superordinate activated first in the early stage, but the activation of information in the basic level speeded up most quickly in the later stage. So we are going to use both behavioral and ERP technique to check the view with a picture-word matching (PW) task.

2   Materials and Methods

2.1   Participants

Twenty undergraduate and graduate students (10 males and 10 females) from Beijing University of Technology participated in this study. All of them finished the picture-word matching task in the behavioral experiment, and other six finished the EEG experiment. Age of the participants was from 20 to 26 years old. All subjects reported normal or corrected-to-normal vision. Subjects received course credits and a small honorarium for their participation. They all provided written, informed consent.

2.2   Materials and Task

Stimulus were 32 color photographs of animals and vehicles, they were selected to be as nearly the same size as possible and each picture had been cut away from its background. They included a variety of animals and vehicles for classification at the superordinate level; a set of cows, sheep, cars and boats for classification at the basic level; and four different photographs for each of eight classification at the subordinate level: water buffalo, milk cows, goat, jumbuckgoat, bus, truck, sailboat and steamboat. There were three sessions and forty-eight trials in each session. In the superordinate condition, distracters were selected from a different superordinate category as the target. For instance, if the word stimulus was "animal", the distracter was a photograph of any kind of vehicle; In intermediate condition, distracters were always from the same superordinate category as the target, for the word stimulus "sheep", the distracter was always another kind of animal; In the subordinate conditions, distracters were always items from the same intermediate category as the target; for instance, if the word stimulus was "water buffalo", the distracter was a photograph of a different kind of "cow". In the present study, we designed the PW task, in which a picture presented first and then a concept word, and participants were asked to judge whether the word matched the picture or not.

2.3   Procedure

Participants viewed a computer monitor from a distance of 80 cm. The stimuli subtended an approximate visual angle of 15. The large presentation size of the stimulus was due to the limitations of the stimulus presentation software. Since images of this size could produce eye movements care and were taken to remove eye movement artifacts from the data sets. Figure 1 shows the procedure of PW task. At the beginning of each trial, a fixation star appeared in the center of the screen for 500 ms followed by a 500 ms blank, then a picture was appeared in the screen for 1000 ms, and also followed by a 500 ms blank, then a concept word was appeared lasting for 1000 ms, finally, a "?" was appeared for 1000 ms to remind participants to response with pressing "k" button to matching words and pressing "j" button to non-matching words. The intervals between trials were 2000 ms with a "+". Participants were asked to remain as still as possible and to minimize blinking and oro-facial movement. Target stimuli and response requirements were held constant across conditions so that sensori-motor contributions to ERP waveforms could be controlled.

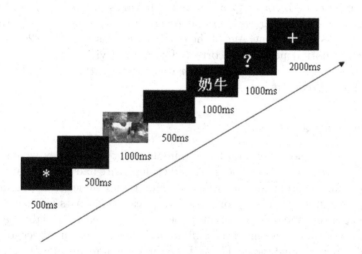

Fig. 1. Procedure of picture-word matching task

2.4   ERP Recording and Analysis

32 channel Ag/AgCl electrodes were used and referenced to linked mastoids. Signals underwent high input impedance amplification (sensorium) and filtering (500 Hz sampling rate: 0.01- to 60-Hz bandpass). Eye artifact was removed from

individual trial epochs and trials in which any of the electro-oculogram (EOG) channels were marked bad and were dropped from the averaging process. ERP data of five participants is available. The mean voltage across the 200 ms before the word stimulus portion was used to baseline correct the subsequent averaged 1000 ms epochs.

3   Results

3.1   Behavioral Performance

A repeated measures analysis of variance (ANOVA) performed on reaction times (RTs) and accuracy rate (ACC) for concept levels (subordinate, basic and superordinate). Removed out of mistaken responses to data and extreme data, the mean response time and mean accuracy rate are shown in Figure 2 and Figure 3.

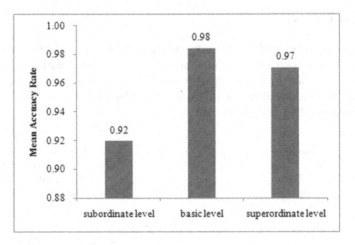

Fig. 2. Mean accuracy rate for picture-word matching task

According to statistics, the results of analysis revealed a main effect of concept level ($F(2, 38) = 15.402$, $P < 0.01$). In PW task, the mean accuracy rate to basic level was significantly higher than subordinate level ($P < 0.01$), and the mean accuracy rate to superordinate level was also significantly higher than subordinate level ($P < 0.01$). However, the mean accuracy rate to superordinate level and to basic level were no significant difference ($P = 0.12$).

A repeated measures ANOVA performed on response times (RTs) for category revealed a main effect of concept level ($F(2, 38) = 23.458$, $P < 0.01$). In PW task, the mean reaction time to basic level was significantly faster than subordinate level ($P < 0.01$), and also was significantly faster than superordinate level ($P = 0.016$), suggesting a typical basic level advantage effect.

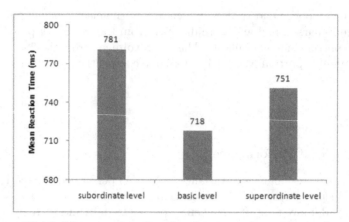

Fig. 3. Mean reaction time for picture-word matching task

3.2   ERP Results

All analyses employed the Huynh-Feldt epsilon correction, which adjusted the degrees of freedom to take into account sphericity assumption violations. The result is presented in Figure 4. The dependent variables were the maximal amplitudes within the four time windows of 100−150, 150−250, 300−500 and 500−600 ms and the corresponding peak latencies.

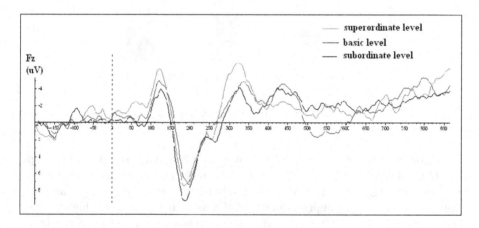

Fig. 4. Fz electrode of average-referenced, grand-averaged ERP waveforms during the picture epoch for superordinate, basic and subordinate level category conditions

• Time window 100−150 ms (N1 component)

A repeated measures ANOVA (superordinate, basic, subordinate) indicated no main effects for latencies. The same analysis on amplitudes showed a main effect of category ($F(2, 9) = 3.309$, $P = 0.04$). From Figure 4, it is clear that amplitudes were larger for superordinate categorizations than subordinate categorizations ($F(1, 4) = 6.68$, $P = 0.04$), there were no differences between amplitudes for superordinate and basic categorizations, basic and subordinate categorizations were also no differences.

- Time window 150–250 ms

A repeated measures ANOVA indicated there were no main effects for latencies. The same analysis on amplitudes showed there was a main effect of category ($F(2, 9) = 6.632$, $P = 0.015$). Analyses of the category levels (subordinate versus basic and subordinate versus superordinate) indicated there was greater positive amplitude for subordinate than basic decisions ($F(1, 4) = 1.896$, $P = 0.045$), and superordinate decisions ($F(1, 4) = 2.248$, $P = 0.032$). Basic and superordinate amplitudes did not differ in this latency range.

- Time window 300–500 ms

A repeated measures ANOVA indicated there were no main effects for latencies. The same analysis on amplitudes revealed there was a main effect of category ($F(2, 9) = 5.412$, $P = 0.03$). Analyses of the category levels (superordinate versus basic level and superordinate versus subordinate level) indicated that there were greater amplitudes for superordinate than basic level categorizations ($F(2, 9) = 3.975$, $P = 0.04$), and also greater than subordinate level categorizations ($F(2, 9) = 1.032$, $P < 0.01$). There were no differences between basic and subordinate categorizations.

- Time window 500–600 ms

A repeated measures ANOVA indicated there were no main effects for latencies. However, the same analysis on amplitudes revealed a main effect of category ($F(2, 9) = 6.487$, $P = 0.02$). And separate analyses of the category levels (basic versus superordinate and basic versus subordinate), the difference between amplitudes for basic and superordinate categorizations approached significance ($F(2, 9) = 1.587$, $P = 0.06$), and it is clear that amplitudes were smaller for basic categorizations than subordinate categorizations ($F(2, 9) = 1.648$, $P = 0.04$), there were no differences on amplitudes between superordinate and subordinate categorizations.

4 Discussion

In some precious study, it is held that basic level object categorizations precede over superordinate categorizations. In keeping with these findings, the behavioral RTs data in this study indicated that response time was fastest for basic categorizations, slightly slower for superordinate and slowest for subordinate categorizations. Basic and superordinate categorizations were undifferentiated in terms of error rate with significantly greater numbers of errors for subordinate categorizations. It is suggested that, under the present experiment, basic and superordinate decisions were of comparable difficulty. With respect to the object categorization processes, three important results were revealed in the present ERP study.

First, superordinate level categorizations produced an enhanced negative defection about 120 ms after the onset of the word stimulus. The negative wave form was consistent in its approximate latency and amplitude with N1 effects found in other studies. This indicated that in the early process, the superordinate level categorizations were the largest to be activated. This might be related to the activation of lexical concepts,it is held that the N1's asymmetrical skewness is modulated by attention [15]. Additionally, its amplitude is influenced by selective attention, and thus it has been used to study a variety of attentional processes [5,12]. As accuracy and attention increases, the amplitude of the N1 increases. It suggests that the amplitude of the N1 is intimately tied to levels of attention. The N1 is greater for stimulus that are attended to versus those that are ignored. In this experiment, the superordinate level words repeated more often in a certain number of times than the basic and subordinate level words, so the superordinate level words attracted more attention, the amplitude of the N1 was also larger than the other two level categorization words, but it was uncertain. Therefore, we need to do a comparative experiment, this experiment does not present the pictures, just present the concept words only. Thus, we mix with some of the other words in the middle of these categories words, these words has nothing to do with the object category. These words are in red font, while the concept words are in black font. Participants are required to respond when they observe a red font. If the result is that in the early process, the superordinate level categorizations will cause a largest negative waveform, it confirms our expectations, that is, the superordinate level categorization words themselves can evoke larger negative waveform due to the number of occurrences. If it is not this result, it may be due to the priming effect of the pictures, because participants were required to match the words with the pictures presented previous. This may result in the superordinate level of maximal activation, but need further confirmation.

Second, the P2 component for the subordinate category level was larger than the basic and superordinate level. The P2 is related to memory and sensory perception conferred upon the attended object [2,6]. In our experiment, there was an enhanced P2 component during 180 ms after a word was presented for subordinate level categorization than superordinate and basic level categorizations, suggesting the subordinate level categorizations need more memory and sensory perception. There might be two reasons, first, from the word frequency, the subordinate categorization words was the lowest frequency of use, therefore it needed to spend more resources to pay attention to them; second, in terms of perception, due to having the same word in the subordinate level of vocabulary, for instance, the word "steamship" and "sailboat" both had a boat word in Chinese. The distinction of these terms was relatively smaller within subordinate level categorization, the difficulty of identifying these words corresponding relatively larger, thus it also needed to invest more resources. In short, subordinate level categorization words were the most difficult to distinguish, so they could evoke a larger P2 component. This indicated that N1 and P2 represented different neural processing mechanisms.

Last, the other important finding of this study was that the amplitudes associated with superordinate level categorizations were larger than basic and subordinate level during 300−400 ms, but sharp decreased in 400−500 ms. However, in this latency range, the amplitudes for basic level categorizations and subordinate level categorizations increased, with slightly larger for basic level categorizations. These results would indicate that the time course of visual categorizations initially involved differentiating between objects at a gross, superordinate level, with finer degrees of differentiation occurring at later processing stages, basic level and subordinate level. These results supported the notion that category classification is processed from top to down. Furthermore, the time span of these results (300 ms post-stimulus) suggested that dissociations between each of the three category levels were related to the categorization and recognition of the objects rather than the processing of low-level stimulus attributes [4]. In their study, Roger and Patterson explained why in the early semantic processing, the latencies were shorter and the amplitudes were larger for superordinate level categorizations than the other two level categorizations. They held that the system produces a "best guess" proportional to the activation of the name unit, the basic-over general-level advantage should vanish and then be reversed−so that, at very fast latencies, people should be more accurate for superordinate relative to basic categorizations, this exactly consistent with the view from top to down. However, during 500−600 ms, the amplitudes for basic level were smaller than superordinate level and subordinate level, in this latency range, there was a basic level advantage, suggesting that the intermediate level required the least resources to distinguish object categorizations. In summary, whereas superordinate level categorizations differed from basic and subordinate level categorizations at an early stage of processing, but basic level differences occur at a later stage of processing.

5   Conclusion

In this study, we used a picture-word matching task with animals and vehicles as experiment materials and explored ERP technology to investigate the neural systems of advantage effect during information retrieval. The behavioral performance showed there was a typical basic level advantage effect in PW task. The ERP result showed that in PW task, about 120 ms after a word presented, the amplitude of N1 in superordinate level was the highest, suggesting a selective attention to the superordinate level. About 180 ms after a word presented there was an enhanced positive waveform for subordinate level, which suggested it might require more memory and sensory perception processing for the level of subordinate. About 320 ms, there was another enhanced negative waveform for superordinate level categorizations, and that might be related to an enhanced semantic processing for the superordinate level. During the time of 500−600 ms, the amplitude for basic level was the weakest, suggesting a basic level advantage at that time. All these results supported the view that concepts in the superordinate level were first be activated in the very early stage, but the activation speeded up most quickly for the concepts in the basic level and a basic level advantage observed in the later stage.

6   Future Work

We are going to use another task of word-picture matching (WP), in which a concept word appeared before a picture, with same materials to further investigate the process of information retrieval form those three levels. We hypothesis that more semantic processing were demanded in the task of PW, but there are more visual processing in the task of WP. We will compare the difference ERPs between these two tasks to test our hypothesis.

Acknowledgments. The research was supported by National Natural Science Foundation of China (No.60875075, 60905027), Beijing Postdoctoral Research Foundation (No. Q6002020201201), Beijing Natural Science Foundation (No.4102007) and the CAS/SAFEA International Partnership Program for Creative Research Teams.

References

1. Zhou, H., Liu, J., Jing, W., Qin, Y., Lu, S., Yao, Y., Zhong, N.: Basic Level Advantage and Its Switching during Information Retrieval: An fMRI Study. In: Yao, Y., Sun, R., Poggio, T., Liu, J., Zhong, N., Huang, J. (eds.) BI 2010. LNCS (LNAI), vol. 6334, pp. 427–436. Springer, Heidelberg (2010)
2. Hillyard, S., Picton, T.: Event-related potentials and selective information processing in man. In: Desmedt, J. (ed.) Cognitive Components in Cerebral Event-Related Potentials and Selective Attention. Clinical Neurophysiology, pp. 1–52 (1979)
3. Jolicoeur, P., Gluck, M.A., Kosslyn, S.M.: Pictures and names: making the connection. Cognitive Psysiology 16(6), 143–175 (1984)
4. Large, M., Kiss, I., McMullen, J.: Electrophysiological correlates of objects categorization: Back to basics. Cognitive Brain Research 20(3), 415–426 (2004)
5. Luck, S.J., Woodman, G.E., Vogel, E.K.: Event-related potential studies of attention. Trends in Cognitive Sciences 4(11), 432–440 (2000)
6. Mangun, G., Hillyard, S.: Mechanisms and models of selective attention. In: Coles, M., Mangun, G. (eds.) Electrophysiology of the Mind, pp. 340–385. Oxford University Press, Oxford (1996)
7. Murphy, G., Brownell, H.H.: Category differentiation in object recognition: typicality constraints on the basic category advantage. Journal of Experimental Psychology: Learning, Memory, and Cognition 11(1), 70–84 (1985)
8. Murphy, G., Lassaline, M.E.: Hierarchical structure in concepts and the basic level of categorization. In: Lamberts, K., Shanks, D.R. (eds.) Knowledge, Concepts and Categories: Studies in Cognition, ch. 3, pp. 93–131. MIT Press, Cambridge (1997)
9. Rosch, E., Mervis, C.B., Gray, W.D., Johnson, D.M., Boyes-Braem, P.: Basic objects in natural categories. Bulletin of the Psychonomic Society 6(NB4), 415 (1976)
10. Rogers, T., Hocking, J., Nopperney, U., Mechelli, A., Gorno-Tempini, M., Paterson, K., Price, C.: Anterior temporal cortex and semantic memory: Reconsiling findings from neuropsychology and functional imaging. Cognitive, Affective, & Behaviroral Neuroscience 6(3), 1–13 (2006)
11. Rogers, T., Patterson, K.: Object categorization: Reversals and explanations of the basic-level advantage. Journal of Experimental Psychology: Gerneral 136(3), 51–69 (2007)

12. Rugg, M.D., Milner, A.D., Lines, C.R., Phalp, R.: Modulations of visual event-related potentials by spatial and non-spatial visual selective attention. Neuropsychologia 25(9), 85–96 (1987)
13. Tanaka, J., Luu, P., Weisbrod, M., Kiefer, M.: Tracking the time course of object categorization using event-related potentials. NeuroReport 10(4), 29–35 (1999)
14. VanRullen, R., Thorpe, S.J.: Is it a bird ? Is it a plane ? Ultra-rapid visual categorization of natural and artifactual objects. Perception 30(6), 655–668 (2001)
15. Wascher, E., Hoffman, S., Sanger, J., Grosjean, M.: Visuo-spatial processing and the N1 component of the ERP. Psychophysiology 46(6), 1270–1277 (2009)

A Skill Learning during Heuristic Problem Solving: An fMRI Study

Zhoujun Long[1,2], Xuyan Wang[1,2], Xiangsheng Shen[1,2], Sanxia Fan[1,2], Haiyan Zhou[1,2], and Yulin Qin[1,2,3]

[1] International WIC Institute, Beijing University of Technology, China
[2] Beijing Key Laboratory of MRI and Brain Informatics, China
[3] Dept. of Psychology, Carnegie Mellon University, USA
yulinq12@gmail.com, zhouhaiyan@bjut.edu.cn

Abstract. In order to investigate the skill learning of heuristics problem-solving, we took simplified 4×4 Sudoku as a new task. Brain activity was recorded when participants solved Sudoku problems with fMRI, and compared before and after plenty of practice. According to the adaptive control of thought-rational (ACT-R) model, we found that the activations in the areas of bilateral prefrontal cortex and posterior parietal cortex decreased by extensive practice. It might indicate that the identification of the problem situation, the problem representation and efficiency of the declarative knowledge extraction were improved greatly in the skill learning of heuristic problem solving.

1 Introduction

Learning is a process of acquiring knowledge and skills, and a lasting change of individual behavior or behavior potential by repeated experience in certain situations. Learning is an important function of the brain, its neural basis is the plasticity of neurons [16]. Although there was a large number of studies about the brain mechanisms of skill learning, included motor learning [8], visual learning and perceptual learning [2,7], classification or the possibility of classification [3,10], mirror reading [14], grammar learning [13] and verb generated task learning [1], the results were not identical, meanwhile there were a lot of controversy. These learning focused on a relatively low level of skill learning such as motor skill learning, sensory and perceptual skill learning, as opposed to the more advanced cognitive skill learning was unclear.

Using the problem-solving paradigms to do behavioral experiments, these paradigms included Hanoi Tower, London Tower, arithmetic puzzles, savage and missionaries and so on. Usually these paradigms took a long time and problem-solving process was more complex. Currently, fMRI was mainly used in the experiments that process-simple, time-short (usually 10 s or less than 20 s), easy-repeat. Therefore, if the early experimental paradigms were used in fMRI experiments, there would be many restrictions. This study used a simplified Sudoku form (4×4 Sudoku) that was the more popular game at home and abroad, it was a new fMRI problem-solving paradigm. This paradigm included a set of

F.M. Zanzotto et al. (Eds.): BI 2012, LNCS 7670, pp. 38–49, 2012.
© Springer-Verlag Berlin Heidelberg 2012

"natural" tasks which were from simple to complex, we explored the different cognitive components in the problem solving process from multiple perspectives, it was suitable for fMRI research in the problem solving. The study used fMRI technology, scanned 4×4 Sudoku tasks in problem solving process.

According to the adaptive control of thought-rational (ACT-R) model, we explored the skill learning process of the problem-solving in the heuristic problem based on the traditional fMRI data analysis. ACT-R model have been proposed and developed by J.R Anderson. It was a human cognitive architecture and compute model, and it was recognized in the international. It was a theoretical system about thinking integration. And it has been applied successful and widely in the field of the cognitive science [11,12]. Therefore, we combined ACT-R model to analyze the collected fMRI data in this experiment.

In this study, we used a 2 (learning effect: Day 1 versus Day 7) × 2 (novelty: new problem versus old problem) × 2 (complexity: simple versus complex) event-related design. In the experiment, the old problem was corresponding to the repeated task, and the new problem was corresponding to the task presented once. We would like to scan the brain when subjects were doing the tasks, to observe the changes of the brain regions activity before and after practice.

2   Materials and Methods

2.1   Subjects

Twenty-one subjects (15 males and 6 females) participated in the present study. Their age ranged from 21 to 26 years. They were undergraduate or graduate students from Beijing University of Technology. They were all right-handed and had no history of neurological or psychiatric disease. Their vision or corrected vision was normal. All subjects signed the informed consent before the experiment. Subjects received proper reward when the experiment completed.

2.2   Experimental Material and Design

4×4 Sudoku was a 4×4 square lattice. Two midlines divided 4×4 square lattice into four boxes. In some grids the figures have been given. Filled figures in the blanks, make each row, each column and each box appeared 1, 2, 3, 4, and only once. In the experiment, subjects were asked to use heuristic rules to complete the tasks. There were the two kind of heuristic rules, which were the simple and the complex heuristic rules, as shown in Figure 1. The simple heuristic rules included the row rule, the column rule and the box rule. The complex heuristic rules included the row-column rule, the row-box rule and the column-box rule.

The experiment adopted the following tasks, which based on the above heuristic rules, as shown in Figure 2. In the simple condition, participants were demanded to find the value of the position with "?" using the simple rules, and in the complex condition, participants were demanded to find the value of the position with "∗" first and then the value in the position of "?" using the complex rules.

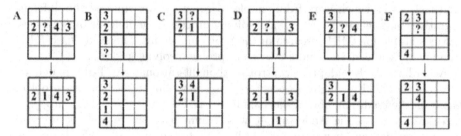

Fig. 1. The example of the row rule (A), the column rule (B), the box rule (C), the row-column rule (D), the row-box rule (E) and the column-box rule (F)

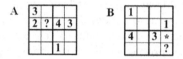

Fig. 2. The 1-step simple task (A) and the 2-step complex task (B)

The experiment was carried out in 7 days. The first scan was performed on Day 1, followed by 5 days practice (Days 2−6). The final scan was performed on Day 7. Each scan took about 1.5 hours, practice took about 1 hour every day. Every day the subjects completed five sessions. Two scanning days there were 32 problems (8 new-simple problems, 8 new-complex problems, 8 old-simple problems and 8 old-complex problems) each session. Five practice days there were 60 problems (10 new-simple problems, 10 new-complex problems, 20 old-simple problems and 20 old-complex problems) each session.

2.3   Procedure

At first the center of the screen appeared the 14 s white "+", it reminded subjects to be ready to answer the task, and then the center of the screen appeared 2 s red "*". After that, the 4×4 Sudoku task appeared. This task presented until subjects presses a button. When the time between the appearence of the task and button-press was less than or equal to 20 s, the task would be presented on the screen. Once beyond 20 s the answer would appear. When subjects pressed the button, the screen would appear the 2 s correct answer. In the end the screen appeared the 10 s white "+". During the 10 s white "+", subjects could have a rest. Procedure of the experiment is shown in Figure 3. In the experiment the answers were given by the data glove. Before the formal experiment, subjects conducted the finger training and the heuristic rules of practice. As to the response of button press, the index finger corresponded to 1, middle finger to 2, ring finger to 3 and little finger to 4. The stimulus was shown by the E-prime software.

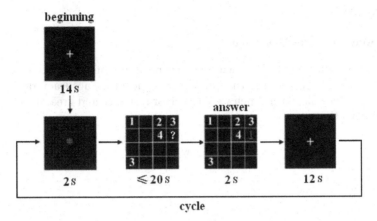

Fig. 3. Procedure of the experiment

2.4 fMRI Procedure

The fMRI measurements were executed on a 3.0 T MR scanner (Siemens Magnetom Trio Tim, Germany) using a quadrature head coil. The experiment used the single shot echo planar imaging sequence which was sensitive to the blood oxygenation level dependent (BOLD) signals. A total of 32 slices of axial images which covered the whole brain. T2*weighted images scanning parameters: FOV = 200 mm × 200 mm, TR = 2 s, Thickness = 3.2 mm, Flip angle = 90°, Disp Factor = 0%, Matrix size = 64 × 64, Voxel size: 3.125 × 3.125 × 3.2 mm^3. Anterior commissures−posterior commissures (AC−PC) located in the 10th slice from bottom to top.

2.5 fMRI Data Analysis

The fMRI data were analyzed with NIS (NeuroImaging Software). The analysis focused on the BOLD signal changes in the regions based on ACT-R model. There are six modules were quite important in ACT-R model and related to Sudoku solving in this study, which were the visual perception module, the procedure module, the declarative memory module, the imaginal module, the goal control module and the manual control module. Since the visual perception module was related to the visual input and the manual module related to the motion, we investigated the brain regions corresponded to the other four modules in detail here. We carried out following fMRI data analysis. First we deleted the first four images of each session in the fMRI data analysis. Preprocessing of the fMRI data included motion correction, normalize to a Talairach brain and smooth (a Gaussian kernel of 6 mm full width at half maximum). Data from 4 participants were deleted because their head shifted more than ± 3 mm or the head rotated more than ± 3°. The remaining 17 subjects' data were used in the fMRI data analysis.

3   Results

3.1   Behavioral Performance

The behavioral data analysis which included response time and accuracy rate. Figure 4 shows mean response time on the left and mean accuracy rate on the right. We removed the data which were the error response and greater than three standard deviations.

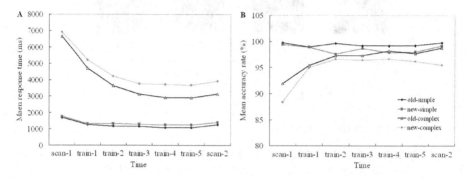

Fig. 4. Mean response time (A) and mean accuracy rate (B)

We conducted repeated measures analysis of variance (ANOVA) on mean response time and mean accuracy rate. For mean response time, we found a significant main effect $(F(1, 20) = 324.982, P < 0.001)$ of complexity, the simple tasks were significantly lower than the complex tasks. There was a significant main effect $(F(1, 20) = 88.649, P < 0.001)$ of learning effect, tasks before practice were significantly lower than after practice. At the same time we found a significant main effect $(F(1, 20) = 59.368, P < 0.001)$ of novelty, the old tasks were significantly lower than the new tasks. We found a significant interaction effect $(F(1, 20) = 67.843, P < 0.001)$ between complexity and of learning effect. We conducted simple effects analysis, found that for the simple tasks, there was a significant effect $(F(1, 20) = 86.84, P < 0.001)$ of learning effect. Mean response time reduced 401.65 ms after practice. For the complex tasks, there was a significant effect $(F(1, 20) = 79.33, P < 0.001)$ of learning effect. Mean response time reduced 3256.88 ms after practice. This showed that there was more significant effect on the complex tasks about practice. We found a significant interaction effect $(F(1, 20) = 15.568, P = 0.001)$ between novelty and learning effect. We conducted simple effects analysis, found that for the new tasks, there was a significant effect $(F(1, 20) = 90.94, P < 0.001)$ of learning effect. Mean response time reduced 1680.50 ms after practice. For the old tasks, there was a significant effect $(F (1, 20) = 82.79, P < 0.001)$ of learning effect. Mean response time reduced 1978.04 ms after practice. This showed that there was more significant effect on the old tasks about practice. We found a significant interaction effect $(F (1,20) = 37.704, P < 0.001)$ between complexity and novelty. We conducted simple effects analysis, found that for the simple tasks, there was a significant effect $(F(1, 20) = 30.04, P < 0.001)$ of novelty. Mean response time reduced 101.10 ms on new and old tasks. For the complex tasks, there was a significant effect $(F(1, 20) = 51.52, P < 0.001)$ of novelty. Mean response time reduced 528.70 ms on new and old tasks. Whether tasks were simple or complex, the differences of mean response time between the new and old tasks which were caused by practice.

As far as mean accuracy rate was concerned, we found a significant main effect $(F(1, 20) = 52.167, P < 0.001)$ of complexity, the simple tasks were significantly higher than the complex tasks. Moreover, there was a significant main effect $(F(1, 20) = 15.855, P = 0.001)$ of learning effect, tasks before practice were significantly higher than after practice. At the same time we found a significant main effect $(F(1, 20) = 23.811, P < 0.001)$ of novelty, the old tasks were significantly higher than the new tasks. There was not the interaction effect between the two among complexity, learning effect and novelty.

3.2   fMRI Results

In Figure 5–Figure 8, horizontal coordinates represent the scan. Scan "-2" is the resting state of the last trial, and scan "-1" is the red "*" presenting in the screen. The averaged value of scan "-2" and scan "-1" is the baseline of BOLD signal; scan "0" is the time that the Sudoku task presented in the screen. Longitudinal coordinates represent BOLD signals of a certain brain region changes relative to baseline. We conducted repeated measures analysis of variance on BOLD signals in the areas of caudate, prefrontal cortex, posterior parietal cortex and anterior cingulate cortex. The results are shown in Table 1. The details of the BOLD signal changes in these brain regions were shown as followed:

• Caudate

We found that the main effect of learning effect wasn't significant in caudate. The main effect of novelty wasn't significant. The main effect of complexity was significant in right caudate, BOLD signals of the complex tasks were higher than the simple tasks, but the main effect of complexity wasn't significant in left caudate. The reason was that caudate corresponded to the procedure module, which formed and extracted the procedural knowledge. For the simple tasks, subjects formed and extracted the procedural memory quickly. But subjects formed and extracted the procedural memory slowly on the complex tasks.

• Prefrontal cortex (PFC)

We found that the main effect of learning effect was significant in prefrontal cortex, BOLD signals of the 1st scan was higher than the 2nd scan. The main effect of novelty wasn't significant. The main effect on complexity was weak significant in right prefrontal cortex, the main effect of complexity was significant in left prefrontal cortex, BOLD signals of the complex tasks were higher than the simple tasks. The reason was that prefrontal cortex corresponded to the declarative memory module, which completed the declarative memory extracted. For the simple tasks, subjects extracted the declarative memory quickly. But subjects extracted the declarative memory slowly on the complex tasks. When

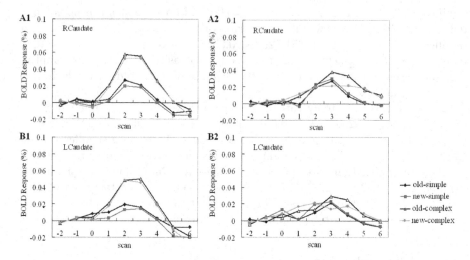

Fig. 5. BOLD signal changes for the right caudate (RCaudate) in the 1st scan (A1) and the 2nd scan (A2), and for the left caudate (LCaudate) in the 1st scan (B1) and the 2nd scan (B2)

subjects answered the new tasks, the position of number was new, subjects needed to reuse the heuristic rules to answer the tasks. However subjects had remembered the old tasks when subjects answered the old tasks. With practice subjects extracted the declarative memory more easily about all tasks.

• Posterior parietal cortex (PPC)

We found that the main effect of complexity was significant in posterior parietal cortex, BOLD signals of the complex tasks were higher than the simple tasks. The main effect of learning effect was significant in posterior parietal cortex, BOLD signals of the 1st scan was higher than the 2nd scan. The main effect of novelty was significant in right posterior parietal cortex, the main effect of novelty was weak significant in left posterior parietal cortex, BOLD signals of the complex tasks were higher than the simple tasks. Posterior parietal cortex corresponded to the imaginal module, which performed problem representation and kept the intermediate state of the questions. For the simple tasks, problem representation was easy, and the intermediate states of the questions were less. But problem representation of the complex tasks was difficult, and the intermediate states of the questions were more. When subjects answered the new tasks, subjects needed to locate the new numbers position and "?" position, subjects needed to reuse the heuristic rules to answer the tasks, problem representation was slow. But subjects had remembered them when subjects answered the old tasks, the answers of the old tasks appeared quickly. With practice problem representation was easy, the intermediate states of the questions decrease, meanwhile the utilization rate of the neurons also increased.

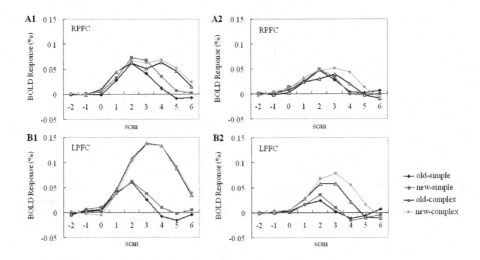

Fig. 6. BOLD signal changes for the right prefrontal cortex (RPFC) in the 1st scan (A1) and the 2nd scan (A2), and for the left prefrontal cortex (LPFC) in the 1st scan (B1) and the 2nd scan (B2)

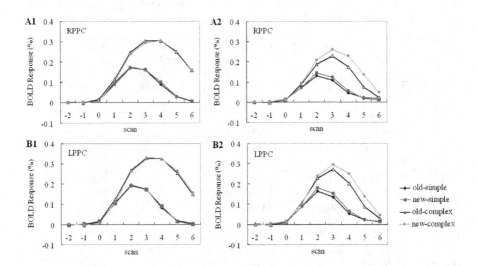

Fig. 7. BOLD signal changes for the right posterior parietal cortex (RPPC) in the 1st scan (A1) and the 2nd scan (A2), and for the left posterior parietal cortex (LPPC) in the 1st scan (B1) and the 2nd scan (B2)

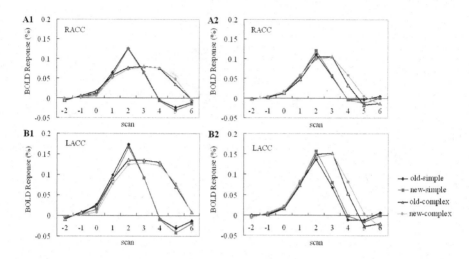

Fig. 8. BOLD signal changes for the right anterior cingulate cortex (RACC) in the 1st scan (A1) and the 2nd scan (A2), and for the left anterior cingulate cortex (LACC) in the 1st scan (B1) and the 2nd scan (B2)

Table 1. The results of repeated measures ANOVA on the BOLD signals in the ACT-R brain regions

Effect		learning effect	complexity	novelty	complexity by learning effect	novelty by learning effect	complexity by novelty
RCaudate	F	0.101	7.615	0.157	2.044	0.025	0.748
	P	0.755	0.014	0.698	0.172	0.877	0.400
LCaudate	F	0.023	2.101	0.418	0.685	0.222	0.482
	P	0.882	0.166	0.527	0.420	0.644	0.498
RPFC	F	8.204	4.124	2.243	9.643	1.177	0.014
	P	0.011	0.059	0.154	0.007	0.294	0.907
LPFC	F	14.07	21.218	2.211	7.297	0.145	0.003
	P	0.002	0.000	0.156	0.016	0.708	0.958
RPPC	F	6.539	36.599	14.46	11.312	6.930	1.030
	P	0.021	0.000	0.002	0.004	0.018	0.325
LPPC	F	5.163	74.716	3.69	13.465	7.576	0.346
	P	0.037	0.000	0.073	0.002	0.014	0.565
RACC	F	0.293	17.319	0.003	0.976	1.387	0.286
	P	0.596	0.001	0.956	0.338	0.256	0.600
LACC	F	0.047	17.308	0.686	0.487	1.683	0.710
	P	0.832	0.001	0.42	0.495	0.213	0.412

- Anterior cingulate cortex (ACC)

We found that the main effect of complexity was significant in anterior cingulate cortex, BOLD signals of the complex tasks were higher than the simple tasks. The main effect of learning effect wasn't significant. The main effect of novelty wasn't significant. The reason was that anterior cingulate cortex corresponded to the goal control module, which kept the target and controlled. For the complex tasks, the target keeping time was long, the goal control was strong. But the target keeping time was short, the goal control was weak on the simple tasks.

4   Discussions

In the fMRI data analysis, we were concerned about the six modules in ACT-R model. Meanwhile subjects solved the 4×4 Sudoku tasks which needed the six modules. But this study was focused on the procedure module, the declarative memory module, the imaginal module and the goal control module. And these modules corresponded to caudate, prefrontal cortex, posterior parietal cortex and anterior cingulate cortex. We would discuss the four brain regions.

Inferior ventral lateral prefrontal cortex corresponded to the declarative memory module, completed the declarative memory extracted. The prefrontal cortex, whose primary function was to guide novice behavior by instantiating the task context and then structuring the sequential execution of task-relevant operations [9]. For the simple tasks, subjects extracted the declarative memory quickly. For the complex tasks, subjects spent more time to retrieve necessary information, such as the heuristic rules. When subjects answered the new tasks, the position of number was new, subjects needed to reuse the heuristic rules to answer the tasks. However subjects had remembered the old tasks when subjects answered the old tasks. With practice subjects extracted the declarative memory more easily about all tasks.

Posterior parietal cortex corresponded to the imaginal module, which completed the problem representation and kept the intermediate state of the questions. Posterior parietal cortex, which was widely viewed as an attentional center of the brain [5,15], subserved a control process that allocated attention to task-specific information processing regions. Its function was that guided information flow by regulating the output of distributed information processing modules during novice performance. After practice, the demand for attentional control was reduced as associations became strong enough to trigger information flow in the absence of attentional modulation [9]. For the simple tasks, problem representation was easy, and the intermediate states of the questions were less. But problem representation of the complex tasks was difficult, and the intermediate states of the questions were more. When subjects answered the new tasks, subjects needed to locate the new numbers position and "?" position, subjects needed to reuse the heuristic rules to answer the tasks, problem representation was slow. But subjects had remembered them when subjects answered the old tasks, the answers of the old tasks appeared quickly. With practice problem representation was easy, the intermediate states of the questions decrease, meanwhile the utilization rate of the neurons also increased.

Caudate corresponded to the procedure module, which formed and extracted the procedural knowledge. More recently, it has been demonstrated that the caudate was highly involved in learning and memory [6]. And anterior cingulate cortex corresponded to the goal control module, which kept the target and controlled. Indeed, much of the recent literature on cingulate function has emphasized its role in communicating a need for greater cognitive control to other executive brain regions [4]. Subjects were trained five days in the experiment. Before and after learning BOLD signal value of two scans which were no difference in caudate and anterior cingulate cortex. In general, with enhancement of practice, activation of caudate and anterior cingulate cortex increased. In other words, when subjects answered the tasks, the formation of the procedural knowledge and the more objectives extraction increased, the target keeping time extended, the goal control would be strong by practice. With the practice continuing, activation of caudate and anterior cingulate cortex decreased. In other words, when the practice achieved a certain degree, the problem-solving process turned automatically, the procedural knowledge extraction decreased, the target keeping time reduced, the goal control would be weak. Because we didn't scan in the middle of training, we guessed that there were not major changes of activation in caudate and anterior cingulate cortex between the 1st scan and the 2cd scan, because the training intensity was high.

We are going to conduct an exploratory analysis to investigate the changes of activities in other related brain regions, which would help us to understand more about the neural mechanism of skill learning during the heuristic problem solving.

Acknowledgements. The research was supported by National Natural Science Foundation of China (No.60875075, 60905027), Beijing Postdoctoral Research Foundation (No. Q6002020201201), Beijing Natural Science Foundation (No.4102007) and the CAS/SAFEA International Partnership Program for Creative Research Teams.

References

1. Alison, H.C., Wynne, A.L.: Practice-related changes in lumbar loading during rapid voluntary pulls made while standing. Clinical Biomechanics 15, 726–734 (2000)
2. Carla, T.F., Bernard, G.: Optic ophasia: evidence of the contribution of different neural systems to object and action naming. Cortex 33, 499–513 (1997)
3. Carol, A.S., Russell, A.P.: Hemispheric asymmetries and individual differences in visual concept learning as measured by functional MRI. Neuropsychologia 38, 1316–1324 (2000)
4. Carter, C.S., Botvinick, M.M., Cohen, J.D.: The contribution of the anterior cingulate cortex to executive processes in cognition. Reviews in the Neuroscience 10, 49–57 (1999)

5. Corbetta, M., Shulman, G.L., Miezin, F.M., Petersen, S.E.: Superior parietal cortex activation during spatial attention shifts and visual feature conjunction. Science 270(5237), 802–805 (1995)
6. Graybiel, A.M.: The basal ganglia: learning new tricks and loving it. Current Opinion in Neurobiology 15(6), 638–644 (2005)
7. Gregor, R., Earl, K.M.: Effects of visual experience on the representation of objects in the prefrontal cortex. Neuron 27, 179–189 (2000)
8. Igor, D., Nicola, G.K.: The time course of motor cortex plasticity after spaced motor practice. Brain Stimulation 4, 156–164 (2011)
9. Jason, M.C., Walter, S.: Neuroimaging studies of practice-related change: fMRI and meta-analytic evidence of a domain-general control network for learning. Cognitive Brain Research 25(3), 607–623 (2005)
10. Anderson, J.R., Fincham, J.M., Douglass, S.: The role of examples and rules in the acquisition of a cognitive skill. Journal of Experimental Psychology-Learning Memory and Cognition 23, 932–945 (1997)
11. Anderson, J.R.: The architecture of cognition. Harvard University Press, Cambridge (1983)
12. Anderson, J.R.: How can the human mind occur in the physical universe? Oxford University Press, USA (2007)
13. Krause, B.J., Hautzel, H., Schmidt, D.: Learning related interactions among neuronal systems involved in memory processes. Journal of Physiology-Paris 99, 318–332 (2006)
14. Mochizuki, K.H., Tsukiura, T., Mochizuki, S.: Learning-related changes of brain activation in the visual ventral stream: An fMRI study of mirror reading skill. Brain Research 1122, 154–160 (2006)
15. Posner, M.I., Petersen, S.E.: The attention system of the human brain. Annual Review of Neuroscience 13, 25–42 (1990)
16. Selene, C., Samuel, J.W.: Neuromagnetic fields reveal cortical plasticity when learning an auditory discrimination task. Brain Research 764, 53–66 (1997)

The Role of Category Label
in Adults' Inductive Reasoning

Xuyan Wang[1,2], Zhoujun Long[1,2], Sanxia Fan[1,2],
Weiyan Yu[1,2], Haiyan Zhou[1,2], and Yulin Qin[1,2,3]

[1] International WIC Institute, Beijing University of Technology, China
[2] Beijing Key Laboratory of MRI and Brain Informatics, China
[3] Dept. of Psychology, Carnegie Mellon University, USA
zhouhaiyan@bjut.edu.cn, yulinq12@gmail.com

Abstract. This study focused on two different views about the role of category label in inductive reasoning: perceptional-similarity-based and conception-based views. We used an inductive reasoning task, possibility judgment for a feature of artificial insect, to record behavioral performance in experiment 1 and brain activity with ERP in experiment 2. Two factors were manipulated: visual similarity of artificial insect, and whether with same label or not. The result suggests that the conception-based view is not supported here. The category label may enhance the perceptual characteristics, since labels have same visual and sound features; but it is hard to deny the role of conceptual information contained by a label to affect the inductive reasoning.

1   Introduction

Inductive reasoning is a process of expanding and inferring knowledge from the known facts to the unknown. It plays a unique role in human cognitive activities [6], with a purpose of summarizing knowledge or experience [13]. People can acquire new knowledge and reduce reliance on memory with inductive reasoning [3] and it is an important part of human high cognitive activities [10]. Usually people don't achieve right conclusions but only infer the likely results from inductive reasoning, which is different from deductive reasoning. Also it is the central link for people to master the uncertain things [11].

One of the primary functions of category is to support inductive reasoning. At present, there are two different views in inductive reasoning about the role on basis of category: the perceptional-similarity-based and the conception-based views. While the category label is the carrier of category knowledge, so there are also two different views of the role of category label in inductive reasoning. Perceptional-similarity-based view believes that category label is only a perceptional feature that supports reasoning, the process of inductive reasoning is to do the judgment by computing the similarity between the source and target stimuli. The conception-based view believes that category label provides a category membership in inductive reasoning, adults should base on the labels to make the

F.M. Zanzotto et al. (Eds.): BI 2012, LNCS 7670, pp. 50–60, 2012.

inference, and the impacts of perceptional similarity should be ignored. Understanding the role of category label in inductive reasoning is helpful for further revealing the mechanism of information processing in the brain of human being, as well as explaining the basis of human brains' cognitive neuroscience.

The earliest study [4] about category label's function in inductive reasoning used a behavioral method by Gelman and Markman in 1986. The participants were shown groups of pictures. There were three pictures in each group, including two test stimuli and one target stimulus. For instance, the target stimulus was a picture of "shark", test stimulus 1 was a "tropical fish" picture, and test stimulus 2 was a pictures of "dolphin". By manipulating the instructions, they made test stimulus 1 and the target stimulus shared the same label, but test stimulus 2 and the target stimulus were perceptual similar. The experimenter told the subjects "this fish (pointing to the picture of "tropical fish") breaths under water" but "this dolphin (pointing to the picture of "dolphin") jumps up to the water surface to breathe". Then the children were asked "Where does this fish (pointing to the picture of "shark") breathe, over or under water?". The results indicated that the four-year-old children thought that the shark breathed more like the tropical fish but not the dolphin, though sharks and dolphins seemed more similar in shape. In the research of Slousky [12], he used the hybrid pictures and artificial linguistic labels as materials. His results demonstrated that the degree of adults' using labels reached a ceiling level, which supported the conception-based view. The study of Murphy and Yamauchi [9,14,15] suggested that category label represented generic information. They discussed the role of category and characteristic similarity in human inductive reasoning with the materials of five characteristic attributes of artificial animals and meaningless categories. They found the category label played a more important role than single feature. Hu cheng's study also showed the same tendency. But Anderson thought the category was a perceptual characteristic [1]. There were many other similar arguments about the two different views as above.

Behavioral method was usually used in previous study, and there was no consistent result about the role of category label in adults' inductive reasoning. In recent years, more and more research use the the method of neural cognitive science to investigate human cognition. We are going to use the technique of ERP to investigate the issue about category label in inductive reasoning in this study.

An event-related potential (ERP) is a measured brain response, that is the direct result of a specific sensory, cognitive, or motor event [7]. ERP is a potential change in brain areas when the brain's sensory systems or someplace of the brain given or canceled a certain stimulation. ERP can be reliably measured by using electroencephalography (EEG), and it is a procedure that measures electrical activity of the brain over time by using electrodes placed on the scalp. The EEG reflects thousands of simultaneously ongoing brain processes. This means the brain's response to a single stimulus or event of interest is not usually visible in the EEG recording in a single trial. So to see the brain's response to a stimulus, the experimenter must conduct many trials (100 or more) and average the results together, causing random brain activity to be averaged out and the relevant waveform to remain, calling the ERP [2]. ERP method is common used in the area of cognitive study, which has a high time resolution with a millisecond timescale and is not traumatic. ERP has a time lock and phase lock relationship with events' process. The integration between the time resolution and the behavior experimental data provides a new perspective for spying out psychological activities. Especially, its integration with reaction time can reflect the cognitive process in real time. ERP waveforms contain a series of positive and negative voltage deflections, calling components, such as P300, N400, PN, RP and so on. The components of ERP are related to different cognitive processing, and we will discuss the relationship of our study later.

2   Experiment 1

2.1   Participants

A total of sixteen college students (healthy, right-handed, Chinese native speaker, normal or corrected-normal vision) participated in this experiment, and received small reward as payment. All participants were given informed consent. Their average age was 22.2±1.54.

2.2   Materials

In the present study, the materials were schematic animals, as shown in Figure 1. There was no label in the condition of "no label". These schematic animals were produced from combinations of four feature dimensions (antennae = crooked/curly/straight, head = square/pentagonal/T-shaped, torso = cruciform/hexagonal/elliptic, tail = lightning/triangular/concave quadrilateral). The labels here were consist of two Chinese characters, and the frequency of them was from seven over ten thousand to sixteen over ten thousand. The characters were randomly combined into labels that actually did not exist, such as "cheng ke". Artificial materials can avoid the influence of familiarity or personal experience effectively. Our reasoning tasks were based on the following four kinds of attributes: genetic, anatomical, perception, and behavior attributes. Specifically, they were: "AEL" in the body, two cavities in the liver, an "F" pattern in the abdomen, and night predation lover respectively. These four attributes were shown randomly. The impact of different attributes was not considered in the analysis.

The meanings of the labels were manipulated as two different animal categories in one group; in the other, the same labels represented names of the animals' attributes. These pictures were paired off as groups and the situations that four attributes were all the same or totally different were wiped off. So the rest groups had one, two, or three same attributes. We assumed that the high similar group had three same attributes and low similar group had only one

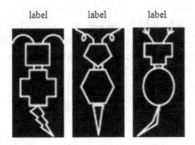

Fig. 1. Materials in this study

same attribute. The consciousness similarity was evaluated by ten college students from Beijing University of Technology. There was a significant difference between high similar and low similar group ($F(2, 239) = 2899.992$, $P < 0.001$).

2.3 Design

The experiment was a 2 (label sharing degree: same label, no label; within subjects) × 3 (consciousness similarity: high similar, low similar; within subjects) factorial design. Participants in the present study were shown schematic pictures of animals side by side and asked to make predictions about the right stimulus on the basis of the left stimulus, as shown in Figure 2. The left picture was "same label" condition and the right was "no label" condition. The possibility that the right animal shared the same reasoning attribute as the left animal was marked with a value from one to five. One meant the possibility was the least, five meant the possibility was the most.

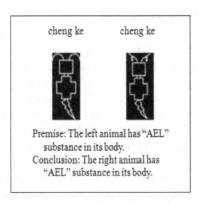 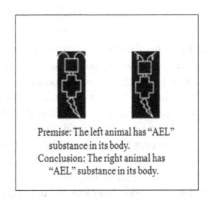

Fig. 2. Examples of the possibility judgment task in this study with left for same label and right for no label

We assumed that in the condition of a fixed category label level, if the participants' confidence of inductive reasoning would not change along with the change of perceptual similarity, then it indicated that the category label expressed a conceptual relationship, participants made the inference on the basis of classificatory member relationship, which meant we supported the conception-based view. However, if the confidence of inductive reasoning changed along with the change of perceptual similarity, then it suggested that we would't support the conception-based view and category label promoted inductive reasoning together with the perceptual information.

2.4 Procedure

The process of the stimulus' presentation is in Figure 3. First, a fixation of a star was presented in the screen for 1 s; after it was the inductive task, which lasted for 2 s; then there were two pictures of animals side by side, in the condition of "same label", the labels would also appeared on the top of the two pictures, but there would be no label in the condition of "no label", the presentation time was at most 10 s, participants should response now by pressing keys, after the response or 10 s, the pictures would disappear. The interval between trials was 1 s.

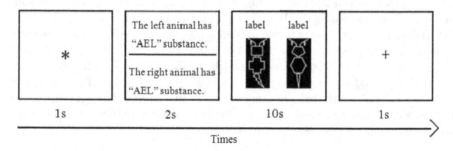

Fig. 3. The process of the stimulus presentation

Before the formal experiment, participants were asked to read the instructions and do tasks on paper to make sure that they understood the tasks. After that, the experiment would continue on computer. There were three parts in the experiment: (i) Key practice. The purpose of "key practice" was to ensure that the participants could give the score quickly and correctly. Keys "blank, Y, 8, 9, P" were corresponding to score "1, 2, 3, 4, 5" respectively. "1, 2, 3, 4, 5" emerged on the screen randomly, participants should press the corresponding keys rapidly with their right hands. Three sessions were requested to finish, each session had 25 practices. We identified a success as participants' mistake number in each session was less than 1, the key practice was over after 3 continuous successes. (ii) Experiment practice. A total of 12 tasks were set for participants, which were the same as formal experiments. (iii) Formal experiments. The formal experiment had 8 sessions, each session included 60 tasks. During the course of the experiment, participants should be concentrated and response as soon as possible. Participants could have a rest after each session. After the experiment, each participant was asked to fill out a questionnaire.

2.5   Results and Discussion

The value diagram of each condition is in Figure 4. We can see from it, the value was higher in "high similar" level than in "low similar" level both in "no label" condition and "same label" condition. And in the same consciousness similarity situation, the value was higher in "same label" condition than in "no label" condition. All dependent measures were analyzed with repeated measures analysis of variance (ANOVA). The results showed that there was a significant main effect on category label factor and perceptual similarity factor ($F(1, 15) = 39.449$, $P < 0.01$ for label effect; $F(1, 15) = 47.135$, $P < 0.01$ for perceptual similarity effect). This meant that participants depended on not only the category label but also the consciousness characteristics to make the inference. Then we did T-test with the data. The results indicated that in the condition of "no label", the value in "high similar" status was significantly higher than the "low similar" status ($t(15) = 7.434$, $P < 0.01$) and in the case of "same label", the value in "high similar" status was also significantly higher than "low similar" status ($t(15) = 5.068$, $P < 0.01$). This demonstrated that the category label was not conceptual information according to the assumption before. Participants made the inference both depended on the label factor and the perceptual similarity factor. When there was a same label or a higher similarity, participants had more confidence to infer the feature from the known animal to the test animal.

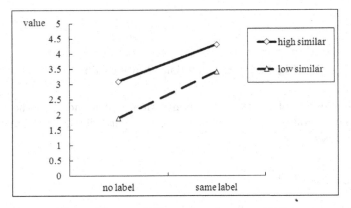

Fig. 4. The possibility value of each condition

The response time diagram of each condition is in Figure 5. As in the diagram, we can see that the response time was slightly shorter when there was a low similarity than a high similarity. We did a T-test ($t(15) = 1.177$, $P = 0.258$), no significant difference existed. This may be because when there was no label, participants made the decision only relying on the pictures' consciousness similarity. But high similarity was defined as three same attributes in four and the low similarity was defined as one same attribute in four, the animal pictures in the two cases were both easy to be recognized, so the response time was almost the same. In "same label" condition, the response time was shorter when there was a high similarity than a low similarity. T-test analysis showed there was a significant difference between the "high similar" condition and the "low similar" condition ($t(15) = 2.607$, $P = 0.02$). This demonstrated that in "same label" condition, the same category label facilitated participants' judgments with the high perceptual similarity. Otherwise, in the same similarity level, the response time in the situation of "same label" was longer than the "no label" condition. The reason was in this case, participants should consider both the label and the similarity factor in "same label" condition but only the similarity factor in "no label" condition. So the response time was longer. These results also illustrated that the participants used both the category label and the perceptual similarity to make the inference.

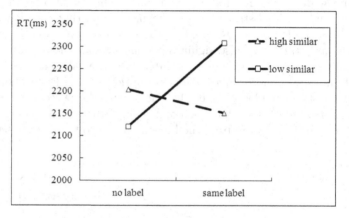

Fig. 5. The response time of each condition

From the results of value and response time, we found that the category label was not a conception, which meant our experiment did not support the conception-based view.

3   Experiment 2

3.1   Participants

A total of ten college students participated in this experiment (healthy, right-handed, Chinese native speaker, normal or corrected-normal vision), and received small reward as payment. All participants were given informed consent. Their average age was 23.4±2.07.

3.2   Materials

Materials in this experiment were the same as those in experiment 1.

3.3 Design

The design in this experiment was basically the same as experiment 1, except the assumption. We tried to study the role of category label by observing the EEG and analyzing the ERP components.

3.4 Procedure

Before the formal experiment, participants did "key practice" and experiment practice as in experiment 1. Then the preparation work about wearing brain cap was done. About the equipment in EEG collected and data analysis, we would make an introduction. The equipment of EEG collected was from German Brain-Products Company, with a 32 conductive recording system constituted by 32 channel BrainAmp MR Amplifier and a BrainCap with 32 conductive electrode caps to record EEG data. The reference electrode was chosen as "Reference" between "Fz" and "Cz" on the top of the head. Scalp resistance in each electrode was controlled less than 6k. "HEOG" and "VEOG" were severally recorded in lateral of the left eye and underside of the right eye. Sampling frequency was 500 Hz. Stimulus presentation was controlled by E-prime 2.0. The rest of the experiment was as experiment 1.

3.5 Results and Discussion

Preliminary results are shown below. We analyzed the forehead brain electrical data. Figure 6 is the oscillogram of the four conditions.

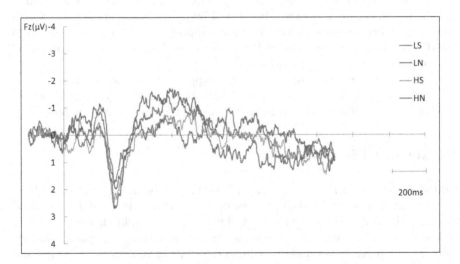

Fig. 6. The oscillogram of the four conditions in experiment 2. Abbreviation: LS-low similarity, the same label condition; LN-low similarity, no label condition; HS-high similarity, the same label condition; HN-high similarity, no label condition.

From Figure 6, we can see a positive wave in the 200−400 ms time window around 300 ms. In Donchin's opinion, the latency of P300 reflects the required time for evaluating the irritants or for classification [8]. The latency increases along with the difficulty of the tasks. From the oscillogram, we can see a longer latency on "same label" level than "no label" level. This meant that category label may be seen as a perceptual characteristic, which made the task easier and promoted the inductive reasoning. In LS and HS, participants devoted less time to characterize the perceptual feature for working memory. However, there was no significant difference after a T-test. This might because a small amount of participants or a not very good data quality. So we should solve the problem in the future.

We can see a negative wave as N400 in the 400−520 ms time window, as shown in Figure 6. N400 was first found in Kutas and Hillyard's study [5] for cognition of words and sentences. It is an endogenous component of ERPs, and is a negative wave in language cognitive event-related potentials, reflecting the cognitive processes for language of the cerebral cortex. By comparing the area of each condition, we found that there was a significant difference between LN and HN ($t(9) = 2.306$, $P = 0.047$). It indicated that in the same category label level, the category label was not a conception according to the assumption in experiment 1, and this consisted with the behavioral results. But the difference between LS and HS was not remarkable, the reason may be the same as above. Also we found that the area of LS and LN was significantly different from each other ($t(9) = -3.215$, $P = 0.011$). This meant when the similarity level was low, the category label played a more important role than in the high similarity. This further showed us that the similarity played a part in inductive reasoning, and the role of category label was influenced by perceptual characteristic, which meant the conception-based view was not supported here. And because N400 reflects the cognitive processes of language processing, so here category label may contain conceptual information.

From the preliminary results, we don't support the conception-based view. The category label may be a perceptual characteristic and may contain conceptual information. But we need a further study to test and verify this point.

4   General Discussion

We did two experiments on the basis of the two different views of the role of category label in adults' inductive reasoning: the perceptional-similarity-based view and the conception-based view. Gelman, et al. thought that the category label provided a conceptual or class relationship, and this relationship was not influenced by perceptual similarity. Also in the study of Slousky, et al., adults' use of label was close to a ceiling level, but Long Changquan and Lu Tianling's study showed a different result. Our behavioral results suggested that the confidence of inductive reasoning changed with the change of perceptional similarity. People's confidence was enhanced with the increase of perceptual similarity degree. So we don't support the conception-based view in the behavioral experiment, but the category label may be a perceptual characteristic and may also provide conceptual information.

The ERP experiment measured the EEG to study the role of category label in adults' inductive reasoning, this was the first time we used an ERP approach on this subject in domestic. From the preliminary results, we did't support the conception-based view as the behavioral results. However, there are some disadvantages in the study, such as the problem in experiment 2. Concerning the ERP components, there are also some arguments about the cognitive activities that different components represent. Only one electrode is analyzed here, which means the results may be not comprehensive. So in the future, we will increase the number of participants, do a comprehensive analysis of the ERP data of the whole brain and the design need to be improved because of the perceptual similarity factor.

5 Conclusion

In this study, we used behavioral and ERP approach to investigate the role of category label in adults' inductive reasoning. Both the behavioral and ERP results didn't support the conception-based view. A category label might be a perceptual characteristic added to attribute reasoning, but it might provide conceptual information either. The proportion of them needs further researches.

Acknowledgement. The research was supported by National Natural Science Foundation of China (No.60875075, 60905027), Beijing Postdoctoral Research Foundation (No. Q6002020201201), Beijing Natural Science Foundation (No.4102007) and the CAS/SAFEA International Partnership Program for Creative Research Teams.

References

1. Anderson, J.R.: The adaptive nature of human categorization. Psychological Review 98(3), 409–429 (1991)
2. Coles, M.G.H., Rugg, M.D.: Event-related brain potentials: an introduction. In: Electrophysiology of Mind. Oxford Scholarship Online Monographs, pp. 1–27 (1996)
3. Fisher, R.: Design of experiments, pp. 202–245. Hafner Publishing Company, New York (1951)
4. Gelman, S.A., Markman, E.M.: Categories and induction in young children. Cognition 23, 183–209 (1986)
5. Kutas, M., Hillyard, S.A.: Reading Senseless Sentences: Brain Potentials Reflect Semantic Incongruity. Science 207, 203–205 (1980)
6. Li, H., Chen, A., Feng, T., Li, F., Long, C.: A brief perspective of the development of induction and its potential mechanism. Psychological Science 27(6), 1457–1459 (2004)
7. Luck, S.J.: An Introduction to the Event-Related Potential Technique. The MIT Press, Boston (2005)

8. McCarthy, G., Donchin, E.: A metric for thought: a comparison of P300 latency and reaction time. Science 211, 77–80 (1981)
9. Murphy, G.L., Ross, B.H.: Predictions from uncertain categorizations. Cognitive Psychology 27, 148–193 (1994)
10. Osherson, D.N., Smith, E.E., Wilkie, O., Lopea, A., Shafir, E.: Category-based induction. Psychological Review 97, 185–200 (1990)
11. Sloman, S.A.: Feature-based induction. Cognitive Psychology 25, 231–280 (1993)
12. Sloutsky, V.M., Lo, Y.F.: How much does a shared name make things similar? Part l: linguistic labels and the development of similarity judgment. Developmental Psychology 35, 1478–1492 (1999)
13. Sloutsky, V.M., Lo, Y.F., Fisher, A.V.: How much does a shard name make things similar: linguistic labels and the development of inductive inference. Child Development 72, 1695–1709 (2001)
14. Yamauchi, T.: Labeling bias and categorical induction: generative aspects of category information. Journal of Experimental Psychology: Learning, Memory and Cognition 31(3), 538–553 (2005)
15. Yamauchi, T., Yu, N.Y.: Category labels versus feature labels: category labels polarize inferential predictions. Memory and Cognition 36(3), 544–553 (2008)

Estimation of Visual Feedback Contribution to Limb Stiffness in Visuomotor Control

Yuki Ueyama and Eizo Miyashita

Department of Computational Intelligence and Systems Science
Interdisciplinary Graduate School of Science and Engineering, Tokyo Institute of Technology
4259 Nagatsuta-cho, Midori-ku, Yokohama, Kanagawa 226-8503, Japan
yuki.ueyama@gmail.com,
eizo@dis.titech.ac.jp

Abstract. The purpose of this work was to investigate contribution of a visual feedback system to limb stiffness. It is difficult to differentiate the visual component from others out of measured data obtained by applying a force perturbation, which is required to estimate stiffness,. In this study, we proposed an experimental procedure consisted of a pair of tasks to investigate the visual feedback component, and showed it as end-point stiffness ellipses at several timings of a movement. In addition, we carried out a numerical simulation of the movement with the perturbation in according with a framework of optimal feedback control model. As results, long axes of the stiffness ellipses of the visual component were modulated to the movement directions and the simulation showed that a positional feedback gain was exponentially increased toward a movement end. Consequently, the visual feedback system is supposed to regulate compliance of a movement direction.

1 Introduction

We investigated a role of visual feedback contribution in biological systems. Our feedback systems are hierarchically composed of several levels, i.e., through mechanical muscle properties, spinal and cerebral reflexes using somatosensory information (i.e., joint angle and velocity), and that using visual information (Fig. 1a). These systems can be depicted as a block diagram (Fig. 1b). A lot of studies have been conducted in order to examine in what aspect the visual information contributes to on-line control of arm movements. However, the visual feedback effect has been considered only in kinematical specialties and plasticity during adaptation learning [1-2]. There may have not been any studies to investigate the effect on dynamical properties such as limb stiffness although it is essential to understand characteristics of the system.

In this study, we proposed an experimental procedure consisted of a pair of tasks in order to investigate the visual feedback effect on the limb stiffness. One of the tasks was a control force perturbation task, in which force perturbation was applied to a monkey's hand using a manipulandum and the hand position was provided as a cursor on a display monitor. The other one was a error cramp visual perturbation task, in

F.M. Zanzotto et al. (Eds.): BI 2012, LNCS 7670, pp. 61–72, 2012.

which force perturbation was also applied, but visual error was dumped by fixing the cursor movement to the direction of the applied perturbation. This task procedure could distinguish influences generated by the somatosensory and visual feedback systems, and the visual feedback effect could be identified as subtraction of the effect of the control task from that of the error cramp task. We showed the effect as stiffness ellipse changes at several timings after external force perturbation onset. Next, we carried out a numerical simulation of the movement using optimal feedback control model [3-4]. It is a plausible control model that could predict variability of movement phenomena such as obstacle avoidance task [5], adaptation to novel tasks [2, 6-7], manipulation of complex object [8] and muscle co-contraction according to the movement accuracy [9]. Moreover, in neural studies in monkey and human, it also has been suggested that primary motor cortex provides a neural substrate for integrating shoulder and elbow motion information into joint torque for fast feedback control [10-11].

As results, the stiffness in the visual error cramp task indicated that effect of the somatosensory feedback were large along to error correcting direction of the trajectory. In contrast, effect of the visual feedback was increased along to the actual trajectories. These suggest that the somatosensory feedback system mainly works as trajectory error correction and the visual feedback systems contribute to reproducing a movement direction or generating a new trajectory. Moreover, our simulation suggested that the visual feedback information might be a trigger to induce precise state estimation.

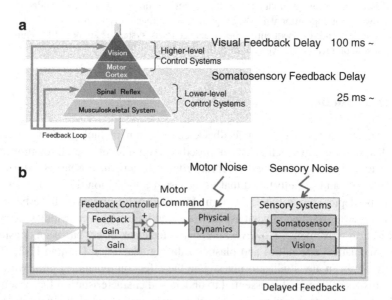

Fig. 1. Illustration of a simplified feedback systems in mammals. (a) Hierarchical feedback systems. (b) Diagram of feedback control systems.

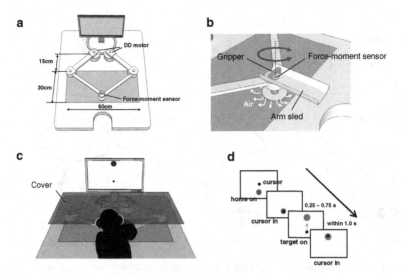

Fig. 2. Illustration of the experimental setup. (a) RANARM has two direct-drive motors and four link bars made of aluminum. A force-moment sensor is attached to the grip of the manipulandum. (b) An arm sled made of aluminum is attached to the rotation axis of the gripper and is free to rotate around the axis. Compressed air is vented under the gripper and joints to generate a floating force. (c) The monkey's hand is covered by a black screen. (d) The task procedure on the computer screen.

2   Material and Methods

2.1   Experimental Apparatus

We have developed RANARM (robotic arm manipulandum for normal and altered reaching movements) that is able to track rapid arm movements and apply efficient force perturbations to a monkey's hand in order to disturb the movement trajectories [12]. RANARM was used as an experimental apparatus in order to measure hand movements and apply force perturbations (Fig. 2a). RANARM is composed of four rigid link bars made of aluminum, and driven by two direct-drive motors with a force–moment sensor attached to a gripper. In addition, RANARM's control enables it to cancel its own dynamics by calculating the inverse dynamics. The gripper position is displayed as a cursor on a display monitor, and the monkey subject is able to move the cursor by controlling the gripper (Fig. 2c). Moreover, the monkey could not see directly the gripper position and arm movements covered by a black screen. To reduce friction between RANARM and a table, compressed air is vented under the gripper and two joints to form a thin layer of air between them (Fig. 2b). During the experiments, an aluminum arm sled was attached to the rotation axis of the gripper, and was free to rotate around the axis. The monkey was seated on a monkey chair with its arm resting on the arm sled in order to maintain the elbow, shoulder, and hand at roughly the same height. Note that the monkey's arm was not fixed to the arm sled.

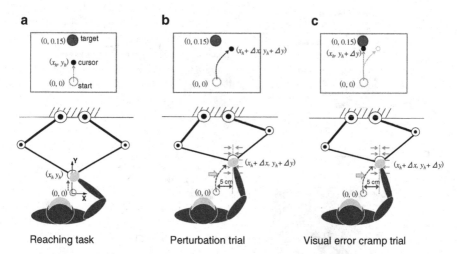

Fig. 3. Experimental tasks. (a) A reaching task without perturbation. (b) A perturbation trial is applied a force to displace monkey's hand right or left from midline in random order. (b) A visual error cramp trial is similar to the perturbation trial. However, the lateral position of the cursor is fixed on the midline.

2.2   Experimental Setup

We examined a reaching task under unpredicted perturbation to a female Japanese monkey (*Macaca fuscata*, weight at 6.0 kg) using RANARM. Our experimental procedure consisted of a pair of tasks in order to investigate the visual feedback effect. One of the tasks was a control perturbation task, in which force perturbation was applied to the monkey's hand using RANARM and the hand position was provided as the cursor on the display monitor (Fig. 2d). The other one was a visual error cramp task, in which force perturbation was also applied, but the visual error was dumped by fixing the cursor movement to the direction of the applied perturbation (Fig. 2c). This task procedure could distinguish influences generated by the somatosensory and visual feedback systems, and the visual feedback effects were identified as subtractions of the effect of the control task from that of the error cramp task.. A local ethics committee approved the experimental protocol and all the experiments were conducted in accordance with guidelines of Tokyo Institute of Technology.

Reaching Task. This task was basically a reaching, in which the subject monkey moved a cursor (black circle with 0.25 cm radius) to a displayed target. The task was divided into four steps (Fig. 2a). First, a home position (red circle with 1.2 cm radius) was appeared at (0, 0) or (0, 0.15) in random order. Note that, the original point (0.0) was 5.4 cm to left and 15.5 cm to forward from the shoulder. Second, subject moved the cursor in the home circle. Third, the home circle was disappeared in 0.25 - 0.75 s after the cursor had been moved in the home circle and a target position (blue circle with 1.8 cm radius) was appeared at 15 cm forward (0, 0.15), or backward (0, 0) positions. Finally, the subject monkey moved the cursor in the target and the home position would be appeared. The subject monkey had to move the cursor in the target within 1s. If the task was accomplished successfully, the monkey would obtain a certain amount of water as a reward with a sound of a solenoid valve. If the task was failed (i.e. the monkey could not move the cursor in the target circle within 1s), the monkey could not get the reward and next home position would be displayed. According to the reward and the sound of the valve, the monkey was able to know whether the trial had been succeeded or not. Since the amount of water the monkey took was controlled on a daily basis, the monkey performed about 1,300 trials in a day.

Control Perturbation Task. In the control perturbation task, we applied small force perturbations to displace monkey's hand right or left from midline in random order at 150 ms after the movement onset as a perturbation trial (Fig. 2b). The amplitude of displacement is 5 cm. The cursor on the display is moved according to the monkey's hand. Note that the maximum force was constrained not to exceed 4.9 N, and the perturbation duration was 300 ms. The perturbation trial was randomly applied in 2.5% of all trials.

Visual Error Cramp Task. Visual error cramp task is similar to the control perturbation task. In this task, as a visual error cramp trial, lateral position of the cursor on the computer display was fixed on the midline even when the perturbation was applied (Fig. 2c). In the visual error cramp trial, the visual feedback error information is not provided to the monkey. The rate of the trial was equal to the perturbation trial.

2.3   Data Acquisition and Analysis

Data Acquisition. The gripper position of the manipulandum and hand force was recorded during the task. The hand force was measured with the force-moment sensor attached on the gripper. All data were sampled at 4,000 Hz and were low-pass filtered at 10 Hz.

Estimation of Limb Impedance. We estimated joint impedance parameters, stiffness, viscosity and inertia, from deviations of trajectories in the perturbation trials from a mean trajectory in the reaching task. We considered that the movement was restricted in horizontal plane. We defined monkey's end-point position as $\mathbf{p} = [x, y]^T$. The original point was set to the movement start position at 5.4 cm left and 15.5 cm forward away from the shoulder. Moreover, the generated hand force vector $\mathbf{F} \in R^2$, which is computed by the joint torque and measurements of a force-moment sensor, is described as $\mathbf{F} = [F_x, F_y]^T$. The deviations of trajectories and the force are denoted by

$$\Delta \mathbf{p} = \mathbf{p} - \mathbf{p}^-, \ \Delta \dot{\mathbf{p}} = \dot{\mathbf{p}} - \dot{\mathbf{p}}^-, \ \Delta \ddot{\mathbf{p}} = \ddot{\mathbf{p}} - \ddot{\mathbf{p}}^-, \ \Delta \mathbf{F} = \mathbf{F} - \mathbf{F}^-,$$

where $\mathbf{p}^- \in R^2, \dot{\mathbf{p}}^- \in R^2, \ddot{\mathbf{p}}^- \in R^2$ are end-point variable vectors of the mean trajectory, and $\mathbf{F}^- \in R^2$ are a mean sensed force vector corresponding to the mean trajectory. The relationship of the deviations of the parameters are represented by

$$\mathbf{I}\Delta\ddot{\mathbf{p}} + \mathbf{B}\Delta\dot{\mathbf{p}} + \mathbf{K}\Delta\mathbf{p} = -\Delta\mathbf{F}, \tag{1}$$

where $\mathbf{K} \in R^{2\times2}$, $\mathbf{B} \in R^{2\times2}$, $\mathbf{I} \in R^{2\times2}$ are stiffness viscosity matrices, respectively. Thus, the equation (1) is transformed to

$$\begin{bmatrix} \mathbf{I} & \mathbf{B} & \mathbf{K} \end{bmatrix} \begin{bmatrix} \Delta\ddot{\mathbf{p}} \\ \Delta\dot{\mathbf{p}} \\ \Delta\mathbf{p} \end{bmatrix} = -\Delta\mathbf{F}. \tag{2}$$

Each element of the impedance (inertia, viscosity, and stiffness) matrices was estimated using the least squares method. We estimated the stiffness at several timings during 25 ms time-window, i.e., 150-175 ms, 200-225 ms and 250-275 ms after the perturbation onset.

2.4 Optimal Feedback Control Model

A Dynamics Model of Sensorimotor Systems. We model the hand as an $m = 1$ [kg] point mass moving in a horizontal plane, with viscosity $b = 10$ [Ns/m] approximating intrinsic muscle damping. The point mass is driven by two orthogonal force actuators that can both push and pull (approximating two pairs of agonist–antagonist muscles). The actuators act as muscle-like first-order low-pass filters of the control signals, with time constant $\tau = 0.05$ [s]. These settings of m, b, and τ were chosen to be compatible with biomechanics of the motor system and were not adjusted to fit the data [13]. Let $\mathbf{v}(t) \in R^2$, $\mathbf{a}(t) \in R^2$, $\mathbf{u}(t) \in R^2$ be the velocity, actuator state, and control signal vectors, respectively. The time index is $t = [0, t_f]$. The plant dynamics in continuous time are modeled as follows:

$$\ddot{\mathbf{p}}(t) = \frac{\mathbf{a}(t) - b\mathbf{v}(t)}{m}, \quad \dot{\mathbf{a}}(t) = \frac{(\mathbf{I} + \sigma_u \varepsilon(t))\mathbf{u}(t) - \mathbf{a}(t)}{\tau}, \tag{3.}$$

where $\varepsilon(t) \in R^2$ is standard Brownian motion. $\sigma_u \in R^{2\times2}$ represents control multiplicative or signal-dependent motor noise [14-15], and is given by the following diagonal matrix:

$$\sigma_u = \begin{bmatrix} c & 0 \\ 0 & c \end{bmatrix},$$

where c is the scaling parameter and set to $c = 0.4$. The scaling parameter was also used to define sensory noise magnitude.

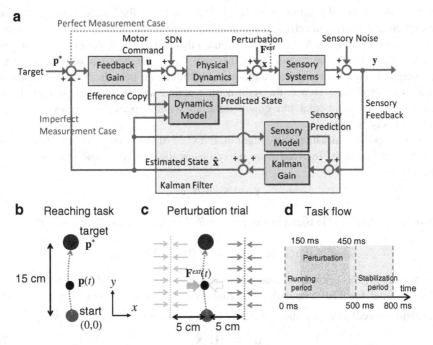

Fig. 4. Simulation model and the task. (a) Block diagram of optimal feedback control model. Optimal controller generates motor commands minimizing a cost function as a state feedback form. Physical dynamics and sensory feedback are disturbed by signal-dependent noise (stood for SDN), and sensory noise, respectively. Forward dynamics model receives the efference copy of the motor command and predicts the future state. A sensory prediction corresponding to the predicted state and sensory feedback are integrated as the estimated state in the framework of Kalman Filter. (b) Illustration of the normal reaching task. (c) The perturbation trial. (d) Task flow in the perturbation trial.

Optimal Feedback Control Problem. In our simulation, the dynamics model is re-written as a discrete-time system using the state space formation:

$$\mathbf{x}_{k+1} = \mathbf{A}\mathbf{x}_k + \mathbf{B}(\mathbf{I} + \sigma_u \varepsilon_k)\mathbf{u}_k \quad (k = 0, 1, \cdots, N-1), \tag{4.}$$

where $\mathbf{x}_k \in R^8$ is a state space vector at time step k defined as

$$\mathbf{x}_k = \begin{bmatrix} \mathbf{p}_k & \mathbf{v}_k & \mathbf{a}_k & \mathbf{p}^* \end{bmatrix}^T. \tag{5.}$$

Here, the target position is denoted by $\mathbf{p}^*$. Thus, N denotes the final time step corresponding to the terminal time t_f. We also need a cost function to define an optimal control problem. Following the previous study [16], the cost function is defined as

$$\sum_{k=N_s+1}^{N} (w_p \|\mathbf{p}_k - \mathbf{p}^*\|^2 + w_v \|\mathbf{v}_k\|^2 + w_a \|\mathbf{a}_k\|^2) + \sum_{k=1}^{N-1} \|\mathbf{u}_k\|^2,$$

where w_p, w_v, w_a are respectively cost weights of the end-point position, velocity and force, and set to $w_p = 1.0 \times 10^6$, $w_v = 1.0 \times 10^4$, $w_a = 1.0 \times 10^2$. According to the cost function, the expected position must be close to the prescribed target position $\mathbf{p}^*$ and the expected velocity and activated muscle state must remain close to 0 during stabilization period ($k = N_s+1, N_s+2, \cdots, N$). On the other hand, the system is free to move unconstrained during the running period ($k = 0, 1, \cdots, N_s$). The last term encourages the energy efficiency during the running and stabilization periods. We set movement duration $t_f = 800$ [ms]. Hence, the stabilization period was assumed to start from 500 ms, since the experimental movement duration without perturbation was observed approximately 500 ms.

In the imperfect measurement situation, the state of the plant $\mathbf{x}_k$ is not directly observable but has to be inferred from noisy observations whose time integral $\mathbf{y}_k \in R^8$ satisfies the following:

$$\mathbf{y}_k = \mathbf{x}_k + \mathbf{\sigma}_y \mathbf{\xi}_k,\tag{6}$$

where $\mathbf{\xi}_k$ is standard Gaussian noise, and $\mathbf{\sigma}_y \in R^{8 \times 8}$ is the sensory noise covariance as

$$\mathbf{\sigma}_y = diag(0.02c, 0.2c, c, 0, 0.02c, 0.2c, c, 0),$$

where c already has been defined as a scaling parameter of signal-dependent noise.

An optimal feedback controller generates motor commands formed a state feedback using a feedback gain matrix $\mathbf{L}_k \in R^{2 \times 8}$ and the estimated state vector $\hat{\mathbf{x}}_k \in R^8$ as

$$\mathbf{u}_k = -\mathbf{L}_k \hat{\mathbf{x}}_k.\tag{7}$$

In the perfect measurement situation when the state could be completely observed, the estimated state equal to the actual state as $\hat{\mathbf{x}}_k = \mathbf{x}_k$. In the imperfect measurement case, the state is estimated by the noisy observation via Kalman filter as

$$\hat{\mathbf{x}}_{k+1} = \mathbf{A}\hat{\mathbf{x}}_k + \mathbf{B}\mathbf{u}_k + \mathbf{K}_k(\mathbf{y}_k - \hat{\mathbf{x}}_k),\tag{8}$$

where $\mathbf{K}_k \in R^{8 \times 8}$ is the Kalman gain which is a function of the uncertainty of the estimated state and the measurement noise, and computed as

$$\mathbf{K}_k = \mathbf{P}_{k|k-1}(\mathbf{P}_{k|k-1} + \mathbf{\sigma}_y \mathbf{\sigma}_y^T)^{-1},\tag{9}$$

where $\mathbf{P}_{k|k-1}$ is the predicted accuracy of the state estimation and given by

$$\mathbf{P}_{k|k-1} = \mathbf{A}\mathbf{P}_{k-1|k-1}\mathbf{A}^T + (\mathbf{B}\mathbf{\sigma}_u \mathbf{u}_k)(\mathbf{B}\mathbf{\sigma}_u \mathbf{u}_k)^T, \quad \mathbf{P}_{k|k} = (\mathbf{I} - \mathbf{K}_k)\mathbf{P}_{k|k-1}.$$

The Kalman gain was computed concurrently at each time step in the simulation, starting with the initial condition $\mathbf{P}_{0|0} = \mathbf{0}$.

External Force Perturbation. We also carried out a simulation influenced by external perturbations. The magnitude of the perturbation was determined to displace the lateral position (x position) to 5 cm or -5 cm, and applied the actuator state as an external force perturbation. Thus, the external force was generated to regulate the lateral position to the displaced position by following:

$$\mathbf{F}^{ext}{}_k = \alpha \begin{bmatrix} \pm 0.05 - x_k \\ 0 \end{bmatrix}, \tag{10}$$

where α is the scaling parameter and set to $\alpha = 10$. The perturbation was applied for 300 ms between 150 and 450 ms after movement onset similar to the experimental situation.

3   Results

3.1   Experimental Result

End-point stiffness ellipses were different in the shapes between the perturbation and visual error cramp trials (Fig. 5a-b). At 150 and 200 ms after the perturbation onset in the visual error cramp trial, the stiffness ellipses were inclined toward the average control trajectory. In contrast, those in the perturbation trial tended to align along actual trajectories. The stiffness eclipses of the visual feedback component at 150 ms after the perturbation onset were largely inclined toward the average control trajectory; however, those at 200 and 250 ms were aligned along the actual trajectories Fig. 5c). Moreover, the velocity profile had two peaks in the perturbation trial while that in the visual error cramp was single-peaked and spread to the later time.

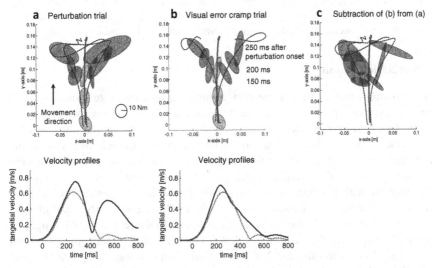

Fig. 5. Hand pathways and end-point stiffness ellipses. Red color shows mean trajectories and stiffness. Blue color shows perturbed trajectories and stiffness at 150, 200, 250 ms after the perturbation onset. In (a) and (b), top and bottom panels show hand pathways and the velocity profiles, respectively. The velocity profiles are only indicated in rightward perturbation, and they are rarely differences from leftward perturbation. (a) The pathways and stiffness ellipses of the perturbation trials. (b) The pathways and stiffness ellipses of the visual error cramp trials. (c) The stiffness ellipses indicate subtractions of the perturbation and visual error cramp trials.

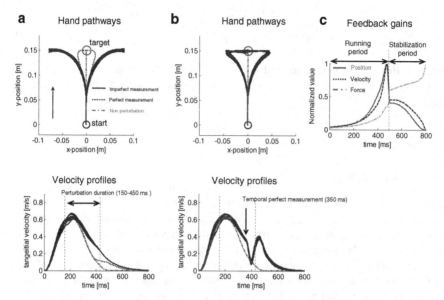

Fig. 6. Simulation results. In (a) and (b), top and bottom panels show hand pathways and the velocity profiles, respectively. The velocity profiles are only indicated in rightward perturbation, and they are rarely differences from leftward perturbation. (a) Simulated trajectories. Blue solid, blue dotted and red dashed-dotted lines indicate imperfect measurement, perfect measurement and non-perturbed cases, respectively. (b) Imperfect measurement trajectories with temporal perfect measurement at 500 ms after movement onset. (c) Feedback gains' profiles.

3.2   Simulation Result

In our simulation, trajectories in the non-perturbed condition were almost straight lines and the velocity profiles were clear bell-shaped similar to the experimental results (Fig. 6a). However, trajectories in the perturbation condition did not reach the target and the velocity profiles spread to the movement end in both directions of the perturbation. On the other hand, trajectories in the perfect measurement condition reached the targets and the lateral displacement was little. Whereat, we carried out an extra simulation with a temporal perfect measurement. In this simulation, the estimated state was updated to the actual state at 350 ms (i.e., 200 ms after perturbation onset). The timing was selected to fit the experimental measurements. Although we did not model explicitly the visuomotor delays or uncertainty in detecting the visual error, the visual delay in our model was considered long enough to update the state from the delayed feedback [5]. In this simulation, the trajectories sudden changed the direction at 400 ms and achieved the target (Fig. 6b).

The position and velocity feedback gains constraining the kinematic achievement were peaked at immediately before the end of the running period (Fig. 6c). In contrast, gains of the force corresponded to the actuator state and the acceleration were higher during the stability period.

4   Discussions

We proposed a pair of experimental tasks that was able to differentiate effects of the visual and somatosensory feedback systems. Using the tasks, we estimated the somatosensory and visual feedback effects onto the limb stiffness. The stiffness by the somatosensory feedback was larger along error correcting direction of the trajectory. In contrast, that by the visual feedback was larger along the direction of actual trajectories. The results suggested that the somatosensory feedback system mainly works as trajectory error corrections and the visual feedback system contribute to regulate compliance of the movement direction. In addition, timely update of the state was required to achieve the task in our simulation. The visual error information might be a trigger to modify the motor command like the intermittent feedback control supposed as a computational model of motor control [17]. On the other hand, the position and velocity feedback gains constraining the kinematic achievement were peaked at immediately before the end of the running period. In contrast, the force gain was higher during the stability period. The actuator state corresponds to the force or acceleration in the model. Considering a musculoskeletal model, it seems to represent the commanded torque [18]. Since the force gain contributed to maintain the stability, the commanded torque may take a role to maintain the stability at movement end in accordance with optimal feedback control model.

In conclusion, we suggested that the visual feedback is a trigger induces enforced estimated error correction or reproduces new motor planning.

References

1. Saijo, N., Gomi, H.: Multiple motor learning strategies in visuomotor rotation. PLoS One 5, e9399 (2010)
2. Izawa, J., Shadmehr, R.: On-line processing of uncertain information in visuomotor control. J. Neurosci. 28, 11360–11368 (2008)
3. Todorov, E., Jordan, M.I.: Optimal feedback control as a theory of motor coordination. Nat. Neurosci. 5, 1226–1235 (2002)
4. Todorov, E.: Optimality principles in sensorimotor control (review). Nature Neuroscience 7, 907 (2004)
5. Liu, D., Todorov, E.: Evidence for the flexible sensorimotor strategies predicted by optimal feedback control. J. Neurosci. 27, 9354–9368 (2007)
6. Izawa, J., Shadmehr, R.: Learning from Sensory and Reward Prediction Errors during Motor Adaptation. PLoS Computational Biology 7, e1002012 (2011)
7. Izawa, J., Rane, T., Donchin, O., Shadmehr, R.: Motor adaptation as a process of reoptimization. J. Neurosci. 28, 2883–2891 (2008)
8. Nagengast, A.J., Braun, D.A., Wolpert, D.M.: Optimal control predicts human performance on objects with internal degrees of freedom. PLoS Comput. Biol. 5, e1000419 (2009)
9. Ueyama, Y., Miyashita, E.: Cocontraction of Pairs of Muscles around Joints Improve an Accuracy of a Reaching Movement: a Numerical Simulation Study. In: 2011 International Symposium on Computational Models for Life Sciences (CMLS 2011), pp. 73–82. American Institute of Physics (2011)

10. Pruszynski, J.A., Kurtzer, I., Scott, S.H.: Rapid motor responses are appropriately tuned to the metrics of a visuospatial task. J. Neurophysiol. 100, 224–238 (2008)

11. Pruszynski, J.A., Kurtzer, I., Nashed, J.Y., Omrani, M., Brouwer, B., Scott, S.H.: Primary motor cortex underlies multi-joint integration for fast feedback control. Nature, 387–390 (2011)

12. Ueyama, Y., Miyashita, E.: A Numerical Simulation Using Optimal Control Can Estimate Stiffness Profiles of a Monkey Arm During Reaching Movements. In: Conf. Proc IEEE The 12th International Workshop on Advanced Motion Control, pp. 1–6 (Year)

13. Winter, D.A.: Biomechanics and motor control of human movement. John Wiley & Sons Inc. (2009)

14. Slifkin, A.B., Newell, K.M.: Variability and noise in continuous force production. Journal of Motor Behavior 32, 141–150 (2000)

15. Harris, C.M., Wolpert, D.M.: Signal-dependent noise determines motor planning. Nature 394, 780–784 (1998)

16. Crevecoeur, F., McIntyre, J., Thonnard, J.L., Lefevre, P.: Movement stability under uncertain internal models of dynamics. Journal of Neurophysiology 104, 1301–1313 (2010)

17. Gawthrop, P., Loram, I., Lakie, M., Gollee, H.: Intermittent control: A computational theory of human control. Biological Cybernetics, 1–21 (2011)

18. Nakano, E., Imamizu, H., Osu, R., Uno, Y., Gomi, H., Yoshioka, T., Kawato, M.: Quantitative examinations of internal representations for arm trajectory planning: minimum commanded torque change model. J. Neurophysiol. 81, 2140–2155 (1999)

Rule Acquisition
in the Proceeding of Heuristic Sudoku Solving

Haiyan Zhou[1,2], Yukun Xiong[1,2], Zhoujun Long[1,2], Sanxia Fan[1,2],
Xuyan Wang[1,2], Yulin Qin[1,2,3], and Ning Zhong[1,2,4]

[1] International WIC Institute, Beijing University of Technology, China
[2] Beijing Key Laboratory of MRI and Brain Informatics, China
[3] Dept. of Psychology, Carnegie Mellon University, USA
[4] Dept. of Life Science and Informatics, Maebashi Institute of Technology, Japan
yulinq12@gmail.com, zhong@maebashi-it.ac.jp

Abstract. To investigate how human brain was involved in explicit rule acquisition during problem solving, with the technique of fMRI, we used a task of simplified Sudoku solving to detect the change of brain activity from a freshman to a rule-acquired solver. Brain activities in the lateral prefrontal, inferior parietal and anterior cingulated cortex increased suggested a goal-directed processing with more accurate representation of problem state and more efficient rule retrieval. The decrease deactivation in the medial prefrontal gyrus might relate to a reduced resource allocation in the later stage; and the signal change pattern of first increasing then decreasing in the superior parietal gyrus might suggest a sensible response for attention to visual perception and recognition during the proceeds.

1 Introduction

Although human being shows an amazing performance in rule learning to solve problems that he/she faces in everyday life, how brain regions are involved in explicit rule acquisition remains undetermined. Since the most efficient strategies for a particular task may not be the most obvious ones to someone encountering the task for the first time, a person might be expected to employ a sequence of strategies as he gains skill in performing the task. Initially, the solver might hit on one of the "obvious" strategies and then gradually progress to more efficient ones with increasing understanding how to solve problems, say problem solving rule acquired finally, as Anzai and Simon statated in their classic research [1]. That study provided a microscopic account of learning in a specific situation (the Tower of Hanoi problem) based on a detailed analysis of a single human problem-solving protocol. They proposed that multiple strategies were used during the proceeding: from selective forward search to incorporated recursive subgoals. Anzai and Simon also argued that the key mechanisms was heuristic search could be employed, which was completely independent of particular tasks and problem-solving environments.

F.M. Zanzotto et al. (Eds.): BI 2012, LNCS 7670, pp. 73–84, 2012.

Recent studies use functional magnetic resonance imaging to investigate how human brain is involved during problem solving, such as task of Tower of Hanoi or Tower of London [2–4], algebraic equation solving [5]. In the general cognitive modeling architecture of adaptive control of thought-rational (ACT-R) proposed by Anderson and his colleagues, several key regions were related to the process of problem solving. Prefrontal cortex (PFC) was related to retrieval of stored information, posterior parietal cortex (PPC) related to changes of problems representation, and anterior cingulated cortex (ACC) related to setting controlling goals [6]. These are consistent with other studies. A number of researchers have found a strong memory response in the prefrontal region [7–9], and others have found the left parietal region reflecting imagery [10, 11]. Some theories of ACC is reflect a control function [12, 13], which is similar to ACT-R, and others consider that ACC is related to error detection [14], and response conflict [15, 16].

More and more researches investigate how human brain involved in rule reasoning or insight. For rule reasoning or inductive reasoning, number series completion is a typical inductive task used with fMRI technique [17, 18], which need to detect the relations between elements to integrate the rule underlying the given number series. Categorization task, in which people abstract the rules that define category membership unconsciously through simple exposure to exemplars of the categories [19], is also used to investigate rule learning [20]. Task of word composition restricted by some constrains [21] or riddle solving [22] is used to investigate insight problems, which means a reorientation of the thinking including breaking of the unwarranted "fixation" and forming novel, task-related associations among the old nodes of concepts or cognitive skills. fMRI research finds that prefrontal played a key role of relational integration during rule learning [20] or inductive reasoning [17, 18]. A brain damaged study showed that the functions dissociate in frontal lobe with key processes for induction in left lateral cortex and in right lateral cortex for monitoring and checking. Anderson and colleagues argued that activity in the lateral inferior prefrontal cortex (LIPFC) reflected retrieval operations, since activation in this region rose only as long as the participants were trying to retrieve the solution and dropped off as soon as the solution was obtained. Furthermore, they also noticed that ACC increased upon the retrieval of a solution, reflecting the need of process that solution [21].

Here we followed the line of Anzai and Simon [1] focused on learning by doing during the proceed of problem solving, and investigate how human brain involved in the process of heuristic search employing, that means the problems solving guided by acquired rules. And the study might provide cognitive inspiration for the development of intelligent system with rule-learning ability. A simplified Sudoku was used in this study, which was simpler than Tower of Hanoi and participant could find out the heuristic rules much easier. Participant could finish a Soduku problem within twenty seconds, a more suitable time scale for an fMRI experiment. Similar to Tower of Hanoi, Sudoku is a knowledge-lean task and will not be affected by the participants' domain knowledge. According to previous research, we expected the region of prefrontal, parietal and ACC would be involved in the proceeding, and stronger activation would be observed in late stage since participant would represent problems state more accurately, retrieve declarative knowledge and control the whole process more intentionally guided by the acquired heuristic rules.

2   Method

2.1   Participants

Twenty-one college students from Beijing University of Technology participated in this study, with averaged age of 24.3 years (from 23-26). All participants were right-handed with normal or corrected-normal vision, and reported with no history of neurological or psychiatric disorders. All of the participants had no experience of Sudoku before their scanning. Written informed consent was obtained from each participant. Two participants' data were deleted since their behavior accuracy was much low. Four more participant's data were deleted because their head shifted more than ±3 mm or the head rotated more than ±3°. Only fifteen participants' data were further analyzed.

2.2   Experimental Design

Task of 4×4 simplified Sudoku was used in this study. A 4×4 Sudoku is a 4×4 matrix to be filled with digits from 1 to 4, so that for each row, each column, and each of four 2×2 boxes, each of the four digits (1, 2, 3 and 4) appears one time. For simplified Sudoku, the experimental tasks in this study, illustrated in Figure 1A, 5 numbers were given, and participants were demanded to find out a proper place with a target value, seen in Figure 1B. There were 2 conditions according to the complexity of heuristic rules: simple problems could be solved by considering information within a single dimension (row, column or 2×2 boxes) of the stimulus, shown in Figure 1C; whereas complex problems required integrating information from multiple dimensions of the stimulus in Figure 1D. Totally 30 simple and 60 complex problems were used in this study.

2.3   Procedure

In this event-related fMRI experiment, the total 90 trials were assigned in one session with random order. As shown in Figure 2, for each trial, a red asterisk in black background appeared 2 s (one scan) in the screen first to cue a new trail starting, and then a 4×4 simplified Sudoku problem was presented with no limited time. The problems would not disappear until participant got an answer. Then a 1 s feedback was followed. At last 10 s inter trial interval (ITI) with a white cross shown in the center of the screen, adjusted with a short time period less than 2 s to make sure each trial had a whole number of scans, to ensure that the BOLD (blood oxygen level-dependent) signal returned to the baseline. Time of the whole session was not limited. Once participants finished all of the 90 problems, the scanning stopped. A data glove with four buttons

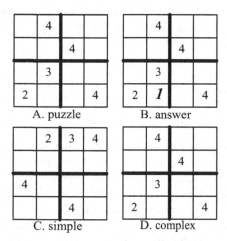

Fig. 1. Sudoku problems (A for a puzzle example and B for its answer) and examples in simple (C) and complex (D) conditions

was used for participant to response. The index, middle, ring and little fingers corresponded to 1, 2, 3, and 4, respectively. Participants had been trained a day before scanning to familiar with the way of finger press. And they were also trained to press three buttons whenever they found the answer. First two of the buttons indicated the location of target (row and column separately), and the last showed the target value. Response accuracy and time were recorded during scanning. After scanning, a questionnaire about heuristic rules discovered by participants during experiments was carried out.

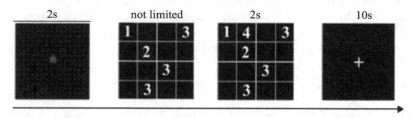

Fig. 2. Procedure for a Sudoku problems solving

2.4 Imaging Scanning and Data Processing

Images were acquired from a 3.0 Tesla MRI system (Siemens Trio Tim; Siemens Medical System, Erlangen, Germany). Both EPI and T1 weighted 3D images were acquired. Functional images were sequenced from bottom to top in a whole brain EPI acquisition. The following scan parameters were used: TE = 31 ms, TR = 2000 ms, flip angle = 90°, matrix size = 64 × 64, field of view = 200 mm × 200 mm, slice thickness = 3.2 mm, number of slices = 32, with AC-PC in the

10th slice from the bottom. The imaging sequence was optimized to detect the BOLD effect including local shimming and 14 s of scan prior to data collection to allow the MR signal to reach equilibrium. In addition, a high resolution, T1 weighted 3D image was acquired (SPGR, TR = 1600 ms, TE = 3.28 ms, flip angle = 90°, matrix size =256 × 256, field of view = 256 mm × 256 mm, slice thickness = 1 mm, number of slices = 192). The orientation of the 3D image was identical to the functional slices.

Data preprocessing were performed using NIS (NeuroImaging Software package; http://kraepelin.wpic.pitt.edu/nis/). After head motion correction, each participant's fMRI BOLD signal data were coregistered to Talairach Coordinate system and spatially smoothed with a 6 mm FWHM Gaussian kernel. For each trial, first a multiple linear regression analysis performed to remove the sources of spurious variances from the signals of six white matter regions; and then the time course of BOLD effect used in data analysis was calculated by computing the ratio of BOLD signal of each scan relative to the baseline of this trial (the averaged BOLD signal across two scans before the task onset of the same trial). For each subject, only the trials with correct response were analyzed and the false trials were deleted.

To investigate the change of brain activity, we divided the whole proceeding into three stages: early stage included the first 20 trials, in which period participant might form heuristic rules by Sudoku solving; the following 30 trials belonged to middle stage and participants might use tentative rules to promote problem solving but not be familiar with the rules in this stage; late stage included the last 40 trials, and participants might be familiar with the rules and could use the heuristic rules much skillfully. Brain regions sensible to the change of processing were revealed by comparing the three stages. Further to observe the change of brain activity with rule acquisition more sensibly and accurately, we next extracted signals of complex trials from the first 12 and the last 8 correct ones and combine every 4 trials' signal as one smaller set to examine the signal change from set 1 to set 5. Every 4 trials combined to make up a Bin, so we got five Bins from very early to the very late period. We summed the signals from scan -1 to scan 7 as the intensity of activation in a region of interest (ROI), and then performed repeated ANOVA (analysis of variance) with Bin as a within factor to investigate the difference within the five Bins.

3   Results

3.1   Behavioral Performance

Repeated 3 (stage: early vs. middle vs. late) × 2 (complexity: simple vs. complex) ANOVA was performed on accuracy rate and response time separately. For accuracy rate, as shown in the left of Figure 3, the main effect of stage was significant ($F(2,28) = 5.211$, $P < 0.05$), the accuracy rate in late stage was higher than that in the early stage ($P < 0.05$). For response time, shown in the right part of Figure 3, there was a main effect of stage ($F(2,28) = 23.387$, $P < 0.001$), and pairwised comparison suggest that the response time in early stage was longer than that in middle ($P < 0.01$) and late ($P < 0.001$) stages, and the response time was also longer in middle stage than that in late stage ($P < 0.001$). The main effect of complexity was significant (F(1,14) = 13.852, $P < 0.01$), and longer time was needed to solve complex problems. The interaction between stage and complexity was also significant (F(2,28) = 5.825, $P < 0.01$).

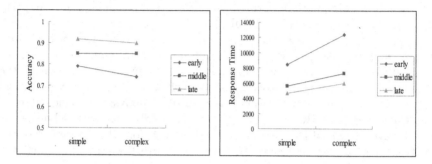

Fig. 3. Behavioral results for accuracy (left) and response time (right)

3.2 Differences of Brain Activity across Stages

With the threshold of $P < 0.0001$ and *cluster size* > 15, we found 12 regions sensible to the difference between the three stages, shown in the left of Figure 4. Wide areas in brain were sensible to stage difference including frontal, parietal, occipital, subcortex and limbic systems. The BOLD effects in these regions were shown in the right of Figure 4. In most of regions the BOLD signal increased at the late stage, such as thalamus, insula/prefrontal gyrus (insula/PFC), anterior cingulated cortex (ACC), superior temporal and inferior parietal lobe (IPL), which suggested a relationship to rule acquisition. And BOLD signals decreased in medial frontal gyrus (MeFG), precuneus/superior parietal lobe (SPL) and subcallosal gyrus might suggest an enhanced efficiency during Sudoku solving.

3.3 Changes Based on Smaller Sets

The analysis of smaller sets was based on the first 12 and last 8 trials in complex condition for each participant. During the proceeding of Sudoku solving, we found three types of signal change. The first type was signal intensity continuously decreasing, such as in the area of medial frontal gyrus (MeFG, shown in Figure 5A). In the very early period deactivation in MeFG was the strongest, and then the signal weakened along the proceeding of Sudoku solving. Repeated ANOVA revealed a significant Bin effect in MeFG ($P < 0.05$). The second type was signal intensity continuously increasing, such as in the area of lateral inferior prefrontal gyrus, inferior parietal lobe and anterior cingulated cortex (insula/PFC, IPL and ACC, shown in Figure 5B, C and D). From Bin 1 to Bin 5, BOLD signal enhanced, and there was a significant difference within the five

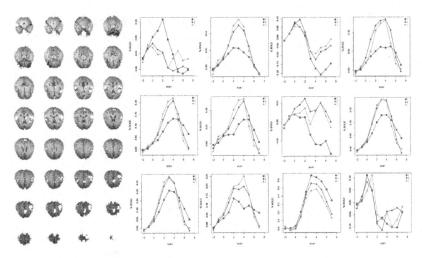

Fig. 4. Activation map by exploratory analysis (left) and BOLD signals in these regions (right). In right, top row indicated BOLD signals from ROI 1 to ROI 4 revealed by exploratory analysis, middle row for form ROI 5 to ROI 8, and bottom row for ROI 9 to ROI 12. The early, middle and late stage were shown in red, blue and green line separately.

Bins for them (insula/PFC, $P < 0.01$; IPL, $P < 0.01$; and ACC, $P < 0.05$). The last type was as shown in Figure 5E, in the area of precuneus/superior parietal gyrus (SPL), the signal went up in the earlier Bins, and then went down at last. The different within the Bins was also significant ($P < 0.01$).

4 Discussion

In the present study, with fMRI technique we used a simplified Sudoku problem to investigate the rule acquisition during problem solving. Behavioral results indicated that participants improved the problem solving strategies with accuracy increased and response time decreased generously. And the difference between simple and complex problems was reduced from early stage to late stage. All these results suggested participant might discover the heuristic rule in the proceedings and could focus on key information to solve Sudoku. We argued that the change of behavior could not own to mechanically repeated operations since there are only 90 trials in our study and participants had no prior experience of Sudoku or similar digit game.

For the materials used in this study, the heuristic rules that most easy to be acquired is to check the number of digits appeared in row, column or 2×2 box. If there are enough information provided, say there are three digits in the same row, column or box, the left digit in the left space location is the answer. That is the condition of simple. And for the condition of complex, information provided in problems is not enough in single dimension, combining information from two dimensions, such as digits in a pair of crossed row and column, row and box or

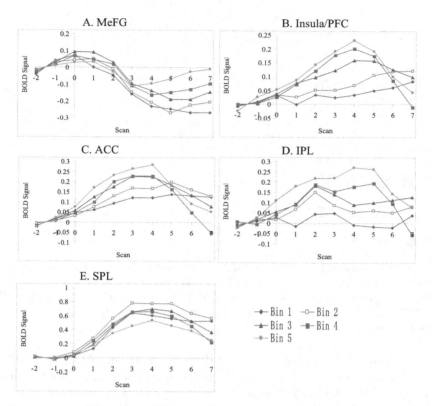

Fig. 5. BOLD signal change from Bin 1 to Bin 5

column and box, would help participants to find the answer in the intersection. In addition, there might be another heuristic rules for complex trials. Because some digits appear three times in different locations in a Sudoku problem, finding out the left location according to one dimension and filling in the repeated digit would get the answer. No matter what kind of heuristic rules acquired at last for a participant, he or she would percept and represent the original stage of problem guided by the rules, and then retrieved a suitable rule to finish the problem. So the processing of Sudoku solving in the late stage were high goal-oriented in a planed way, same as Anzai and Simon emphasized in their study.

The fMRI results enhances our view of rule acquisition in this study. By exploratory analysis, we find prefrontal, posterior parietal and anterior cingulated gyrus were sensitive to the performance from early to late stage in the proceedings, and the BOLD signal in these regions enhanced in the later stage, which are consistent with our expectation. In the analysis based on smaller set, BOLD signals in these areas became narrow and high from Bin 1 to Bin 5. As stated above, guided by the heuristic rules, perception and representation of problem state would be more accurate with a meaningful pattern, which increased the activity in posterior parietal cortex; by comparing problem state and condition of rule application, suitable rules acquired and stored in long-term memory were retrieved to solve problem, which related to the activity in prefrontal; and the whole process might be controlled and directed by anterior cingulated cortex. There are rich interconnections between parietal and dorsolateral prefrontal areas [23], and numerous neuroimage research found coactivation of prefrontal, parietal and the dorsal anterior cingulated gyrus during spatial working memory and problem solving [24, 3, 21, 4]. An executive control network, mainly anchored in the dorsal lateral prefrontal cortex, and posterior parietal cortex, including part of dorsal anterior cingulated cortex, is proposed that the network is crucial for actively maintaining and manipulating information in working memory for rule-based problem solving and for decision making in the context of goal-directed behavior [25, 26]. Recent research of resting state shows that spontaneous fluctuations in these regions were high consistent and related [27, 28]. Our results suggest that these areas play key roles jointly for rule acquisition in the proceedings of problem solving. To be noted that the change pattern in these regions is not consistent with the effect of practice, in which a decreasing signals is always observed. As mentioned above, the proceeding of Sudoku solving in this study is a processing of rule acquisition, although rule application more and more familiar later, the process is far away from skilled with practicing.

Some other wide areas are also involved in the proceedings. Ventral medial frontal gyrus seems involved in the processing of rule acquisition. BOLD signal in this area were deactivated, and the intensity weakened in the later stage. This area is one of the typical regions of default mode network (DMN), in which active signal detected in resting state and deactivated in most task state [29, 30]. The function of medial prefrontal gyrus was argued to be associated with self-related and social cognitive processes [31, 32], value-based decision making [33] and emotion regular [34]. But more and more research thought that DMN, as an intrinsic network in brain, contributed to interpreting, responding to and predicting environmental demands during information processing, which were accorded well with the allocation of the brain's energy resources. The decreased deactivation in medial fontal gyrus observed here might illuminate the less resource was allocated after heuristic rules have acquired.

Another area to be noted is the superior parietal gyrus. In the Bin analysis, it's very interesting to find that BOLD signal in this area first was low, and then enhanced but decreased along the proceeds. This region is linked together with the occipital gyrus, and it is involved in visual information reception and spatial orientation. This area might be related to visual and task input in this study. At the beginning of proceeds, participants needed relative less resource to percept the digits and their locations since they were not sensitive to the visual information. With the improved strategies, they payed more attention to the relationship between digits and their locations, so an increased activation appeared. But participants became more and more familiar with the digits patterns, a decreased activation was observed in the later stage, which might reflect the process of practice.

4.1 Summary

In summary, to investigate how human brain was involved in rule acquisition during problem solving, with the technique of fMRI, we used a task of simplified Sudoku solving to detect the change of brain activity from a freshman to a rule-acquired solver. Three kinds of brain activities or mechanisms were related to the process of rule acquisition: lateral prefrontal, inferior parietal and anterior cingulated cortex were increased suggesting a goal-directed processing with more accurate representation of problem state and more efficient rule retrieval. The decreased deactivation in medial prefrontal gyrus might relate to a reduced resource allocation in the later stage; and signal change pattern of first increase then decrease in the superior parietal gyrus suggested a sensible response for visual perception and recognition change during the proceeds.

Acknowledgments. This research was supported by the CAS/SAFEA International Partnership Program for Creative Research Teams, National Natural Science Foundation of China (No.60875075, 60905027), Beijing Natural Science Foundation (No.4102007), and Beijing Postdoctoral Research Foundation (No. Q6002020201201).

References

1. Anzai, Y., Simon, H.: The theory of learning by doing. Psychological Review 86(2), 124–140 (1979)
2. Anderson, J.R., Albert, M.V., Fincham, J.M.: Tracing problem solving in real time: fmri analysis of the subject-paced tower of hanoi. Journal of Cognitive Neuroscience 17(8), 1261–1274 (2005)
3. Fincham, J.M., Carter, C.S., van Veen, V., Stenger, V.A., Anderson, J.R.: Neural mechanisms of planning: A comuptational analysis using event-related fmri. Proceedings of the National Academy Sciences 99(5), 3346–3351 (2002)
4. Newman, S.D., Carpernter, P.A., Varma, S., Just, M.A.: Frongal and parietal participatation in problem solving i the tower of london: fmri and comuputational modeling of planning and high-level perception. Neuropsychoologia 41, 1668–1682 (2003)
5. Qin, Y.L., Carter, C.S., Silk, E.M., Stenger, V.A., Fissell, K., Goode, A., Anderson, J.R.: The change of the brain activation patterns as children learn algebra equation solving. Proceedings of the National Academy Sciences 101(15), 5686–5691 (2004)
6. Anderson, J.R., Fincham, J.M., Qin, Y., Stocco, A.: A central circuit of the mind. Trends in Cognitive Sciences 12(4), 136–143 (2008)
7. Cabeza, R., Dolcos, F., Graham, R., Nyberg, L.: Similarities and differneces in the neural correlated of episodic memory retrieval and working memory. Neuroimage 16, 317–330 (2002)
8. Donaldson, D., Petersen, S., Ollinger, J., Buchner, R.: Dissociating state and item components of recognition memory using fmri. Neuroimage 13, 129–142 (2001)
9. Fletcher, P.C., Henson, R.N.A.: Frontal lobes and human memory: insights from neuroimaging. Brain 124, 849–881 (2001)
10. Dehaene, S., Piazza, M., Pinel, P., Cohen, L.: Three parietal circuits for nunber processing. Cognitive Neuropsychology 20, 487–506 (2003)

11. Reichle, E., Carpenter, P., Just, M.: The neural basis of strategy and skill in sentence-picture verification. Cognitive Psychology 40, 261–295 (2000)
12. D'Esposito, M., Detre, J., Alsop, D., Shin, R., Atlas, S., Grossman, M.: The neural basis of the central executive system of working memory. Nature 378(16), 279–281 (1995)
13. Posner, M., Dehaene, S.: Attentional networks. Trends in Neurosciences 17(2), 75–79 (1994)
14. Gehring, W., Goss, B., Coles, M., Meyer, D., Donchi, E.: A neural systemfor error detection and compensation. Psychological Science 4(6), 383–390 (1993)
15. Carter, C., Macdonald, A., Botvinick, M., Ross, L., Stenger, V., Noll, D., Cohen, J.: Parsing executive processes: Strategic versus evaluative functions of the anterior cingulate cortex. Proceedings of the National Academy Sciences 97(4), 1944–1948 (2000)
16. Yeung, N., Botvinick, M., Cohen, J.: The neural basis of error detection: Conflict monitoring and the error-related negativity. Psychological Review 111(4), 931–959 (2004)
17. Jia, X., Liang, P., Lu, J., Yang, Y., Zhong, N., Li, K.: Common and dissociable neural correlates associated with component processes of inductive reasoning. Neuroimage 56, 2292–2299 (2004)
18. Goel, V., Dolan, R.: Differential involvement of left prefrontal cortex in inductive and deductive reasoning. Cognition 93(3), 109–121 (2004)
19. Reber, A.: Implicit learning of artificial grammers. Journal of Verbal Learning and Verbal Behavior 6(6), 855–863 (1967)
20. Strange, B., Henson, R., Friston, K., Dolan, R.: Anterior perfrontal cortex mediates rule learning in humans. Cerebral Cortex 11, 1040–1046 (2001)
21. Anderson, J.R., Anderson, J.F., Ferris, J.L., Fincham, J.M., Jung, K.J.: The lateral inferior prefrontal cortex and anterior cingulate cortex are engaged at different stages in the solution of insight problems. Proceedings of the National Academy Sciences 106(26), 10799–10804 (2009)
22. Luo, J., Niki, K.: Function of hippocamupus in "insight" of problem solving. Hippocampus 13, 316–323 (2003)
23. Petrides, M., Pandya, D.: Projections to the fontal cortex form the posterior parietal region in the rhesus monkey. Journal of Comparative Neurology 228, 105–116 (1984)
24. Cabeza, R., Nyberg, L.: Imaging cognition ii: An empireical review of 275 pet and fmri studies. Journal of Cognitive Neuroscience 12(1), 1–47 (2000)
25. Menon, V.: Large-scale brain networks and psychopathology: a unifying triple network model. Trends in Cogntive Science 15(10), 483–506 (2011)
26. Koechlin, E., Summerfield, C.: An information theoretical approach to prefrontal executive function. Trends in Cogntive Science 11(6), 229–236 (2007)
27. Shirer, W., Ryali, S., Rykhlevskaia, E., Menon, V., Greicius, M.: Decoding subject-driven cognitive states with whole-brain connectivity patterns. Cerebral Cortex 22(1), 158–165 (2012)
28. Raichle, M.: Two views of brain function. Trends in Cognitive Sciences 14(4), 180–190 (2010)
29. Greicius, M., Krasnow, B., Reiss, A., Menon, V.: Functional connectivity in the resting brain: A network analysis of the default mode hypothesis. Proceedings of the National Academy Sciences 100(1), 253–258 (2003)
30. Raichle, M.E., McLeod, A.M., Snyder, A.Z., Powers, W.J., Gusnard, D.A., Shulman, G.L.: A default mode of brain function. Proceedings of the National Academy Sciences 98(2), 676–682 (2001)

31. Spreng, R., Mar, R., Kim, A.: The common neural basis of autobiographical memory, perception, navigation, theory of mind, and the default mode: A quantitative meta-analysis. Journal of Cognitive Neuroscience 21(3), 489–510 (2009)
32. Amodio, D., Frith, C.: Meeting of minds: the medial frontal cortex and social cognition. Nature Reviews Neuroscience 7, 268–277 (2006)
33. Rangel, A., Camerer, C., Read, P.: A framework for studing the neurobiolgoy of value-based decision making. Nature Reviews Neuroscience 9, 543–556 (2008)
34. Etkin, A., Egner, T., Kalisch, R.: Emotional processing in anterior cingulate and medial prefrontal cortex. Trends in Cognitive Sciences 15(2), 85–93 (2010)

BatGaze: A New Tool to Measure Depth Features at the Center of Gaze during Free Viewing

Redwan Abdo A. Mohammed, Samah Abdulfatah Mohammed,
and Lars Schwabe

Universität Rostock, Dept. of Computer Science and Electrical Engineering,
Adaptive and Regenerative Software Systems, 18051 Rostock, Germany
{redwan.mohammed,samah.mohammed,lars.schwabe}@uni-rostock.de

Abstract. The human visual system still outperforms any artificial vision system in terms of generalization. One approach to build human-level artificial vision systems is to formulate learning principles and then let the artificial system self-organize under natural stimulation. More specifically, learning probabilistic generative models of visual signals is considered a promising approach. The latent variables in such models may then eventually turn out to reflect meaningful aspects of scene descriptions such as features of depths images, surface properties, etc. Using luminance and depth information, which itself is only indirectly available to the human visual system, is a promising approach to learn artificial vision systems. So far, the proper stimulus material was only available from a few studies employing range imaging in static scenes, but the luminance and depth features at the center of gaze during free viewing are simply not know. We combined mobile eye tracking and depth imaging in order to record such missing stimulus material. Here we report on this newly developed system, called BatGaze, and on a first experimental validation of it. We believe that it will become a very valuable tool for mapping the visual environment of free viewing humans.

1 Introduction

While machine vision is a mature field with many industrial applications, artificial vision systems still fall short in terms of generalization when compared to the human visual system. The human visual system may be slow and built with sluggish components, but it works well under various lightning conditions and in many contexts. This is probably due to the vast amount of prior knowledge humans bring into interpreting visual scenes. Most computational vision researchers, who aim at reverse engineering the principles behind biological visual systems, adopted the hypothesis that the environmental signals shape biological visual systems. In other words, according to this approach the goal is not build a biologically inspired vision system, but to engineer the learning mechanisms of biologically inspired vision systems and then let them learn based on natural signals.

F.M. Zanzotto et al. (Eds.): BI 2012, LNCS 7670, pp. 85–96, 2012.

Much work has been invested into the statistical modeling of natural luminance images [1]. The rational behind many such approaches is that latent variables in generative probabilistic models of these luminance images will eventually correspond to meaningful scene descriptions in terms of, for example, properties of surfaces, objects. etc. Thus, once a structure for a probabilistic model of luminance images has been set up, the remaining task is to perform a model selection given natural images using, for example, Maximum Likelihood learning.

It was shown, however, that eye movements are far from a random sampling. It was even suggested that the statistics of natural images differ at the center of gaze when compared to random sampling [2]. Thus, taking into account eye movements is essential for shaping artificial vision systems via natural images. Another line of research has investigated the depth structure of natural scenes using range sensors [3,4]. This depth structure is not directly accessible to the human visual system and needs to be inferred using stereo vision or other depth cues. Some statistical aspects of depth images as well as the relation between depth and luminance images have been investigated before [4], but the statistical properties of depth images at the center of gaze during free viewing are not clear. For example, simple questions such as "Do humans look more often to high contrast edges due to depth gaps than to edges due to texture borders?" have not been addressed yet.

We argue that characterizing the statistical properties of luminance and depths images at the center of gaze during free viewing is an important next steps in characterizing natural visual stimuli in order to learn, for example, better generative models of visual signals, which artificial visual systems can then invert to perform human-level visual computations. We have developed BatGaze, a new tool to measure luminance and depth images at the center of gaze. We combined a mobile eye tracker with a new and light-weight depth sensor from Asus, developed recording software and alignment procedures to analyze the recorded image streams, and performed an experimental validation of this system. In analogy to bat echolocation we call this system BatGaze.

This paper is organized as follows: First, in Section 2, we describe the BatGaze system in terms of the hardware setup, the software we developed, and the synchronization procedures. Then, in Section 3, we describe the features we extracted from the luminance and depth images. These features are then used in Section 4 in the experimental validation. We close with a discussion of the benefits of this system for mapping the visual environment of freely viewing and behaving humans.

2   The BatGaze System

The BatGaze system combines an eye tracker (Figure 1a) with the new lightweight depth sensor Asus Xtion Pro Live from Asus (Figure 1b). The eye tracker is equipped with a camera to record the eye movements and a scene camera. After calibration the gaze points are given in coordinates of this scene camera. The Asus depth sensor was mounted next to the eye tracker's scene camera (Figure 1c), and it records depth images and RGB luminance images. The image streams of the Asus camera are already aligned to each other. We then developed procedures and tools to align them to the scene camera in order to obtain proper coordinates of the gaze point matched in space and time to the image streams from the Asus camera. Here we describe the details of the hardware setup, the software and processing, and the alignment in space and time.

2.1 Hardware Setup

The Mobile SMI Eye Tracker. SensoMotoric Instruments (SMI, smivision.com) offers to researchers state-of-the-art eye tracking systems. It was our choice for recording the gaze data, because of its easy access to the raw data (gaze location, pupil position, pupil diameter, etc.). Our analyses were all done offline, but the eye tracker also gives online access to this data. The eye tracker uses two cameras (Figure 1a): The first is used to track the pupil and the second camera records the scene view. The gaze position is reported with a sampling rate of 50 Hz and a reported accuracy of 0.5°-1°. The scene camera comes with three lenses (8, 6 and 3.6 mm). The default 3.6 mm lens provides a viewing angle of ±31° horizontally and ±22° vertically. The scene camera resolution is 752 × 480. All specifications are taken from [5]. We used the 3.6 mm lens to record indoor scenes, mostly in our labs, where the observed objects are within 3m distance. Then, to avoid parallax error, we calibrated in a distance within 1-1.5 m. We used a calibration with 5 points so that the SMI recording software can compute the gaze location in scene camera coordinates from the recorded pupil images.

The Asus Xtion Depth Camera. Depth sensing technology is now widely applied in commercial video games and computer vision applications. As a side effect, new applications such as markerless full body tracking become available to many researchers via low price consumer devices such as the Microsoft Kinect camera. Among the various sensors available the choice between different brands has to be made by respecting their specifications and the requirements of our BatGaze system. Options available to us were: the Asus Xtion Pro/Pro Live camera, the Microsoft Kinect, and a time-of-flight (TOF) camera from PMDTec (pmdtec.com). We selected the Asus Xtion Pro Live (Figure 1b) for two reasons: First, the camera does not need an external power supply as it is powered via USB, unlike the Kinect or the PMD TOF, which demand for external power supply. This makes the Asus Xtion Pro Live much more mobile and portable. Second, the Asus camera is much smaller than the Kinect and TOF and also weights less (~170g), which makes it easier to mount it onto the head of a subject. The Asus Xtion Pro Live has three sensors: an infrared (IR) emitter with IR receiver to sense depth via the structured light principles and an RGB camera. The camera supports registration of depth and RGB frames in hardware and synchronized audio recording. It is most suitable for indoor environments. The camera has an effective depth sensing distance between 0.8m and 3.5m while

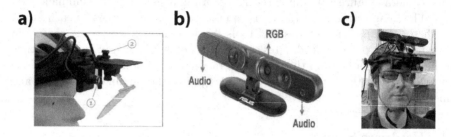

Fig. 1. Illustration of the BatGaze hardware setup. **a)** Eye tracker from SMI (smivision.com). The field of view is not occluded as the eye tracking camera and the corresponding scene camera are mounted out of sight from the subject. **b)** Asus Xtion Pro Live camera, which captures depths images using the structured-light principle as well as RGB images. **c)** Our setup with a depth camera (here: the predecessor of the Asus Xtion Pro Live, which only recorded depth but no RGB images) mounted on the mobiel SMI eye tracker.

the lenses effective angle is 58° horizontally and 45° vertically, which satisfies most computer vision application requirements. Asus released it with a complete SDK, which includes the OpenNI APIs.

Combining the SMI Eye Tracker with the Asus Xtion Depth Camera
We first removed the base of the depth camera and mounted it on the front upper part of the helmet of the eye-tracker. We adjusted its position so that the RGB lenses of both cameras align vertically as much as possible. Then, we fixed the depth camera on the helmet using a tape and ensured that during free viewing the depth camera will not be moved or shacked. This is a very important part of our system setup. Any shifting in the depth camera position during an experiment will affect the alignment and registration process. To ease the movement of the subject during the experiment, we built two shelves to be carried on the back: one for a laptop connected to eye-tracker and the other for another laptop connected to Xtion camera. Before starting the calibration of the eye-tracker camera we checked the captured views from both cameras. If necessary, we readjusted the camera position to record the same view. The next step is the calibration of the eye-tracker camera using SMI's iViewX software. The depth camera does not need any calibration, but we usually ensure uniform light conditions.

2.2   Software Setup: Recording Software and Processing Toolchain

Asus ships the camera with the NiViewer tool, which records from all sensors of the camera. It can be configured via a configuration file. The recorded streams are saved in a custom file format (*.oni), which is accessible to the OpenNI software. In a previous version of the BatGaze system we used the predecessor of the Asus camera and developed a custom recording software, but with the new

Asus Xtion Pro Live it turned out that the NiViewer software is sufficient for our needs. We always recorded RGB images with a resolution of 640x480 at 25 fps. We developed a custom player for oni-files (OniPlayer), which can read, process and render scenes and depth frames from oni-files. Most importantly, it converts images into a custom binary format for further processing using MATLAB [6]. Finally, we also developed a custom software called (XtionRecorder) that can stream directly from the Xtion camera for online processing.

2.3 Temporal Synchronization

The depth camera delivers the depth map and the RGB frames already synchronized with timestamps. The scene camera of the eye tracker also delivers RGB frames as well as gaze locations, both with timestamps. All synchronization was done offline. When both cameras were recording, we generated two special events in time, which were recorded by both cameras: a "clapper board" at the beginning and end of recording. More specifically, we did the alignment using the timestamps of both cameras, where both are given in microseconds. For the depth camera, let

- $\mathbf{Z}$ be a three-dimensional matrix of n depth frames from the Asus camera; $\mathbf{Z}$ has size of $640 \times 480 \times n$ (width $\times$ height $\times$ frames),
- $\mathbf{R}$ be a matrix of n RGB frames from the Asus camera; $\mathbf{R}$ has a size of $640 \times 480 \times 3 \times n$ (width $\times$ height $\times$ RGB channels $\times$ frames),
- T_Z be a function T_Z : Frames $\rightarrow$ Timestamps to obtain the timestamps for each depth frame,

and for the eye-tracker camera, let

- $\mathbf{S}$ be a matrix of m frames from the scene camera; S has size of $752 \times 480 \times 3 \times m$ (width $\times$ height $\times$ RGB channels $\times$ frames),
- $\mathbf{G}$ be a matrix of m gaze points from the SMI system, one for each frame from the scene camera; $\mathbf{G}$ has size of $2 \times m$ (x/y gaze point position $\times$ frames), and
- T_S be a function T_S : Frames $\rightarrow$ Timestamps to obtain the timestamps for each frame.

The recording of depth data is started always some seconds later than the recording with the eye-tracker camera, and stopped always first, so that we have $n < m$. For each recording we identified reference frames i_Z^{ref} and i_S^{ref} for the depth and scene camera, respectively, by manually inspecting the frames around the first "clapper board" event. Then, a frame from the scene camera, i_S, was assigned to a frame from the depth camera, i_Z, where the difference in timestamps was smallest, i. e.

$$i_Z(i_S) := argmin_i |t_Z(i) - t_S(i_S)|$$
$$t_Z(i) = T_Z(i) - T_Z\left(i_Z^{ref}\right)$$
$$t_S(i) = T_S(i) - T_S\left(i_S^{ref}\right)$$

Then, we generated a new pair of aligned streams with equal length. The results of this temporal alignment were double-checked with the software "Kinovea" (kinovea.org), which supports frame-by-frame inspection of videos. Finally, we double-checked temporal alignment by inspecting the alignment of the second "clapper board" event at the end of the recording. Failures of alignment for this second event would be indicative of technical problems with the timestamps from either the SMI or Asus system.

2.4 Spatial Registration of Images

After the frames have been aligned temporally, they are also aligned spatially. We aligned each pair of frames using a transformation obtained from a pair of frames in the beginning of the recording, i. e. we assume that the spatial relation of the two cameras does not change in the course of a recording. The geometrical aligning of images is termed image registration, and many algorithms are available for that. We registered the scene frames of both cameras using a simple registration of two 2D images.

If (x, y) is a pixel in the eye trackers scene camera and (x', y') is a pixel in the Asus scene camera, we make the Ansatz

$$\begin{bmatrix} r_1 & r_2 & t_1 \\ r_3 & r_4 & t_2 \\ s_1 & s_2 & 1 \end{bmatrix} \times \begin{bmatrix} x \\ y \\ 1 \end{bmatrix} = \begin{bmatrix} x' \\ y' \\ 1 \end{bmatrix}$$

where

$$\begin{bmatrix} r_1 & r_2 \\ r_3 & r_4 \end{bmatrix} = \begin{bmatrix} \cos\theta & -\sin\theta \\ \sin\theta & \cos\theta \end{bmatrix}$$

is a rotation matrix, $[t_1\ t_2]^T$ is a translation vector, and $[s_1\ s_2]^T$ accounts for scaling/shrinking. MATLAB already offers a solution to this transformation problem (2D image registration), which is based on manually identifying pairs of matching points in the two images. The resulting transformations are then applied to the gaze positions, which are in the coordinates of the scene camera from the eye tracker, in order obtain their coordinates in the Asus scene camera. Figure 2 shows an example of a spatial registration.

3 Analysis Methods

3.1 A Simple Local Feature for Depth Images: Gap Discontinuity

A gap discontinuity in a depth image is a significant depth difference between two points implying that they are lying on different surfaces. We used the algorithm from [7], which can detect such discontinuities by computing the maximum difference in depth at a pixel and its 8 neighbors. For a pixel at x, y with depth value $z(x, y)$ let

$$N_{x,y} = \{z_i \mid i = 1, 2, ..., 8\}$$

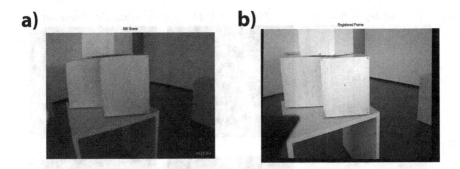

Fig. 2. Example of a spatial registration. **a)** Frame from the scene camera of the eye tracker, after registration to the image from the Asus scene camera. **b)** Corresponding image from the Asus scene camera. The small green dots are the identified points for matching the images.

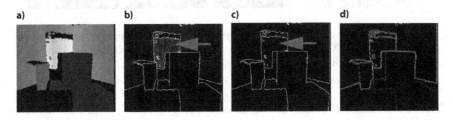

Fig. 3. Example of a depth map and the computed gap discontinuities. **a)** Depth map recorded with the Asus sensor. **b)** G_{map} before thresholding. **c)** G_{map} after thresholding with a constant threshold ($T = 1$). **d)** G_{map} after thresholding with an adaptive threshold (see text for details).

denote the depth values of the 8 neighbors, then

$$G_{map}(x, y) = \max \{|\, z(x, y) - z_i \,|: z_i \in N_{x,y}\}.$$

Figure 3a shows an example of a depth map recorded with the Asus sensor. Figure 3b shows the corresponding G_{map} before thresholding, and Figure 3c after thresholding, i. e. the $G_{map}(x, y)$ was set to 0 if it was below a fixed threshold T (here: $T = 1$). Note the removed noise at the distant surface (see red arrow). We also applied an adaptive threshold to avoid the manual selection of a value for T by trial and error. We first calculated T as the minimum nonzero value in G_{map}. Then we used an adaptive thresholding algorithm (see http://homepages.inf.ed.ac.uk/rbf/HIPR2/adpthrsh.htm) with a 5×5 window and local mean filtering. The new thresholded G_{map} is shown in Figure 3d.

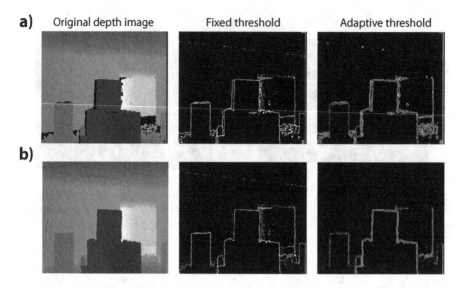

Fig. 4. Example of the gap discontinuity map applied to both the raw depth map and filled-in depth map. **a)** Original depth frame and corresponding G_{map}. **b)** Same as a), but for the filled-in depth map.

The fundamental problem of the structured light principle implemented in the Asus depth sensor is a so-called shadowing behavior, i. e. the black pixels around some corners and gap discontinuities (see Figure 3a). We applied a simple correction, namely by filling in the depth values from the nearest neighboring pixel. Figure 4 shows the depth and associated gap discontinuity maps before and after this filling in. In the presence of depth shadows the pixels with invalid information are known, and we excluded them from the computation of the gap discontinuity map (Figure 4a). When the filled-in depth image is used, all pixels in a neighborhood contribute to G_{map} (Figure 4b). A first visual inspection suggests that this heuristic may serve to overcome some problems with depth shadows, but more work is needed to investigate possible shortcomings of these "imputed" values. In our analysis, we used the filled-in depth maps and double-checked that all results (Figure 5) are qualitatively invariant to this procedure.

3.2   Features of the Luminance Images

The luminance images were first transformed into gray-scale images. Then, each gray-scale image is linearly decomposed into a set of edge feature responses to Gabor filters with different orientations. We used orientations $\theta = \{0°, 15°, \ldots, , 165°\}$, but only one spatial frequency and two spatial phases.

Within each image we subtracted the mean from the filter responses to each orientation, and normalized the responses to the interval between -1 and 1. These filter responses are used in the next section to characterize the patches in the luminance images at the center of gaze.

4 Experimental Validation

Here we report the experimental validation of the BatGaze system. We explicitly instructed subjects, who were freely walking around a table with boxes on top of the table, to direct their gaze to either the edges or the surfaces of the boxes ("look at edges" vs. "look at surfaces"). The rational for these instructions was to collect ground truth data: Obviously, we expected that an analysis of the structure of the depth images at the center of gaze will uncover a higher probability of inspecting edges in the edge condition as compared to surfaces, and vice versa in the surface condition.

4.1 Experimental Design

Subjects executed the two task conditions "look to edges" and "look to surfaces", while they were freely walking around the table with boxes on top of the table in a big hall. A total of 3 boxes were assembled on top of the table. The eye tracker was calibrated before each experiment using a 5-point calibration target. While the subjects were performing the task we recorded the gaze positions, the scene frames and the depth frames on one computer. The overall duration of a single recording was 80s on average. Subjects were given verbal instructions. In the first condition ("look to edges"), subjects were instructed to look only to the edges of the boxes. In the second condition ("look to surfaces"), subjects were instructed to look only to surfaces. Three subjects (the authors of this study) participated multiple times in each conditions.

4.2 Results: Depth Features at the Center of Gaze

The recorded data was analyzed by computing the probability of finding a gap discontinuity (a value of G_{map} above the threshold) in a neighborhood of 25, 49 and 81 pixel around the gaze location. This was done for both conditions. Figure 5 shows the estimated probabilities and confirms, as expected, that the probability of finding a gap discontinuity in the "look at edges" condition is higher than in the "look at surfaces" condition. Also note that the probability for a gap discontinuity increases with increasing neighborhood size while is remains largely constant in the surface condition. This is due to the fact that the surfaces of the boxes in our study was rather large compared to the largest neighborhood, and that the subjects presumably looked at the center of the surfaces. These results

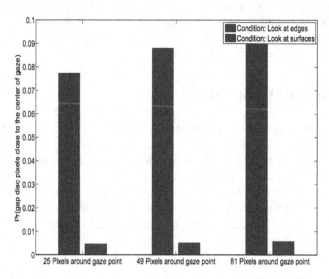

Fig. 5. Bar plot for the depth features around the gaze point in the two experimental conditions. Shown are the probabilities of finding gap discontinuity around gaze point.

validate that the BatGaze system is working as anticipated. Future work can now address the accuracy of the whole system, which will probably be only limited by the accuracy of the eye tracker.

4.3   Results: Luminance Features at the Center of Gaze

In order to characterize the features in the luminance images at the center of gaze we first selected 500 consecutive frames from the middle of a block for each condition. Then we transformed each frame into gray-scale images. Each gray-scale image is linearly decomposed into a set of edge feature responses to the Gabor filters with different orientations. In this analysis, however, we used only the responses to horizontal and vertical filters.

We then compiled histograms for the responses to these Gabor filters from the pixels around the gaze point in each condition. Figure 6a,b show these histograms and reveal that the probability of horizontal or vertical edges being present, i. e. non-zero filter responses, around the center of gaze is much higher in the "look at edges" compared to the "look at surfaces" condition. This holds true for both horizontal (red bars) and vertical edges (blue bars).

In order to further highlight this difference between conditions, we also generated "combined histograms", where we did not distinguish between the orientations of the Gabor filters. Figure 7 shows clearly that in the "look at edges" condition the non-zero filter responses are much more frequent for all sizes of the neighborhood.

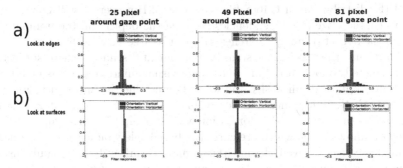

Fig. 6. Normalized histograms for the Gabor features in the vertical=blue and horizontal=red directions at the center of gaze in the two experimental conditions. **a)** Condition "look at edges". **b)** Condition "look at surfaces".

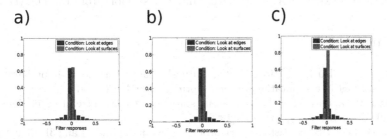

Fig. 7. Normalized histograms for the combined Gabor features (vertical and horizontal) in the experimental conditions. **a–c)** Different neighborhoods (25, 49 and 81 pixel).

5 Discussion

In summary, we have presented a new system, the BatGaze system, which can be used to measure luminance *and* depth features at the center of gaze. The rationale for building such a system is to inform computational vision research about these features, so that generative models of visual signals could be learned. We have described in depth the technical aspects of this system, the software we have developed, and the analysis procedures. In addition, we have also performed an experimental validation. This validation yielded expected results, namely that edge-like structures in depth and luminance images are more frequent at or around the center of gaze when subjects look at edge like structures, and vice versa when they look at surfaces. We performed this test in order to obtain some ground truth data for the BatGaze system.

Our experimental results reported here do not yet fully exploit the fact that we recorded the depth data and the luminance images simultaneously. For example, the results in Figure 5 were compiled from only depth information, and the results in Figures 6 and 7 make use of only luminance information. For both types of data the task condition is an important factor as it affects the probability of gaps and the distribution of Gabor filter responses. However, it will now be of interest to characterize the dependencies between the depth and the luminance features in the subset of images patches sampled by free viewing humans.

We plan to use the BatGaze system in experimental studies, where subjects are not instructed to look at certain points in a visual environment. Instead, the subjects will conduct certain tasks, and we will determine the informative image features in both the luminance and depth images at visual field locations they fixate on. Collecting such depth information will also help to improve models for *predicting* eye movements, which are currently based solely on features obtained from luminance images even though the human visual system certainly uses top-down post-recognition information to guide eye movements.

Acknowledgments. The first two authors, R. A. A. M. and S. A. M., contributed equally to this work. R. A. A. M. receives a DFG fellowship from DFG GRK 1424 MuSAMA, S. A. M. received financial support from the DAAD.

References

1. Hyvärinen, A., Hurri, J., Hoyer, P.O.: Natural Image Statistics – A probabilistic approach to early computational vision. Springer, London (2009)
2. Reinagel, P., Zador, A.M.: Natural scene statistics at the centre of gaze. Network (Bristol, England) 10(4), 341–350 (1999)
3. Potetz, B., Lee, T.S.: Statistical Correlations Between 2D Images and 3D Structures in Natural Scenes. Journal of Optical Society of America, A 7(20), 1292–1303 (2003)
4. Yang, Z., Purves, D.: Image/source statistics of surfaces in natural scenes. Network: Computation in Neural Systems 14(3), 371–390 (2003)
5. SMI iView X system manual version 2.7 (March 2011)
6. MATLAB. version 7.10.0 (R2010a). The MathWorks Inc., Natick, Massachusetts (2010)
7. Hoover, X.J.A., Jean-Baptiste, G.: An Experimental Comparison of Range Image Segmentation Algorithms. IEEE Transactions on Pattern Analysis and Machine Intelligence 18 (1996)

A Brain Informatics Approach to Explain the Oblique Effect via Depth Statistics

Redwan Abdo A. Mohammed and Lars Schwabe

Universität Rostock, Dept. of Computer Science and Electrical Engineering,
Adaptive and Regenerative Software Systems, 18051 Rostock, Germany
{redwan.mohammed,lars.schwabe}@uni-rostock.de

Abstract. Natural vision systems still outperform artificial vision systems in terms of generalization. Therefore, many researchers turned to investigate biological vision systems in order to reverse engineer them and implement their principles into artificial vision systems. An important approach for developing a theory of vision is to characterize the visual environment in statistical terms, because this may provide objective yard sticks for evaluating natural vision systems using measures such as, for example, the information transmission rates achieved by natural vision systems. Most such studies focused on characterizing natural luminance images. Here we propose to investigate natural luminance images together with corresponding depth images using information-theoretical measures. We do this using a database of natural images and depth images and find that certain oriented filter responses convey more information about relevant depth features than other oriented filters. More specifically, we find that vertical filter responses are much more informative about gap and orientation discontinuities in the depth images than other filters. We show that this is an inherent property of the investigated visual scenes, and it may serve to explain parts of the oblique effects.

1 Introduction

Understanding how the brain is processing complex visual signals is a challenging problem in vision science. Some vision scientists turned to investigating the statistical structures of natural images in order to obtain statistical models of them. Then, with added "normative" assumptions about the potential goal of visual processing such as redundancy reduction, optimal coding, or optimal statistical inference predictions about the organization of natural vision systems can be derived.

It is well known that the statistics of natural images follow particular regularities. The distribution of the amplitude across spatial frequency in natural scenes follows a power law, i. e. the average amplitude at spatial frequency f falls as $\frac{1}{f^\alpha}$ with, for example, $\alpha \approx 2$ or $\alpha \approx 1$, where the particular value of α varies among individual images [1,2,3]. Furthermore the statistics of filter responses turned out to provide powerful and general models [4]. Related studies found that in natural images, including both natural landscapes and man-made environments,

F.M. Zanzotto et al. (Eds.): BI 2012, LNCS 7670, pp. 97–106, 2012.
© Springer-Verlag Berlin Heidelberg 2012

vertical and horizontal orientations are more frequent than oblique [5]. Rothkopf et al. showed that when learning basis functions of a sparse generative model the distribution of orientations when fitting Gabor functions to the obtained basis functions shows an asymmetry, which may serve to explain the dominance of horizontally and vertically oriented filters (the oblique effect) in the center of the visual field with increasingly meridional directions in the periphery[6].

In this paper, we employ information-theoretic measures to quantify the dependence between the oriented filter responses to luminance images and the features computed from corresponding depth images. We will arrive at an alternative explanation of the oblique effects, namely that it is rooted in the information from luminance images about depth features. Our approach goes beyond the analysis of the luminance images by incorporating depth images, similar to a few pioneering studies [7,8]. We also find an asymmetry between the orientations of the oriented filters, but compared to other optimal coding theories our explanation of this asymmetry is different: In our interpretation it emerges, because we think of the distribution of oriented filters as being optimized to encode information about the depth features and not as a code for the optimal reconstruction of the luminance images. This may be important for image transmission, or the energy-efficient transmission of information in nervous systems, but our results suggest that another optimality criteria for information-based "normative" approaches to understand natural vision systems shall be taken into account, namely the faithful representation of relevant features, where here we consider properties of depth images as relevant.

This paper is organized as follows: First, we describe the material and methods including the image material (Sec. 2). Then, we present the results of our analysis, where we first compare the spatial correlations of the luminance and depth images for different types of scenes (Sec. 3.1) and then the dependency for responses of oriented filters and depth features as quantified by the mutual information.

2   Material and Methods

2.1   Description of the Datasets

Our analysis is based on a collection of images obtained originally from Stanford University [9] (see Fig. 1). The total number of images in this database is 400. The 2D color pixel images were recorded with a high resolution 1704×2272 pixel (width × height), but the depth images with a resolution of 305×55 pixel (width × height). All images were inspected manually by us and then labeled as either "forest scene", "city scene", or "landscape scene". Only 12 images were labeled as landscape scenes, and we did not include them in our analysis. 80 scenes were labeled as city scenes, and the remaining ones as forest scenes. Therefore, we compared only forest and city scenes.

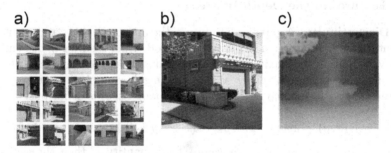

Fig. 1. Examples from the image collection. **a)** Pixel images of city scenes. **b)** RGB luminance image. **c)** Depth map.

2.2 Features in the Luminance Images

The luminance images were first transformed into gray-scale images. Then, each gray-scale image is linearly decomposed into a set of edge feature responses to Gabor filters with different orientations. More specifically, the Gabor function is given by

$$G\left(x,y\right) = \exp\left(-\frac{\hat{x}^2 + \gamma^2\hat{y}^2}{2\sigma^2}\right)\cos\left(2\pi\frac{\hat{x}}{\lambda} - \psi\right)$$

with $\hat{x} = x\cos\theta + y\sin\theta$ and $\hat{y} = -x\sin\theta$. We used orientations $\theta = \{0°, 15°, \ldots, , 165°\}$, but only one spatial frequency $\lambda = 6.1$ (and $\sigma = 3.4$) and two spatial phases $\psi \in \{0, \pi/2\}$. We set $\gamma = 1$. Within each image we subtracted the mean from the filter responses to each orientation, and normalized the responses to the interval between -1 and 1. Figure 3 shows the histogram of such normalized responses for selected orientations.

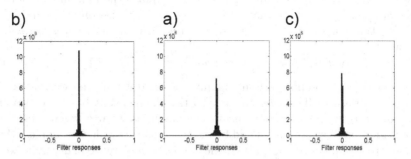

Fig. 2. Histograms of the Gabor filter responses with three different orientations. **a)** Histogram of the Gabor filter responses in the vertical, **b)** oblique, and **c)** horizontal orientation.

2.3   Features in the Depth Images

Gap Discontinuity. A gap discontinuity in the underlying 3D structure is a significant depth difference in a small neighborhood. We measure gap discontinuity μ_{GD} by computing the maximum difference in depth between the depth of a pixel in the depth image and the depth at its eight neighboring pixel. Here, we considered the methods presented in [10]; μ_{GD} for a point (x, y) is defined as:

$$\mu_{GD}(x,y) = \max\{ \mid z(x,y) - z(x+i, y+j) \mid : -1 \le i, j \le 1\}, \tag{1}$$

where $z(x, y)$ represents a depth value. This quantity is then thresholded to generate a binary gap discontinuity map. In our analysis, we have empirically chosen a threshold $\mu_{GD}(x, y) > T_d$ where $T_d = 0.5$. Fig. 3b shows an illustration of a gap discontinuity map.

Surface Orientation Discontinuity. An orientation discontinuity is present when two surfaces meet with significantly different 3D orientations. Orientation discontinuity was measured using surface normal analysis. Here, we considered the methods presented in [11,10]. The orientation discontinuity measure μ_{OD} is computed as the maximum angular difference between adjacent unit surfaces normal. First, a three dimensional point cloud was constructed from the X, Y, Z coordinates for each pixel in a depth image. Then, each pixel is represented by a pixel patch $P_{(x,y,z)}$ compiled from the eight neighboring points in the point cloud. Finally, the unit surfaces normal are computed for each patch $P_{(x,y,z)}$ using Singular Value Decomposition (SVD).

More specifically, for an image patch $P_{(x,y,z)}$ the orientation discontinuity is defined as

$$\mu_{OD}(P_{(x,y,z)}) = \max\left\{ \alpha\left(normal(P_{(x,y,z)}), normal\left(P_{(x+i,y+j,z+k)}\right)\right) : -1 \le i, j, k \le 1 \right\}, \tag{2}$$

where $normal(P_{(x,y,z)})$: is a function, which computes the unit surface normal of a patch $P_{(x,y,z)}$ in 3D coordinates using Singular Value Decomposition (SVD), α is a function computing the angle between adjacent unit surfaces normal. It is given by

$$\alpha(P_1, P_2) = \arccos(normal(P_1) \cdot normal(P_2)). \tag{3}$$

max is function to compute the maximum angular difference between adjacent unit surfaces normal. This measure is also thresholded, but based on two criteria, namely i) an *angular criterion*: the maximum angular difference between adjacent unit surfaces normal should be more than a threshold $T_{\theta 1}$ and less than $T_{\theta 2}$, and ii) a *distance-based criterion*: the maximum difference in depth between a point and its eight neighbor's μ_{GD} should be less than a threshold T_d.

In our analysis, we have empirically chosen $T_{\theta 1} = 20°$, $T_{\theta 2} = 160°$ and $T_d = 0.5$, respectively. Fig. 3b shows an illustration of an orientation discontinuity map.

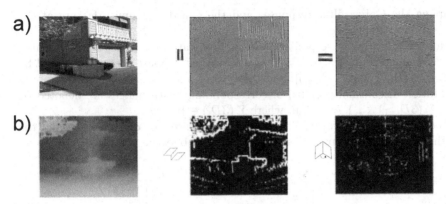

Fig. 3. Examples for features in luminance and depth images. **a)** A gray-scale image convolved with two Gabor filters selective for the same spatial frequency, but different orientation. **b)** A depth map (left) decomposed into its discontinuity maps: gap discontinuity map (middle) and orientation discontinuity map (right).

2.4 Analysis Methods

Spatial Correlations. The correlation between pixels is probably the simplest statistical characterization of images. It reveals how spatial dependencies in images fall off with distance. The luminance and depth values are each given by a single number. Based on these numbers we estimated the correlation coefficient as a function of the distance between any two pixels, i. e.

$$\text{corr}(d) := \text{corr}(X_1, X_2) = \frac{\text{cov}(X_1, X_2)}{\sqrt{\text{var}(X_1)\,\text{var}(X_2)}}, \tag{4}$$

where X_1 and X_2 are two random variables representing two gray-scale/depth values of two pixels separated by d pixel. Here,

$$\text{cov}[X_1, X_2] = E[X_1 X_2] - E[X_1]\,E[X_2] \tag{5}$$

$$\text{var}[X] = E[X^2] - E[X]^2 \tag{6}$$

are the covariance and variance, respectively. $E[\cdot]$ denotes the expectation, which we estimated by the sample mean.

Mutual Information. The mutual information (MI) between two variables is the amount of information that one variable contains about another. It is a graded quantification of the statistical dependencies between two random variables beyond second order. We used MI as a dependency measure between luminance and depth images. The luminance images are first linearly decomposed into a set of edge feature responses to Gabor filters in different orientations (see Figure 3a). For the depth images we computed gap and orientation discontinuities (see Figure 3b). Then, we estimated the MI between the discretized filter responses for each oriented filter and the binary discontinuity feature by sampling the Gabor filter responses and the gap discontinuity feature at the corresponding image location.

More specifically, the responses of Gabor filters at orientation θ were computed for all luminance images $I_1...I_n$. This orientation response vector is denoted by $X_\theta = [X_\theta(I_{i=1}),...,X_\theta(I_{i=n})]$, and the discontinuity maps (combined gap and orientation discontinuity maps) of corresponding depth images are denoted by $Y = [Y(3D_{i=1}),...,Y(3D_{i=n})]$, where $Y(3D_i) \in \{0,1\}$.

The dependency between all luminance responses for orientation θ and the depth discontinuity maps is measured by the MI between X_θ and Y

$$MI_\theta(X_\theta;Y) = \sum_{x,y} \Pr_{X_\theta,Y}(x,y) \log\left(\frac{\Pr_{X_\theta,Y}(x,y)}{\Pr_{X_\theta}(x)\Pr_Y(y)}\right), \qquad (7)$$

where $\Pr_{X_\theta,Y}(x,y)$ is the joint probability distributions calculated using a joint histogram, and $\Pr_{X_\theta}(x)$ and $\Pr_Y(y)$ are the marginal probabilities. The θ subscript emphasizes the fact that the MI is a function of orientation.

3   Results

3.1   Spatial Correlations

The luminance and depth images clearly differ in terms of their spatial correlations, which is illustrated in Figure 4a-c and summarized in Figure 5. Consider the example luminance image and the corresponding depth image: While the gray-scale values of the pixels in the luminance image along a horizontal line (see arrow) is variable (Figure 4c, blue line) the corresponding depths are almost constant (Figure 4c, green line). This suggests that the 3D environment is spatially more homogeneous than it appears from the luminance images.

The spatial correlation over many images reveals a scene-dependence: The correlations in the luminance and depth city scenes are more extended than in forest scenes (Figure 5, green lines vs. blue lines). This is due to the presence

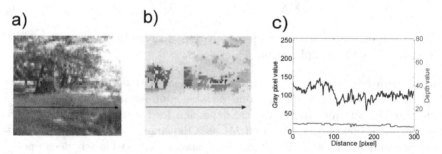

Fig. 4. Illustration to compare the changes in luminance values and depth values. **a, b)** Color and depth image of an example scene. **c)** Gray-scale and depth values of the pixels along the black arrow in panels a, b.

of many spatially extended surfaces in the city scenes such as walls, streets, etc, while there are many depth discontinuities in forest scenes such as due to trees. On the other hand, the correlation in the depth images in the city scenes are more extended than in the corresponding luminance images (green dashed vs. green solid line). The same is true for forest scenes (blue dashed vs. blue solid line), which means that the 3D environment is generally more homogeneous than evident from the luminance images.

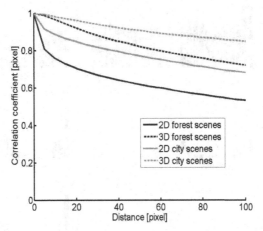

Fig. 5. Spatial correlation as a function of distance measured in pixel. The pixel pairs selected for estimating this function were selected randomly from all possibly pixel pairs in an image with the corresponding distance in pixels.

3.2 Mutual Information between Filter Responses and Discontinuities

The results of the mutual information analysis for *gap discontinuities* are shown in Fig. 6a,b for two different thresholds. The general pattern of the orientation-dependence does not differ much between the two threshold values we selected (Fig. 6a vs. Fig. 6b), but a scene-dependence shows up: In forest scenes the responses of the vertically oriented filters are much more informative about the gap discontinuities than for other oriented filters. This is not a surprise but expected, because the forest scenes have many trees with vertically oriented trunks, which are present in both the luminance and the depth images. When considering the *orientation discontinuities* separately (Fig. 6c), we do not find such a strong scene-dependence, but again a dominance of vertically oriented filter responses, i. e. they are more informative about orientation discontinuities than responses of other oriented filters. It is interesting to note that the information of the responses in horizontally oriented filters is lower in forest scenes compared to oblique and vertically oriented filters (in particular when compared to city scenes), which is probably due to the presence tree branches and trunks, but almost no horizontal gap discontinuities. Finally, the overall summary of

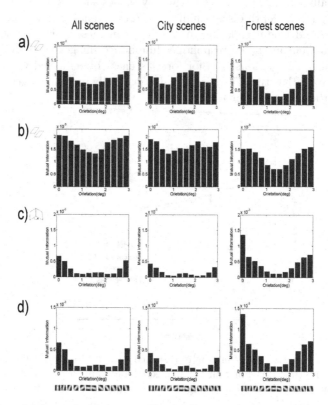

Fig. 6. Mutual information between oriented filter responses and orientation filter responses and 3D gap discontinuities with different thresholds T_d. **a)** T_d=0.5 m and **b)** T_d=0.1 m. **c)** Information about orientation discontinuities. **d)** Information about a "joint" discontinuity, i. e. either a gap or an orientation discontinuity.

our analysis is shown in Fig. 6d, where we computed the MI between the filter responses and a "joint" depth feature, i. e. the presence of either a gap or an orientation discontinuity.

4   Summary and Conclusion

We have analyzed the dependency between luminance and depth images features in natural scenes using mutual information. We find that the dependencies differ according to the type of visual environments. Most interestingly, we find that response of vertical filters carry most information about 3D discontinuities. This can explain the preferred processing of vertical orientations, but not because the corresponding orientations are more frequent in the luminance images, but because they are more informative about ecologically relevant depth features.

This is in contrast to other efficient coding hypotheses. More specifically, such hypotheses state that the visual system shall encode the stimuli from the sensory periphery most efficiently. This could be done by transforming these stimuli into neural representations, which are less redundant such as factorial codes. Other hypotheses about the visual system state that it implements statistical models of the environment. In that way of thinking vision is "inverse graphics", but finding and learning proper statistical models and inverting them is a current research topic.

Our approach, which at this point does *not* use an explicit statistical model, can be viewed as a hybrid of the efficient coding approach and the use of generative statistical models: We determine, using information-theoretic measures, the potentially informative features in the luminance images and argue that those should be encoded most reliable and robust, but we do not postulate any particular neural code. Thus, while our results suggest an asymmetry in orientation processing as evident in the oblique effect, we cannot yet predict how exactly that should be reflected in the early human visual system.

We explicitly refer to the properties of depth images, and it may be tempting to integrate such information directly into generative statistical models of the visual scenes. However, we intentionally did not formulate such models, because the whole idea of vision being "inverse graphics" may serve as a good guidance for computer vision, but it is still only a hypothesis as to weather biological visual systems implement such models, or if they follow other strategies. We argue that our results suggest that future natural image analysis may revitalize and refine the pioneering studies of depth and the corresponding luminance images [7,8], because this way important constraints for any theory of visual processing can be obtained. Our work is also an important first towards building generative models for natural images, which explicitly take into account 3D properties of the visual environments and, most importantly, we suggest that a new series of analysis shall empirically measure the corresponding prior probabilities over latent variables in such geometrically motivated models.

References

1. Field, D.J.: Relations between the statistics of natural images and the response properties of cortical cells (1987)
2. Simoncelli, E.P., Olshausen, B.A.: Natural image statistics and neural representation. Annu. Rev. Neurosci. 24(1), 1193–1216 (2001)
3. Burton, G.J., Moorhead, I.R.: Color and spatial structure in natural scenes. Applied Optics 26(1), 157–170 (1987)
4. Zhu, S.C., Mumford, D.: Prior learning and gibbs reaction-diffusion. IEEE Trans. Pattern Anal. Mach. Intell. 19, 1236–1250 (1997)
5. Van Hateren, J.H., Van Der Schaaf, A.: Independent component filters of natural images compared with simple cells in primary visual cortex. Proceedings of the Royal Society B Biological Sciences 265(1394), 359–366 (1998)
6. Rothkopf, C.A., Weisswange, T.H., Triesch, J.: Learning independent causes in natural images explains the spacevariant oblique effect. In: IEEE 8th International Conference on Development and Learning, ICDL 2009, pp. 1–6 (June 2009)
7. Potetz, B., Lee, T.S.: Statistical Correlations Between 2D Images and 3D Structures in Natural Scenes. Journal of Optical Society of America, A 7(20), 1292–1303 (2003)

8. Yang, Z., Purves, D.: Image/source statistics of surfaces in natural scenes. Network: Computation in Neural Systems 14(3), 371–390 (2003)

9. Ng, A.Y., Saxena, A., Sun, M.: Make3d: Learning 3d scene structure from a single still image. IEEE Transactions of Pattern Analysis and Machine Intelligence (PAMI) 30(5), 824–840 (2009)

10. Yokoya, N., Levine, M.D.: Range image segmentation based on differential geometry: a hybrid approach. IEEE Transactions on Pattern Analysis and Machine Intelligence 11(6), 643–649 (1989)

11. Hoover, X.J.A., Jean-Baptiste, G.: An experimental comparison of range image segmentation algorithms. IEEE Transactions on Pattern Analysis and Machine Intelligence 18, 673–689 (1996)

An Agent Model for Temporal Dynamics Analysis of a Person with Chronic Fatigue Syndrome

Azizi Ab Aziz[1,2], Faudziah Ahmad[2], and Houzifa M. Hintaya[2]

[1] ITU-UUM Asia Pacific Centre of Excellence for Rural ICT Development
Universiti Utara Malaysia, 06010 UUM, Sintok, Kedah Malaysia
[2] Bio-Inspired Agent Research Group, Artificial Intelligence Laboratory,
School of Computing, College of Arts & Sciences, Universiti Utara Malaysia
06010 UUM, Sintok, Kedah Malaysia
{aziziaziz,fudz,s809389}@uum.edu.my

Abstract. This paper presents a dynamic agent model of chronic fatigue syndrome for an individual. Chronic fatigue syndrome is the most common name to define a group of cognitive and medical disorders caused by persistent fatigue. Based on several personal characteristics, viral infection, and a representation of events (i.e. psychological and physiological stressors), the agent model can simulate whether a human agent that experience certain scenarios will fall into a chronic fatigue condition. A number of well-known relations between events and the course of chronic fatigue are summarized from the literature and it is shown that the model exhibits those patterns. In addition, the agent model has been mathematically analyzed to find out which stable situations exist. Finally, it is pointed out how this model can be used in therapy, supported by a software agent.

Keywords: Agent Based Modeling, Human Aware System, Cognitive Modeling, Chronic Fatigue Syndrome.

1   Introduction

Chronic fatigue syndrome (CFS) is a disorder that causes extreme fatigue. It is estimated that the illness caused about 20,000 dollar per person with CFS in lost productivity which totals to 9.1 billion dollar per year in the United States [1,15]. Symptoms of CFS include fatigue for six months or more and experience on other problems such as muscle pain, memory problems, headaches, pain in multiple joints, sleep problems, sore throat and tender lymph nodes [6,16]. Although fatigue is a human experience, and many people report experiencing chronic fatigue intermittently, CFS is different and not very common. The hallmark post-conditions of CFS are overwhelming fatigue and weakness that make it extremely difficult to perform routine and daily tasks, like getting out of bed, dressing, and even eating [10,12]. Moreover, fatigue may worsen with physical or mental activity, but does not improve with rest. In addition, a study found that CFS patients report a heavy psychosocial burden [3,9]. Although

F.M. Zanzotto et al. (Eds.): BI 2012, LNCS 7670, pp. 107–118, 2012.

much work has been dedicated to understand the CFS mechanism, little attention has been paid to a computational modeling angle on how a person with certain risks can experience chronic fatigue. The aim of this paper is to present a computational model that can be used to simulate the dynamics of CFS under influence of stressful events and related personal profiles.

The paper is organized as follows; Section 2 describes several theoretical concepts of CFS. From this point of view, a formal model is designed (Section 3). Later in Section 4, a number of simulation traces are presented to illustrate how the proposed model satisfies the expected outcomes. In Section 5, a mathematical analysis is performed in order to identify possible equilibria in the model, followed by verification of the model against formally specified expected overall patterns, using an automated verification tool (Section 6). Finally, Section 7 concludes the paper.

2   Important Concepts in CFS

Before presenting the model, the main characteristics of CFS as known from the literature are described. Therefore, the key step in the development of a model to represent potential CFS is to understand how this condition may occur. First, the predisposed factors such as *negative personality* and *periodic activity* (for strenuous task) are often related to a number of reported cases in CFS [1,6,12,13, 18]. In many cases, these factors will amplify the effect from the environment, especially with the present of *psychological* and *physiological* stressors. Very often, the physiological (e.g., noise, work) and psychological (e.g., frustration, cognitive pressure, threat) reactions to predisposed factors will tend to produce additional condition known as *demands*. These include emotional and work demands, which later will cause *mental load* (e.g. workplace stress). With continued mental load at the residing environment (e.g. workplace) and under intense influence from stressors and predisposed factors, a person will develop the unnecessary stress (*short* and *long term stress*) that will cause both stress (cognitive) and physical exhaustion and suppress body's ability from producing a *balance immune level* against a number of diseases (e.g. viral infection) [5, 14,].

Deterioration in a human's immune system against viral infections is another prevalence factor for a person with CFS. It was reported that some cases of CFS begin with a flu-like infection [8,11]. When the immune system is over taxed by high levels of stress, its ability to fight off other types of illnesses becomes compromised. This results a person with the risk of chronic fatigue vulnerable (*susceptible*) towards a number of viral infections such as Epstein-Barr virus [16], Human Herpesvirus (HHV) [12], retroviruses and enteroviruses [11]. It was reported that a small perturbation in immunological stimuli may cause major fluctuation in endocrine status [8,16]. Physical exhaustion is, for the most part created by choice. Typically, the *exhaustion* that comes shortly after a person slows down is expected and the recovery efforts of relaxation are planned. However, stress exhaustion is not planned and normally caused by thoughts and feelings of that person rather than the situation related to it [1,17]. For example, a person who experience stress as a result of a lost job may become cognitively exhausted as a result of worry, while another person may choose to take the lost in a positive perspective. In many reported cases, when these types of exhaustion are combined with a lack of adequate nutrition, proper care and treatment, stress (cognitive) exhaustion is exceptionally debilitating [7,11,17].

Prolonged exhaustion will cause another state called as *fatigue* (lethargy). It is a state of awareness describing a range of afflictions, usually associated with mental and/or physical weakness and it varies from a general state of lethargy to a specific work induced condition [7]. In addition, fatigue is a non-specific symptom and often reported by the person itself instead of being observed by others. In a long run, direct and constant exposure towards long-term exhaustion and fatigue will allow the development of *chronic fatigue*. During this stage, a person will experience unexplained and persistent fatigue unrelated to exertion and not substantially relieved by rest. Moreover, in most cases, people report critical reductions in levels of physical activity, and a reduction in the complexity of activity has been observed. Through a cognitive perspective, one of the meta-analysis research findings concluded cognitive symptoms were principally resultants of decreased attention and reaction time [1, 10,13, 16].

In short, the following relations can be identified from the literature: (1) a series of psychological and physiological stressor events can lead to the formation of mental load and long term stress; (2) periodic activity and low job control will increase the risk of work and emotional demand ; (3) negative personality factors aggravate the effect of stressor events on the potential onset of demand and stress;(4) long term stress will reduce a normal immune system production that alleviate the risk of viral susceptibility, and later will increase the risk of chronic fatigue and, (5) a combination of long-term fatigue and long-term exhaustion will exacerbate the risk of having a CFS.

3   Modeling Approach

This section discusses the details of the dynamic model. The characteristics of the proposed model are heavily inspired by the research discussed in the previous section on CFS. In particular, this model combines ideas from research in affective disorder, prevention medicine, artificial intelligence, and dynamic modeling. Those ideas are encapsulated to simulate how a person is fragile towards stressors, and possibly further develops a CFS condition. All of these concepts (and their interactions) are discussed in the following paragraphs in this section. In this model, eight main components are interacting to each other to simulate temporal dynamics in CFS. These components are grouped as predisposed factors, stressors, viral infection, demand, stress, exhaustion, fatigue and immune function (refer to Figure 1).

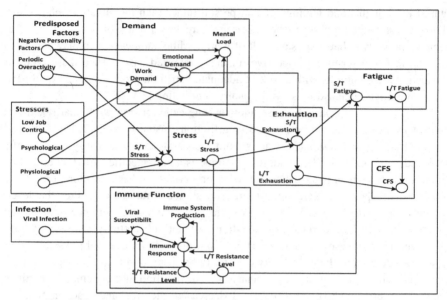

Fig. 1. Global Relationships of Variables Involved in the Formation of CFS

Once the structural relationships in the model have been determined, the model can be formalized. In the formalization, all nodes are designed in a way to have values ranging from 0 (low) to 1 (high). This model involves a number of instantaneous and temporal relations, which will be discussed in greater detailed below.

3.1   Instantaneous Relations

The instantaneous relations are derived from several formulae, namely; work (Wd), and emotional (Ed) demand, mental load (Ml), viral susceptibility (Vs), immune system production (Ip), immune response (Ir), and short-term (stress (Ss),resistance level (Sr), exhaustion (Se), and fatigue (Sf)). These relations were designed as given by the following formulae. First, the state of work demand will be explained. The state work demand (Wd) is used to express what a person feels when facing too much work (periodic work activity,(Po)) and unable to prioritize job loads (low job control,(Lj)).

$$Wd(t) = \alpha_w.Po(t) + (1 - \alpha_w).\,Lj(t) \tag{1}$$

$$Ed(t) = \beta_e.\,Np(t) + (1 - \beta_e).\,Ps(t) \tag{2}$$

$$Ml(t) = [\,\mu_m.\,Ed(t) + (1 - \mu_m).\,Wd(t)\,]\,.\,Np(t) \tag{3}$$

Emotional demand (Ed) is influenced by negative personality (Np) and psychological stressors (Ps). Together with negative personality, both work and emotional demand will later influence the development of mental load (Ml). Short-term stress depends on the relation between mental load, negative personality, psychological and physiological (*Ph*) stressors. Note that if a person has a very low negative personality level, it will reduce the formation of short term stress.

$$Ss(t) = [\omega_{s1}. Ps(t) + \omega_{s2}. Ml(t) + \omega_{s3}. Ph(t)].Np(t) \tag{4}$$

$$Vs(t) = Vi(t). (1 - [\kappa_v.Sr(t) + (1-\kappa_v).Lr(t)]) \tag{5}$$

$$Ip(t) = \omega_i. Ip_{norm} + (1-\omega_i). Ir(t). Ip_{norm} \tag{6}$$

Other important conditions are viral susceptibility (*Vs*) and immune system production (*Ip*). Viral susceptibility relates to the viral infection (*Vi*), short and long term viral resistance (*Sr* and *Lr*). Immune system production depends on the interaction between the normal immune production level (*Ip_norm*) within a person and the condition of long-term resistance.

$$Ir(t) = [\gamma_i. Vs(t) + (1-\gamma_i). Ls(t)]. Ip(t) \tag{7}$$

$$Sr(t) = \alpha_s. Sr_{norm} + (1-\alpha_s). Ir(t). Sr_{norm} \tag{8}$$

$$Se(t) = \lambda_{e1}. Ed(t) + \lambda_{e2}. Wd(t) + \lambda_{e3}. Ls(t) \tag{9}$$

$$Sf(t) = Se(t). (1 - Lr(t)) \tag{10}$$

The combination of viral susceptibility, long-term stress, and immune system production will later influence immune response (*Ir*). Short-term resistance level (*Sr*) is also having a similar behavior with immune system production, but it is related to the interaction in a normal resistance level (*Sr_norm*). Short-term exhaustion (*Se*) is generated by simulating potential effects weighted sum of emotional demand, work demand and long-term stress. The interaction between short-term exhaustion and long-term stress determines the level of short-term fatigue (*Sf*). For all instantaneous relations, parameters $\alpha_w, \beta_e, \mu_m, \omega_{s1}, \omega_{s2}, \omega_{s3}, \kappa_v, \omega_i, \gamma_i, \alpha_s, \lambda_{e1}, \lambda_{e2}$ and λ_{e1} provide a proportional contribution in respective relations.

3.2   Temporal Relations

Long term stress (*Ls*) is primarily contributed the accumulation exposure towards short term stress, while the accumulated short-term resistance produces long-term viral resistance (*Lr*). The formation of long-term exhaustion and fatigue are modeled using the presence of short-term exhaustion and fatigue respectively.

$$Ls(t+\Delta t) = Ls(t) + \lambda_{ls}. (Ss(t) - Ls(t)). Ls(t).(1-Ls(t)).\Delta t \tag{11}$$

$$Lr(t+\Delta t) = Lr(t) + \beta_{lr}.(Sr(t) - Lr(t)). Lr(t).(1-Lr(t)).\Delta t \tag{12}$$

$$Le(t+\Delta t) = Le(t) + \beta_{le}. (Se(t) - Le(t)). Le(t). (1 - Ls(t)). \Delta t \tag{13}$$

$$Lf(t+\Delta t) = Lf(t) + \beta_{lf}. (Sf(t) - Lf(t)). Lf(t). (1 - Lf(t)). \Delta t \tag{14}$$

Finally, consistent exposure of long-term exhaustion and fatigue will increase the level of chronic fatigue syndrome (*Cf*).

$$Cf(t + \Delta t) = Cf(t) + \beta_{cf} \cdot (Pc(t) - Cf(t)) \cdot Cf(t) \cdot (1 - Cf(t)) \cdot \Delta t \qquad (15)$$

Where $Pc(t) = \left(\frac{1}{1+e^{(-\lambda * yf(t)-\tau)}} - \frac{1}{1+e^{(\lambda * \tau)}} \right) * \left(1 + e^{-\lambda * \tau} \right)$, and

$Yf(t) = Lf(t) + Le(t)$

To compute the combination effect (Pc) of long-term exhaustion and fatigue, a continuous logistic function is used, where λ is a steepness and τ a threshold parameter. In this choice, a common practice is followed (logistic function) but other types of combination functions can be specified as well. Note that the change process is measured in a time interval between t and $t + \Delta t$. In addition to all this, the rate of change for all temporal specifications are determined by flexibility rates λ_{ls}, β_{lr}, β_{le}, β_{lf}, and β_{cf}. Using all defined formulas, a simulator was developed for experimentation purposes; specifically to explore interesting patterns and traces that explains the behaviour of the human agent model.

4   Simulation Results

In this section, the model was executed to simulate a large number of conditions of individuals. With variation of these conditions, some interesting patterns can be obtained, as previously defined in the earlier section. In order to visualize related patterns, three fictional humans are shown: a healthy individual (A), an individual with a moderate potential risk of chronic fatigue (B), and an individual with a high risk of chronic fatigue (C). Table 1 shows the initial values for each respective individual.

Table 1. Initial Values for the Simulation Experiments

Individual	Negative Personality	Periodic Activity	Low Job Control	Viral Infection
A	0.1	0.2	0.1	0.2
B	0.3	0.4	0.5	0.4
C	0.7	0.8	0.7	0.6

For both psychological and physiological stressors, two conditions were introduced, one with a very high constant stressor, and with no stressor event. These events simulate the condition of where a person was facing a sudden change in his or her life. In addition to this, there are several parameters that can be varied to simulate different characteristics. However, in this simulation, we used the following settings: $t_{max} = 500$ (to represent a monitoring activity up to 200 days), $\Delta t = 0.3$, regulatory rates = 0.5 and flexibility rates = 0.2. These settings were obtained from several experiments to determine the most suitable parameter values for the model. For the sake of brevity, this section will only discuss the results of individual A and C. First, the simulation of person with low risk in CFS is shown (Figure 2).

Case #1: A Healthy Person (Low Risk in CFS)
For a healthy person (A), despite the high intensity of stressors (both psychological and physiological) in the first half of the simulation trace, he or she manages to reduce future development of long-term fatigue and exhaustion.

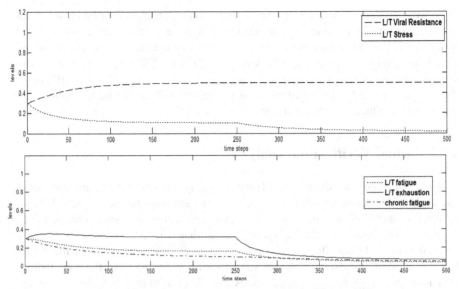

Fig. 2. Simulation Results of Person with Low Risk in CFS

Fig. 2 shows a gradual reduction in a long-term stress, fatigue, and exhaustion while improving resistance against viral infection. In addition, it can be seen all temporal effects are decreasing rapidly after the absent of negative events. This person tends to be stable and reduce the risk of having chronic fatigue [10].

Case #2: A Person with a High Risk in CFS
Obviously, during this simulation, a highly vulnerable person (C) experiences CFS faster and higher compared to person A and B. The result from this simulation trace is consistent with a number of findings in prior works related to the CFS (see Figure 3) [6, 7, 14, 18].

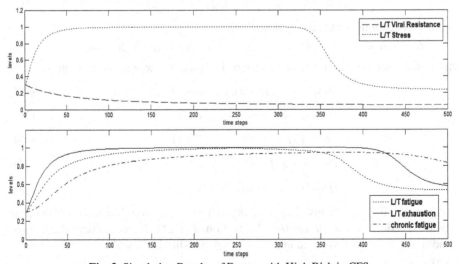

Fig. 3. Simulation Results of Person with High Risk in CFS

To wrap up these experimental results, the simulation traces described above satisfactorily explain the relations as summarized in Section 2. In all simulation traces, it is shown that persons with a positive personality (less neurotic), high job control and capable to manage the assigned tasks develop less often CFS compared those who are not. It is consistent with a number of findings as reported in [6, 9].This distillation of above evidences and traces illustrates that this model reflects the basic relations that are known to influence CFS, given certain criteria of events and personality attributes.

5   Formal Verification Analysis

In this section the equilibria are analyzed that may occur under certain conditions. The equilibria describe situations in which a stable situation has been reached. These equillibria conditions are interesting to be explored, as it is possible to explain them using the knowledge from the theory or problem that is modelled. As such, the existence of reasonable equilibria is also an indication for the correctness of the model. This can be done to assume constant values for all variables (also the ones that are used as inputs). Then in all of the equations the reference to time t can be left out, and in addition the differential equations can be simplified by cancelling, for example $Cf(t+\Delta t)$ against $Cf(t)$. One important assumption should be made; all exogenous variables are having a constant value. Assuming all parameters are non-zero, this leads to the following equations where an equilibrium state is characterized by:

$$dLs(t)/dt = \lambda_{ls} . (Ss - Ls). Ls.(1\text{-}Ls) \tag{16}$$

$$dLr(t)/dt = \beta_{lr}.(Sr - Lr). Lr.(1\text{-}Lr) \tag{17}$$

$$dLe(t)/dt = \beta_{le} . (Se - Le) . Le . (1 - Ls) \tag{18}$$

$$dLf(t)/dt = \beta_{lf} . (Sf - Lf). Lf . (1 - Lf) \tag{19}$$

$$dCf(t)/dt = \beta_{cf} . (Pc - Cf) . Cf . (1 - Cf) \tag{20}$$

Next, the equations are identified describing

$$dLs(t)/dt = 0, dLr(t)/dt = 0, dLe(t)/dt=0, dLf(t)/dt =0, dCf(t)/dt = 0$$

Assuming both adaptation rates are equal to 1, therefore, these are equivalent to;

$$(Ss = Ls) \vee (Ls = 0) \vee (Ls=1) \tag{21}$$

$$(Sr = Lr) \vee (Lr=0) \vee (Lr=1) \tag{22}$$

$$(Se = Le) \vee (Le=0) \vee (Ls=1) \tag{23}$$

$$(Sf = Lf) \vee (Lf =0) \vee (Lf=1) \tag{24}$$

$$(Pc = Cf) \vee (Cf=0) \vee (Cf=1) \tag{25}$$

From here, a first of conclusions can be derived where the equilibrium can only occur when the $Ls=1$, $Ss=Ls$, or $Ls=0$ (refer to Equation 21). By combining these three conditions, it can be re-written into a set of relationship in $(A \vee B \vee C) \wedge (D \vee E \vee F)$ expression:

$$(Ss= Ls \lor Ls = 0 \lor Ls=1) \land (Sr= Lr \lor Lr=0 \lor Lr=1) \land$$
$$(Se = Le \lor Le=0 \lor Ls=1) \land (Sf = Lf \lor Lf =0 \lor Lf=1) \land \qquad (26)$$
$$(Pc = Cf \lor Cf=0 \lor Cf=1)$$

This expression can be elaborated using the *law of distributivity* as $(A \land D) \lor (A \land E)$ $\lor,..,\lor (C \land F)$.

$$(Ss= Ls \land Sr= Lr \land Lr=0 \land Se = Le \land Sf=Lf \land Pc=Cf) \lor, ...,\lor \qquad (27)$$
$$(Ls=1 \land Lr = 1 \land Lf =1 \land Cf =1)$$

This later provides possible combinations equillibria points to be further analyzed. However due to the huge amount of possible combinations, (in this case, $3^5 = 243$ possibilities), it makes hard to come up with a complete classification of equilibria. However, for some typical cases the analysis can be pursued further.

Case # 1: $Ls=1 \land Lr = 1 \land Lf =1 \land Cf =1$
For this case, by equation (5) it follows that,
$$Vs = Vi . (1 - [\kappa_v.Sr + (1- \kappa_v)])$$
and hence by equation (7)
$$Ir = [\gamma_i. Vs + (1 - \gamma_i)]. Ip(t)$$
Moreover, from (9) it follows that
$$Se = \lambda_{e1}. Ed + \lambda_{e2}. Wd + \lambda_{e3}$$
Finally, from (10), it follows
$$Sf = 0$$

Case # 2: $Lr = 0$
From equation (5) it follows that this is equivalent to
$$Vs = Vi . (1 - \kappa_v.Sr)$$
and from (10) it follows that
$$Sf = Se$$

Case #3: $Ls = 0$
For this case, from equation (7) it follows that the case is equivalent to:
$$Ir = [\gamma_i. Vs)]. Ip$$
Assuming $\lambda e1$ and $\lambda e2 > 0$,   this is equivalent to:
$$Se= \lambda_{e1}. Ed + \lambda_{e2}. Wd$$

6   Automated Verification

In order to verify whether the model indeed generates results that adherence to psychological literatures, a set of properties have been identified from related literatures. These properties have been specified in a language called Temporal Trace Language (TTL). TTL is built on atoms referring to states of the world, time points, and traces. This relationship can be presented as *holds(state(γ, t), p)* or *state(γ, t)|= p*, which means that state property p is true in the state of trace γ at time point t [4]. It is also comparable to the *Holds*-predicate in the Situation Calculus. Based on that concept, dynamic properties can be formulated using a hybrid sorted predicate logic approach, by using quantifiers over time and traces and first-order logical connectives such as $\neg$, $\wedge$, $\vee$, $\Rightarrow$, $\forall$, and $\exists$. A number of simulations including the ones described in Section 4 have been used as basis for the verification of the identified properties and were confirmed. Note that tb and te are the initial and final time points of the simulation period.

VP1: Monotonic Increase of CFS

For all time points t1 and *t2* between *tb* and *te* in trace γ1
if at t1 the value of   the CFS is R1 and at t2 the value of the CFS is R2 and t1 < t2, then R1 ≤ R2.

   P1 ≡∀γ: TRACE, ∀R1, R2: REAL, t1,t2:TIME, ∀A1:AGENT
   [state(γ,t1)l= chronic_fatigue_syndrome(A1, R1) &
    state(γ,t2)l= chronic_fatigue_syndrome (A1, R2) &
    tb ≤   t1 ≤ te & tb ≤ t2 ≤ te & t1< t2 ⇒ R1 ≤ R2]

By checking property VP1, one can verify whether a person's CFS increases monotonically over a certain time interval. For example, the person's long-term stress turned out to increase over the second half of the trace for person that have experienced intense conditions that causes prolonged fatigue and exhaustion.

VP2: Higher Resistant Level against Long Term Fatigue

For all time points t1 and t2 in trace γ,
If at t1 the level of long term resistance of agent A1 is m1, and m1 ≥ 0.8 (high) and at time point t2 the   level of the long term fatigue of agent A1 is m2 and t2 ≥   t1+d, then m2   ≤ 0.4 (low).

   P2 ≡ ∀γ:TRACE, ∀t1, t2:TIME, ∀m1, m2, d:REAL , ∀A1:AGENT
   state(γ, t1)l= long_term_resistance(A1, m1) &
   state(γ, t2)l= long_term_fatigue(A1, m2) &
   m1 ≥ 0.8 & t2= t1+d ⇒   m2 ≤ 0.4

Property VP2 can be used to check whether higher resistance level against viral infection buffers the person's long term fatigue. It is checked whether if the long term resistance in agent A1 is high (a value higher or equal to 0.8), then the long term fatigue level of agent A1 will have a low value after some time (having a value below or equal to 0.4). The property succeeded on the traces, where the resistance level against viral infection was higher or equal to 0.8.

VP3: Monotonic Decrease of CFS for Any Individual When Low Job Control, Low Viral Infection, Negative Personality Factor and Psychological Stressors are Reduced

When a person manages to control job, reduce possible viral infection, think positively, and avoid potential psychological stressors throughout time, then the person will reduce the level of CFS in future.

   VP3 ≡ ∀γ:TRACE,t1,t2:TIME,D1,D2,E1,E2,F1,F2,G1,G2,H1,H2:REAL,X:AGENT

[state(γ, t1)|= low_job_control(X, D1) &
 state(γ, t2)|= low_job_control (X, D2) &
 state(γ, t1)|= viral_infection(X,E1) &
 state(γ, t2)|= viral_infection (X,E2) &
 state(γ, t1)|= negative_personality(X,F1) &
 state(γ, t2)|= negative_personality (X,F2) &
 state(γ, t1)|= psychological_stressors(X,G1) &
 state(γ, t2)|= psychological_stressors (X,G2) &
 state(γ, t1)|= chronic_fatigue_syndrome (X,H1) &
 state(γ, t2)|= chronic_fatigue_syndrome (X,H2) & t' > t &
 D2 ≥ D1 & E1 ≥ E2 & F1 ≥ F2 & G1 ≥ G2] ⇒ H2 ≤ H1

Property VP3 can be used to verify person's condition when negative factors (e.g., low job control, viral infection, negative personality, and psychological stressors) that cause CFS are decreasing throughout time [8,14].

7 Conclusion

The grand challenge addressed in the research that is reported in this paper is to develop a software agent that is capable of monitoring individuals' condition in certain events. In this paper, a first step has been taken. A model has been developed that is able to explain the development of CFS based on personal characteristics and stressor events. A mathematical analysis has been performed to demonstrate the occurrence of equilibrium conditions, fundamentally beneficial to describe convergence and stable state of the model. In addition, the simulation results have been verified based on several properties using Temporal Trace Language environment. The proposed model provides a basic building block in designing a software agent that will support the human. Future work of this agent and model integration will be specifically focus how interactions and sensing properties can be further developed and enriched, to promote a better way to fluidly embedded this into any monitoring and health informatics system [2].

References

1. Afari, N., Buchwald, D.: Chronic Fatigue Syndrome: A Review. Psychiatry 160, 221–236 (2003)
2. Aziz, A.A., Treur, J.: Modelling Dynamics of Social Support Networks for Mutual Support in Coping with Stress. In: Nguyen, N.T., Katarzyniak, R.P., Janiak, A. (eds.) New Challenges in Computational Collective Intelligence. SCI, vol. 244, pp. 167–179. Springer, Heidelberg (2009)
3. Bagnall, A., Whiting, P., Richardson, R., Sowden, A.: Interventions for the Treatment and Management of Chronic Fatigue Syndrome/ Myalgic Encephalomyelitis. Qual. Saf. Health Care 11, 284–288 (2002)
4. Bosse, T., Jonker, C.M., van der Meij, L., Sharpanskykh, A., Treur, J.: Specification and Verification of Dynamics in Agent Models. International Journal of Cooperative Information Systems (18), 167–1193 (2009)

5. Christley, Y., Duffy, T., Martin, C.: A Review of the Definitional Criteria for Chronic Fatigue. Journal of Evaluation in Clinical Practice 18, 25–31 (2010)
6. Courjaret, J., Schotteb, C., Wijnantsc, H., Moorkensc, G., Cosyns, P.: Chronic Fatigue Syndrome and DSM-IV Personality Disorders. Journal of Psychosomatic Research 66, 13–20 (2009)
7. Dick, M., Sundin, J.: Psychological and Psychiatric Causes of Fatigue. Australian Family Physician 32(11) (2003)
8. Goodnick, P.J.: Chronic Fatigue and Related Immune Deficiency Syndromes, Washington, DC, vol. 40 (2001)
9. Harvey, S., Wadsworth, M., Hotopf, M., Wessely, S.: The Relationship between Prior Psychiatric Disorder and Chronic Fatigue: Evidence from a National Birth Cohort Study. Psychol. Med. 38(7), 933–940 (2008)
10. Harvey, S., Wessely, S.: Chronic Fatigue Syndrome: Identifying Zebras Amongst the Horses. BMC Med. 7(58) (2009)
11. Harvey, S., Wessely, S.: Commentary Open Access Chronic Fatigue Syndrome: Identifying Zebras Amongst the Horses. BMC Medicine 7, 58 (2009)
12. Hempel, S., Chambers, D., Bagnall, A., Forbes, C.: Risk Factors for Chronic Fatigue Syndrome/myalgic Encephalomyelitis: a Systematic Scoping Review of Multiple Predictor Studies. Psychological Medicine, 1–12 (2007)
13. Kai-Wen, C.: A Study of Stress Sources among College Students in Taiwan. Journal of Academic and Business Ethics, 1–6 (2010)
14. Kocalevent, R., Hinz, A., Brähler, E., Klapp, B.: Determinants of Fatigue and Stress. BMC Research Notes 4, 238 (2011)
15. Lin, J., Resch, S., Brimmer, D., Johnson, A., Kennedy, S., Burstein, N., Simon, C.: The Economic Impact of Chronic Fatigue Syndrome in Georgia: Direct and Indirect Costs. Cost Effectiveness and Resource Allocation (9), 1 (2008)
16. Maes, M., Twisk, F.: Chronic Fatigue Syndrome: Harvey and Wessely's (Bio) Psychosocial Model versus a Bio (Psychosocial) Model Based on Inflammatory and Oxidative and Nitrosative Stress Pathways. BMC Medicine 8, 35 (2010)
17. Moustaka, E.: Sources and Effects of Work-related Stress in Nursing. Health Science Journal 4(4), 210–216 (2010)
18. Nater, U., Jones, J., Lin, J., Maloney, E., Reeves, W., Heim, C.: Personality Features and Personality Disorders in Chronic Fatigue Syndrome: A Population-Based Study. Psychother Psychosom. 79, 312–318 (2010)

A Naïve Hypergraph Model of Brain Networks

Zhijiang Wang[1,2], Jiming Liu[1,2,3], Ning Zhong[1,2,4],
Yulin Qin[1,2,5], Haiyan Zhou[1,2], Jian Yang[1,2], and Kuncheng Li[6,2]

[1] International WIC Institute, Beijing University of Technology, China
[2] Beijing Key Laboratory of MRI and Brain Informatics, China
[3] Dept. of Computer Science, Hong Kong Baptist University, China
[4] Dept. of Life Science and Informatics, Maebashi Institute of Technology, Japan
[5] Dept. of Psychology, Carnegie Mellon University, USA
[6] Dept. of Radiology, Xuanwu Hospital, Capital Medical University, China
wang.zj.ross@gmail.com

Abstract. This paper extended the concept of motif by maximum cliques defined as "hyperedges" in brain networks, as novel and flexible characteristic network building blocks. Based on the definition of hyperedge, a naïve brain hypergraph model was constructed from a graph model of large-scale brain functional networks during rest. Nine intrinsic hub hyperedges of functional connectivity were identified, which could be considered as the most important intrinsic information processing blocks (or units), and they also covered many components of the core brain intrinsic networks. Furthermore, these overlapped hub hyperedges were assembled into a compound structure as a core subsystem of the intrinsic brain organization.

1 Introduction

Recent studies have demonstrated that the brain is hierarchically organized as a complex network of interconnected neurons or regions on multiple spatial and time scales [1–3]. With graph theory, many important statistical characteristics have been revealed underlying the large-scale brain organization [1], e.g., the small-world property, power-law degree distribution and modular/community with hubs architecture, which are also shared by various biological, social, technological and other natural system networks. As Bressler et al. [3] suggest, it is a big progress to be aware that cognition results from dynamic interactions of distributed brain areas operating in large-scale networks, not attributable to isolated operations of single brain areas. Accordingly, it is necessary to detect the complex organizational principles of the brain topological organization.

Resting-state network studies have identified local intrinsic spatial patterns at subsystem levels underlying the large-scale brain functional organization, and as reviewed by Menon et al. [4], there are three core neurocognitive intrinsic networks, i.e., the executive control network (ECN), salience network (SN) and default mode network (DMN). On the other hand, the current graph-theoretical analysis of brain networks mainly includes connectivity measuring

F.M. Zanzotto et al. (Eds.): BI 2012, LNCS 7670, pp. 119–129, 2012.

and pattern finding over both global and local topological scales. Clustering co-efficient and average shortest path distance [5], or local efficiency and global efficiency [6, 7], are two pairs of local and global topological connectivity mea-sures, and can quantify a network's capability to transfer information locally and globally, respectively. The small-world organization, characterized by both high clustering coefficient and short path distance [5], has been widely demon-strated in both functional [8–11] and anatomical [12–14] brain networks, which can support both segregated/specialized and distributed/integrated information processing [2]. Studies have also demonstrated a modular or community struc-ture [15, 16] and hierarchical clusters [9] in the large-scale brain organization, which actually exhibited several semi-global organizational principles. Addition-ally, in detection of low-level local structures (lower than specific subsystem level), motifs, as characteristic network building blocks, significantly occur in brain networks with neuroanatomical data [17]. However, there are still two challenges. First, the results are highly dependent on a prior definition of motif (the number of vertices and all possible connection styles) that makes motifs lack of much flexibility in size. Second, motifs of a network are a set of generalized elementary local patterns without specific context information.

The present study aimed to develop a novel large-scale brain connectivity model based a naïve definition of local multiple relationship among vertices. Here, we have hypothesized that every brain region is engaged in a range of joint multiple interactions within different groups of brain regions and serves as multiple cognitive roles. In the motif theory, each node is actually involved in multiple possible motifs with a number of its neighbors in a network. In the present work, we utilized a concept of "hyperedge" linking a group of vertices based on hypergraph theory and suggested a naïve definition of hyperedge by maximum cliques as an extension of motif concept, which could be independent of the number of vertices and the definition of basic connection styles. This is also different from the "superedge" in Costa et al. [18, 19], who defined by a gener-alized connectivity between pairs of nodes with taking into account the number of paths of different lengths between two nodes, not a multiple relationship for a group of nodes (the number of nodes >2). Furthermore, a naïve hypergraph model was constructed from a graph model of large-scale brain networks. Based on this novel brain connectivity model, we identified important or hub local structures in terms of hyperedges and hub nodes interacting through the hyper-edges in the large-scale bran networks, and they covered many components of the core intrinsic brain networks, i.e., the DMN and ECN.

2   Data Acquisition and Preprocessing

2.1   Data Acquisition

Twenty-four healthy subjects (12 males, 12 females; 24.2 ± 1.8 years old, right-handed) from Beijing University of Technology were scanned on a 3.0 Tesla Siemens MR with the parameters: repetition time/echo time = 2000/31 ms, thickness/gap = 3.2/0 mm, matrix = 64 × 64, axial slices number = 32 and field of view = 200 × 200 mm². The written informed consent was obtained from each subject. All subjects were scanned prior, during and after a flashing checkerboard over the three sessions, lying quietly for 10 min and 20 s, 5 min and 10s, and 10 min and 20 s, respectively. All subjects exhibited a maximum displacement of less than 1.5mm at each axis and an angular motion of less than 1.5° for each axis. During the first and last resting sessions, all subjects were instructed to close their eyes and relax. Gradient-echo echoplanar imaging (EPI) data depicting blood oxygen level-dependent (BOLD) contrast were acquired over sessions. In the present paper, we only focused on the resting state during the first session with 307 volumes. To allow for magnetization equilibrium and subjects' adaptation to the circumstances, the first 7 volumes of EPI sequence were discarded.

2.2 Data Preprocessing

Images were first preprocessed using the software package of statistical parametric mapping (SPM8, http://www.fil.ion.ucl.ac.uk/spm). First, all the images were corrected for the acquisition time delay by slice timing and head motion, and then were spatially normalized to the Montreal Neurological Institute (MNI) EPI template and resampled to 3 mm cubic voxels, without smoothing. After those, each brain was then parcellated into 89 cortical and sub-cortical regions using a brain functional atlas (totally 90 regions) [20]. Of note, all the functionally defined regions of interest (ROIs) were resampled to 3 mm cubic voxels, but the number of voxels within an ROI of the left executive control network (LECN) was only less than 3 and overlapped with other ROIs, so we discarded to use this ROI in this study. Furthermore, each regional time series were acquired by averaging the time series over all voxels within each ROI, and filtered into the frequency range of 0.01~0.08 Hz to reduce the effects of low-frequency drift and high-frequency noise, followed by a multiple linear regression analysis to remove several sources of spurious variances from the estimated head-motion profiles (six parameters obtained from head-motion correction) and global signal [21]. The residual of the linear regression was considered the neuronal-induced signal of each corresponding region.

3 Construction of a Naïve Hypergraph Model of Brain Networks

3.1 Principles of a Naïve Hypergraph Model

It is useful to construct a hypergraph model from a graph structure, because hypergraph theory can be used to reveal implicit topological properties in a structured thinking, although it is impossible to create extra descriptions about a network or system through this kind of conversion. In a graph, a link or edge relates a pair of nodes, but in a hypergraph, known as a generalization of graph, the edges relate any number (>0) of nodes and are called "hyperedge", and represent multiple relations over any number of nodes or vertices. A hypergraph G is formally defined as an ordered pair (V, E), where $V = \{v_1, v_2, ..., v_N\}$ is a set of nodes, and $E = \{e_1, e_2, ..., e_M\}$ is a set of hyperedges, such that $e_i \in 2^V \setminus \varnothing$ and $\bigcup_i e_i = V$. In the present work, a naïve hypergraph model G is constructed from graphs, where V is defined by the graph nodes, and E is defined by the graph maximum cliques. The underlying principle is that, any graph structure can be decomposed into a set of maximum cliques, which could be regard as elementary communication blocks or units and an extension of network motifs further. For example, Figure 1 shows some examples of the defined hyperedge, in which all the maximum cliques covered by different colors represent different hyperedges.

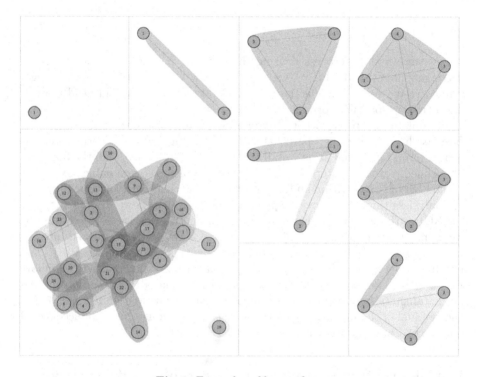

Fig. 1. Examples of hyperedges

3.2   A Naïve Hypergraph Model Based on Graph Models of Brain Networks

This process included the definition of graph model of brain networks and hypergraph model construction from the graph model. First, the 89 ROIs of the brain functional parcellation were defined as nodes. Edges were determined by whether the statistic significance of functional connectivity between any pair of ROIs exceeded a significance threshold. To measure the functional connectivity between any two brain regions, we calculated Pearson correlation coefficients between any two residual BOLD time series extracted from the two ROIs, followed by a Fisher's r-to-z transformation to improve the normality of the correlation coefficients [22]. Then, a temporal correlation matrix R (89×89) was obtained for each subject. To examine whether each inter-regional correlation was significantly positive, right-tailed one-sample t-tests were performed for all the possible 3916 (i.e., $89 \times 88/2$) pairwise correlations across subjects. We further controlled a false discovery rate (FDR) at 5% level over all the interregional functional connectivity tests ($P(R>0)<0.05$), which thresholded the correlation matrices into a binarized matrix, whose element was set to 1 if the corresponding test was significant and 0 otherwise. As a result, the basic graph mode of brain functional networks was defined, characterizing the globally positive or synchronous couplings over the whole brain. According to the hypergraph model introduced in section 3.1, we finally constructed a naïve brain hypergraph model over the brain networks. The 89 ROIs of the brain functional parcellation were defined as nodes $V = \{v_1, v_2, ..., v_N, N = 89\}$, and the totally maximum cliques of the brain networks were defined as hyperedges $E = \{e_1, e_2, ..., e_M\}$. The distributed brain regions communicated through the hyperedges as the elementary information processing blocks or units.

4   Eigenvector Centrality of the Brain Hypergraph Model and Hubs

Eigenvector centrality has been long used to measure the importance of a node in social network [23], supposing that every nodal centrality is a linear combination of its neighbors centralities. The centrality score of vertex v_i in the graph G can be defined as $x_i = \lambda^{-1} \sum_j a_{ij} x_j$, where $a_{ij} = 1$ if v_i is linked to v_j and $a_{ij} = 0$ otherwise. Thus, the eigenvector equation can be defined by $Ax = \lambda x$, where $A = (a_{ij})_{N \times N}$ and $x = \{x_1, x_2, ..., x_N\}$. Bonacich et al. [24] have further extended the concept of graph eigenvector centrality to hypergraphs for both nodes and hyperedges. The hypergraph HG is represented by an incidence matrix $B_{M \times N}(HG) = E \times V = \{b_{ij}\}$, where $b_{ij} = 1$ if $v_j \in e_i$ and $b_{ij} = 0$ if $v_j \in e_i$. Let vectors x and y be the centrality scores for the hyperedges and nodes, respectively. Then, we define the following equations for x and y.

$$[BB^T - diag(BB^T)]x = \lambda x$$

$$[B^T B - diag(B^T B)]y = \lambda y$$

In general, there would be many different eigenvalues λ corresponding to different eigenvector solutions. However, by the Perron-Frobenius theorem [25, 26], only the largest eigenvalue λ_{max} can guarantee the corresponding eigenvector to be positive, which implies a solution of all positive centrality scores. As a result, we can calculate the eigenvector centrality scores for all nodes and hyperedges of the hypergraph model HG. Then, we can identify the important nodes named as hub nodes and important hyperedges named as hub hyperedges by higher centrality in ranking their eigenvector centrality and thresholded after a standard normalization, $Z_i^u = (u_i - <u>)/std(u), u = x, y$.

5   Results

5.1   Hub Nodes

Figure 2(a) shows the top ranked nodes with the highest centrality of the naïve brain hypergraph model, thresholded by $Z^y > 1.5$. Even using such a relaxed threshold, the hub nodes are regularly located in the left and right executive control network (LECN and RECN) as well as right basal ganglia (Basal_Ganglia.1), and covered a few components of the DMN or "task-negative" network (Fox et al., 2005). Both the ECN and DMN are two important intrinsic networks in the brain. Figure 2(b) shows the top ranked nodes with the highest centrality of the brain graph model, thresholded by $Z^y > 1.5$. Consistently, the ECN regions served as important or hub nodes in the brain networks. But the differences are that the components of the salience network (SN) serve as hubs in the brain graph model as well. Of note, the SN, as another core intrinsic network, covered many components of the "task-positive" network based on a study by Fox et al. [21]. These results further indicate that the two important intrinsic resting-state networks, the "task-positive" and "task-negative" networks, may serve as the hubs in brain networks.

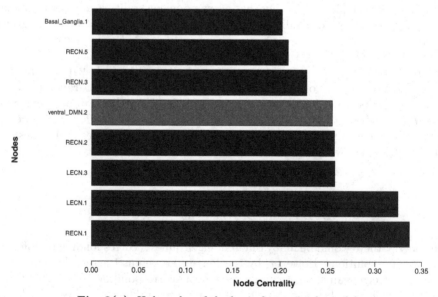

Fig. 2(a). Hub nodes of the brain hypergraph model

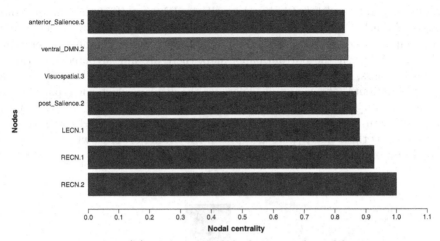

Fig. 2(b). Hub nodes of the brain graph model

5.2   Hub Hyperedges

Figure 3 shows the top ranked hyperedges with the highest centrality thresholded by $Z^x > 2$. The intrinsic hub hyperedges, presented by the maximum cliques of

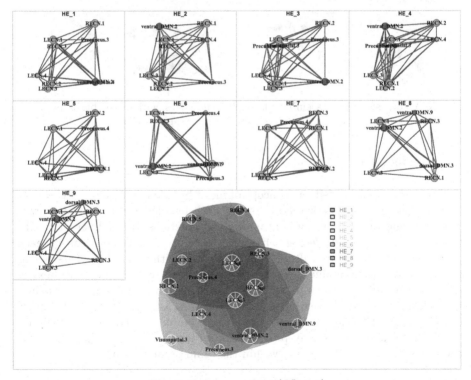

Fig. 3. Hub hyperedges $(Z^x > 1.5)$

the brain graph model and indexed by HE_1, HE_2, ..., HE_9, are mainly composed of the ECN regions as well as some DMN regions. In the other words, the components of ECN dominated all of the hyperedges in number, interacting with the DMN. At the bottom panel map, there are nine hyperedges filled by different colors, in which nodes are linked through the hyperedges. Each node has two attributes of size and pie colors for the display, which correspond to the nodal centrality scores and belonged hyperedges, respectively. Every region can be involved in different hyperedges. Figure 4 shows a compound core structure assembled by these hub hyperedges within the brain networks, which is mapped on a brain template and visualized in axial and sagittal views.

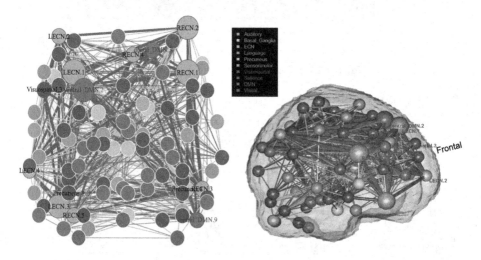

Fig. 4. A core structure assembled by hub hyperedges within the brain networks mapped on a brain template. Left: axial view; Right: sagittal view.

6   Discussion

In this paper, we extended the concept of motif by maximum cliques defined as "hyperedges" in brain networks. Here, we have hypothesized that every brain region is engaged in a range of joint multiple interactions within different groups of brain regions in multiple cognitive roles. Actually, in the motif theory, each node can be involved in multiple possible motifs with a number of its neighbors. However, the maximum cliques of graph model seem to be more flexible local meta-patterns and can better characterize elementary building blocks in a network. Further, we defined all maximum cliques as hyperedges, and a naïve brain hypergraph model was constructed from a graph model of large-scale brain resting-state networks. It may provide a novel insight to study the large-scale interregional functional coupling within the brain organization.

Based on the hypergraph eigenvector centrality analysis, we identified nine intrinsic hub hyperedges, which could be regarded as the most important information processing blocks (or units), and covered many components of the core intrinsic brain networks, i.e., the DMN and ECN (see Fig. 3). The ECN, a frontoparietal system, shows strong coactivation during a wide range of cognitively demanding task, and is crucial for actively maintaining and manipulating information in working memory (Menon, 2011). The DMN is a set of regions which are more active during rest than task [27, 28], is dynamically negatively correlated with the ECN [21]. From quantifying brain metabolic activity by PET, the components of the DMN are more activated [28]. However, in the present work, the hyperedges composed of the ECN components and a few DMN components dominated in the large-scale resting-state brain network in the sense of hub hyperedges. Cole et al. [29] have also demonstrated that the highest global connectivity also occurs in the ECN and DMN, in accordance with our hub results in both graph and hypergraph models. The difference is that our results may suggest more advantages in the ECN in terms of nodal and hyperedge eigenvector centrality. More importantly, we directly identified the important or hub local structure not only isolated nodes, and further extracted a compound structure assembled by these overlapped hub hyperedges, which should serve as a core subsystem of the large-scale intrinsic brain organization.

Three important issues remain to be addressed in the future. First, the assembled core subsystem could not be simply thought as an overlapped compound structure. It needs to be figured out how these hyperedges assemble into higher-level subsystems and how the ECN, DMN and SN interact through the inter-hyperedges communication. Second, as described above, it is impossible to create extra descriptions about a network or system with constructing a hypergraph model based on a graph model, because the original graph representation is limited to binary relationships. On the other hand, most basic cognition should be arised from highly-complex multiplex coordinations over the distributed brain cortex, thus the construction of real hyperedges should be seriously explored based on real multiple relations over distributed brain regions in the future. Last, it is necessary to investigate compound hyper-structures on the basis of a hypergraph model, since it may benefit for revealing implicitly complex connectivity patterns of brain origination and provide deep insights into understanding the topological principles of the cerebral cortex.

Acknowledgments. The authors are grateful to the anonymous referees for their valuable comments and references. This work is partially supported by the National Natural Science Foundation of China under Grant (No.60875075, 60905027), Beijing Natural Science Foundation (No. 4102007) and the CAS/SAFEA International Partnership Program for Creative Research Teams.

References

1. Sporns, O., Chialvo, D.R., Kaiser, M., Hilgetag, C.C.: Organization, development and function of complex brain networks. Trends in Cognitive Sciences 8, 418–425 (2004)

2. Bassett, D.S., Bullmore, E.D.: Small-world brain networks. Neuroscientist 12, 512–523 (2006)
3. Bressler, S.L., Menon, V.: Large-scale brain networks in cognition: emerging methods and principles. Trends in Cognitive Sciences 14, 277–290 (2010)
4. Menon, V.: Large-scale brain networks and psychopathology: a unifying triple network model. Trends in Cognitive Sciences 15, 483–506 (2011)
5. Watts, D.J., Strogatz, S.H.: Collective dynamics of "small-world" networks. Nature 393, 440–442 (1998)
6. Latora, V., Marchiori, M.: Efficient behaviour of small-world networks. Phys. Rev. Lett. 87, 198701 (2001)
7. Latora, V., Marchiori, M.: Economic small-world behaviour in weighted networks. Euro. Phys. JB. 32, 249–263 (2003)
8. Eguíluz, V.M., Chialvo, D.R., Cecchi, G.A., Baliki, M., Apkarian, A.V.: Scale-free brain functional networks. Phys. Rev. Lett. 94, 018102 (2005)
9. Salvador, R., Suckling, J., Coleman, M.R., Pickard, J.D., Menon, D., Bullmore, E.D.: Neurophysiological architecture of functional magnetic resonance images of human brain. Cereb. Cortex 15, 1332–1342 (2005a)
10. Achard, S., Salvador, R., Whitcher, B., Suckling, J., Bullmore, E.D.: A resilient, low-frequency, small-world human brain functional network with highly connected association cortical hubs. J. Neurosci. 26, 63–72 (2006)
11. Van den Heuvel, M.P., Stam, C.J., Boersma, M., Hulshoff Pol, H.E.: Small-world and scale-free organization of voxel-based resting-state functional connectivity in the human brain. Neuroimage 43, 528–539 (2008)
12. Hagmann, P., Kurant, M., Gigandet, X., Thiran, P., Wedeen, V.J., Meuli, R., Thiran, J.P.: Mapping the structural core of human cerebral cortex. PLoS ONE 2, e597 (2007)
13. He, Y., Chen, Z.J., Evans, A.C.: Small-world anatomical networks in the human brain revealed by cortical thickness from MRI. Cereb. Cortex 17, 2407–2419 (2007)
14. Iturria-Medina, Y., Sotero, R.C., Canales-Rodriguez, E.J., Aleman-Gomez, Y., Melie-Garcia, L.: Studying the human brain ananatomical network via diffusion-weighted MRI and graph theory. NeuroImage 40, 1064–1076 (2008)
15. Sporns, O., Honey, C.J., Kötter, R.: Identification and classification of hubs in brain networks. PLoS Biology 2, e1049 (2004)
16. He, Y., Wang, J., Wang, L., Chen, Z.J., Yan, C., Yang, H., Tang, H., Zhu, C., Gong, Q., Zang, Y., Evans, A.C.: Uncovering intrinsic modular organization of spontaneous brain activity in humans. PLoS ONE 4, e5226 (2009)
17. Sporns, O., Kötter, R.: Motifs in brain networks. PLoS Biology 2, e369 (2004)
18. Costa, L.F., Rodrigues, F.A.: Superedges: connecting structure and dynamics in complex networks. arXiv:0801.4068v2 (2008)
19. De Vico Fallani, F., Rodrigues, F.A., Costa, L.F., Astolfi, L., Cincotti, F., Mattia, D., Salinari, S., Babiloni, F.: Multiple pathways analysis of brain functional networks from EEG signals: an application to real data. Brain Topogr. 23, 344–354 (2011)
20. Shirer, W.R., Ryali, S., Rykhlevskaia, E., Menon, V., Greicius, M.D.: Decoding subject-driven cognitive states with whole-brain connectivity patterns. Cere. Cortex (2011), doi: 10.1093/cercor/bhr099
21. Fox, M.D., Snyder, A.Z., Vincent, J.L., Corbetta, M., Van Essen, D.C., Raichle, M.E.: The human brain is intrinsically organized into dynamic, anticorrelated functional networks. Proc. Natl. Acad. Sci. U.S.A. 102, 9673–9678 (2005)
22. Jenkins, G.M., Watts, D.G.: Spectral Analysis and Its Applications. Holden-Day, San Francisco (1968)

23. Bonacich, P.: Techinique for analyzing overlapping memberships. Sociological Methodology 4, 176–185 (1972)
24. Bonacich, P., Holdren, A.C., Johnston, M.: Hyper-edges and multidimensional centrality. Social Networks 26, 189–203 (2004)
25. Perron, O.: Zur Theorie der Matrices. Mathematische Annalen 64, 248–263 (1907)
26. Frobenius, G.: Üeber Matrizen aus nicht negativen Elementen. Sitzungsber, pp. 456–477. Königl. Preuss. Akad. Wiss, Berlin (1912)
27. Shulman, G.L., Fiez, J.A., Corbetta, M., Buckner, R.L., Miezin, F.M., Raichle, M.E., Petersen, S.E.: Common blood flow changes across visual tasks: II. decreases in cerebral cortex. J. Cognit. Neurosci. 9, 648–663 (1997)
28. Raichle, M.E., Macleod, A.M., Snyder, A.Z., Powers, W.J., Gusnard, D.A., Shulman, G.L.: A default mode of brain function. Proc. Natl. Acad. Sci. U.S.A. 98, 676–682 (2001)
29. Cole, M.W., Pathak, S., Schneider, W.: Identifying the brain's most globally connected regions. NeuroImage 49, 3132–3148 (2010)

The Effect of Individual Psychological Characteristics on Creativity Revelation: Emphasis with Psychological Empowerment and Intrinsic Motivation

Do Young Choi[1], Kun Chang Lee[2,*], and Seong Wook Chae[3]

[1] Solution Business Unit, LG CNS Co., Ltd, Seoul 100-725, Republic of Korea
[2] SKK Business School, WCU Department of Interaction Science,
Sungkyunkwan University, Seoul 110-745, Republic of Korea
[3] SKK Business School, Sungkyunkwan University, Seoul 110-745, Republic of Korea
{dychoi96,kunchanglee,seongwookchae}@gmail.com

Abstract. Creativity is considered as one of critical strategic resources of organizations for long term sustainable growth as well as improvement of short term performances. This paper suggests the individual creativity revelation model, which mainly focuses on the causal relations among individual psychological characteristics – psychological empowerment and intrinsic motivation - and individual creativity revelation processes – exploration and exploitation. The empirical results showed that psychological empowerment and intrinsic motivation are related positively with the creativity revelation processes. Furthermore, this research notably showed the interplay between exploration and exploitation in the perspective of creativity revelation processes, which indicated that exploitation could be revealed by the exploration.

Keywords: Creativity, Psychological empowerment, intrinsic motivation, Exploration, Exploitation.

1   Introduction

Researches on creativity have been lively conducted in the various fields, and also creativity has variety of the definition and research methods in accordance with research areas and their interests. Recently, creativity researches have paid attention to the organizational behavior and business management because creativity has been widely considered as important assets for the organizational enhancement or business performance improvement [1-2]. Furthermore, it has been considered as one of critical strategic resources of business organization for the improvement of short term performances and for keeping organizations' long term sustainable growth at the same time. Specifically, in the perspective of organizational learning or organizational adaptation, researches have paid attention to creative problem solving processes or creating new business competitiveness and organizational competences. Accordingly,

---

* Corresponding author.

F.M. Zanzotto et al. (Eds.): BI 2012, LNCS 7670, pp. 130–139, 2012.

researchers have gradually enlarged their research scope from individual level to team level, organizational level, and even to inter-organizational level.

In order to verify influencing factors on creativity within organization or business, there are several kinds of research perspectives – researches focusing on personal characteristics to find out influencing factors on creativity [3-4]; researches focusing on environmental characteristics [5-6]; researches of creativity with perspective of problem solving processes [7]. When we consider that creativity could be revealed not only by personal characteristics, but also by interactions among individuals, working environment, and business environment, investigation of creativity revelation within organization has great significance. Therefore, several researchers has taken notice of exploitation and exploration, which are significant processes of organizational learning and organizational adaptation, as innovation processes or creativity revelation processes [8]. In consequence, researches on interplay among exploitation and exploration, and researches on its affecting mechanism to creativity have been conducted [9].

This paper addresses to verify the effects of individual characteristics on individual creativity revelation processes – exploitation/exploration - and creativity. Specifically, this paper pays attention to the psychological empowerment and intrinsic motivation among personal characteristics influencing on individual creativity revelation processes and on individual creativity itself.

2   Theoretical Foundations and Hypotheses

2.1   Creativity, Exploitation, and Exploration

Since Guilford [10] suggested the importance of creativity in the year of 1950, several researchers of various research fields have conducted creativity studies. However, there is no generally agreed definition because researchers have different definitions based on their own unique research interests. According to the definition of Amabile [11], creativity could be defined as processes which produce innovative outcomes by creating something new. When we consider the creativity research level, researchers have enlarged their research level from individual level to team level, organizational level, or inter-organizational level [12-13]. Meanwhile, there are several influencing factors on individual level creativity according to the previous studies. Typically, Woodman et al. [13] insisted that cognitive awareness, personal characteristics, intrinsic motivation, and expertise knowledge of individuals were considered as influencing factors on individual creativity. They also addressed influencing factors on individual creativity in the perspective of team level and organizational level – organizational cohesiveness, diversity, culture, resources, and organizational structure. They strongly insisted that creativity could be revealed by interactions among all factors of all levels. Meanwhile, a group of researchers have paid attention to the creativity revelation processes based on the interaction of influencing factors. Specifically, researchers consider exploitation process and exploration process as critical processes which create new ideas and new knowledge in the perspective of creativity [9]. This paper mainly pays attention to the causal relations among individual creativity and exploitation/exploration as creativity revelation processes.

2.2   Psychological Empowerment and Intrinsic Motivation

According to the Bennis [14], empowerment could be considered as task capability owned by empowered individuals who conduct skillfully their tasks under collaboration with colleagues . That is, empowered individuals are considered as a person who tries to improve his/her interest, challenge and creativity on his/her tasks. Also, Voget & Murrell [15] insisted that empowered organizations has distinct characteristic of high level autonomy for decision making. The members of empowered organization have mission, values, trust, and responsibility of mutual acceptance. They intend to put efficient information sharing and promoting of human resources above something in order to produce highly qualified performances, and consequently they intend to expand decision making authority from specific hierarchy to generalized hierarchy. When we consider psychological empowerment, it could be significant to recognize that members of organization have power for conducting their tasks and for making decisions. That is, the individuals' recognition of power comes from self-efficacy which authorizes members of organization to have control power or influencing power regarding their tasks or their own situations [16]. Like this, emphasis on members' intrinsic motivation for power and understanding of empowerment are regarded as psychological empowerment [17]. Researchers have emphasized psychological perspectives by understanding empowerment psychologically [18-21].

Meanwhile, when we consider intrinsic motivation, it is generally considered that two kinds of motivation exist; intrinsic motivation and extrinsic motivation. According to the research of Amabile [11] and the research of Barron & Harrington [22], intrinsic motivation could be regarded as significant factors for creativity. That is, intrinsic motivation can be defined as the motivational state which their works themselves attract individuals of organization, regardless of external compensations [23]. Individuals who are encouraged by intrinsic motivation intend to have passion for their work. And consequently, they could have highly contribution to their work [24].

2.3   Research Model and Hypotheses

This paper tries to investigate the causal relations among individual psychological characteristics individual creativity revelation processes. Figure 1 shows our research model which covers our research questions. Our research model has five constructs – psychological empowerment and intrinsic motivation in the perspective of individual psychological characteristics, exploration and exploitation in the perspective of creativity revelation processes, and finally individual creativity. According to our model, individual psychological characteristics – psychological empowerment and intrinsic motivation – could be assumed to have positive effect on individual creativity based on the previous studies. Furthermore, our model addressed that psychological empowerment, intrinsic motivation, could have positive effect on individual creativity through the mediation of creativity processes – exploitation and exploration – also based on the concrete literature [8-9, 13, 17, 23]. And notable thing of our model is the interplay between exploration and exploitation as explanation of creativity revelation process itself. According to our model, creativity revelation processes – exploration and exploitation – could have positive effect on individual creativity. In addition, exploitation could be affected by exploration for its own characteristics.

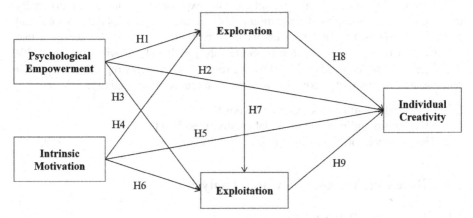

Fig. 1. Individual Creativity Revelation Model

Through empowerment, individuals of organization conduct actively and autonomously their work and tasks, and consequently they intend to experience work immersion and job satisfaction. Moreover, they intend to have creative response to the change of environment by conducting their tasks rapidly and flexibly, and they could realize creativity and innovation up to the level which organization request [25-26]. In addition, Gretz & Drozdeck [27] addressed empowerment as finding best decision-making method, problem solving with synergetic interactions, and capability of producing new ideas. Also, Kinlaw [28] explained that the processes of continuous achievement for developing influence capability through empowerment. And Bennis [14] regarded that individuals could improve their challenge, interest, and creativity on work through empowerment. Therefore, we have derived the following research hypotheses with regard to the causal relations among psychological empowerment and creativity processes – exploration and exploitation.

H1.   Psychological empowerment influences exploration positively.
H2.   Psychological empowerment influences individual creativity positively.
H3.   Psychological empowerment influences exploitation positively.

As already explained in the previous studies, intrinsic motivation could be regarded for positive affecting factor on individual creativity and its revelation processes [11, 22]. Intrinsic motivation could attract individuals of organization and individuals highly encouraged by intrinsic motivation could highly contribute to their work creatively [24]. Therefore, we have derived the following research hypotheses with regard to the causal relations among intrinsic motivation and creativity processes – exploration and exploitation.

H4.   Intrinsic motivation influences exploration positively.
H5.   Intrinsic motivation influences individual creativity positively.
H6.   Intrinsic motivation influences exploitation positively.

Creativity revelation processes – exploitation and exploration – comes from originally innovation and organizational adaptation [8], which are both considered as significant processes of innovation and new knowledge creation. It is generally accepted that innovative activity and innovation processes are tightly related with creativity [29-32]. Therefore, we can derive the following research hypotheses regarding the causal relations among creativity revelation processes and individual creativity.

H7.   Exploration influences exploitation positively.
H8.   Exploration influences individual creativity positively.
H9.   Exploitation influences individual creativity positively.

3   Research Methodology and Analysis

3.1   Sample and Data Collection

Survey method was adopted in order to investigate the individual creativity revela-tion model which this paper suggested. Measurement items from proven and reliable literature were adapted and re-developed for the research and 7-point Li-kert-scale were used for surveys. We adapted thirteen measurement items from the researches by Ettlie & O'Keefe [33] regarding individual creativity. In order to measure psychological empowerment, nine measurement items were adapted from Spreitzer [21], and three survey items for intrinsic motivation from Amabile [11], respectively. Also regarding exploration and exploitation, the measurement items from Prieto et al. [34] were adapted. After making the survey questionnaire and collecting data from university students, 304 appropriate responses were used for the statistical analysis.

3.2   Measures

Statistical analyses based on PLS(Partial Least Squares) were conducted in order to verify this paper's research model. And we used SmartPLS 2.0 software in order to test hypotheses. PLS could be regarded as a appropriate method in the areas of struc-tural equation modeling of which the theory and variables' relations are weak.

Reliability and validity analyses were conducted in order to verify consistency of the measurement items with our intent. The values of Cronbach alpha of all constructs are higher than 0.7, which indicates they have a high internal consistency. Firstly, the t-test for factor loading was reviewed in order to verify convergent validity. Further-more, convergent and discriminant validity were assessed in order to examine compo-site reliability and AVE(Average Variance Extract). Table 1 shows the convergent and discriminant validity results. Also table 2 presents the correlation matrix among five constructs and the square root of AVE on the diagonal and the discriminant valid-ity were assured from the analyses.

Table 1. Reliability and Convergent Validity

Construct	Measurement Item	Factor Loading	Cronbach's α	Composite Reliability	AVE
Creativity	CR1	0.7147	0.9415	0.9496	0.6320
	CR2	0.8178			
	CR3	0.7541			
	CR4	0.7898			
	CR5	0.8116			
	CR7	0.7962			
	CR8	0.7942			
	CR10	0.7777			
	CR11	0.8645			
	CR12	0.8154			
	CR13	0.7997			
Exploitation	ET1	0.7735	0.8610	0.8963	0.5908
	ET2	0.8088			
	ET3	0.7528			
	ET4	0.7564			
	ET5	0.8054			
	ET6	0.7104			
Exploration	ER1	0.8557	0.8550	0.8963	0.6341
	ER2	0.8068			
	ER3	0.7342			
	ER4	0.8197			
	ER5	0.7593			
Intrinsic Motivation	MT1	0.8275	0.8032	0.8837	0.7170
	MT2	0.8633			
	MT3	0.8491			
Psychological Empowerment	PE4	0.8070	0.8871	0.9142	0.6401
	PE5	0.8169			
	PE6	0.7316			
	PE7	0.8313			
	PE8	0.7951			
	PE9	0.8144			

Table 2. Discriminant Validity

Construct	CR	ER	ET	MT	PE
CR	0.7950				
ER	0.7058	0.7963			
ET	0.5856	0.6802	0.7686		
MT	0.5995	0.6220	0.5603	0.8468	
PE	0.6011	0.6885	0.7345	0.5432	0.8001

CR: Creativity,   ET: Exploitation,   ER: Exploration,   MT: Intrinsic Motivation,   PE: Psychological Empowerment

3.3   Analysis and Results

The hypotheses of the model this paper suggested were verified by coefficients of path and R^2 as presented in the figure 2. The coefficients of path address how strong the relations are among respondent variable and explanatory variables. In addition, the values of each R^2 indicate the amount of variance explained by the explanatory variables.

The model shows that the R^2 values of all constructs are higher than the 10% which is recommended [35]. This result supports strongly the posited causal relations among variables. The R^2 value of individual creativity, which is the last respondent variable explained by all independent variables turns out to be 55.7% and that of exploitation was 60.8%, and that of exploration was 56.1%. Table 3 shows the summary of the research hypothesis test results. As shown in the table 3, hypothesis 9 was not accepted. But, other hypotheses were all accepted.

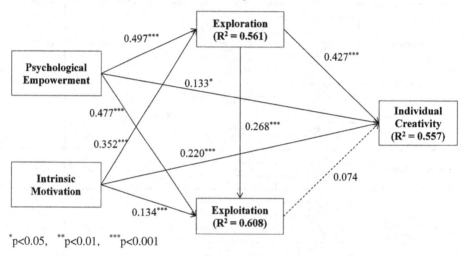

Fig. 2. Research Results

Table 3. Summary of Hypotheses Test Results

H-No.	Path Name	Path Coefficient	t-Value	Result
H1	PE → ER	0.4974	10.0451[***]	Accept
H2	PE → CR	0.1333	1.7632[***]	Accept
H3	PE → ET	0.4766	8.7981[***]	Accept
H4	MT → ER	0.3518	7.0992[***]	Accept
H5	MT → CR	0.2201	3.6586[***]	Accept
H6	MT → ET	0.1344	2.8832[***]	Accept
H7	ER → ET	0.2684	4.1117[***]	Accept
H8	ER → CR	0.4266	6.2172[***]	Accept
H9	ET → CR	0.0742	1.0358	Reject

CR: Creativity, ET: Exploitation, ER: Exploration, MT: Intrinsic Motivation, PE: Psychological Empowerment

*p<0.05, **p<0.01, ***p<0.001

4   Discussion and Concluding Remarks

This paper suggested the individual creativity revelation model, which mainly focuses on the causal relations among individual psychological characteristics – psychological empowerment and intrinsic motivation, and individual creativity revelation processes – exploration and exploitation.

Through the results of PLS(Partial Least Squares) analyses, we found that psychological characteristics of individuals which consisted of psychological empowerment and intrinsic motivation have the statistically significant effect on the individual creativity and the creativity revelation processes – exploration and exploitation. Nonetheless, we could find out that the effects of individual creativity revelation processes – exploration and exploitation –on individual creativity were not in accordance with our assumptions based on the previous researches. Specifically, exploration could affect directly to individual creativity, however, exploitation could not affect directly to individual creativity. We can infer that this result was caused by the task characteristics given to the university students. That is, it is considered that the tasks given to them were relatively related to the tasks which required newly generation ideas from them. Therefore, we could not conclude that exploitation did not affect directly on individual creativity. The significantly notable result of the research is the interplay between exploration and exploitation in the perspective of individual creativity revelation processes. As we assumed, the result showed that exploration could affect to exploitation directly, which indicated that exploitation could be revealed by the exploration.

Through the empirical research of this paper, we can have several consideration points for individual creativity management. Firstly, we can conclude that psychological empowerment affects positively on creativity revelation processes and individual creativity. That is, the working environment with psychological empowerment encourages individuals to be immersed in task solving and new knowledge creation through creativity revelation processes. Therefore, when we consider empowerment in working environment, managers should pay attention to build working environment and cultures individuals to have psychologically autonomy. Secondly, intrinsic motivation can be also considered as significant factor affecting to individual creativity. Practically, managers should encourage intrinsic motivation to the individuals as well as external motivation. Thirdly, managers should have sense of balance between exploration and exploitation with regard to creativity management. As we could find out the interplay between exploration and exploitation, managers should understand that exploration could be base for exploitation. Therefore, managers of organizations should manage exploration and exploitation with ambidexterity perspectives.

Nevertheless, there are several limitations and considerations for future research. Firstly, this research considers only two individuals' psychological factors for addressing creativity revelation processes and individual creativity. There may exist many affecting factors on individual creativity and several considerable variables on creativity revelation processes. In the future study, more factors should be considered such as social interactions, environmental interactions. Secondly, this paper conducted survey from university students, which has limitations to be generalized.

Therefore, future study should extend the surveys into more realistic business environment such as business organizations.

Acknowledgment. This research was supported by WCU(World Class University) program through the National Research Foundation of Korea funded by the Ministry of Education, Science and Technology (Grant No. R31-2008-000-10062-0).

References

1. Amabile, T.M.: Creativity in context. Westview, Boulder (1996)
2. Madjar, N., Oldham, G.R., Pratt, M.G.: There's no place like home? The contributions of work and nonwork creativity support to employees' creative performance. Academy of Management Journal 45, 757–767 (2002)
3. Fodor, E.M., Carver, R.A.: Achievement and power motives, performance feedback, and creativity. Journal of Research in Personality 34, 380–396 (2000)
4. Wolfradt, U., Pretz, J.E.: Individual differences in creativity: Personality, story writing, and hobbies. European Journal of Personality 15, 297–310 (2001)
5. Amabile, T.M., Conti, R.: Changes in the Work Environment for Creativity during Downsizing. Academy of Management Journal 42, 630–640 (1999)
6. Pirola-Merlo, A., Mann, L.: The relationship between individual creativity and team creativity: aggregating across people and time. Journal of Organizational Behavior 25, 235–257 (2004)
7. Tardif, T.Z., Sternberg, R.J.: What Do We Know About Creativity? In: Sternberg, R.J. (ed.) The Nature of Creativity: Contemporary Psychological Perspectives, pp. 429–440. Cambridge University Press, Cambridge (1988)
8. March, J.G.: Exploration and Exploitation in Organizational Learning. Organization Science 2, 71–87 (1991)
9. Taylor, A., Greve, H.R.: Superman or the Fantastic Four? Knowledge Combination And Experience in Innovative Teams. Academy of Management Journal 49, 723–740 (2006)
10. Guilford, J.P.: The structure of intellect. Psychological Bulletin; Psychological Bulletin 53, 267 (1956)
11. Amabile, T.M.: A model of creativity and innovation in organizations. Research in Organizational Behavior 10, 123–167 (1988)
12. Kurtzberg, T.R., Amabile, T.M.: From Guilford to creative synergy: Opening the black box of team level creativity. Creativity Research Journal 13, 285–294 (2001)
13. Woodman, R.W., Sawyer, J.E., Griffin, R.W.: Toward a Theory of Organizational Creativity. Academy of Management Review 18, 293–321 (1993)
14. Bennis, W.G.: Good managers and good leaders. Across the Board 21, 7–11 (1984)
15. Voget, J.F., Murrell, K.L.: Empowerment in Organization. Pfeiffer & Company, San Diego (1990)
16. Conger, J.A., Kanungo, R.N.: The empowerment process: Integrating theory and practice. Academy of Management Review, 471–482 (1988)
17. Spreitzer, G.M.: Psychological empowerment in the workplace: Dimensions, measurement, and validation. Academy of Management Journal, 1442–1465 (1995)
18. Corsun, D.L., Enz, C.A.: Predicting psychological empowerment among service workers: The effect of support-based relationships. Human Relations 52, 205–224 (1999)

19. Eylon, D., Herman, S.: Exploring empowerment: One method for the classroom. Journal of Management Education 23, 80–94 (1999)
20. Kirkman, B.L., Rosen, B.: Powering up teams. Organizational Dynamics (2000)
21. Spreitzer, G.M., De Janasz, S.C., Quinn, R.E.: Empowered to lead: The role of psychological empowerment in leadership. Journal of Organizational Behavior 20, 511–526 (1999)
22. Barron, F.B., Harrington, D.M.: Creativity, intelligence, and personality. Annual Review of Psychology 32, 439–476 (1981)
23. Deci, E.L., Ryan, R.M.: Intrinsic Motivation and Self Determination in Human Behavior. Plenum Press, New York (1985)
24. Amabile, T.M.: The social psychology of creativity: A componential conceptualization. Journal of Personality and Social Psychology 45, 357–376 (1983)
25. Gandz, J., Bird, F.G.: The ethics of empowerment. Journal of Business Ethics 15, 383–392 (1996)
26. Kirkman, B.L., Rosen, B.: Beyond self-management: Antecedents and consequences of team empowerment. Academy of Management Journal, 58–74 (1999)
27. Gretz, K.F., Drozdeck, S.R.: Empowering innovative people. Probus Publishing Company, Chicago (1992)
28. Kinlaw, D.C.: The practice of empowerment: making the most of human competence. Gower Publishing Company, Hampshire (1995)
29. Audia, P.G., Goncalo, J.A.: Past Success and Creativity over Time: A Study of Inventors in the Hard Disk Drive Industry. Management Science 53, 1–15 (2007)
30. He, Z.-L., Wong, P.-K.: Exploration vs. Exploitation: An Empirical Test of the Ambidexterity Hypothesis. Organization Science. 15, 481–494 (2004)
31. Kanter, R.M.: When a thousand flowers bloom: Structural, collective, and social conditions for innovation in organization. Research in Organizational Behavior 10, 169–211 (1988)
32. Scott, S.G., Bruce, R.A.: Determinants of innovative behavior: A path model of individual innovation in the workplace. Academy of Management Journal, 580–607 (1994)
33. Ettlie, J.E., O'Keefe, R.D.: Innovative attitudes, values, and intentions in organizations. Journal of Management Studies 19, 163–182 (1982)
34. Prieto, I.M., Revilla, E., Rodriguez-Prado, B.: Managing the knowledge paradox in product development. Journal of Knowledge Management 13, 157–170 (2009)
35. Falk, R.F., Miller, N.B.: A primer for soft modeling. The University of Akron, Akron (1992)

Modeling and Optimization of Information Retrieval for Perception-Based Information

Alexander Ryjov

Chair of Mathematical Foundations of Intelligent Systems,
Department of Mechanics and Mathematics,
Lomonosov' Moscow State University
119899 Moscow Russia
ryjov@intsys.msu.ru

Abstract. The properties of human beings as a "measurement device" have been studied in this article. It is assumed that the person describes the properties of real objects in the form of linguistic values; the human's descriptions of objects make a data base of some data management system. Is it possible to define the indices of quality of information retrieval in such fuzzy (linguistic) databases and to formulate a rule for the selection of such a set of linguistic values, use of which would provide the maximum indices of quality of information retrieval? It is shown that it is possible to introduce indices of the quality of information retrieval in fuzzy (linguistic) databases and to formalize them. It is shown that it is possible to formulate a method of selecting the optimum set of values of qualitative attributes which provides the maximum quality indices of information retrieval. Moreover, it is shown that such a method is stable, i.e. the natural small errors in the construction of the membership functions do not have a significant effect on the selection of the optimum set of values.

1 Introduction

It is difficult even to imagine Internet or Web Intelligence or big data analysis [1] without human's participation in processes of description of the real objects, information retrieval and management, interpretation of the results. This article is focusing on modeling and optimization some of these processes. The properties of human beings as a "measurement device" have been studied. It is assumed that the person describes the properties of real objects in the form of linguistic values. The subjective degree of convenience of such a description depends on the selection and the composition of such linguistic values. Let us explain this on a model example [7].

Example 1.   Let it be required to evaluate the height of a man. Let us consider two extreme situations.
Situation 1.   It is permitted to use only two values: "small" and "high".
Situation 2.   It is permitted to use many values: "very small", "not very high", ... , "not small and not high", ... , "very high".

F.M. Zanzotto et al. (Eds.): BI 2012, LNCS 7670, pp. 140–149, 2012.

Situation 1 is inconvenient. In fact, for many men both the permitted values may be unsuitable and, in describing them, we select between two "bad" values.

Situation 2 is also inconvenient. In fact, in describing height of men, several of the permitted values may be suitable. We again experience a problem but now due to the fact that we are forced to select between two or more "good" values. Could a set of linguistic values be optimal in this case?

One object may be described by different experts (persons). Therefore it is desirable to have assurances that the different experts describe one and the same object in the most "uniform" way.

On the basis of the above we may formulate the first problem as follows:

Problem 1. Is it possible, taking into account certain features of the man's perception of objects of the real world and their description, to formulate a rule for selection of the optimum set of values of characteristics on the basis of which these objects may be described? Two optimality criteria are possible:

Criterion 1. We regard as optimum those sets of values through whose use man experiences the minimum uncertainty in describing objects.

Criterion 2. If the object is described by a certain number of experts, then we regard as optimum those sets of values which provide the minimum degree of divergence of the descriptions.

This problem may be reformulated as a problem of construction of an optimal information granulation procedure from point of view of criterion 1 and criterion 2.

It is shown that we can formulate a method of selecting the optimum set of values of qualitative indications (collection of granules [7]). Moreover, it is shown that such a method is stable, i.e. the natural small errors that may occur in constructing the membership functions do not have a significant influence on the selection of the optimum set of values. The sets which are optimal according to criteria 1 and 2 coincide.

What gives us the optimal set of values of qualitative attributes for a solution of the practical tasks? For the answer to this question let us assume that the human's description of an objects make a data base of some data management system. In this connection the following problem arises.

Problem 2. Is it possible to define the indices of quality of information retrieval in fuzzy (linguistic) databases and to formulate a rule for the selection of such a set of linguistic values, use of which would provide the maximum indices of quality of information retrieval?

2   Basic Concepts of a Fuzzy Linguistic Scales

The model of an estimating of real object's properties by a person as the procedure of measuring in fuzzy linguis-tic scale (FLS) has been analyzed at first time in [3] and described in details in [4]. The set of scale values of some FLS is a collection of fuzzy sets defined on the same universum.

Let us consider t fuzzy variables with the names a_1, a_2, ..., a_t, specified in one universal set (Fig. 1). We shall call such set the scale values set of a FLS.

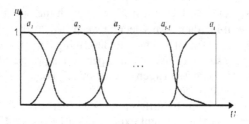

Fig. 1. The scale values set of a FLS

Let us introduce a system of limitations for the membership functions of the fuzzy variables comprising s_t. For the sake of simplicity, we shall designate the membership function a_j as μ_j. We shall consider that:

1. $\forall \mu_j (1 \leq j \leq t) \exists U_j^1 \neq \varnothing$, where $U_j^1 = \{u \in U : \mu_j(u) = 1\}$, U_j^1 is an interval or a point;

2. $\forall j (1 \leq j \leq t)$ μ_j does not decrease on the left of U_j^1 and does not increase on the right of U_j^1 (since, according to 1, U_j^1 is an interval or a point, the concepts "on the left" and "on the right" are determined unambiguously).

Requirements 1 and 2 are quite natural for membership functions of concepts forming a scale values set of a FLS. In fact, the first one signifies that, for any concept used in the universal set, there exists at least one object which is standard for the given concept. If there are many such standards, they are positioned in a series and are not "scattered" around the universe. The second requirement signifies that, if the objects are "similar" in the metrics sense in a universal set, they are also "similar" in the sense of FLS.

Henceforth, we shall need to use the characteristic functions as well as the membership functions, and so we shall need to fulfil the following technical condition:

3. $\forall j (1 \leq j \leq t)$ μ_j has not more than two points of discontinuity of the first kind.

For simplicity, let us designate the requirements 1-3 as L.

Let us also introduce a system of limitations for the sets of membership functions of fuzzy variables comprising s_t. Thus, we may consider that:

4. $\forall u \in U \exists j (1 \leq j \leq t) : \mu_j(u) > 0$;

5. $\forall u \in U \sum_{j=1}^{t} \mu_j(u) = 1$.

Requirements 4 and 5 also have quite a natural interpretation. Requirement 4, designated the *completeness* requirement, signifies that for any object from the universal set there exists at least one concept of FLS to which it may belong. This means that in our scale values set there are no "holes". Requirement 5, designated the *orthogonally* requirement, signifies that we do not permit the use of semantically similar concepts or synonyms, and we require sufficient distinction of the concepts used. Note also that this requirements is often fulfilled or not fulfilled depending on the method used for constructing the membership functions of the concepts forming the scale values set of a FLS [7].

For simplicity, we shall designate requirements 4 and 5 as G.

We shall term the FLS with scale values set consisting of fuzzy variables, the membership functions of which satisfy the requirements 1-3, and their populations the requirements 4 and 5, a *complete orthogonal FLS* and denote it $G(L)$.

As can be seen from example 1 (Section 1), the different FLS have a different degree of internal uncertainty. Is it possible to measure this degree of uncertainty? For complete orthogonal FLS the answer to this question is yes.

To prove this fact and derive a corresponding formula, we need to introduce a series of additional concepts.

Let there be a certain population of t membership functions $s_t \in G(L)$. Let $s_t = \{\mu_1, \mu_2, \ldots, \mu_t\}$. Let us designate the population of t characteristic functions $\hat{s}_t = \{h_1, h_2, \ldots, h_t\}$ as the most similar population of characteristic functions, if $\forall j (1 \le j \le t)$

$$h_j(u) = \begin{cases} 1, & \text{if } \mu_j(u) = \max_{1 \le i \le t} \mu_i(u) \\ 0, & \text{otherwise} \end{cases} \tag{1}$$

It is not difficult to see that, if the complete orthogonal FLS consists not of membership functions but of characteristic functions, then no uncertainty will arise when describing objects in it. The expert unambiguously chooses the term a_j, if the object is in the corresponding region of the universal set. Some experts describe one and the same object with one and the same term. This situation may be illustrated as follows [8]. Let us assume that we have scales of a certain accuracy and we have the opportunity to weigh a certain material. Moreover, we have agreed that, if the weight of the material falls within a certain range, it belongs to one of the categories. Then we shall have the situation accurately described. The problem lies in the fact that for our task there are no such scales nor do we have the opportunity to weigh on them the objects of interest to us.

However we can assume that, of the two FLS, the one having the least uncertainty will be that which is most "similar" to the space consisting of the populations of characteristic functions. In mathematics, distance can be a degree of similarity. Is it possible to introduce distance among FLS? For complete orthogonal FLS it is possible.

The semantic statements formulated by us above may be formalized as follows.

Let $s_t \in G(L)$. For the measure of uncertainty of s_t we shall take the value of the functional $\xi(s_t)$, determined by the elements of $G(L)$ and assuming the values in $[0,1]$ (i.e. $\xi(s_t) : G(L) \to [0,1]$), satisfying the following conditions (axioms):

A1. $\xi(s_t) = 0$, if s_t is a set of characteristic functions;

A2. Let $s_t, s_t' \in G(L)$, t and t' may be equal or not equal to each other. Then $\xi(s_t) \le \xi(s_t')$, if $d(s_t, \hat{s}_t) \le d(s_t', \hat{s}_t')$.

(Let us recall that $\hat{s}_t$ is the set of characteristic functions determined by (1) closest to s_t.).

Do such functional exist? The answer to this question is given by the following theorem [7].

Theorem 1 (theorem of existence). Let $s_t \in G(L)$. Then the functional

$$\xi(s_t) = \frac{1}{|U|} \int_U f\left(\mu_{i_1}(u) - \mu_{i_2}(u)\right) du, \qquad (2)$$

where

$$\mu_{i_1}(u) = \max_{1 \le j \le t} \mu_j(u), \quad \mu_{i_2}(u) = \max_{1 \le j \le t, j \ne i_1} \mu_j(u) \qquad (3)$$

f satisfies the following conditions:
F1. $f(0)=1, f(1)=0$;
F2. f does not increase –
is a measure of uncertainty of s_t, i.e. satisfies the axioms A1 and A2.

There are many functional satisfying the conditions of Theorem 1. They are described in sufficient detail in [7]. The simplest of them is the functional in which the function f is linear. It is not difficult to see that conditions F1 and F2 are satisfied by the sole linear function $f(x) = 1 - x$. Substituting it in (2), we obtain the following simplest measure of uncertainty of the complete orthogonal FLS:

$$\xi(s_t) = \frac{1}{|U|} \int_U (1 - (\mu_{i_1}(u) - \mu_{i_2}(u))) du, \qquad (4)$$

where $\mu_{i_1}(u)$, $\mu_{i_2}(u)$ are determined by the relations (3).

Let us define the following subset of function set L:

$\overline{L}$ is a set of functions from L, which are part-linear and linear on $\overline{U} = \{u \in U : \forall j (1 \le j \le t)\ 0 < \mu_j(u) < 1\}$;

$\hat{L}$ is a set of functions from L, which are part-linear on U (including $\overline{U}$). The following theorems are hold [3].

Theorem 2. Let $s_t \in G(\overline{L})$. Then $\xi(s_t) = \dfrac{d}{2|U|}$, where $d = |\overline{U}|$.

Theorem 3. Let $s_t \in G(L)$. Then $\xi(s_t) = c\dfrac{d}{|U|}$, where $c < 1$, $c =$ Const.

Finally, we present the results of the analysis of our model, when the membership functions which are members of the given collection of fuzzy sets, are not given with absolute precision, but with some maximal inaccuracy δ (Fig. 3). Let us call this particular situation the δ-model and denote it by $G^\delta(L)$.

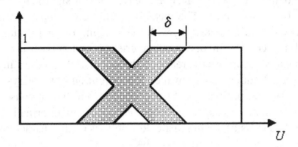

Fig. 2. Presentation of $G^\delta(L)$.

In this situation we can calculate the top ($\overline{\xi}(s_t)$) and the bottom ($\underline{\xi}(s_t)$) valuations of the degree of fuzziness.

The following theorem is hold [7].

Theorem 4. Let $s_t \in G^\delta(L)$. Then $\underline{\xi}(s_t) = \dfrac{d(1-\delta)^2}{2|U|}$, $\overline{\xi}(s_t) = \dfrac{d(1+2\delta)}{2|U|}$, where $d = |U|$.

By comparing the results of the theorem 2 and theorem 5, we see that for small significances δ, the main laws of our model are preserved. Therefore, we can use our technique of estimation of the degree of fuzziness in practical tasks, since we have shown it to be stable.

3   A Model of Information Retrieval in Fuzzy (Linguistic) Data Bases

The database of system is a basis of information model of a subject area. The quality of this basis is expressed, in particular, through parameters of the information retrieval. If the database containing the linguistic descriptions of objects of a subject area allows to carry out qualitative and effective search of the relevant information then the system will work also qualitatively and effectively.

3.1   Concepts of Loss of Information and of Information Noise in Fuzzy Data Bases

As well as in section 2, we shall consider that the set of the linguistic meanings can be submitted as $G(L)$.

In our study of the process of information searches in data bases whose objects have a linguistic description, we introduced the concepts of loss of information ($\Pi_X(U)$) and of information noise ($H_X(U)$). These concepts apply to information searches in these data bases, whose attributes have a set of significances X, which are modelled by the fuzzy sets in s_t. The meaning of these concepts can informally be described as follows. While interacting with the system, a user formulates his query for objects satisfying certain linguistic characteristics, and gets an answer according to his search request. If he knows the real (not the linguistic) values of the characteristics, he would probably delete some of the objects returned by the system (information noise), and he would probably add some others from the data base, not returned by the system (information losses). Information noise and information losses have their origin in the fuzziness of the linguistic descriptions of the characteristics.

These concepts can be formalized as follows.

Let's consider the case $t=2$. Let's fix the number $u^* \in U$ and introduce following denotes:

- $N(u^*)$ is the number of objects, the descriptions of which are stored in the data base, that possess a real (physical, not linguistic) significance equal to u^*;
- N^{user} - the number of users of the system.

Then

- $N_{a_1}(u^*) = \mu_{a_1}(u^*)N(u^*)$ - the number of data base descriptions, which have real meaning of some characteristic equal u^* and is described by source of information as a_1;
- $N_{a_2}(u^*) = \mu_{a_2}(u^*)N(u^*)$ - the number of the objects, which are described as a_2;
- $N_{a_1}^{user}(u^*) = \mu_{a_1}(u^*)N^{user}$ - the number of the system's users who believe that u^* is a_1;
- $N_{a_2}^{user}(u^*) = \mu_{a_2}(u^*)N^{user}$ - the number of the users who believe that u^* is a_2.

That's why under the request "To find all objects which have a meaning of an attribute, equal a_1" (let's designate it as $\langle I(O)= a_1\rangle$) the user gets $N_{a_1}(u^*)$ descriptions of objects with real meaning of search characteristic is equal to u^*. Under these circumstances $N_{a_1}^{user}(u^*)$ users do not get $N_{a_2}(u^*)$ object descriptions (they carry loses). It goes about descriptions of objects which have the meaning of characteristic equal u^*, but described by sources as a_2. By analogy the rest $N_{a_2}^{user}(u^*)$ users get noise ("unnecessary" descriptions in the volume of given $N_{a_1}(u^*)$ descriptions).

Average individual loses for users in the point u^* under the request are equal

$$\pi_{a_1}(u^*) = \frac{1}{N^{user}} N_{a_1}^{user}(u^*) \times N_{a_2}(u^*) = \mu_{a_1}(u^*)\mu_{a_2}(u^*)N(u^*) \tag{5}$$

By analogy average individual noises in the point u^*

$$h_{a_1}(u^*) = \frac{1}{N^{user}} N_{a_2}^{user}(u^*) \times N_{a_1}(u^*) = \mu_{a_1}(u^*)\mu_{a_2}(u^*)N(u^*) \tag{6}$$

Average individual information loses and noises, given under analyzed request ($\Pi_{a_1}(U)$ and $H_{a_1}(U)$ accordingly) are naturally defined as

$$\Pi_{a_1}(U) = \frac{1}{|U|} \int_U \pi_{a_1}(u)du , \; H_{a_1}(U) = \frac{1}{|U|} \int_U h_{a_1}(u)du$$

It's obvious that

$$\Pi_{a_1}(u^*) = H_{a_1}(u^*) = \frac{1}{|U|} \int_U \mu_{a_1}(u)\mu_{a_2}(u)N(u)du \tag{7}$$

By analogy for the request $\langle I(O)= a2 \rangle$ or from symmetry considerations we can get that in this case average loses and noises are equal ($\Pi_{a_2}(U) = H_{a_2}(U)$) too and are equal the right part of (7). Under information loses and noises appearing during some actions with characteristic which has the set of significance $X = \{a_1, a_2\}$ (($\Pi_X(U)$ and $H_X(U)$)) we naturally understand

$$\Pi_X(U) = p_1\Pi_{a_1}(U) + p_2\Pi_{a_2}(U) \; H_X(U) = p_1 H_{a_1}(U) + p_2 H_{a_2}(U)$$

where p_i ($i = 1,2$) - the probability of some request offering in some i-meaning of the characteristic.

It's obvious that as $p_1 + p_2 = 1$, then

$$\Pi_X(U) = H_X(U) = \frac{1}{|U|} \int_U \mu_{a_1}(u)\mu_{a_2}(u)N(u)du \tag{8}$$

Let's consider general case: t- meanings of the retrieval attribute. We can generalize the formula (10) in case of t meanings of the retrieval attribute the following way [5]:

$$\Pi_X(U) = H_X(U) = \frac{1}{|U|} \sum_{j=1}^{t-1}(p_j + p_{j+1}) \int_U \mu_{a_j}(u)\mu_{a_{j+1}}(u)N(u)du \tag{9}$$

where $X = \{a_1, ..., a_t\}$, p_i ($i = 1,2, \; ... \;, t$) - the probability of some request offering in some i- meaning of the characteristic.

3.2   The Several Properties of Loss of Information $\Pi_X(U)$ and of Information Noise $H_X(U)$

Theorem 5. Let $s_t \in G(\overline{L})$, $N(u) = N = Const$ and $p_j = \frac{1}{t}$ ($j=1, ..., t$). Then

$$\Pi_X(U) = H_X(U) = \frac{ND}{3t|U|}, \text{ where } D = |\overline{U}|.$$

Corollary 1. Let the restrictions of the theorem 5 are true. Then

$$\Pi_X(U) = H_X(U) = \frac{2N}{3t}\xi(s_t).$$

For proof of the Corollary is enough to compare theorems 2 and 5.

We can generalize corollary 1 for $s_t \in G(L)$. The following theorem is hold.

Theorem 6. Let $s_t \in G(L)$, $N(u) = N = Const$ and $p_j = \frac{1}{t}$ ($j=1, ..., t$). Then

$$\Pi_X(U) = H_X(U) = \frac{c}{t}\xi(s_t), \text{ where } c \text{ is a constant with depends from } N \text{ only.}$$

The proof of theorems 5 and 6 are given in [6].

This theorems showing that the volumes of losses of the information and of information noise arising by search of the information in a linguistic (fuzzy) databases are coordinated with a degree of uncertainty of the description of objects. It means that describing objects by an optimum way (with minimization of degree of uncertainty) we provide also optimum search of the information in databases.

3.3   The Stability of Loss of Information $\Pi_X(U)$ and of Information Noise $H_X(U)$

By analogue with section 2, we can construct the top ($\overline{\Pi}_X(U), \overline{H}_X(U)$) and bottom ($\underline{\Pi}_X(U), \underline{H}_X(U)$) valuations of the $\Pi_X(U)$ and $H_X(U)$.

The following theorems and corollaries are hold [5].

Therem 7. Let $X = \{a_1,...,a_t\}$, $s_t \in G^\delta(\overline{L})$, $N(u)=N=Const$ and $p_j = \frac{1}{t}$ ($j=1, ..., t$). Then

$$\underline{\Pi}_X(U) = \underline{H}_X(U) = \frac{ND(1-\delta)^3}{3t|U|} \tag{10}$$

where $D = |\overline{U}|$.

Corollary 2. Let the restrictions of the theorem 7 are true. Then

$$\underline{\Pi}_X(U) = \underline{H}_X(U) = \frac{2N}{3t}(1-\delta)\underline{\xi}(s_t) \tag{11}$$

Therem 8. Let $X = \{a_1,...,a_t\}$, $s_t \in G^\delta(\bar{L})$, $N(u)=N=Const$ and $p_j = \frac{1}{t}$ $(j=1, ..., t)$.
Then

$$\overline{\Pi}_X(U) = \overline{H}_X(U) = \frac{ND(1-\delta)^3}{3t|U|} + \frac{2ND\delta}{t|U|} \qquad (12)$$

where $D = |\bar{U}|$.

Corollary 3. Let the restrictions of the theorem 8 are true. Then

$$\overline{\Pi}_X(U) = \overline{H}_X(U) = \frac{2N}{t(1+2\delta)}\left[\frac{(1-\delta)^3}{3} + 2\delta\right]\xi(s_t) \qquad (13)$$

By comparing the results of the theorem 5 and theorems 7 and 8 or the corollary 1 and corollaries 2 and 3, we see that for small significances δ, the main laws of our model of information retrieval are preserved. Therefore, we can use our technique of estimation of the degree of uncertainty and our model of information retrieval in fuzzy (linguistic) data bases in practical tasks, since we have shown it to be stable.

References

[1] Big data: The next frontier for innovation, competition, and productivity. McKinsey Global Institute (2011), http://www.mckinsey.com/Insights/MGI/Research/Technology_and_Innovation/Big_data_The_next_frontier_for_innovation

[2] Pfanzagl, J.: Theory of Measurement, 2nd edn. Physica-Verlag (1971)

[3] Ryjov, A.: The Degree of Fuzziness of Fuzzy Descriptions. In: Krushinsky, L.V., Yablonsky, S.V., Lupanov, O.B. (eds.) Mathematical Cybernetics and its Application to Biology, pp. 60–77. Moscow University Publishing, Moscow (1987) (in Russian)

[4] Ryjov, A.: Fuzzy Linguistic Scales: Definition, Properties and Applications. In: Reznik, L., Kreinovich, V. (eds.) Soft Computing in Measurement and Information Acquisition, pp. 23–38. Springer (2003)

[5] Ryjov, A.: The Information Retrieval in Fuzzy Data Bases. In: Proceedings of the Fifth International Fuzzy Systems Association World Congress, Seoul, Korea, vol. 1, pp. 477–480 (1993)

[6] Ryjov, A.: On degree of fuzziness and its application to intelligent information systems. Intelligent Systems 1, 205–216 (1996) (in Russian)

[7] Ryjov, A.: The Principles of Fuzzy Set Theory and Measurement of Fuzziness, 116 p. Dialog-MSU, Moscow (1998)

[8] Ryjov, A., Belenki, A., Hooper, R., Pouchkarev, V., Fattah, A., Zadeh, L.A.: Development of an Intelligent System for Monitoring and Evaluation of Peaceful Nuclear Activities (DISNA), IAEA, STR-310, Vienna, 122 p (1998)

Sleep Physiological Dynamics Simulation with Fuzzy Set

Yu-Wen Chen and Hsing Mei

Web Computing Lab., Department of Computer Science and Information Engineering,
Fu Jen Catholic University
{eric99,mei}@csie.fju.edu.tw

Abstract. Neuroscientists have investigated into the functional-structural mechanisms of sleep for a long time. However, the sleep physiology is so complex that the relations to brain structure are still mostly unknown. In this paper, we integrate the brain sleep switch model with fuzzy methodology, more specifically, combining the the mutual inhibition system of the sleep switch with a rule-based fuzzy reasoning system. Based on the extension of sleep switch, a model for sleep physiological dynamics is proposed. In addition, we implement the sleep mechanisms and integrate them into an object-oriented brain simulator. With the brain simulator, we can demonstrate sleep dynamics of the brain network with 3D-rendering system is demonstrated. The sleep physiological dynamics in brain become more intuitive and easier to realize.

Keywords: sleep physiology, fuzzy methodology, brain, simulation.

1   Introduction

The sleep switch model is the most famous model which illustrates the functional-structural behavior of sleep [1]. The sleep switch adopts an abstract flip-flop to describe changes of the sleep-related brain components which cause transitions among different states during wakefulness and sleep. Related studies also discovered mechanisms and operating patterns of sleep in the human brain; such as pathways of neurotransmitters, mutual inhibition mechanism, and firing patterns of neuron clusters. The sleep switch model is considered as the candidate tool to demonstrate the brain sleep physiology. However, the sleep switch model cannot describe the dynamics of sleep in detail because some essential parts are still missing, such as quantification of neurotransmitter and the threshold of the sleep switch control. Instead of investigated into brain sleep physiology, most researchers discover activity patterns from external observations, and describe internal operations without quantified data.

Fuzzy concept and methodology are popular in several domains, such as electrical controlling, temperature regulating, decision making, and artificial intelligence. Coincidentally, fuzzy could be applied to describe some behavior in the brain. Fuzzy concept is good at modeling learning behavior and the growth of understanding. Since the pattern of the brain operations are not as rigorous as the computer, fixed reactions modeling of the brain simply cannot apply in various environments. The fuzzy theory provides a reasoning methodology with flexibility and vagueness.

F.M. Zanzotto et al. (Eds.): BI 2012, LNCS 7670, pp. 150–161, 2012.

Inspired by the vagueness of the brain and fuzzy methodology, we combine the sleep switch model with the fuzzy theory to propose a feasible method to model the internal sleep brain operations. We also use 3D-rendering visualization system to present sleep physiological dynamics with a brain simulator. In next section, we will introduce the sleep mechanisms and model. Then, describe the fuzzy concept and its applications. In section 4, we illustrate how to combine the fuzzy theory with the sleep switch model. The design and implementation of the simulator is introduced in section 5.

2   Background

The brain sleep dynamics simulation requires knowledge of sleep physiology and fuzzy control. In this section, these related backgrounds are discussed.

2.1   Sleep

Sleep is an essential state of most animals including mammal, birds or even invertebrates. The characteristics of sleep include reducing the body movement, lack of consciousness and decreasing the sensitivity and reaction to external stimuli. Sleep can help the body growth or recovery, such as revitalizing immune systems, increasing the growth of skeletal-muscular systems and reorganize memory of the brain. Regular sleep is necessary for health and survival especially for human beings. The quality of sleep will affect not only physiological but also psychological situations.

There are two phases of sleep: namely Rapid Eye Movement (REM); and Non-Rapid Eye Movement (NREM) sleep. The American Academy of Sleep Medicine (AASM) further defines three stages of the NREM sleep (four stages previously). These three stages are N1; N2; and N3. The N3 stage is also called Slow-Wave Sleep (SWS) [2]. By analyzing captured physiological signals, sleep science professionals can determine the subject's sleep stage or even diagnose sleep problems [14, 15].

2.2   The Sleep Switch Model

In 2001, Saper, Chou and Scammell [1] proposed a sleep mechanism named flip-flop switch, which describes the sleep/wake state transitions based on the concept of mutually inhibitory circuits. The sleep switch is a homeostatic regulating system of sleep, which describes changes between different systems, including neurotransmitter and their pathways will cause different sleep/wake stages and stabilize the state transitions of wakefulness and sleep. It can be divided into three main systems: The ascending arousal system, the NREM sleep-promoting system and the REM sleep-promoting system. Each system contains different neurochemicals, brain regions and networks. Interactions (excitation/inhibition) between these systems can regulate wakefulness, NREM and REM sleep of the brain.

- **Ascending Arousal System:** Ascending arousal models are based on observations from Moruzzi and Magoun [3]. They discovered that activities of paramedian reticular formation, especially in the midbrain; cause the state of arousal. Subsequent studies also found that a group of tissue at the junction of the caudal midbrain and rostral pons plays a critical role on maintaining wakefulness. Based on these discoveries, studies found that cell groups at the mesopontine junction project monoaminergic and cholinergic neurotransmitter to the forebrain. In detail, there are two major types of neurons involved in the wake-promoting system; the cholinergic neuron and the monoaminergic neuron. Cholinergic neurons are found in pedunculopontine nucleus (PPT) and laterodorsal tegmental nucleus (LDT). There existing projecting pathways not only from the mesopontine junction to the thalamic relay nucleus, intraluminal and reticular thalamic nucleus, but also to the lateral hypothalamus, basal forebrain, and prefrontal cortex [4]. Cholinergic neurons fire rapidly during wakefulness and REM sleep, and fire much slower in the state of NREM sleep. Thus firing of cholinergic neurons is considered help promoting cortical activities [5]. The monoaminergic neurons include several nucleus and project different neurotransmitter to the forebrain. Neurons of the locus coeruleus (LC) contain noradrenaline (NA), neurons of the dorsal and median raphe nucleus contain serotonin (5-HT), neurons adjacent to the dorsal raphe nucleus contain dopamine (DA) and neurons of the tuberomammillary nucleus (TMN) contain histamine (HIST). These monoaminergic cells have similar projecting targets and firing patterns. The pathway contains the brainstem, lateral hypothalamus, basal forebrain, and cerebral cortex. Neurons of this group generally fire most rapidly during wakefulness, less active during NREM sleep, and almost silent in the state of REM sleep. On the other hand, there's another kind of neurons in posterior half area of the lateral hypothalamus, these neurons produces neuropeptides named orexin (or hypocretin). Some studies found that there are excitatory receptors in cell groups of the arousal system such as TMN, basal forebrain, raphé nucleus and mesopontine reticular formation.

  The orexin neurons fire during wakefulness and fire briskly during some survival-related behaviors, such as exploration of environment and foraging behaviors in hungry animals. Thus, the orexin neurons are suggested that play an important role in promoting arousal from the sleep and stabilizing the state of wakefulness.

- **NREM Sleep-Promoting System:** In 1996, Sherin et al found that a group of neurons in the ventrolateral preoptic nucleus (VLPO) and which control the activity of the TMN during sleep [6, 7]. Moreover, this phenomenon is not observed during wakefulness. The VLPO contains inhibitory neurotransmitters named GABA (or γ-Aminobutyric acid) and Galanin. Neurons of the VLPO release these two neurotransmitters and inhibit components of the ascending arousal system such as the LC, TMN, raphe nucleus and lateral hypothalamic area [8]. Another research found decrease of NREM, REM, and total sleep time from animals with lesions of the VLPO [9]. These observations suggested that the VLPO is important in promoting sleep and which contains pathway to innervate the wake-promoting system. On the other hand, neurons of the VLPO release the GABA and Galanin to inhibit components of the wake-promoting system. Oppositely they are also be inhibited by neurotransmitter projected from the wake-promoting system, such as acetylcholine, norepinephrine, dopamine and serotonin. That is, the sleep- and wake-promoting systems are mutually antagonistic.

- **REM Sleep-Promoting System:** In 1950s, the REM sleep was discovered and defined, subsequent studies started to research the mechanism of the REM sleep. Currently, the pedunculopontine nucleus (PPT) and laterodorsal tegmental nucleus (LDT) at the junction of the midbrain and pons are considered to be critical for the REM sleep [10]. Further, researchers found other factors and define two kinds of neurons: REM-on and REM-off neurons. In addition to the PPT and LDT, the sublaterodorsal nucleus (SLD) and precoeruleus region (PC) are classified as the REM-on neurons. The REM-off neurons includes ventral periaqueductal gray matter(vlPAG) and lateral pontine tegmentum (LPT), which are considered the main region of preventing REM sleep, because vlPAG and LPT receive inputs from the extended VLPO and the lateral hypothalamus [11]. Similar to the relationship between the VLPO and ascending arousal system, the REM-on and REM-off neurons have a mutually inhibitory relationship; interactions between them will cause the on/off switching of the REM sleep.

The flip-flop switch can model the mutually antagonistic relationship among the above systems. Switches of electrical circuits have the characteristic of rapid and complete state transitions. In the brain, transition of sleep states must be quick enough to increase the chance of survival, thus two halves of the 'switch' must inhibit the other side strongly and have stabilizing mechanism to avoid the intermediate states. On the other hand, large scale effects, such as circadian regulation and accumulated homeostatic need for sleep, are also important in regulate balance of mutual inhibition. With the slower large scale effect, state transition of the switch can keep dynamic equilibrium. Thus, damage or lesions of the sleep-related systems may break the balance and cause sleep problems, such as insomnia, narcolepsy or other sleep disorders.

2.3   Fuzzy Concept and Fuzzy Logic

The fuzzy logic comes from "fuzzy set theory" proposed by Lotfi A. Zadeh in 1965 [12]. Traditional logic represents clear and specific logic of contexts, that is, completely true or completely false (i.e. two-value or binary logic). Fuzzy defines logical values in a range and allows values between 0 to 1 rather than "0 or 1" (many-valued logic or probabilistic logic). Fuzzy reasoning, extended from the fuzzy logic, which is similar to human reasoning; it provides approximate results from incomplete or ambiguous data to deal with problems that difficult to solve by traditional logic methods. It has been applied to many applications, such as control theory, and artificial intelligence; that used to handle applications of logics with truth values range between completely true and false.

To implement a fuzzy reasoning system, fuzzy set and membership function should be designed first. Membership functions contain linguistic variables and truth values. Variables in mathematics are usually numerical values; in fuzzy logic applications, the non-numeric linguistic variables are often used to be the expression of rules and facts [13].

Fuzzy reasoning is usually based on rules, which described as IF-THEN rules or fuzzy associative matrices. In addition, operators of boolean logic such as AND, OR, NOT are able to use in fuzzy logic. With fuzzy sets and logical operators, we can design rules for the reasoning system. For example, a rule-based fuzzy regulating system of room temperature can be defined like this:

Rule 1: **IF** *temperature is very cold* **THEN** *stop air conditioning*
Rule 2: **IF** *temperature is normal* **OR** *little hot* **THEN** *maintain air conditioning*
Rule 3: **IF** *temperature is hot* **THEN** *speed up air conditioning*

After designing fuzzy sets and rules, the reasoning system will have abilities to make decisions according to status of environments.

In Brain Informatics field, some related studies [14, 15] have applied fuzzy methodology and neuron network approaches to classify sleep stages from measured physiological signals, such as brain wave, eye movement and muscular tone, etc. In this research, we apply fuzzy approach into the human brain in nucleus-level, attempting to speculate sleep stages according activity of sleep-related nucleus.

3   Design of the Sleep Switch

The 'flip-flop switch' describes the mutually antagonistic relationship among neurons of wake, NREM, and REM promoting systems. There are three sleep states: wakefulness, NREM sleep, and REM sleep; and two state transitions (that is, two switches) in this model:

- **Wake-Sleep Switch:** The wake-sleep switch is affected by mutual inhibitory interactions of monoaminergic system (wake-promoting) and the VLPO (sleep-promoting) system. For example, when activity of VLPO is strong, the monoaminergic system will be inhibited and weaker. As the pressure of change is heavy enough; the switch will change rapidly to NREM sleep state. However, the direct inhibition of these neuron groups is relatively unstable [16]. In the human brain, there exist neuron groups which are responsible for stabilizing the wake-sleep switch, such as orexin neurons in LHA and neurons of extended VLPO.

- **REM-NREM Switch:** After switching to the NREM sleep state, the REM-NREM switch will be launched and start to regulate REM and NREM states of the brain. The main neuron groups are SLD/PC(REM-on) and vlPAG/LPT (REM-off). Similar to previous switch, the mutual inhibitory interaction produces the REM-NREM flip-flop switch and promotes state transitions. On the other hand, either REM-on or REM-off neurons are controlled by other neurotransmitter systems respectively. For example, the noradrenergic, serotoninergic and orexin neurons inhibit REM sleep by exciting REM-off neurons; whereas cholinergic neurons and the VLPO promote REM sleep by inhibit REM-off neurons.

We combine the Wake-Sleep switch and REM-NREM switch into a single system. Figure.1 shows the integration of two switches and the relationship between wake-promoting, sleep-promoting, REM-on, and REM-off neuron groups. In this study, the design and implementation of sleep case will base on this integrated switch model.

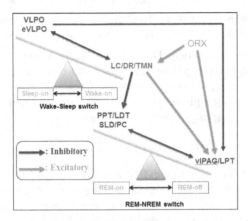

Fig. 1. Integrated Sleep Switches and Relationship between Neurons

Mutual Inhibitory Interactions: To implement the integrated sleep switches, we should firstly design the mutual inhibitory mechanism of neuron and neurotransmitters. When a nucleus is active, it will project neurotransmitter to other brain regions through specific pathways. The amount of neurotransmitters depends on number of single projection and the projection cycle. On the other hand, neurons of nucleus contain receptors of different neurotransmitters. That is, each nucleus is affected by specific neurotransmitter either excitatory or inhibitory. Therefore we describe this phenomenon for each nucleus as follow:

$$n(t) = \alpha(t) \times A(t) \tag{1}$$

$$\gamma(t) = \begin{cases} \overline{E}_n(t) \\ \overline{I}_n(t) \end{cases} \tag{2}$$

$$\overline{E}_n(t) = \frac{\sum_{j=1}^{Ne} n_j(t)}{N_e} \quad , \quad \overline{I}_n(t) = \frac{\sum_{j=1}^{Ni} n_j(t)}{N_i} \tag{3}$$

In the above equations, $A(t)$ represents activity of the nucleus, which is, projecting number in a unit time (1/t). $\alpha(t)$ is the transmission amount of the neurotransmitter of each projection (molecular weight). $n(t)$ is the amount of neurotransmitter projected by nucleus per unit time (molecular weight/t). With the first formula, we can get the number of each neurotransmitter in a unit time. The $\gamma(t)$ is the proportion of excitatory and inhibitory of nucleus, which depends on excitatory/inhibitory activities from other nucleus. $\bar{E}_n(t)$ is the average number of excitatory neurotransmitters, and $\bar{I}_n(t)$ is the average number of inhibitory neurotransmitters.

For example, the sleep-promoting neurons are inhibited by wake-promoting neurons (i.e. DR, LC and TMN nucleus) and excited by neurons of extended VLPO. Thus, the parameters of $\bar{E}_n(t)$ must take activity of extend VLPO into account (for sleep-promoting neurons, extended VLPO are excitatory); and consider activities of wake-promoting neurons as parameters of $\bar{I}_n(t)$ (for sleep-promoting neurons, wake-promoting neurons are inhibitors). During each iteration, the system calculates the number of serotonin; norepinephrine; histamine; and other related neurotransmitters according to active values of these nucleuses. Then, we can use these results to calculate the excitatory-inhibitory proportion. Finally, the activity value of each nucleus of next iteration $A(t+1)$ is shown as follow:

$$A(t+1) = A(t) \times \gamma(t) \tag{4}$$

However, from above formulas we can find that if the weight of one side of the switch is very heavy, the other side will keep suppressing without any chance to move the switch. Thus, there must an external controlling mechanism to regulate the balance of the switch. In this study, we add the decay coefficient $\Phi(t)$ into the formula of calculating activities of nucleus as follow:

$$A(t+1) = [A(t) \times \gamma(t)] \times (1 - \Phi(t)) \tag{5}$$

Whether in wake, NREM or REM sleep states the decay coefficient is always available. In the beginning of each state, the $\Phi(t)$ will be initialized. As time goes by, this coefficient increases over time. The $\Phi(t)$ will weaken the activity of dominant neurons and relieve the inhibition of the other side of sleep switch. Finally, the pressure of the inhibited side will be stronger and make the switch change to other sleep states. In our simulation, the initial state is set to "wakefulness"; and Table 1 shows initial value of each nucleus and neurotransmitters.

Table 1. Initial Values of Nucleus and Neurotransmitters

Nucleus	Activity($A(t)$)	Neurotransmitter	Amount ($\alpha(t)$)
DR	1.0	Serotonin	0.4
LC	1.0	Noradrenaline	0.4
TMN	1.0	Histamine	0.4
PPT	0.3	Acetylcholine	0.6
LDT	0.3	Orexin	0.2
LHA	1.0	GABA	0.5
VLPO	0.1		
SLD/PC (REM-on)	0.1		
vlPAG/LPT (REM-off)	0.1		

4   Combination of Fuzzy Theory and Sleep Switch

The sleep switch model describes the homeostatic regulation mechanisms of sleep in the human brain. However, the threshold of sleep switches can only be inferred by collect statistics data from observing subjects. In this study, we take the fuzzy theory as a tool to calculate the threshold of the sleep switches. The fuzzy system is consisted of three parts as follow:

Fuzzifier: Before starting fuzzy reasoning, the inputs should be converted into fuzzy sets. Thus the first step is to define membership functions of inputs and controlling operations. In the sleep case, we select four kinds of nucleus as inputs (activities of wake-promoting, sleep-promoting, REM-on, and REM-off neurons), and use the change of "sleepy index" as controlling operations. On the other hand, we defined the activity of nucleus with three states: rapid, slow and stop. We also set the control of sleepy index with three states: increase, maintain and decrease. After setting states of each element, then we define membership functions of each state. Parameters of fuzzy sets are set as follow:

- Firing rate of nucleus

  1. Rapid: $F_{Rapid} = \int_{0.6}^{0.8} (5x-3)/x + \int_{0.8}^{1} 1/x$

  2. Low: $F_{Low} = \int_{0.1}^{0.4} (2.5x)/x + \int_{0.4}^{0.6} 1/x + \int_{0.6}^{0.7} ((-10)x+7)/x$

  3. Stop: $F_{Stop} = \int_{0.1}^{0.2} ((-10)x+2)/x$

- Control of sleepy index

  1. Increase: $S_{Increase} = \int_{0}^{1} (x)/x$

  2. Maintain: $S_{Maintain} = \int_{-0.5}^{0} (2x+1)/x + \int_{0}^{0.5} ((-2)x+1)/x$

  3. Decrease: $S_{Decrease} = \int_{-1}^{0} (-x)/x$

- Control of REM index

  1. Increase: $R_{Increase} = \int_{0}^{1} (x)/x$

  2. Maintain: $R_{Maintain} = \int_{-0.5}^{0} (2x+1)/x + \int_{0}^{0.5} ((-2)x+1)/x$

  3. Decrease: $R_{Decrease} = \int_{-1}^{-0.5} 1/x + \int_{-0.5}^{0} (-(\frac{8}{5}x)+0.2)/x$

After finishing defining the membership functions of all inputs and controlling operations, the fuzzy set can be used in the fuzzy reasoning system.

- **Rule-Based Fuzzy Logic System:** Fuzzy system must provide rules for reasoning. The general format of rule is "IF A THEN B". The A is called "premise" (or condition) and the B is called "consequence" of the rule. If the rule is composed by multiple premise, we can combine premises with operators such as AND, OR or XOR, etc. For example, we define activity of wake-promoting neurons as input x_1, sleep-promoting neurons as input x_2 and REM-on neurons as input x_3. And then we use the fuzzy sets from the fuzzifier to define rules as follow:

Rule1: **IF** *[(*Wake-Promoting Nucleus *is* Rapid) **AND** *(*Sleep-Promoting Nucleus *is* (Low **OR** Stop)) **AND** *(*REM-Promoting Nucleus *is* Stop)] **THEN** **Decrease** Sleepy Index

Rule2: **IF** [(Wake-Promoting Nucleus *is* (Low **OR** Stop) **AND** *(*Sleep-Promoting Nucleus *is* Rapid) **AND** *(*REM-Promoting Nucleus *is* Stop)] **THEN** **Increase** Sleepy Index

Rule3: **IF** [(Wake-Promoting Nucleus *is* Stop) **AND** *(*Sleep-Promoting Nucleus *is* Low) **AND** *(*REM-Promoting Nucleus *is* Rapid)] **THEN** **Increase** REM Index

Rule4: **IF** [(Wake-Promoting Nucleus *is* Stop) **AND** *(*Sleep-Promoting Nucleus *is* Low) **AND** *(*REM-Promoting Nucleus *is* (Low **OR** Stop))] **THEN** **Decrease** REM Index

After defining rules, the system can start reasoning following these rules. During each iteration, the fuzzy system receives inputs (that is, activity of each nucleus) from the homeostatic regulating system and applies received inputs into each rule to calculate the membership functions of the consequence. The system will get several bounded membership functions from each rule, and then combine these functions with union operation. Finally, we can get a new function from the fuzzy reasoning system.

- **Defuzzifier:** After getting the combinational membership function of controlling operations, we must convert the fuzzy set into a single explicit output (or called "crisp value") so that the system can process the follow-up control. In this study we use the most common used method to get the output value: calculating the central area of the membership function.

The output value from the fuzzy reasoning system will be used to control the sleepy index. The workflow can be described as Figure.2:

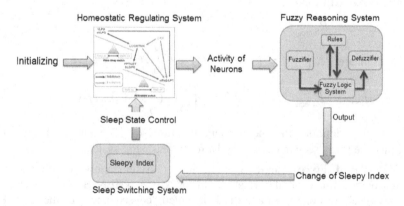

Fig. 2. The Workflow of Sleep Switches and Fuzzy Reasoning System

The homeostatic regulating system processes the mutual inhibitory interactions of each nucleus. After calculating activity values of nucleus, these values will be sent to the fuzzy reasoning system as inputs. The fuzzy system receives the inputs and starts the rule-based fuzzy reasoning. When the fuzzy reasoning is completed, there will be a single output from the reasoning system. That is, the change of sleepy index. This value increases, maintains or decreases the sleepy index of the switching system. When the sleepy index exceeds a certain threshold, the switching system will change the sleep state of the simulated brain. The sleep simulating algorithm can be described with pseudo code as follow:

```
SIMULATE_SLEEP_DYNAMICS(time t, sleepNetwork $s ,list $allNucleus[])
1  while time(t) < t_end
2        do sleepyIndex ← GET-CURRENT-SLEEPY-INDEX(s);
3           REMIndex ← GET-CURRENT-REM-INDEX(s);
4           for each nucleus n ∈ allNucleus[]
5                       do changedList[] ← CALCULATE-INHIBITION-
EXCITATION(t,n);
6           changedSleepyIndex ← FUZZY-REASONING-SLEEP(changedList[]);
7           changedREMIndex ← FUZZY-REASONING-REM(changedList[]);
8           nextState      ←    CALCULATE-NEXT-STATES(changedSleepyIndex,
                                              changedREMIndex);
9           update SLEEP-INDEX(s,changedSleepyIndex);
10          update REM-INDEX(s,changedREMIndex);
11          update STATE(s, nextState);
12          update Nucleus-List(changedList[],allNucleus[]);
13 end while
```

Given a networks, which contains value of sleepy index, REM index and sleep state at time t. List allNucleus[] contains value of nucleus' activity and projecting amount of neurotransmitters at time t (see Table 1). Firstly, the brain simulator calculates the inhibition/excitation results of each nucleus. Next, the changed values will be sent to the fuzzy reasoning system; then the fuzzy system produces outputs, which represents changes of the sleepy and REM index. Finally, the simulator will check changed values of sleepy/REM index and determine whether the sleep switches will change or not. If the switches change, the sleep state of brain simulator will also be modified.

5   Brain Simulator Based Implementation

To complete the simulation, implementation of above systems into a simulator is required. In this paper, we use a brain network simulator suggested by Tseng, Lu, and Mei [17]. The brain simulator is an open-sourced project, which adopts object-oriented (OO) methodologies to design and implement brain components, brain regions, neurotransmitters and brain networks. In addition to anatomical structure, the brain simulator also integrates functional structures and operational models of the brain. This simulator adopted of case-based incremental delivery developmental process to increase the elasticity and flexibility of the brain simulator framework itself. With the case-based method, developers can add new functions or behavior models into the brain simulator according to their requirements. Besides providing Back-end integration, the simulator also supports front-end rendering of the brain network, including 3D-rendering functions and interactive visualization. With supports of the 3D graphics, presenting the sleep behavioral models will be more intuitive and easier to understand. Currently, this simulator has integrated models of Alzheimer's disease and has basic structure of brain networks; in this study, we integrate sleep behavior models and the fuzzy system into the brain simulator and show the sleep physiological changes of the brain with user interfaces and the 3D-rendering system. Figure.3 shows a snapshot of the simulation. After initializing, the user interface will present the sleep states, activity of each nucleus, and projecting pathways of neurotransmitters. The activity changes of Wake/Sleep/REM Promoting Neurons are shown in Figure. 4.

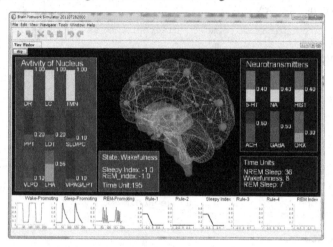

Fig. 3. Screenshot of the Brain Simulator

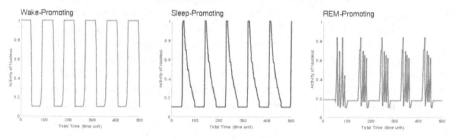

Fig. 4. Activity Changes of Wake-, Sleep and REM Promoting Neurons

6   Conclusion and Future Work

In this study, we focus on combining the sleep switch model and fuzzy theory to provide a possible methodology for resolving problems to formulate the sleep switch and mutual inhibition mechanism among nucleus of the human brain. Moreover, we implement these models and methodology with techniques of computer science, and then present changes of the brain network with 3D-rendering system to make these models more intuitive and easier to understand. However, currently we can only simulate general cases of sleep behaviors by gradually regulating fuzzy sets of nucleus status and controlling strategies. Thus, some training methods are required, such as pattern recognition from input data, and machine learning technologies. With input data and appropriate training methodologies, it may be possible to generate various fuzzy sets, and finally achieve personalization. In summary, this study is still ongoing; more in-depth studies and improvement are required, such as rationality of theoretical models of sleep, more appropriate fuzzy sets and controlling strategies, and take other behavior models into account (i.e. Alzheimer's disease, cognitive or memory). Each improvement will enhance our works and make our methodology more reasonable and comprehensive. Finally, we hope that this study can inspire more related research and encourage people joining the development making more contributions for discovering the secrets of the sleep physiology.

References

1. Saper, C.B., Chou, T.C., Scammell, T.E.: The sleep switch: hypothalamic control of sleep and wakefulness. TRENDS in Neurosciences 24(12), 726–731 (2001)
2. Siegel, J.: The REM Sleep-Memory Consolidation Hypothesis. Science 294(5544), 1058–1063 (2001)
3. Moruzzi, G.: Brainste mreticular formation and activation of the EEG. Electroencephalography and Clinical Neurophysiology 1(1-4), 455–473 (1949)
4. Hallanger, A.E.: The origins of cholinergic and other subcortical afferents to the thalamus in the rat. The Journal of Comparative Neurology 262(1), 105–124 (1987)
5. El Mansari, M., Sakai, K., Jouvet, M.: Unitary characteristics of presumptive cholinergic tegmental neurons during the sleep-waking cycle in freely moving cats. Experimental Brain Research 76(3), 519–529 (1989)
6. Sherin, J.E.: Activation of ventrolateral preoptic neurons during sleep. Science 271, 216–219 (1996)
7. Thomas, C., Chou, A.: Afferents to the Ventrolateral Preoptic Nucleus. The Journal of Neuroscience 22(3), 977–990 (2002)
8. Sherin, J.E.: Innervation of histaminergic tuberomammillary neurons by GABAergic and galaninergic neurons in the ventrolateral preoptic nucleus of the rat. The Journal of Neuroscience 18, 4705–4721 (1998)
9. Lu, J.: Effect of lesions of the ventrolateral preoptic nucleus on NREM and REM sleep. The Journal of Neuroscience 20, 3830–3842 (2000)
10. Lu, J.: A putative flip-flop switch for control of REM sleep. Nature, 589–594 (2006)
11. Boissard, R.: The rat ponto-medullary network responsible for paradoxical sleep onset and maintenance: a combined microinjection and functional neuroanatomical study. European Journal of Neuroscience 16(10), 1959–1973 (2002)
12. Zadeh, L.: Fuzzy sets. Information and Control 8, 338–353 (1965)
13. Zadeh, L.: Fuzzy Sets, Fuzzy Logic, and Fuzzy Systems. World Scientific Books (1996)
14. Held, C.M., Heiss, J.E., Estévez, P.A., Perez, C.A., Garrido, M., Algarín, C., Peirano, P.: Extracting fuzzy rules from polysomnographic recordings for infant sleep classification. IEEE Transactions on Biomedical Engineering 53(10), 1954–1962 (2006)
15. Held, C.M., Estevez, P.A., Perez, C.A., Holzmann, C.A., Perez, J.P.: Classification of sleep stages in infants: a neuro fuzzy approach. IEEE Engineering in Medicine and Biology Magazine 21(5), 147–151 (2002)
16. Clifford, B., Saper, P.: Sleep State Switching. Neuron 68(6), 1023–1042 (2010)
17. Tseng, W.-H., Lu, S.-Y., Mei, H.: On the Development of a Brain Simulator. In: Pan, J.-S., Chen, S.-M., Nguyen, N.T. (eds.) ICCCI 2010, Part II. LNCS, vol. 6422, pp. 258–267. Springer, Heidelberg (2010)

Parallels between Machine and Brain Decoding

Lorenzo Dell'Arciprete[1], Brian Murphy[2], and Fabio Massimo Zanzotto[1]

[1] Artificial Intelligence Research, University of Rome Tor Vergata, Rome, Italy
fabio.massimo.zanzotto@uniroma2.it
[2] Machine Learning Department, Carnegie Mellon University, Pittsburgh, USA
brianmurphy@cmu.edu

Abstract. We report some existing work, inspired by analogies between human thought and machine computation, showing that the informational state of a digital computer can be decoded in a similar way to brain decoding. We then discuss some proposed work that would leverage this analogy to shed light on the amount of information that may be missed by the technical limitations of current neuroimaging technologies.

1 Introduction

Analogies have often been drawn between machine computation and human thought. In computer science biological principles are sometimes appealed to when designing machines. For instance in cybernetics [1], artificial adaptive machines – that is machines that can control their states – have been studied with respect to the adaptivity of natural living organisms. And both the Von Neumann architecture [2], and the neural-based computing architecture originally introduced by Turing [3] show the influence of concepts coming from the study of the mind and of the brain. In contemporary cognitive sciences the analogy is also widespread, a computational theory of mind [4] being central to the "cognitive revolution" in the second half of the last century. For example in the work of Chomsky [5, 6] we see cognitive operations (in this case linguistic) being rooted in formal mathematical models, and in various guises this idea continues to be an influential model for understanding cognition more generally (see e.g. [7]).

Here we try to explore whether the analogy may provide *concrete* insights into the nature of the task of decoding brain states from neuroimaging data, describing in this paper some preliminary work that might inform the fields of cognitive neuroscience, and machine learning from neuroimaging data.

In neural decoding analyses, we take recordings of brain activity, which are noisy and limited in resolution, and use machine learning methods to determine which patterns of activity consistently co-occur with the cognitive states and processes that are active in the minds of participants. One could take a similar "black box", data-driven approach to reading the informational state of a computer, by learning the relationship between particular computational tasks and snapshots of its contemporary RAM contents. But of course in the case of a computer, unlike in the human brain, the ground-truth is well-defined: the

F.M. Zanzotto et al. (Eds.): BI 2012, LNCS 7670, pp. 162–174, 2012.

precise informational state of the machine is known at all times, and the distinction between process (code) and representation (data) is unambiguous. Previous papers have demonstrated that such decoding of RAM-states is possible for classical computational tasks [8, 9] and that it is even possible to produce real chip scanners that could capture RAM activation images [10].

In this paper, we propose to use the more cognitively realistic tasks of linguistic processing for classification of semantic and syntactic categories (analogous to cognitive-neuroscience studies [11–15]). In our view, observing this computational task can give concrete insights on the task of decoding neuroimaging data. In section 2 we discuss how such an analysis could give us a better handle on the limitations of resolution imposed by physiological properties of the brain and technical limitations of imaging devices: since in computer decoding we have access to the "true" informational state, we can investigate the extent to which we may be missing information in the relatively impoverished brain data to which we have access. In section 3, we describe the computational task of linguistic processing from the distributional perspective. In section 4, we estimate the size of the brain areas involved in particular linguistic processing tasks. And, finally, in section 5, we discuss the experiments on decoding computational processing while exploring different blurring levels. With this experiments, we aim to investigate how decoding performances decrease with blurring. This is an useful insight for the understanding of brain state decoding.

2   Modelling Resolution Limitations of Imaging Technologies

Current neuroimaging methods have impressive spatial and temporal resolution, but are still working at a level far from the actual physical phenomenon of interest: millions or billions of single neuron firing events. For example, MEG has a temporal resolution that can capture the full temporal dynamics of neuronal firing, but spatially a single channel may aggregate the activity of the order of 10^9 individual neurons.[1] EEG is further limited in that its sensors are sensitive to larger overlapping areas of cortex, and that the low-pass filtering properties of the skull make higher frequencies hard to record. Turning to fMRI, its effective sampling rate of under 0.5Hz (due to the sluggish blood-oxygen level response) is well below the firing rates found in neurons (ca. 10-1000Hz), and even at higher limits of its spatial resolution (voxels of size 1mm^3) it still samples the order of 10^4 neurons at a time.[2] Capabilities for recording individual neuron activity is limited to very small numbers of cells, typically under 100 and is usually random in the particular neurons it samples in a brain locality of interest. As a result we do not have a detailed understanding of the functional activity of large neuronal populations, nor consequently how the patterns of activity seen in neuroimaging experiments relate to it. Furthermore, from the machine learning perspective,

---

[1] Assuming 100-300 channels, and 100 billion neurons in total.

[2] Assuming cortex covered by ca. 700,000 voxels of size 1mm^3.

we do not have a handle on how impoverished our data is, relative to the full neuronal population activity that we would ideally have access to.

Here we propose to make use of the computer-brain analogy in the following way. We will choose cognitive tasks that are studied in neuroscience, and can be emulated successfully by a computer – in this case detecting the semantic and syntactic categories involved in noun-phrase composition. While such a task is being performed by the computer we will take snapshots of RAM state. Given this very rich data, we expect that high-accuracy decoding should be achievable. The question we will then ask of the data, is how much accuracy is degraded as the input data is downsampled in ways that reflect neuroimaging technologies, such as MEG, EEG or fMRI.

3   Computer-Based Distributional Semantic Processing

Processing natural language is one of the key activities of artificial intelligence. Many morphological, syntactic, and semantic formal models are available. Even if many of these approaches are not *cognitively inspired*, we can rely on a good basis of computational models to experiment with our idea of a comparative study between brain activities and machine activities.

Among the others, distributional semantics is an attractive model for our comparative study. Unlike symbolic formal semantics for natural language [16], word meaning is represented in the memory as vectors of real numbers. These vectors can be easily seen as activation images like the activation images of the brain. These idea of observing vectors as images has been also used in the slightly different context of distributed knowledge representation (see [17]). The recently revitalized trend of compositional models for distributional semantics [18–22] produces interesting computational processing models for semantic interpretation of natural language utterances. This is a semantic process and the model along with the distributional semantic vectors can be easily seen as activation images.

The rest of the section is organized as follows. First, section 3.1 introduces to distributional semantic principles and to linear compositional distributional semantic models. Then, section 3.2 describes how these computational models can be easily transformed in activation matrices and, consequently, activation images.

3.1   A Linear Compositional Distributional Semantic Model

Lexical distributional semantics has been largely used to model word meaning in many fields as computational linguistics [23, 24], linguistics [25], corpus linguistics [26], and cognitive research [27]. The fundamental hypothesis is the distributional hypothesis (DH): "similar words share similar contexts" [25]. Recently, this hypothesis has been operationally defined in many ways in the fields of physiology, computational linguistics, and information retrieval [28–30].

Given the successful application to words, distributional semantics has been extended to word sequences. This has happened in two ways: (1) via the reformulation of DH for specific word sequences [31]; and (2) via the definition of compositional distributional semantics (CDS) models [18, 19]. These are two different ways of addressing the problem.

Lin and Pantel [31] propose the *pattern distributional hypothesis* that extends the distributional hypothesis for specific patterns, i.e. word sequences representing partial verb phrases. Distributional meaning for these patterns is derived directly by looking to their occurrences in a corpus. Due to data sparsity, patterns of different length appear with very different frequencies in the corpus, affecting their statistics detrimentally. On the other hand, compositional distributional semantics (CDS) propose to obtain distributional meaning for sequences by composing the vectors of the words in the sequences [18, 19]. This approach is fairly interesting as the distributional meaning of sequences of different length is obtained by composing distributional vectors of single words.

A compositional distributional semantic model aims to compute the distributional meaning of word sequences by composing distributional vectors of individual words. Focussing on 2-word sequences, e.g., z =*close contact*, the CDS model has to compute the distributional vector z for the entire sequence using the distributional vectors u and v of, respectively, *close* and *contact*.

Among all the models, we focus here on the generic *additive* model that sums the vectors u and v in a new vector z:

$$Au + Bv = z \tag{1}$$

where A and B are two square matrices capturing a particular syntactic relation R between the two words, e.g., adjective-noun (JN) for *close contact*. This linear model for semantic processing is extremely interesting as A and B activated by u and v can be easily seen as activation images.

For a good CDS model, we estimate matrices A and B using the methodology described in [20]. We can then have different CDS models for different syntactic relations. In the experiments, we use three different pairs of matrices for three different syntactic relations: adjective-noun (JN), noun-noun (NN), and verb-noun (VN).

3.2   Image-Based Interpretation

Linear CDS are then interesting computational semantic processing models as we can easily interpret them as activation images. This idea is sketched in Figure 1. The original matrices A and B represent a Composition Matrix that is in active process. The Stimulus Vector, that represents the two distributional vectors for the two words, activate the process by producing the Activated Computation Matrix. This latter is then transformed in the final composition distributional vector. Looking the process in this way, we can easily derive an image representing the active state of the semantic composition computational model.

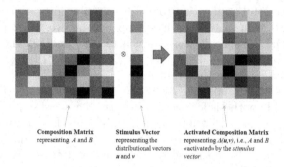

Composition Matrix   Stimulus Vector   Activated Composition Matrix
representing A and B representing the   representing $\Delta(u,v)$, i.e., A and B
   distributional vectors   «activated» by the *stimulus*
   u and v *vector*

Fig. 1. Compositional Distributional Semantics: Activation of the Compositional Matrix

We can derive the above view by looking at the linear equations of the model:

$$Au + Bv = \begin{bmatrix} a_{0,0} & a_{0,1} & a_{0,2} & \cdots & a_{0,n} \\ a_{1,0} & a_{1,1} & a_{1,2} & \cdots & a_{1,n} \\ a_{2,0} & a_{2,1} & a_{2,2} & \cdots & a_{2,n} \\ & & \ddots & & \\ a_{n,0} & a_{n,1} & a_{n,2} & \cdots & a_{n,n} \end{bmatrix} \begin{pmatrix} u_0 \\ u_1 \\ u_2 \\ \vdots \\ u_n \end{pmatrix} + \begin{bmatrix} b_{0,0} & b_{0,1} & b_{0,2} & \cdots & b_{0,n} \\ b_{1,0} & b_{1,1} & b_{1,2} & \cdots & b_{1,n} \\ b_{2,0} & b_{2,1} & b_{2,2} & \cdots & b_{2,n} \\ & & \ddots & & \\ b_{n,0} & b_{n,1} & b_{n,2} & \cdots & b_{n,n} \end{bmatrix} \begin{pmatrix} v_0 \\ v_1 \\ v_2 \\ \vdots \\ v_n \end{pmatrix} =$$

$$= \begin{bmatrix} a_{0,0}u_0 + b_{0,0}v_0 & a_{0,1}u_1 + b_{0,1}v_1 & a_{0,2}u_2 + b_{0,2}v_2 & \cdots & a_{0,n}u_n + b_{0,n}v_n \\ a_{1,0}u_0 + b_{1,0}v_0 & a_{1,1}u_1 + b_{1,1}v_1 & a_{1,2}u_2 + b_{1,2}v_2 & \cdots & a_{1,n}u_n + b_{1,n}v_n \\ a_{2,0}u_0 + b_{2,0}v_0 & a_{2,1}u_1 + b_{2,1}v_1 & a_{2,2}u_2 + b_{2,2}v_2 & \cdots & a_{2,n}u_n + b_{2,n}v_n \\ & & \ddots & & \\ a_{n,0}u_0 + b_{n,0}v_0 & a_{n,1}u_1 + b_{n,1}v_1 & a_{n,2}u_2 + b_{n,2}v_2 & \cdots & a_{n,n}u_n + b_{n,n}v_n \end{bmatrix} \begin{pmatrix} 1 \\ 1 \\ 1 \\ \vdots \\ 1 \end{pmatrix} =$$

$$= \Delta(u,v) \begin{pmatrix} 1 \\ 1 \\ 1 \\ \vdots \\ 1 \end{pmatrix} = z$$

The above derivation describes how it is possible to model the activation of the A and B matrices as a separate step that is done before the final sum. The matrix $\Delta(u, v)$ is then a matrix representing the activation of A and B with respect to the input vectors u and v. Matrices $\Delta(u, v)$ are then easily transformed in activation images as done in [8, 9].

3.3 Decoding Tasks for Computational Semantic Processing

The previous compositional and distributional semantic processing model opens two possible decoding tasks:

T_1) decoding the kind of composition, e.g., deciding whether activation images $\Delta(\boldsymbol{u}, \boldsymbol{v})$ are related to JN, NN, or VN semantic composition activity;

T_2) decoding the semantic types of the involved vectors $\boldsymbol{v}$ and $\boldsymbol{u}$ in the composition looking at the activation matrix $\Delta(\boldsymbol{u}, \boldsymbol{v})$, e.g., decide *animals* vs. *tools*.

4   Estimating the Size of Correlated Brain Areas

We have the opportunity to use the two computational semantic processing tasks to investigate our primary problem. We need now to understand the size of the brain areas that are related to these two tasks. The literature suggests that the two most relevant areas are:

- Brocas area for the syntactic composition task (T_1)
- the fusiform gyri for the animal-vs-tool task (T_2)

We need now to estimate the size of each area in order to tune the size of the computational semantic composition matrices A and B.

4.1   Deciding on Scale of Neural Areas

To model the scale of the neural decoding problem, we should first consider several candidates for basic units of neural hardware: neurons, minicolumns, and macrocolumns.

Neurons instantaneously can be either on or off (like a bit). The cerebrum (that is the cerebral hemispheres, or neocortex), is where the great majority of higher cognition takes place, and it contains about 20 billion of neurons. The precise number varies with age and gender, and estimates are affected by the methodologies adopted by each study. Pakkenberg and colleagues [32] found a wide range across individuals (also of similar ages), from 15 billion to 32 billion, with the mean for females at 18 billion, and for males at 23 billion. Stark and colleagues [33] have very similar average figures for females and males (20 billion and 23 billion). Here we choose a particularly careful whole-brain estimate which found an average of 16 billion over four individuals [34].

Minicolumns are collections of about 100 neurons (so there are 200 million in the cerebrum). One byte could be used to represent the firing rate of each of these neural assemblies [35].

Macrocolumns (also termed hypercolumns, or simply cortical columns) are larger collection of neurons that contain approximately 5000-10000 neurons (so 3 million in cerebrum) [36]. Optimistically, macrocolumns are the smallest structure (3mm deep, spaced at 0.5mm) that can be detected individually with fMRI or MEG. We estimate that the state of a single macrocolumn would require one or more bytes to be represented.

4.2 Dimensions of Relevant Brain Areas

Based on these cortical densities, and volume estimates for functionally relevant parts of the brain, we can estimate the dimensionality needed to model them (see table 1). These numbers are estimated as such. The young healthy brain

Table 1. Brain areas in bytes

Cerebrum	neurons	minicolumns	macrocolumns
size	$2 \cdot 10^{10}$	$2 \cdot 10^8$	$3 \cdot 10^6$
Ram size (instantaneous)	2.5Gb	200MB	3MB
Fusiform gyri (2.8% of cerebrum)			
N	$5.6 \cdot 10^8$	$5.6 \cdot 10^6$	$8.4 \cdot 10^4$
Ram size (instantaneous)	452Mb	4.5 MB	68 kB
Brocas areas (0.5% of cerebrum)			
size	$1 \cdot 10^8$	$1 \cdot 10^6$	$1.5 \cdot 10^4$
Ram size (instantaneous)	80Mb	0.8MB	12kB

has a volume of about 1250 cm^3 (see [37]). The cortical activity detected by fMRI, MEG and EEG is in the cortex, or grey matter surface of the brain tissues. Estimates of grey/white matter proportions vary, and here we use the figure of 1.35 derived from [38] (estimated over 80 individuals of both genders). Taking this ratio, and the estimated volumes from [34], we estimate the amount of grey matter in a typical participant to be approximately 710 cm^3, containing 16 billion neurons. This leads to an estimate of cerebral neural density of 23 million neurons per cm^3, which we assume to be uniform. This density can be used to estimate the number of neurons (and hence micro- and macrocolumns) in a functionally relevant part of the brain.

For the semantic category decoding task we take the fusiform gyri (left and right, part of Brodmann area 37), which have a grey matter volume of approximately 20cm^3 [37]. These areas are involved in high level processing of visual categories (including distinguishing between pictures of living vs non-living things), and which have been shown to have a similar discriminative activity in linguistic tasks (with word stimuli), even in congenitally blind participants who have no visual experience [39].

For the syntactic task, we consider Broca's area, which is generally agreed to be central to processing linguistic structures [40]. Here we take this to cover the pars opercularis and pars triangularis (Brodmann areas 44 and 45) of the left inferior frontal gyrus, with grey-matter volume of 5cm^3 [41].

5   Experimental Investigation

5.1   Experimental Set-Up

Classification Tasks. Two classification tasks have been designed in the context of compositional distributional semantics processing.

The first one aims at distinguishing between the different syntactic relations among the concepts being composed. We considered three syntactic relations: noun-noun (NN), adjective-noun (JN) and verb-object (VN). As specified in Section 3.1, the three classes of compositions are performed by means of different pairs of matrices A and B. The data set included 100 term pairs for each class, selected at random from the set of terms whose distributional vectors were produced. The set was split into a 70% training set and a 30% testing set, uniformly distributed among the three classes. For this experiment, the classifiers were used in the context of a multi-class classification.

In the second experiment, only the JN syntactic relation was considered, but the adjective-noun pairs were chosen among two different semantic domains. The domains are those of *animals* versus *objects*. *Aggressive anteater* and *shy reindeer* are examples of the *animals* class, while *elegant dress* and *modern pot* are examples of the *objects* class. In this case, the experiment tried to relate the composition process to a semantic domain rather than to a syntactic relation. While this task could have been performed on nouns only, we still used noun-adjective pairs to work in the same setting of the first experiment and of the general model presented in the paper. The data set included 123 pairs for each class, and was again split into uniformly distributed 70% training set and a 30% testing set.

Feature Extraction from Activation Images. For learning and applying a classifier, we need to extract specific features from images generated using the activation matrices $\Delta(u, v)$. We then used two major classes of features: chromatic and energetic. Chromaticity features express the color properties of the image. They determine, in particular, a n-dimensional vector representation of the 2D chromaticity histograms. Since chromaticity is invariant against changes in the illuminant color, the intensity information can also be evaluated using simple color histograms, one for each color component R, G and B and the luminance L. Energy features emphasize the background properties and their composition. They are extracted by generating a texture-energy image, and calculating the energy images for the three color channels R, G and B. A more detailed discussion of the theoretical and methodological aspects behind each feature set are presented in [42].

Classifier Learners. For finally building the classifiers of the *"cognitive task"* that the machine is performing, we used three alternative machine learning models. This is useful to see whether or not results are confirmed for any kind of classification method. We then used: a decision tree based learner [43], a simple Naive Bayes classifier (for more information see [44]), and, finally, an instance based learner (IBk) [45]. These machine learning methods have been used in the context of Weka [46].

The three models are different. Decision tree learners capture and select the best features for doing the classification. Naive Bayes learners instead use a simple probabilistic model that considers all the features to be independent.

The instance based learner defines a distance in the feature space, does not make any abstraction of the samples, and classifies new instances according to the distance of these new elements with respect to training samples. While the first model makes a sort of feature selection, the second and the third use all the features for taking the final decision.

Distributional Vector Extraction. Finally, we describe how the distributional vectors were obtained for all experiments of this paper. Raw frequency distributional vectors were obtained from the UKWaC British English web corpus[3]. We considered as contextual window the sentence in which each target word or linguistic unit occurs. Features are contextual words and the weighting scheme is term frequency times inverse document frequency ($tf \times idf$). We applied a crude feature selection using $tf \times idf$ and keeping the first 10.000 dimensions. The resulting distributional vectors constitute a high dimensional vector space model. An SVD reduction with $k = 250$ was then applied to the vector space to build our final distributional vector set.

Learning of the Compositional Matrices. For learning the compositional matrices A and B, we used the methodology described in [9]. As we operated in English, we used the definitions in WordNet [47] to extract training instances for the dictionary-based method. We extracted bigram training instances that follow three syntactic structures, i.e. noun-noun (NN-WN), adjective-noun (JN-WN) and verb-object (VN-WN). Respectively, we used 1220, 6131, and 1317 triples to learn different A and B matrices for NN, JN, and VN. For the details of the methodology, refer to [9].

Dimension of the CDS Matrices. The CDS process is represented by an activation matrix of 500x250 decimal values (in double format, i.e. 8 bytes each). This leads to a byte matrix of size 4000x250, for a total of 1000000 bytes ($\sim$1 MB). Looking at Table 1, the modeled process has an order of magnitude similar to what we would get by observing the Broca's area or the fusiform gyri at the level of the minicolumns. Applying a blurring factor $\sim$10 to the resulting images can simulate the observation at the level of the macrocolumns.

5.2   Results and Analysis

Tables 2 and 3 report the results of the experiments. Both are organized in the same way. The first column reports the different blurring levels we experimented on. The second and third columns give an estimate of the corresponding level of blurring that would arise by observing the brain at the levels of minicolumns and macrocolumns respectively. The estimates are based on the orders of magnitude reported in table 1 for the sizes of the brain areas. The last three columns report the results of the classification task obtained by the three considered classifiers.

---

[3] http://trac.sketchengine.co.uk/wiki/Corpora/UKWaC

Table 2. Test 1: classify JN vs NN vs VN

RAM blurring factor	Minicolumns blurring factor	Macrocolumns blurring factor	Decision Tree	Naive Bayes	IBk
1	1	-	96.67%	98.89%	98.89%
2	2	-	95.56%	98.89%	96.67%
4	4	-	96.67%	98.89%	96.67%
10	10	1	93.33%	98.89%	92.22%
100	100	10	88.89%	92.22%	94.44%

The results of the first experiment are reported in Table 2. The accuracies scored by all the classifiers are very high, even though the task requires a multi-class classification. This comes from the fact that in this experiment both the inactive process (matrices A and B) and the input stimuli (vectors u and v) are different. The introduction of blurring factors has an impact on the results, but still allows for high accuracies.

Table 3. Test 2: classify animals vs objects

RAM blurring factor	Minicolumns blurring factor	Macrocolumns blurring factor	Decision Tree	Naive Bayes	IBk
1	1	-	59,46%	75,68%	54,05%
2	2	-	63,51%	70,27%	64,86%
4	4	-	62,16%	70,27%	63,51%
10	10	1	60,81%	66,22%	52,70%
100	100	10	51,35%	52,70%	54,05%

The results of the second experiment are reported in Table 3. In this case the accuracies are much lower, especially considering that this task requires a binary classification. The introduction of blurring factors has different impacts, depending on the considered classifier. The Naive Bayes classifier is the one that scores higher accuracies, but its performances degrade rapidly when introducing higher blurring levels. The other two classifiers, instead, score lower accuracies, but are less affected by the introduction of blurring factors. In fact, they seem to benefit from a slight blurring.

Notice that the activation matrices in themselves appear to contain enough information to perform a correct classification. In fact, the same experiment run using the explicit activation matrices as features yields an accuracy of 100% for Naive Bayes and IBk, and 91.89% for Decision Trees.

These results are very encouraging, and we hope to build upon them in future work. A priority will be to directly compare our simulations of decoding performance with classification accuracies achieved for neuroimaging data recorded during similar tasks. We also hope to examine the dimension of time (in which EEG and MEG have an advantage over fMRI) and compare the effect of different trade-offs of temporal and spatial resolution that neuroimaging technologies provide.

References

1. Wiener, N.: Cybernetics: Or the Control and Communication in the Animal and the Machine. MIT Press, Cambridge (1948)
2. von Neumann, J.: First draft of a report on the EDVAC. IEEE Ann. Hist. Comput. 15, 27–75 (1993)
3. Turing, A.: Intelligent machinery. In: Meltzer, B., Michie, D. (eds.) Machine Intelligence, vol. 5, pp. 3–23. Edinburgh University Press, Edinburgh (1969)
4. Putnam, H.: Minds and Machines. In: Hook, S. (ed.) Dimensions of Mind, pp. 130–164. Collier Books, New York (1960)
5. Chomsky, N.: Syntactic Structures. The Hague, Mouton (1957)
6. Chomsky, N.: A Review of B. F. Skinner's Verbal Behavior. Language 35, 26–58 (1959)
7. Pinker, S.: How the Mind Works. Norton and Company (2009)
8. Zanzotto, F.M., Croce, D.: Reading What Machines "Think". In: Zhong, N., Li, K., Lu, S., Chen, L. (eds.) BI 2009. LNCS (LNAI), vol. 5819, pp. 159–170. Springer, Heidelberg (2009)
9. Zanzotto, F.M., Croce, D.: Comparing EEG/ERP-Like and fMRI-Like Techniques for Reading Machine Thoughts. In: Yao, Y., Sun, R., Poggio, T., Liu, J., Zhong, N., Huang, J. (eds.) BI 2010. LNCS, vol. 6334, pp. 133–144. Springer, Heidelberg (2010)
10. Prezioso, S., Croce, D., Zanzotto, F.M.: Reading what machines "think": a challenge for nanotechnology. Journal of Computational and Theoretical Nanoscience 8, 1–6 (2011)
11. Haxby, J.V., Gobbini, M.I., Furey, M.L., Ishai, A., Schouten, J.L., Pietrini, P.: Distributed and overlapping representations of faces and objects in ventral temporal cortex. Science 293, 2425–2430 (2001)
12. Murphy, B., Baroni, M., Poesio, M.: EEG responds to conceptual stimuli and corpus semantics. In: Proceedings of EMNLP, pp. 619–627. ACL (2009)
13. Murphy, B., Poesio, M., Bovolo, F., Bruzzone, L., Dalponte, M., Lakany, H.: EEG decoding of semantic category reveals distributed representations for single concepts. Brain and Language 117, 12–22 (2011)
14. Chan, A.M., Halgren, E., Marinkovic, K., Cash, S.S.: Decoding word and category-specific spatiotemporal representations from MEG and EEG. NeuroImage 54, 3028–3039 (2011)
15. Sudre, G., Pomerleau, D., Palatucci, M., Wehbe, L., Fyshe, A., Salmelin, R., Mitchell, T.: Tracking Neural Coding of Perceptual and Semantic Features of Concrete Nouns. NeuroImage 62, 451–463 (2012)
16. Montague, R.: English as a formal language. In: Thomason, R. (ed.) Formal Philosophy: Selected Papers of Richard Montague, pp. 188–221. Yale University Press, New Haven (1974)
17. Plate, T.A.: Distributed Representations and Nested Compositional Structure. PhD thesis (1994)
18. Mitchell, J., Lapata, M.: Vector-based models of semantic composition. In: Proceedings of ACL 2008: HLT, pp. 236–244. Association for Computational Linguistics, Columbus (2008)
19. Jones, M.N., Mewhort, D.J.K.: Representing word meaning and order information in a composite holographic lexicon. Psychological Review 114, 1–37 (2007)
20. Zanzotto, F.M., Korkontzelos, I., Fallucchi, F., Manandhar, S.: Estimating linear models for compositional distributional semantics. In: Proceedings of the 23rd International Conference on Computational Linguistics, COLING (2010)

21. Baroni, M., Zamparelli, R.: Nouns are vectors, adjectives are matrices: Representing adjective-noun constructions in semantic space. In: Proceedings of the 2010 Conference on Empirical Methods in Natural Language Processing, pp. 1183–1193. Association for Computational Linguistics, Cambridge (2010)
22. Guevara, E.: A regression model of adjective-noun compositionality in distributional semantics. In: Proceedings of the 2010 Workshop on GEometrical Models of Natural Language Semantics, pp. 33–37. Association for Computational Linguistics, Uppsala (2010)
23. McCarthy, D., Carroll, J.: Disambiguating nouns, verbs, and adjectives using automatically acquired selectional preferences. Comput. Linguist. 29, 639–654 (2003)
24. Manning, C.D., Raghavan, P., Schütze, H.: Introduction to Information Retrieval. Cambridge University Press, Cambridge (2008)
25. Harris, Z.: Distributional structure. In: Katz, J.J., Fodor, J.A. (eds.) The Philosophy of Linguistics. Oxford University Press, New York (1964)
26. Firth, J.R.: Papers in Linguistics. Oxford University Press, Oxford (1957)
27. Miller, G.A., Charles, W.G.: Contextual correlates of semantic similarity. Language and Cognitive Processes VI, 1–28 (1991)
28. Lund, K., Burgess, C.: Producing high-dimensional semantic spaces from lexical co-occurrence. Behavior Research Methods, Instrumentation, and Computers 28, 203–208 (1996)
29. Pado, S., Lapata, M.: Dependency-based construction of semantic space models. Computational Linguistics 33, 161–199 (2007)
30. Deerwester, S.C., Dumais, S.T., Landauer, T.K., Furnas, G.W., Harshman, R.A.: Indexing by latent semantic analysis. Journal of the American Society of Information Science 41, 391–407 (1990)
31. Lin, D., Pantel, P.: DIRT-discovery of inference rules from text. In: Proceedings of the ACM Conference on Knowledge Discovery and Data Mining (KDD 2001), San Francisco, CA (2001)
32. Pakkenberg, B., Gundersen, H.J.: Neocortical neuron number in humans: effect of sex and age. Journal of Comparative Neurology 384, 312–320 (1997)
33. Stark, A., Toft, M., Pakkenberg, H., Fabricius, K., Eriksen, N., Pelvig, D., Møller, M., Pakkenberg, B.: The effect of age and gender on the volume and size distribution of neocortical neurons. Neuroscience 150, 121–130 (2007)
34. Azevedo, F.A.C., Carvalho, L.R.B., Grinberg, L.T., Farfel, J.M., Ferretti, R.E.L., Leite, R.E.P., Jacob Filho, W., Lent, R., Herculano-Houzel, S.: Equal numbers of neuronal and nonneuronal cells make the human brain an isometrically scaled-up primate brain. Journal of Comparative Neurology 513, 532–541 (2009)
35. Buxhoeveden, D.P., Casanova, M.F.: The minicolumn hypothesis in neuroscience. Brain: A Journal of Neurology 125, 935–951 (2002)
36. Mountcastle, V.B.: The columnar organization of the neocortex. Brain: A Journal of Neurology 120, 701–722 (1997)
37. Raz, N., Gunning-Dixon, F., Head, D., Rodrigue, K.M., Williamson, A., Acker, J.D.: Aging, sexual dimorphism, and hemispheric asymmetry of the cerebral cortex: replicability of regional differences in volume. Neurobiol. Aging. 25, 377–396 (2004)
38. Gur, R.C., Turetsky, B.I., Matsui, M., Yan, M., Bilker, W., Hughett, P., Gur, R.E.: Sex differences in brain gray and white matter in healthy young adults: correlations with cognitive performance. J. Neurosci. 19, 4065–4072 (1999)
39. Mahon, B.Z., Anzellotti, S., Schwarzbach, J., Zampini, M., Caramazza, A.: Category-specific organization in the human brain does not require visual experience. Neuron 63, 397–405 (2009)

40. Hagoort, P.: On Broca, brain, and binding: a new framework. Trends in Cognitive Sciences 9, 416–423 (2005)
41. Yamasaki, S., Yamasue, H., Abe, O., Suga, M., Yamada, H., Inoue, H., Kuwabara, H., Kawakubo, Y., Yahata, N., Aoki, S., Kano, Y., Kato, N., Kasai, K.: Reduced gray matter volume of pars opercularis is associated with impaired social communication in high-functioning autism spectrum disorders. Biol. Psychiatry 68, 1141–1147 (2010)
42. Alvarado, P., Doerfler, P., Wickel, J.: Axon^2 - a visual object recognition system for non-rigid objects. In: IASTED International Conference-Signal Processing, Pattern Recognition and Applications (SPPRA), pp. 235–240. Rhodes, IASTED (2001)
43. Quinlan, R.J.: C4.5: Programs for Machine Learning. Morgan Kaufmann Series in Machine Learning. Morgan Kaufmann (1993)
44. John, G.H., Langley, P.: Estimating continuous distributions in bayesian classifiers, pp. 338–345 (1995)
45. Aha, D.W., Kibler, D., Albert, M.K.: Instance-based learning algorithms. Mach. Learn. 6, 37–66 (1991)
46. Witten, I.H., Frank, E.: Data Mining: Practical Machine Learning Tools and Techniques with Java Implementations. Morgan Kaufmann, Chicago (1999)
47. Miller, G.A.: WordNet: A lexical database for English. Communications of the ACM 38, 39–41 (1995)

Detecting Emotion from EEG Signals
Using the Emotive Epoc Device

Rafael Ramirez and Zacharias Vamvakousis

Department of Information and Communication Technologies
Universitat Pompeu Fabra
Roc Boronat 138, 08018 Barcelona, Spain
{rafael.ramirez,zacharias.vamvakousis}@upf.edu

Abstract. The study of emotions in human-computer interaction has increased in recent years in an attempt to address new user needs. At the same time, it is possible to record brain activity in real-time and discover patterns to relate it to emotional states. This paper describes a machine learning approach to detect emotion from brain activity, recorded as electroencephalograph (EEG) with the Emotic Epoc device, during auditory stimulation. First, we extract features from the EEG signals in order to characterize states of mind in the arousal-valence 2D emotion model. Using these features we apply machine learning techniques to classify EEG signals into high/low arousal and positive/negative valence emotional states. The obtained classifiers may be used to categorize emotions such as happiness, anger, sadness, and calm based on EEG data.

1 Introduction

The study of emotions in human-computer interaction has increased in recent years. This is due to the growing need for computer applications capable of detecting the emotional state of users [17]. Motivated by every day interaction among humans, a great part of the research in this area has explored detecting emotions from facial and voice information. Under controlled situations, current emotion-detection computer systems based on such information are able to classify emotions with considerable accuracy [18]. However, emotions are not always manifested by means of facial expressions and voice information. Psychologists distinguish between physiological arousal, behavioral expression, and the conscious experience of emotions. Facial and voice information is related only to behavioral expression which can be consciously controlled and modified, and which interpretation is often subjective. Thus, other approaches to detect emotion have been proposed which focus on different physiological information such as heart rate, skin conductance, and pupil dilation [18,16]. A still relatively new field of research in affective brain-computer interaction attempts to detect emotion using electroencephalograms (EEGs) [2,3]. There have been several approaches to EEG-based emotion detection, but there is still little consensus about definite conclusions.

F.M. Zanzotto et al. (Eds.): BI 2012, LNCS 7670, pp. 175–184, 2012.

In this paper we describe an approach to detecting emotion from electroencephalogram signals measured with a (low-cost) Emotiv EPOC headset. We present to subjects auditory stimuli from a library of emotion-annotated sounds and record their response EEG activity. We then filter and process the signal in order to extract emotion-related features and apply machine learning techniques to classify emotional states into high/low arousal and positive/negative valence (e.g. happiness is a state with high arousal and positive valence, whereas sadness is a state with low arousal and negative valence). Our approach differs from previous works in that we do not rely in subject self-reported emotional states during stimuli presentation. Instead, we use a library of emotion-annotated sounds publicly available for emotional research. Figure 1 illustrates the different steps of our approach.

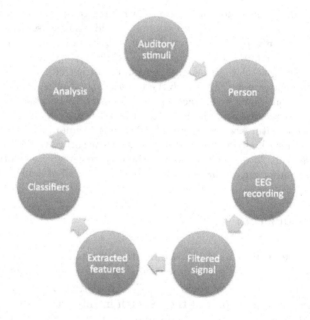

Fig. 1. Schematic view of the system

The rest of the paper is organized as follows: Section 2 presents background to this research. Section 3 described the data collection process and methods. In Section 4 we describe our approach to EEG-based emotion classification and report the results, and finally Section 5 presents some conclusions and further research.

2   Background

The firing of neurons in the brain trigger voltage changes. The electrical activity measured by the electrodes in an EEG headset corresponds to the field potentials resulting from the combined activity of many individual neuronal cells in the brain cortex. However, the measured cortical activity is distorted by the tissue and skull between the electrodes and the neurons. This introduces noise and reduce the intensity of the recorded signals. In despite of this, EEG measurements still provide important insight into the electrical activity of the cortex.

The frequency of EEG measurements ranges from 1 to 80Hz, with amplitudes of 10 to 100 microvolts [9]. Signal frequencies have been divided into different bands, since specific frequency waves are normally more prominent in particular states of mind. The two most important frequency waves are the alpha waves (8-12Hz) and the beta waves (12-30Hz). Alpha waves predominantly originate during wakeful relaxation mental states, and are most visible over the parietal and occipital lobes. Intense alpha wave activity have also been correlated to brain inactivation. Beta wave activity, on the other hand, is related to an active state of mind, most prominent in the frontal cortex during intense focused mental activity [9].

Alpha and beta wave activity may be used in different ways for detecting emotional (arousal and valence) states of mind in humans (more details later). Choppin [3] propose to use EEG signals for classifying six emotions using neural networks. Choppin's approach is based on emotional valence and arousal by characterizing valence, arousal and dominance from EEG signals. He characterize positive emotions by a high frontal coherence in alpha, and high right parietal beta power. Higher arousal (excitation) is characterized by a higher beta power and coherence in the parietal lobe, plus lower alpha activity, while dominance (strength) of an emotion is characterized as an increase in the beta / alpha activity ratio in the frontal lobe, plus an increase in beta activity at the parietal lobe.

Oude [14] describes an approach to recognize emotion from EEG signals measured with the BraInquiry EEG PET device. He uses a limited number of electrodes and trains a linear classifier based on Fishers discriminant analysis. He considers audio, visual and audiovisual stimuli and trains classifies for positive/negative, aroused/calm and audio/visual/audiovisual.

Takahashi [18] use a headband of three dry electrodes to classify five emotions (joy, anger, sadness, fear, and relaxation) based on multiple bio-potential signals (EEG, pulse, and skin conductance). He trains classifiers using support vector machines and reports the resulting classifying accuracy both using the whole set of bio-potential signals, and solely based on EEG signals.

Lin at al. [10] apply machine-learning techniques to categorize EEG signals according to subject self-reported emotional states during music listening. They propose a framework for systematically seeking emotion-specific EEG features and exploring the accuracy of the classifiers. In particular, they apply support vector machines to classify four emotional states: joy, anger, sadness, and pleasure.

3   Data Collection

EEG data in this study were collected from 6 healthy subjects (3 males and 3 females) with average age of 30.16 during listening to emotion-annotated sounds.

For collecting the data we used the Emotiv EPOC headset, recently released by the Emotiv Company [7]. This headset consists of 14 data-collecting electrodes and 2 reference electrodes, located and labeled according to the international 10-20 system [12]. Following the international standard, the available locations are: AF3, F7, F3, FC5, T7, P7, O1, O2, P8, T8, FC6, F4, F8 and AF4. Figure 2 shows the 14 Emotiv EPOC headset electrode positions. The EEG signals are transmitted wirelessly to a laptop computer.

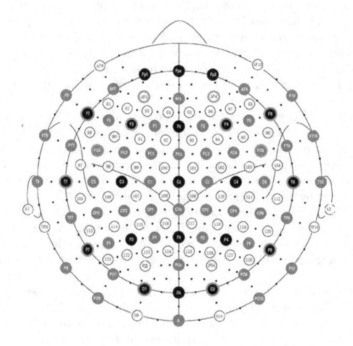

Fig. 2. Emotiv EPOC headset electrode positioning

Subjects were instructed to look at a cross in the a computer screen and to remain seated during the experiment. Subjects listened to selected sounds from the IADS library of emotion-annotated sounds [1] which is available for emotion research. Based on the annotations provided by the stimuli databases, we selected 12 sound stimuli situated in the extremes on the arousal-valence emotion plane: three positive/aroused, three positive/calm, three negative/calm, and three negative/aroused. The stimuli were selected to be as much as possible on the extremes of the two-dimensional emotion plane and as unanimous as possible, since we do not consider self-reporting information to cater for person-dependent deviations.

Initially, the subjects are informed about the experiment procedure and instructed to follow the usual guidelines during stimuli presentation (e.g. do not blink or move). Once this was done, 12 sound stimuli are randomly presented each one for five seconds and a 10 second silent rest is inserted between stimuli.

The purpose of the 10 second silent rests is to set a neutral emotional state of mind in between stimuli.

4   Data Classification

4.1   Feature Extraction

As mentioned in the previous section, in EEG signals the alpha (8-12Hz) and beta (12-30Hz) bands are particular bands of interest in emotion research for both valence and arousal [13]. The presence of EOG artifacts (eye movement/blinking) is most dominant below 4Hz, ECG (heart) artifacts around 1.2Hz, and EMG (muscle) artifacts above 30Hz. Non physiological artifacts caused by power lines are normally present above 50Hz [6,5].

Thus, fortunately a byproduct of extracting the alpha and beta frequencies is that much of the noise present in EEG signals is considerably reduced. We apply bandpass filtering for extracting alpha and beta frequency bands. Using Fourier frequency analysis, the original signal is split up in frequencies in order to remove specific frequencies, before transforming back the signal with only the frequencies of interest. For this research, we apply the bandpass filter implementation provided by the OpenVibe software [15].

From the EEG signal of a person, we determine the level of arousal, i.e. how relaxed or excited the person is, by computing the ratio of the beta and alpha brainwaves as recorded by the EEG. We measure the EEG signal in four locations (i.e. electrodes) in the prefrontal cortex: AF3, AF4, F3 and F4 (see Figure 2). As mentioned before, beta waves are associated with an alert or excited state of mind, whereas alpha waves are more dominant in a relaxed state. Alpha activity has also been associated to brain inactivation. Thus, the beta/alpha ratio is a reasonable indicator of the arousal state of a person.

In order to determine the valence level, i.e. negative or positive state of mind, we compare the activation levels of the two cortical hemispheres. This is motivated by psychophysiological research which has shown the importance of the difference in activation between the cortical hemispheres. Left frontal inactivation is an indicator of a withdrawal response, which is often linked to a negative emotion. On the other hand, right frontal inactivation may be associated to an approach response, or positive emotion.

As mentioned before, high alpha activity is an indication of low brain activity, and vice versa. Thus, an increase in alpha activity together with a decrease in beta waves may be associated with cortical inactivation [13]. F3 and F4 are the most used positions for looking at this alpha activity, as they are located in the prefrontal lobe which plays a crucial role in emotion regulation and conscious experience.

Although previous research suggests that hemispherical differences are not an indication of affective valence (feeling a positive or negative emotion), it has been suggested that it is an indication of motivational direction (approach or withdrawal behavior to the stimulus) [8]. In general, however, affective valence is related to motivational direction. Therefore, comparing hemispherical activation seems to be a reasonable method to detect valence. Thus, we estimate the valence value in a person by computing and comparing the alpha power a and beta power b in channels F3 and F4. Specifically,

$$valence = a_{F4}/b_{F4} - a_{F3}/b_{F3}.$$

4.2   Learning Task

In this section we describe our approach to training and evaluating classifiers for the task of detecting the emotional state of mind of a person given the person's observed EEG data. We approach this problem as a two 2-class classification problem. In particular, we apply machine learning techniques to classify high/low arousal and positive/negative valence emotional states. The obtained classifiers can be used to classify emotions such as happiness, anger, sadness, and calm. Figure 3 shows these emotions in the arousal/valence plane.

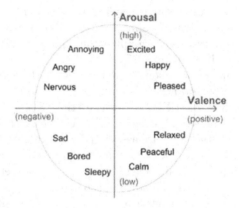

Fig. 3. Emotional states and their positions in the valence/arousal plane

We are interested in inducing two classifiers of the following forms:

$$ArousalClassifier(EEGdata([t, t + c])) \rightarrow \{high, low\}$$

and

$$ValenceClassifier(EEGdata([t, t + c])) \rightarrow \{positive, negative\}$$

where $EEGdata([t, t + c])$ is the EEG data observed at time interval $[t, t + c]$ and $\{high, low\}$ and $\{positive, negative\}$ are the sets of emotional states to be discriminated. The results reported in this paper are obtained with c=1s and with increments of t of 0.0625s. For each subject in the EEG data sets we train a separate classifier.

4.3 Algorithms

In this paper we evaluate two classifiers, Linear Discriminant Analysis (LDA) [11] and Support Vector Machines (SVM) [4], for classifying an emotion state for each EEG segment. Linear discriminant analysis and the related Fisher's linear discriminant are methods used in statistics, pattern recognition and machine learning to find a linear combination of features which characterizes or separates two or more classes of objects or events. The resulting combination may be used as a linear classifier. LDA is closely related to regression analysis, which also attempt to express one dependent variable as a linear combination of other features. In regression analysis however, the dependent variable is a numerical quantity, while for LDA it is a categorical variable (i.e. the class label).

On the other hand, SVM is one of the most popular supervised learning algorithms for solving classification problems. The basic idea in SVM is to project input data onto a higher dimensional feature space via a kernel transfer function, which is easier to be separated than that in the original feature space. Depending on input data, the iterative learning process of SVM would eventually converge into optimal hyperplanes with maximal margins between each class. These hyperplanes would be the decision boundaries for distinguishing different data clusters. Here, we use linear and radial basis function (RBF) kernel to map data onto a higher dimension space. The results reported are obtained using the LDA and SVM implementations in the OpenVibe software [15].

We evaluated each induced classifier by performing the standard 10-fold cross validation in which 10% of the training set is held out in turn as test data while the remaining 90% is used as training data. When performing the 10-fold cross validation, we leave out the same number of examples per class. In the data sets, the number of examples is the same for each class considered, thus by leaving out the same number of examples per class we maintain a balanced training set.

4.4 Results

Given that we are dealing with 2-class classification tasks and that the number of instances in each class is the same, the expected classification accuracy of the default classifier (one which chooses the most common class) is 50% (measured in correctly classified instances percentage). For the high-versus-low arousal, and the positive-versus-negative valence classifiers the average accuracies obtained for SVM with radial basis function kernel classifier were 77.82%, and 80.11%, respectively. For these classifiers the best subject's accuracies were 83,35%, and 86.33%, respectively. The correctly classified instances percentage for each subject and each learning method is presented in Figures 4 and 5.

4.5 Discussion

The difference between the results obtained and the accuracy of a baseline classifier, i.e. a classifier guessing at random confirms that the EEG data contains sufficient information to distinguish between high/low arousal and positive/negative

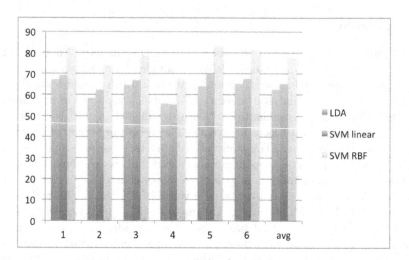

Fig. 4. Classifiers (LDA, SVM with linear kernel, and SVM with radial basis function kernel) accuracies for high-versus-low arousal for all subjects

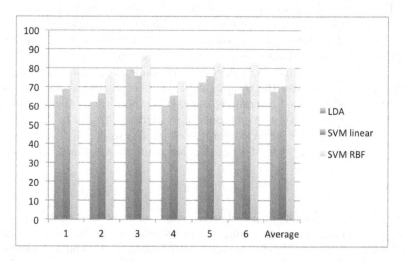

Fig. 5. Classifiers (LDA, SVM with linear kernel, and SVM with radial basis function kernel) accuracies for positive-versus-negative valence for all subjects

valence states, and that machine learning methods are capable of learning the EGG patterns that distinguish these states. It is worth noting that both learning algorithm investigated (LDA and SVM) produced better than random classification accuracies. This supports our statement about the feasibility of training classifiers using the Emotiv Epoc for the tasks reported.

The accuracy of the classifiers for the same task for different subjects varies significantly, even using the same learning method. Subjects producing high accuracies with one learning method tend to produce high accuracies with the other learning methods. These uneven accuracies among subjects may be due to different degrees of emotional response between different individuals, or to the amount of noise for different subjects. In any case, it has been reported that there exists considerable variation in EEG responses among different subjects.

It is worth mentioning that in all the experiments performed we provided no self-assessment information about the emotional states by the subjects. This contrasts with other approaches (e.g. [10]) where EEG data is categorized according to subject self-reported emotional states. Incorporating self-assessment information would very likely improve the accuracies of the classifiers.

5 Conclusion

We have explored and compared two machine learning techniques for the problem of classifying the emotional state of a person based on EEG data using the Emotiv Epoc headset. We considered two machine learning techniques: linear discriminant analysis and support vector machines. We presented the results of the induced classifiers which are able to discriminate between high-versus-low arousal and positive-versus-negative valence. Our results indicate that EEG data obtained with the Emotiv Epoc device contains sufficient information to distinguish these emotional states, and that machine learning techniques are capable of learning the patterns that distinguish these states. Furthermore, we proved that it is possible to train successful classifiers with no to self-assessment of information about the emotional states by the subjects. As future work, we are particularly interested in systematically exploring different feature extraction methods and learning methods in order to improve the accuracy of the induced classifiers.

Acknowledgments. This work is supported by the Spanish TIN project DRIMS (TIN2009-14274-C02-01).

References

1. Bradley, M.M., Lang, P.J.: International Affective Digitized Sounds (IADS): Stimuli, Instruction Manual and Affective Ratings. The Center for Research in Psychophysiology, University of Florida, Gainesville, FL, USA (1999)
2. Chanel, G., Kronegg, J., Grandjean, D., Pun, T.: Emotion Assessment: Arousal Evaluation Using EEG's and Peripheral Physiological Signals. In: Gunsel, B., Jain, A.K., Tekalp, A.M., Sankur, B. (eds.) MRCS 2006. LNCS, vol. 4105, pp. 530–537. Springer, Heidelberg (2006)
3. Choppin, A.: Eeg-based human interface for disabled individuals: Emotion expression with neural networks. Masters thesis, Tokyo Institute of Technology, Yokohama, Japan (2000)
4. Cristianini, N., Shawe-Taylor, J.: An Introduction to Support Vector Machines. Cambridge University Press (2000)

5. Coburn, K., Moreno, M.: Facts and artifacts in brain electrical activity mapping. Brain Topography 1(1), 37–45 (1988)
6. Fatourechi, M., Bashashati, A., Ward, R.K., Birch, G.E.: EMG and EOG artifacts in brain computer interface systems: A survey. Clininical Neurophysiology (118), 480–494 (2007)
7. Emotiv Systems Inc. Researchers, http://www.emotiv.com/researchers/
8. Harmon-Jones, E.: Clarifying the emotive functions of asymmetrical frontal cortical activity. Psychophysiology 40(6), 838–848 (2003)
9. Kandel, E.R., Schwartz, J.H., Jessell, T.M.: Principles of Neural Science. Mc Graw Hill (2000)
10. Lin, Y.-P., Wang, C.-H., Jung, T.-P., Wu, T.-L., Jeng, S.-K., Duann, J.-R., Chen, J.-H.: EEG-Based Emotion Recognition in Music Listening. IEEE Transactions on Biomedical Engineering 57(7) (2010)
11. Mika, S., et al.: Fisher Discriminant Analysis with Kernels. In: IEEE Conference on Neural Networks for Signal Processing IX, pp. 41–48 (1999)
12. Niedermeyer, E., da Silva, F.L.: Electroencephalography, Basic Principles, Clinical Applications, and Related Fields, p. 140. Lippincott Williams & Wilkins (2004)
13. Niemic, C.P.: Studies of emotion: A theoretical and empirical review of psychophysiological studies of emotion. Journal of Undergraduate Research 1, 15–18 (2002)
14. Bos, D.O.: EEG-based Emotion Recognition: The Influence of Visual and Auditory Stimuli
15. OpenViBE: An Open-Source Software Platform to Design, Test, and Use Brain-Computer Interfaces in Real and Virtual Environments. MIT Press Journal Presence' 19(1), 35–53 (2010)
16. Partala, T., Jokiniemi, M., Surakka, V.: Pupillary responses to emotionally provocative stimuli. In: ETRA 2000: Proceedings of the 2000 Symposium on Eye Tracking Research & Applications, pp. 123–129. ACM Press, New York (2000)
17. Picard, R.W., Klein, J.: Toward computers that recognize and respond to user emotion: Theoretical and practical implications. Interacting with Computers 14(2), 141–169 (2002)
18. Takahashi, K.: Remarks on emotion recognition from bio-potential signals. In: 2nd International Conference on Autonomous Robots and Agents, pp. 186–191 (2004)

An Efficient Visibility Graph Similarity Algorithm and Its Application on Sleep Stages Classification

Guohun Zhu[1,3], Yan Li[1,3], and Peng Paul Wen[2,3]

[1] Department of Mathematics and Computing, University of Southern Queensland
[2] Faculty of Engineering and Surveying, University of Southern Queensland
[3] Centre for Systems Biology, University of Southern Queensland
Toowoomba, QLD 4350, Australia
{Guohun.Zhu,Yan.Li,Peng.Wen}@usq.edu.au

Abstract. This paper presents an efficient horizontal visibility directed graph similarity algorithm (HVDS) by taking the advantages of two synchronization measuring methods in graph theory: phase locking value (PLV) and visibility graph similarity (VGS). It develops a new linear horizontal visibility graph constructing algorithm, analyzes its constructing complexity, and tests its feature performance via the sleep stages identification application. Six features are extracted, separately, from HVDS, PLV and VGS as the input to a support vector machine to classify the seven sleep stages. 11,120 data segments are used for the experiments with each segment lasts 30 seconds. The training sets are selected from a single subject and the testing sets are selected from multiple subjects. 10-cross-validation is employed to evaluate the performances of the PLV, VGS and HVDS methods. The experimental results show that the PLV, VGS and HVDS algorithms produce an average classification accuracy of 72.3%, 81.5% and 82.6%, respectively. The speed of the HVDS is 39 times faster than the VGS algorithm.

Keywords: Computational complexity, phase locking value, horizontal visibility directed graph similarity, classification sleep stage, synchronization.

1 Introduction

Synchronization is a common phenomenon in the human brain. Several synchrony measurements based on electroencephalography (EEG) signals have been presented in recent years. Cross correlation [1] and coherence function [2] are two simple and linear methods to measure the interdependency between two channels of EEGs in both time and frequency domains. Nonlinear synchronization approaches, such as phase locking value (PLV) [3], synchronization likelihood (SL) [4] and visibility graph similarity (VGS) [5], appear more powerful to solve the problems of time series signals.

Several existing nonlinear synchronization methods have been successfully used to study EEG signals, especially the sleep EEG signals. Aijun He [6] proposed a PLV method for sleep stages identification. Acharya [7] then applied the concept to

F.M. Zanzotto et al. (Eds.): BI 2012, LNCS 7670, pp. 185–195, 2012.
© Springer-Verlag Berlin Heidelberg 2012

classify the levels of fatigue and sleepiness. Ferri [8] showed that there were high levels of synchronization in the slow-wave sleep EEG signals by means of a SL method, and also showed that the synchronization of EEG slow-waves during sleep has the features of a small-world network [9]. Aksahin [10] used a coherence function to classify the sleep apnea syndromes.

A VGS based method has shown a much better performance than the coherence function and SL methods on measuring the synchrony of time series signals [5]. It uses the cross correlation to evaluate the degree sequence from two visibility graphs (VGs). A VG is a mapping from a time series signal to a graph based on its geometric visibility features. It is widely used to study human heartbeat dynamics [11, 12], Alzheimer's disease [13] , currency exchange rate [14] and environmental problem [15]. However, a VGS based method has never been applied to study EEGs in the literature. It is probably because the computation of constructing a VG is very slow and it can't process large data points in one data segment. For example, BrainWave software [16] can't process more than 512 data points in one segment.

This paper presents an efficient horizontal visibility directed graph similarity (HVDS). The proposed HVDS method performs better than the VGS, and has a faster computing speed than the PLV. In order to compare their performances, the three synchrony measuring methods, PLV, VGS and HVDS, are applied to test sleep stages classification. For each of the three algorithms, firstly, two channels of EEG data (Fpz-Cz and Pz-Oz) and one EOG (the horizontal) signal are used and filtered in delta and theta bands. Secondly, six synchronization features are extracted and forwarded as the input to a support vector machine algorithm, LIBSVM [17], to classify the seven sleep stages. There are 1390 segments of data forming the training set, and totally 11120 segments of data from four subjects are used for testing. The performances of the PLV, VGS and HVDS algorithms are then compared in the paper.

This paper is organized as follows: the experimental data are briefly introduced in the next section. The proposed horizontal visibility directed graph similarity (HVDS) algorithm and other several synchronization measuring methods, such as PLV, VGS and FHVG, are introduced in Section 3. Section 4 presents the experiment results. Finally, the conclusions are drawn in Section 5.

2   The Experimental Data

The experimental data used in this paper were obtained from the public Sleep-EDF database [14], which is part of Physionet data bank [18]. Because sleep is a complex and important biological process for humans, efficient automatically identifying the sleep stages is still very challenging [19].

Four data recordings from subjects: sc4002e0, sc4012e0, sc4102e0 and sc4112e0, were used in this paper. The data were recorded in 1989 from two healthy males and two healthy females between the age of 21 and 35. The recorded data of a subject was saved in an EDF-File and each file of the sleep recordings included one horizontal EOG, two EEG channels (Fpz-Cz and Pz-Oz), submental electromyogram (EMG) envelope, oronasal airflow, and rectal body temperature. The first three signals were sampled at 100 Hz. This paper selected three signals: the two EEG channels signals and the EOG recording, to perform an automatic sleep stage classification. The interval of each segment (or epoch) in this study was defined as 30 seconds, and thus each signal in one segment contains 3000 data points.   The sleep stages of these segments were labeled with one of the seven classes: Awa (wakefulness), St1 (sleep stage 1), St2 (sleep stage 2), St3 (sleep stage 3), St4 (sleep stage 4), REM (rapid eye-movement) and MVT (REM sleep plus the duration of body movement).

Note that the size of recording of sc4112e0 has only 2780 segments although others three recordings are beyond 2800 segments. Therefore, this study only uses the segments from 1 to 2780 for all four subjects, with a total of 11,120 data segments.

3   The Methodology

The procedure of the proposed method is shown in Fig.1. Note that the synchrony measures include three methods, the PLV, VGS and HVDS, that are processed separately. The LIBSVM involves the training stage and the testing stage, with the size of training data is only 12.5% of the size of testing sets.

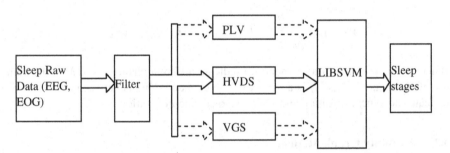

Fig. 1. Algorithm Diagram

3.1   Preprocessing

The raw sleep EEG and EOG signals as shown in Fig.1 are filtered by a band pass FIR filter. Based on the sleep EEG characteristics [20], two bands of waves, delta band (0.5-4 Hz) and theta band (4-8Hz), are most influential. The two bands of data are, therefore, filtered out on each segment, individually, and used in this study.

3.2   Mean Phase Locking Value Method

Phase locking value (PLV) is also called the phase synchronization index.   It assumes that two time series, $x_1(t)$ and $x_2(t)$, are synchronized if their phase difference of $\theta_1(t)$ and $\theta_2(t)$ satisfies the following equation:

$$| m\theta_1(t) - n\theta_2(t) |= constant \qquad (1)$$

In this study, $m = n = 1$, because the sources of signals come from the same brain and with the same sampling frequency. The algorithm is divided into two steps. The first step is to estimate the phase of the input time series $x_i(t)_{i=1..N}$. The phase of a signal can be calculated either with a Hilbert transform method or a wavelet approach [15]. This paper uses the Hilbert method. Each data point of the time series has a Hilbert phase:

$$\theta_i(t) = \left(\frac{\tilde{x}_i(t)}{x_i(t)} \right) \tag{2}$$

Where $\tilde{x}(t)$ is the Hilbert transform of $x(t)$:

$$\tilde{x}(t) = \frac{1}{\pi} p.v. \int_{-\infty}^{+\infty} \frac{x(t')}{t-t'} dt' \tag{3}$$

Where $p.v$ denotes the Cauchy principal value.

The second step calculates the quantification of the mean phase locking value between channels, $\theta_i(t)$ and $\theta_j(t)$.

$$\rho(i,j) = |\frac{1}{N} \sum_{t=1}^{N} e^{i(\theta_i(t)-\theta_j(t))}|; \quad i, j \in [1..M] \tag{4}$$

Where N is the length of a segment; i, j indicate different channels and M is the number of channels used; $\rho(i,j)$ is a matrix whose element value is between 0 to 1, with 0 indicates no synchronization and 1 for an exact synchronization.

3.3   Visibility Graph Method

The visibility graph (VG) method is a powerful tool for time series analyses. It maps a time series, $x(t)_{(t=1...n)}$, to a graph **G**, and characterizes the data point x_i, with the degree of a node v_i in **G**. The degree v_i is the number of connected edges of v_i in **G**.

In the literature, given any two points (t_i, x_i) and (t_j, x_j), the edge between v_i and v_j has two rules to be defined in VG. The first rule proposed by Lacasa, et al. [21] is named as a visibility graph. The nodes, v_i and v_j, in a VG are connected if and only if:

$$\forall k \in (i,j); \quad \frac{(x_j - x_k)}{j-k} > \frac{(x_j - x_i)}{j-i} \tag{5}$$

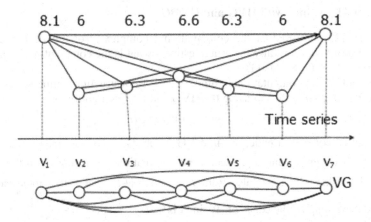

Fig. 2. Illustration of the time series (upper part) into its visibility graph (bottom part)

Fig. 2 shows a time series *{8.1,6.0,6.3 ,6.6 , 6.3,6.0,8.1}* and it's visibility graph. v_1 is the first node of the graph corresponding to *8.1*. The time series is characterized with a degree sequence in VG. For example, the degree sequence of VG in Fig. 2 is *{6,3,4,4,4,3,6}* .

The second rule was introduced by Luque, et al. [22] which was named as a horizontal visibility graph (HVG). The arcs, v_i to v_j , in a HVG is existed if and only if:

$$\forall k \in (i, j) ; \quad x_i > x_k \quad \text{and} \quad x_j > x_k \tag{6}$$

One of the HVG versions is the directed graph which was named as horizontal visibility directed graph (HVDG) in [22]. HVDG is always acyclic (without cycle), which implies that the out degree of the first node (or terminal node if in a reverse direction) is always zero. An out-degree $d(v_i)$ is the number of arc connections from v_i to others nodes.

Fig.3 shows a time series *{8.1,6,6.3, 6.5, 6.3,6,8.1}* and it's HVDG. The out degree sequence in Fig. 3 is *{0,1,2,2,1,1,4}* .

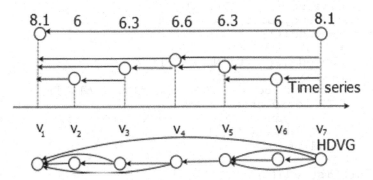

Fig. 3. Illustration of the time series (upper part) into its HVG (bottom part)

3.4   Fast Algorithms with HVG and HVDG

Gutin et al. [23] proved that the computational complexity of identifying a HVG graph is linear. This naturally raises a question - what is the computational complexity to construct a VG or a HVG?

Let us look at the computational complexities of constructing a time series with n points of data to an n-node VG using the HVG and HVGS algorithms.

Lemma 1: The complexity of constructing a VG is $O(n^3)$.

Proof: Let us consider a node, v_i , in a VG graph, **G**.   To determine whether there is an edge between v_i and v_j , according to equation (5), it requires |j-i| comparisons for the task.   Since j is also from $1, ..., i-1, i+1, ... n$,   the total executing time for determining all the edges of v_i in **G** is $1+2+...+n-1 = \dfrac{n(n-1)}{2}$.

As there are n nodes to be considered, the total complexity of constructing a VG is $\dfrac{\left(n^3 - n^2\right)}{2}$.   □

Since a HVG graph is a sub-graph of a VG [19], the HVG algorithm based on equation (6) would have the same complexity of the VG, which indicates that both HVG and VG algorithms are very slow, and are impossible to be applied for many applications, especially for real time applications.

For example, the VG algorithm is implemented as a function in BrainWave software package [22]. The execution of the function is very slow, and any data points that are more than the size of 512 samples are truncated. For the sleep-EDF dataset, the   length of each segment is 2780 or 3000 data points. Apparently a more efficient algorithm is required to process the dataset.

To overcome the computational complexity problem in equations (5) and (6), this paper proposes an improved HVG algorithm: fast HVG (FHVG). The key concept of the FHVG is that a maximal pole (value) is always visible to its neighbor's maximal pole, even the distance in between is more than two nodes.   All the maximal values in a time series are stored in a sorting list which is named "SortList" in the FHVG algorithm, and it is empty when the index is zero.

```
Algorithm:   FHVG (Fast constructing HVG)
Input: a time series   X[1..n]
Output: Adjacency List   Node[1..n]
1     SortList.add(1)
2     For i=2 to n
3         Connect Node[i] to Node[i-1]
4         If X[i]>X[i-1]   then
5             Search Loc while SortList[0..Loc]<X[i]
6             IF Loc>0 then
7                 Connect Node[i] to Node[SortList[1..Loc]]
8                 Remove [1..Loc] from SortList
9             End if
10        End if
11        SortList.add(i)
12    End For
```

Now let us analyze the computational complexity of the FHVG. Firstly, let us introduce a result based on Corollary 9 and Corollary 19 from Gutin [23] on the HVG.

Lemma 2 [23]: The maximum number of edges in an HVG on n vertices is *2n-3*, which represents the time series in the forms of

$X = \{ ...; 8; 6; 4; 2; 1; 3; 5; 6; 7; 9; ...\}$ or $X = \{...; 9; 7; 5; 3; 1; 2; 4; 6; 8; ...\}$

Now let us consider the computational complexity of the FHVG.

Lemma 3: The complexity of constructing a F*VHG is O(n)*.

Proof: It is clear that the worst case of the computational complexity is equal to the execution time calculating the loop between line 2 and line 5 in Algorithm FHVG. The cycle time for computing the line 5 is equal to the cycle time of line 8 in the worst case. Therefore, the worst case is when the HVG has the maximum edges. According to Lemma 2, the average cycle time of executing line 8 occurs at most three times. The total execution complexity, therefore, is *3(n - 1)*.   □

Note that the output of the FHVG algorithm is either a directed graph or an undirected graph depending on the cycle time of executing line 3 and the line 7. If the connection between two nodes is an arc, then the output of the algorithm is a directed graph. Otherwise, if it is an edge, then the output is an undirected graph. That indicates that the FHVG algorithm can be used as the same way as the HVG and HVDG algorithms and its computation complexity is the same as the HVG.

3.5   Visibility Graph Similarity Method

The Visibility Graph Similarity (VGS) algorithm was introduced by Ahmandlou and Adeli based on the visibility graph algorithm [11]. Like the PLV algorithm, it is used to measure the generalized synchronization among multiple signals. It is divided into three steps. Firstly, any two input time series signals, $x(t)$ and $y(t)$, are mapped into two VGs, G_x and G_y. The second step is to calculate the degree sequences of $d(G_x)$ and $d(G_y)$, respectively. The degree of $d(v_i)$ is the number of edges connected to v_i. Lastly the synchronization of $x(t)$ and $y(t)$ is calculated based on the degree sequences, $d(G_x)$ and G_y, using their cross correlation:

$$S(x, y) = \left| \frac{Cov(D_x, D_y)}{\sigma_{D_x} \sigma_{D_y}} \right| \qquad (7)$$

Where Cov(x, y) is the covariance of $x(t)$ and $y(t)$, and σ_x is the standard deviation of $x(t)$. The value of S(x, y) are in the range of [0..1]. The index of the VGS algorithm is the average of S in each channel.

The VGS algorithm has been proved to be more powerful than the coherence method or the SL method for analyzing certain types of Chaos signals [11]. However, the VGS algorithm doesn't work for some other types of signals. Here gives an example to show that the VGS algorithm yields an incorrect result about the synchronization between two signals. Considering two time series signals, $x_1 = \{7,1,2,4,2,1,7\}$ and $x_2 = \{6,2,1,4,1,2,6\}$, their degree sequences of the VG are the same: $D_1 = D_2 = \{4,3,3,6,3,3,4\}$. From calculating equation (7), we have: $S(x_1,x_2) = 1$. This result indicates that x_1 and x_2 are exactly synchronized each other - which is not true in this case.

3.6   Horizontal Visibility Directed Graph Similarity Method

To overcome the above problem, this study proposes a horizontal visibility directed graph similarity (HVDS) algorithm derived from the VGS algorithm. The HVDS algorithm improves its performance with three aspects. Firstly, it constructs a HVG instead of a VG . As proved in Lemma 3, the FHVD algorithm performs faster. The second improvement is to use an out degree sequence from a HVG rather than the degree sequence from a VG. The last improvement is to replace equation (7) with equation (8).

$$S(x,y) = \frac{Cov(D_x, D_y)}{\sigma_{D_x} \sigma_{D_y}} \tag{8}$$

The value range of S(x, y) is now in [-1...1]. If x and y are desynchronized, the value of S(x, y) is -1, otherwise 1 if they are synchronized. The synchronization index, S(x), of the HVDS is the average of S in each channel.

Let us consider the previous example again. The out degree sequence of the HVDG is $D_1 = \{0,1,2,2,1,2,4\}$, $D_2 = \{0,1,2,3,1,2,3\}$. From calculating equation (8), we get: $S(x_1,x_2) = 0.78$, The result is consistent with the observation of the signals, $x_1 = \{7,1,2,4,2,1,7\}$ and $x_2 = \{6,2,1,4,1,2,6\}$.

4   The Experimental Results

To evaluate the performances of the three synchronization methods discussed in Section 3, the experiments were conducted with Java programming language. The Sleep EDF-file data mentioned in Section 2 was converted into the ASCII format. The LIBSVM classifier [17] was applied to classify the sleep stages after the synchronization index feature matrices are exacted, separately, by the PLV, VGS and HVDS algorithms, from the Sleep-EDF dataset.

The Sleep-EDF dataset was divided into two data sets. One is the training set which comes from all odd numbers, such as 1, 3, 5 ... 2789, of segments in subject sc4012e. The other data set is the testing set which is from all the four subjects, with each having 2780 segments. After the synchronization index matrices as the feature representations of the two EEG and EOG signals were extracted, the extracted features were sent as the input of a support vector machine (SVM) algorithm in a SVM tool, LIBSVM, for training. As there are seven types of sleep stages, the multiple classification algorithm was applied.

The accuracy rates for the sleep stages classification using the PLV, VGS and HVDS methods are shown in Table 1, when the training data set was from subject sc4012e. The results using the four subjects were compared. The best classification accuracy of 86.33% was obtained for subject sc4112e0.

Table 1. Classification accuracy of the PLV, VGS , HVDS algorithms, plus LIBSVM, using sc4012e0 as the trainning set

Subject	Classification accuracy		
	PLV+LIBSVM	VGS+LIBSVM	HVDS+LIBSVM
sc4002e0	66.00%	73.24%	73.71%
sc4012e0*	81.65%	84.14%	84.82%
sc4102e0	65.86%	83.56%	84.68%
sc4112e0	75.68%	84.86%	86.33%
average	72.30%	81.45%	82.64%

Symbol * indicates that   the training data are from that subject

The 10-fold cross-validation is used to evaluate the testing results on each subject as shown in Table 2. The classification accuracy rate of the HVDS algorithm is highest among three synchrony measuring methods for all four subjects.

Table 2. Classification accuracy with 10-fold cross validation

Subject	Classification accuracy		
	PLV+LIBSVM	VGS+LIBSVM	HVDS+LIBSVM
sc4002e0	66.00%	74.96%	76.00%
sc4012e0	63.17%	84.10%	84.82%
sc4102e0	65.86%	84.28%	85.25%
sc4112e0	75.68%	84..35%	86.69%
average	67.68%	81.11%	83.19%

According to Tables 1 and 2, the accuracy rates for individual subjects were only slightly affected by a different training set for the VGS and HVDS methods. In contrast, the accuracy rate of the PLV was strongly affected by a different training set. The average accuracy of the HVDS is more close to the accuracy rate by an expert's evaluation, which is 83±3% [24]. The HVDS with LIBSVM also has a higher accuracy than the power spectral density with an artificial neural network method, which is at most 76.40% on six sleep stages for the same Sleep EDF dataset [19].

Table 3. Computational time for feature extracting (including I/O time)

Algorithms	PLV	VGS	HVDS
Running time	0.42s	95.09s	2.41s

The computation times using the three synchronization measuring methods are evaluated and shown in Table 3, which does not include the SVM running time. All experiments are implemented on a computer with 3.0G Hz Inter CoreTM Duo E8400 processor and 4GB of RAM.

From Table 3, it can be observed that the HVDS method is 39 times faster than the VGS, but 5 times slower than the PLV due to the running time in HVDS includes the executing cross correlation time. Each 30-second of a segment only needs 8.03ms for obtaining its sleep stage with the HVDS algorithm.

5   Conclusion

Although synchronization methods, such as coherence function, the PLV and SL, are widely used to study the sleep stages, the accuracy of multi sleep stages classification by these methods are not previously reported in the literature. This paper is the first to apply the VGS to analyze EEG sleep signals. This paper is also the first to report the PLV accuracy of classifying the sleep stages.

Moreover, this paper is also the first to discuss the computational complexity of constructing a VG although the VG algorithm has been widely used for analyzing biological signals. To improve the performance of constructing a VG or a HVG, this paper presents a linear constructing algorithm based on the horizontal visibility graph, the fast HVG, which is 39 times faster than the original VG algorithm. This paper compares three synchrony measuring methods: PLV, VGS and HVDS, with a support vector machine classifier, LIBSVM, to identify seven classes of sleep stages with 11120 segments. The results show that the accuracy of the HVDS classification method is the highest among those of the VGS and PLV, and the accuracy of the HVDS is only slightly affected by a different training data. These results suggest that the proposed HVDS method is promising and can be used for online sleep stages classification.

References

1. Apostol, G., Creutzfeldt, O.D.: Crosscorrelation between the activity of septal units and hippocampal EEG during arousal. Brain Research 67, 65–75 (1974)
2. Colter, N., Shaw, J.C.: Eeg coherence analysis and field dependence. Biological Psychology 15, 215–228 (1982)
3. Rosenblum, M.G., Pikovsky, A.S., Kurths, J.: Phase Synchronization of Chaotic Oscillators. Physical Review Letters 76, 1804–1807 (1996)
4. Stam, C.J., van Dijk, B.W.: Synchronization likelihood: an unbiased measure of generalized synchronization in multivariate data sets. Phys. D 163, 236–251 (2002)
5. Ahmadlou, M., Adeli, H.: Visibility graph similarity: A new measure of generalized synchronization in coupled dynamic systems. Physica D: Nonlinear Phenomena 241, 326–332 (2012)
6. He, A., Yang, X., Yang, X., Ning, X.: Phase Synchronization in Sleep Electroencephalogram. In: 2007 IEEE/ICME International Conference on Complex Medical Engineering (CME 2007), pp. 1421–1424 (2007)

7. Acharya, A., Kar, S., Routray, A.: Phase synchronization based weighted networks for classifying levels of fatigue and sleepiness. In: 2010 International Conference on Systems in Medicine and Biology (ICSMB), pp. 265–268 (2010)

8. Ferri, R., Rundo, F., Bruni, O., Terzano, M.G., Stam, C.J.: Regional scalp EEG slow-wave synchronization during sleep cyclic alternating pattern A1 subtypes. Neuroscience Letters 404, 352–357 (2006)

9. Ferri, R., Rundo, F., Bruni, O., Terzano, M.G., Stam, C.J.: Small-world network organization of functional connectivity of EEG slow-wave activity during sleep. Clinical Neurophysiology 118, 449–456 (2007)

10. Akşahin, M., Aydın, S., Fırat, H., Eroğul, O.: Artificial Apnea Classification with Quantitative Sleep EEG Synchronization. Journal of Medical Systems 36, 139–144 (2012)

11. Shao, Z.-G.: Network analysis of human heartbeat dynamics. Applied Physics Letters 96, 073703 (2010)

12. Dong, Z., Li, X.: Comment on Network analysis of human heartbeat dynamics. Applied Physics Letters 96, 266101–266102 (2010)

13. Ahmadlou, M., Adeli, H., Adeli, A.: New diagnostic EEG markers of the Alzheimer's disease using visibility graph. Journal of Neural Transmission 117, 1099–1109 (2010)

14. Yang, Y., Wang, J., Yang, H., Mang, J.: Visibility graph approach to exchange rate series. Physica A: Statistical Mechanics and its Applications 388, 4431–4437 (2009)

15. Elsner, J.B., Jagger, T.H., Fogarty, E.A.: Visibility network of United States hurricanes. Geophys. Res. Lett. 36, L16702 (2009)

16. Stam, C.J.: http://home.kpn.nl/stam7883/brainwave.html

17. Chang, C.-C., Lin, C.-J.: LIBSVM: a library for support vector machines. ACM Transactions on Intelligent Systems and Technology 2, 21–27 (2011)

18. Goldberger, A.L., Amaral, L.A.N., Glass, L., Hausdorff, J.M., Ivanov, P.C., Mark, R.G., Mietus, J.E., Moody, G.B., Peng, C.-K., Stanley, H.E.: PhysioBank, PhysioToolkit, and PhysioNet: Components of a New Research Resource for Complex Physiologic Signals. Circulation 101, e215–e220 (2000)

19. Ronzhina, M., Janoušek, O., Kolářová, J., Nováková, M., Honzík, P., Provazník, I.: Sleep scoring using artificial neural networks. Sleep Medicine Reviews 16, 251–263 (2012)

20. Rechtschaffen, A., Kales, A.: A manual of standardized terminology, techniques and scoring systems for sleep stages of human subjects. In: Office, U.G.P. (ed.) Public Health Service, Washington DC (1968)

21. Lacasa, L., Luque, B., Ballesteros, F., Luque, J., Nuño, J.C.: From time series to complex networks: The visibility graph. Proceedings of the National Academy of Sciences 105, 4972–4975 (2008)

22. Luque, B., Lacasa, L., Ballesteros, F., Luque, J.: Horizontal visibility graphs: Exact results for random time series. Physical Review E 80, 046103 (2009)

23. Gutin, G., Mansour, T., Severini, S.: A characterization of horizontal visibility graphs and combinatorics on words. Physica A: Statistical Mechanics and its Applications 390, 2421–2428 (2011)

24. Chapotot, F., Becq, G.: Automated sleep–wake staging combining robust feature extraction, artificial neural network classification, and flexible decision rules. International Journal of Adaptive Control and Signal Processing 24, 409–423 (2010)

Information-Theoretic Based Feature Selection
for Multi-Voxel Pattern Analysis of fMRI Data

Chun-An Chou[1,2], Kittipat "Bot" Kampa[1,2], Sonya H. Mehta[1,4,5],
Rosalia F. Tungaraza[1,5], W. Art Chaovalitwongse[1,2,5],
and Thomas J. Grabowski[1,3,5]

[1] Integrated Brain Imaging Center, University of Washington, Seattle, USA
[2] Industrial & Systems Engineering, University of Washington, Seattle, USA
[3] Neurology, University of Washington, Seattle, USA
[4] Psychology, University of Washington, Seattle, USA
[5] Radiology, University of Washington, Seattle, USA

Abstract. Multi-voxel pattern analysis (MVPA) of functional magnetic
resonance imaging (fMRI) data is an emerging approach for probing the
neural correlates of cognition. MVPA allows cognitive representations and
processing to be modeled as distributed patterns of neural activity, which
can be used to build a classification model to partition activity patterns
according to stimulus conditions. In machine learning, MVPA is a very
challenging classification problem because the number of voxels (features)
greatly exceeds the number of data instances. Thus, there is a need to select informative voxels before building a classification model. We introduce a feature selection method based on mutual information (MI), which
is used to quantify the statistical dependency between features and stimulus conditions. To evaluate the utility of our approach, we employed several linear classification algorithms on a publicly available fMRI data set
that has been widely used to benchmark MVPA performance [1]. The
computational results suggest that feature selection based on the MI ranking can drastically improve the classification accuracy. Additionally, high-
ranked features provide meaningful insights into the functional-anatomic
relationship of neural activity and the associated tasks.

1 Introduction

Multi-voxel pattern analysis (MVPA) is an emerging approach for studying
the relationship between cognition and brain activity measured by functional
magnetic resonance imaging (fMRI). fMRI measures blood oxygenation level-
dependent (BOLD) signal that arises from the interplay of blood flow (and blood
oxygenation) and changes in neural activity [2]. In task-based studies, changes in
neural activity are assumed to be experimentally induced, with fMRI time series
data reflecting the response to stimuli (e.g., activation of cognitive representations) at locations (i.e., voxels) across the brain. The hemodynamic response to
neural activity is slow (on the order of seconds) but predictable, allowing the
observed BOLD signal of a given stimulus (or stimulus block) to be adequately
modeled by a canonical response function and summarized by a single value.

F.M. Zanzotto et al. (Eds.): BI 2012, LNCS 7670, pp. 196–208, 2012.

A common objective of MVPA is to build a pattern classification model of BOLD responses at informative voxels to predict cognitive representations associated with experimental conditions (e.g., the responses to different categories of visual stimuli). One of the first studies to consider a pattern analysis approach with fMRI data was performed by Haxby et al. [1]. They investigated whether distributed and overlapping multi-voxel response patterns in the ventral temporal (VT) cortex of the brain could be identified for eight different categories of objects that were shown to the subject: 1) faces, 2) houses, 3) cats, 4) bottles, 5) scissors, 6) shoes, 7) chairs, and 8) 'scrambled pictures'. From a machine learning perspective, this is a straightforward pattern classification problem.

Because in most studies, the number of voxels to be analyzed is far greater than the number of data instances (stimuli), using all voxels to build a classification model will likely result in overfitting. Thus, it is important to select *informative voxels* before using them to build a classification model. In this paper, we introduce an information-theoretic feature selection approach using mutual information (MI) as a feature-ranking metric. MI is a measure to quantify mutual dependence of two random variables, such as between a feature and class label, or between features [3]. MI has been widely applied to feature ranking and selection problems [4] in many areas of research, for instance, fMRI analysis [5–7], image registration [8], gene expression [9], computer-aided diagnosis [10], etc. MI has advantages over traditional correlation analysis methods (e.g., Pearson's correlation coefficient) which are only sensitive to a linear dependence between two variables, whereas MI can capture the higher degree of dependency between the variables that takes into account both joint and marginal probability distributions of the variables. Moreover, in multi-class classification problems like the MVPA problem considered herein, the class label can be cast as a random variable that naturally makes MI an appropriate candidate for such problems. Although MI has been used in fMRI analysis [5–7, 11], MI has not been broadly considered in the application of MVPA to fMRI analysis [12–17]. Unlike multivariate MI (between the class label and the joint feature set) [6], we propose using an univariate MI as an individual feature ranking measure in MVPA. The latter approach can be seen as a relaxed version of the former, and is relatively less expensive in computation, as univariate MI considers each voxel independently. We show experimentally that our proposed method can achieve accuracy levels comparable to or exceeding other proposed machine learning approaches.

The overall MVPA framework proposed here is illustrated in Figure 1. The first step is to preprocess the fMRI data to obtain corrected and representative values from BOLD times series at each voxel. The second step is feature ranking, which sorts the voxels based on the importance indices of MI and classification accuracy of individual voxels. Subsequently, pattern classification is performed using cross-validation by training, validating, and testing on separate data.

The organization of the paper is as follows. In Section 2, we describe the background of MVPA of fMRI data. In Section 3, we present the proposed MVPA framework with an information-theoretic approach to rank and select informative voxels, and briefly describe the state-of-the-art widely used machine learning

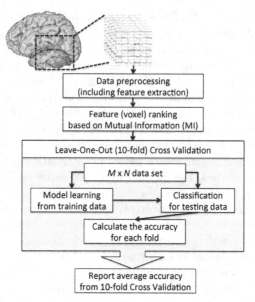

Fig. 1. The MVPA framework of fMRI data analysis

algorithms used in this study. In Section 4, we present the experimental results of applying our method to the benchmark data set and compare them with classification results using other feature selection approaches. In Section 5, we conclude this work.

2   Background

Conventional statistical analysis of fMRI data has relied on a mass univariate framework in which the response at each brain location (operationally, each image voxel) is considered independently. However, numerous studies have demonstrated that 'mental representations' may in fact be embedded in a distributed neural population code captured in the activity pattern across multiple voxels [1, 18, 13]. If this is the case, successful analysis of fMRI data will require consideration of the joint contribution of brain space (operationally, across multiple image voxels). To address this possibility, MVPA approaches, adapted from machine learning and pattern recognition techniques, have been applied to fMRI data to elucidate the neural basis of cognition.

Often researchers are interested in performing "cognitive state decoding" (i.e., classification of 'cognitive representations' into discrete categories of stimulus conditions). This subset of MVPA entails several steps: feature extraction, feature selection, and pattern classification. For fMRI data, features are commonly operationalized as voxels, and their selection is important from the standpoint of interpreting the relationship between brain anatomy and cognitive processes. Feature extraction is a procedure to characterize the temporally-evolving response to a stimulus at a voxel, often with a summary value such as a regression coefficient. Feature selection is a procedure to identify and select the subset of voxels that are informative to use with the classifier. Pattern classification is a procedure to train a classification algorithm to create a decision/classification model that best separates the stimulus categories within the multidimensional space defined by the selected features (voxels). Linear classifiers are often preferred because of their interpretability, with an above chance decoding accuracy indicating the presence of information at an 'explicit' level (e.g., not requiring further nonlinear neural computation).

3   Materials and Methods

3.1   fMRI Data Processing and Feature Extraction

In this study, we used the Haxby data set[1], a benchmark data set in [1]. In Haxby's block-design experiment, there were 10 fMRI runs; in each run, eight stimulus blocks, each displaying image exemplars from a different conceptual category as described above, were displayed to the subject in a random order. The fMRI data were collected from a GE 3T scanner. One image of brain activity in the data set (consisting of $64 \times 64 \times 40$ voxels) was acquired every repetition time (TR) of 2.5 seconds. Thus, there are a total of 9 TRs (=22.5/2.5) in each block, yielding 720 data instances for the data set (10 runs × 8 blocks × 9 TRs). In our study, we only focused on the predetermined region (region of interest, ROI) of 577 thresholded voxels with task-related variance in the VT cortex, as opposed to the whole brain space of 43,193 voxels.

Figure 2 illustrates the feature extraction for the fMRI time series data in the VT cortex. To characterize the BOLD response to a given stimulus condition, a general linear model (GLM) was applied, and coefficient parameters β were estimated by fitting a GLM with different predictors for each stimulus block. In this study, the predictors were modeled with a boxcar and a boxcar convolved with a canonical hemodynamic response function (HRF), respectively [2]. The boxcar effectively gives the same effect as averaging the brain response in the box. The HRF has been used to characterize the temporally-evolving BOLD signal change in response to a brief stimulus. In this experiment, we used a double-Gamma function provided by SPM [19], with the default settings, for the HRF.

We performed standard data preprocessing steps to attenuate noise and to improve spatial alignment of time series data, including motion correction and linear detrending. We also standardized (z-scored) the data by subtracting the mean and dividing by the standard deviation of the time series signal at each voxel. We refer interested readers to [2, 20] for more details.

---

[1] Downloaded from http://code.google.com/p/princeton-mvpa-toolbox/

3.2   Data Notation

At each voxel, the BOLD time series data was fitted by a HRF, and coefficient parameters β (associated to different stimuli) are now used as feature values of the voxel. In Figure 2, the corresponding data representation is transformed from the original temporal data in a 3-dimensional voxel space to a 2-dimensional input matrix X.

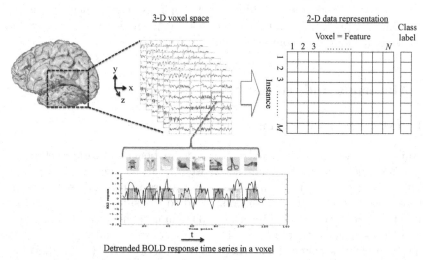

Fig. 2. An illustration of spatio-temporal fMRI data in the VT cortex with an example of a BOLD times series in response to eight different images at a single voxel. The collected fMRI data after preprocessing is transformed into a instance × feature data representation matrix.

Denote an input data matrix X, whose size is $M \times N$, where M is the number of data instances (the total number of presented stimuli) and N is the number of features (voxels). The (i, j) element of the matrix X, $x_j^{(i)}$, represents the real-valued coefficient parameter β of the ith data instance at the jth voxel. It is helpful to view $x_j^{(i)}$ as the ith sample of the jth feature random variable X_j, the jth column of X. Similarly, $X^{(i)}$, the ith row of X represents the collection of coefficients from all the voxels. Let the class label (i.e., stimulus category in MVPA) $c^{(i)} \in \{1, ..., K\}$ denote the ith sample of the class label random variable C, where K is the total number of stimulus categories. In the dataset, each sample $c^{(i)}$ is known precisely according to the experiment design for each data instance i.

3.3   Mutual Information for Feature Ranking

Mutual information (MI) of two random variables measures the statistical dependence of the two random variables. In the feature selection context, MI between the class label random variable C and the jth feature X_j, $I(C; X_j)$ is calculated for all the features $j \in \{1, ..., n\}$ and subsequently sorted in a descending order. The MI between the discrete random variable C and the continuous random variable X_j can be expressed by:

$$MI(C; X_j) = \sum_{c=1}^{K} \int_{X_j} p(c, x_j) \log \left(\frac{p(c, x_j)}{p(c)p(x_j)} \right) dx_j,$$

where $p(c, x_j)$ (short-handed for $p(C = c, X_j = x_j)$) is a joint distribution of both discrete and continuous variables C and X_j, which can be calculated more conveniently using the chain rule $p(c, x_j) = p(c)p(x_j|c)$. The estimator $\hat{p}(x_j|c)$ of the conditional term $p(x_j|c)$ can be calculated by a kernel density estimation technique, called the *Parzen-Rosenblatt* window method:

$$\hat{p}(x_j|c) = (\sum_{i=1}^{M} \delta_c(c^{(i)}) \mathcal{K}(\frac{x_j - x_j^{(i)}}{w})) / (w \sum_{i'=1}^{M} \delta_c(c^{(i')})),$$

where $\delta_x(y)$ is the Kronecker delta function, where $\delta_x(y) = 1$ when $x = y$ and 0 otherwise, $\mathcal{K}(\cdot)$ is the kernel, and w is the bandwidth. In this particular case, the kernel function is chosen to be a Gaussian kernel, and thus the bandwidth becomes the standard deviation. $p(c)$ is derived from marginalizing out x_j, $p(c) = \int_{x_j} p(c)p(x_j|c)dx_j$, and $p(x_j)$ can be obtained from $p(x_j) = \sum_{c=1}^{K} p(c)p(x_j|c)$.

After the MI between the class labels and all features are computed, the column of the input matrix X is sorted in a descending order with respect to its corresponding MI value (index). This will be the order of features fed to each of classifiers to be discussed in the subsequent section.

3.4 Classification Algorithms

In this section we will discuss 3 classifiers widely used in MVPA:

Gaussian Naive Bayes Classifier (GNB). A naive Bayes (NB) classifier [21] is a probabilistic classifier based on Bayes' theorem with a strong assumption that each feature is independent, namely, "independent feature model".

Logistic Regression Classifier (LR). Logistic regression (LR) classifier is a linear discriminative classifier [22], whose underlying intuition is to separate the data instances into 2 groups by a hyperplane. LR works substantially well in the scenario where the feature-to-instance ratio is high, fitting well with the description of fMRI data in general. Although the LR's cost function is originally formulated for binary classification, the extension for multi-class classification can be done using a one-vs-all paradigm.

Support Vector Machines (SVM). Support vector machine (SVM) is arguably the most widely used algorithm to analyze fMRI data [14, 15, 20, 16, 17] because it performs well on the data with high feature-to-instance ratio. SVM is a linear discriminative classifier which not only separates data into two groups by a hyperplane, but also maximizes the margin between the two classes, and it is hence best described by a "maximum margin classifier". The notion of margin lends robustness and good generalization to SVM, making it one of the most popular classifiers. In this experiment, a multi-class SVM is implemented using a pair-wise strategy. For the sake of interpretability, a linear SVM is used throughout the experiment.

3.5   Performance Evaluation

In our experiments, accuracy is defined as the percentage of correctly predicted data instances over the total data instances. A leave-one-run-out (10-fold) cross validation is employed for training and assessment of classification accuracy. The accuracy (avg_accur) refers to the averaged accuracy among 10 folds as mentioned in the rest of the paper. In addition, the performance is reported using two criteria. First, $best\_accur = \max_n avg\_accur(n)$ refers to the best accuracy from the accuracy curve. Second, $overall\_accur = \frac{1}{N} \sum_{n=1}^{N} avg\_accur(n)$ refers to the normalized area under the accuracy curve, measuring how well the classifier performs when considering the overall range of the number of included voxels.

4   Experimental Results

In this section, we first explain the whole process of the experiment in detail and thereafter discuss the results. First, the data set is preprocessed as described in Section 3.1. Then an ROI within the brain is defined based on theoretically-informed expectations and/or evidence of its selective involvement in the experimental task. In this experiment, we focus primarily on the VT cortex, mentioned in section 3.1, but also roughly explore the whole brain for comparison. Let the extracted feature matrix in the ROI be denoted by X. We first compute the quantity $\mathcal{M}_j$ (e.g., MI) between the known class label C and each feature (voxel) X_j. The ranked feature matrix X_{ranked} is obtained by ranking X according to the quantity $\mathcal{M}_j, \forall j \in \{1, ..., N\}$ with some criteria such as descending or ascending order. While we are primarily focussing on ranking the features using MI in a descending order (MI-$descend$) (i.e. from the lowest to highest MI index.), we additionally rank the features using more interesting criteria as listed below:

1. MI in ascending order (MI-$ascend$): The features are ranked with MI in an ascending order rather than descending order.
2. SVM-accuracy in descending order (acc-$descend$): First, the accuracy obtained from using SVM with feature vector containing only one single feature at a time is calculated as a measure. The features are then ranked by the measure in a descending order.
3. SVM-accuracy in ascending order (acc-$ascend$): Similar to acc-descend except it is ranked in an ascending order.
4. Shuffle order ($shuffle$): The feature order is randomly shuffled.

Ultimately, we are interested in seeing the performances in terms of accuracy when adding the feature to a classifier $\mathcal{A}$ one by one until all the features are

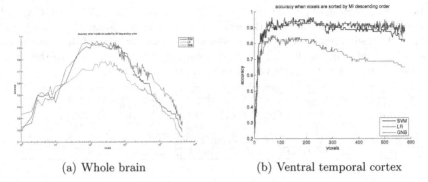

(a) Whole brain   (b) Ventral temporal cortex

Fig. 3. Comparisons of accuracies from three classification algorithms when using HRF as the basis to decompose the response. The voxels in the whole brain (a) and ventral temporal cortex (b) are sorted in a descending order based on MI index.

used. That is, the first n features of X_{ranked}, denoted by $X_{ranked}(1 : n)$, are input to $\mathcal{A}$, and the accuracy $avg\_accur(n)$ can be calculated from the results. The experiment continues from $n = 1$ to N. The Haxby data set, after feature extraction, provides 80 data instances (refer to Section 3.1), which may not be appropriate when separated into training, validation, and testing data sets. Therefore, a 10-fold cross-validation regime is employed to take into account such a limitation. In such a regime, the data set is divided into 10 folds, each having eight data instances from eight different stimulus categories. At each time, a fold is retained as a testing data set while the remaining 9 folds are further divided into a validation data set (1 fold) and a training data set (8 folds). The training set and the validation set are used to learn the model parameter Θ and the regularization parameter λ respectively for the classifier $\mathcal{A}$. Thus, the accuracy $avg\_accur(n)$ will be obtained by averaging 10 single-fold classification accuracy.

In this study, we are interested in assessing a specific/consistent instantiation of the ranking of voxels, thus the ranking is only performed once using all 10 folds of data. We are aware that by doing so the information of the test data set is being *peeked*, introducing the possibility of favorably biasing classification accuracy. However, the accuracy reported here is always the average across the 10 folds, so the effect of *peeking* should be minimal at most. To confirm this, we replicated our procedure but ranked the voxels on the training data only. The results are practically identical to those obtained from ranking all data, and therefore only the former results are reported in this paper. Subsequently, the details of experiments and their results are discussed.

4.1 Investigating Brain Activation of the Whole Brain vs VT Cortex

We compared the accuracy curves of GNB, LR, and SVM classifiers using the *MI-descend* to rank the HRF features. The results shown in Figure 3(a) and Table 1 indicate that LR yielded the best overall accuracy and maximum accuracy. The

Table 1. Comparison of percent of accuracy obtained from three classifiers: GNB, LR, and SVM, when all the voxels in the whole brain are ranked using *MI-descend*. Some parts of the results reported in [17] are shown in the last two rows of the table. In case where the number of voxels used in the original paper is not identical to that in our experiment, we put the original voxel number in the parenthesis.

n	5	20	40	60	100	200	500	1000	43193	$best\_accur$
GNB	50	60	66.25	72.50	71.25	77.50	77.50	68.75	13.75	78.75
LR	47.50	72.50	81.25	93.75	93.75	92.50	88.75	86.25	26.25	96.25
SVM	50	61.25	82.50	88.75	90.00	93.75	92.50	83.75	18.75	95.00
SVM+w_{SVM}	38.47	58.47	60.28(33)	63.19(50)	62.78	64.44	n/a	69.86	n/a	69.86
RFO+w_{SVM}	39.44	59.17	62.22(33)	64.17(50)	69.17	71.25	n/a	72.22	n/a	72.22

Table 2. Comparison of percent of accuracy obtained from three classifiers: GNB, LR, and SVM, when all the voxels in the VT cortex are ranked using *MI-descend*

	VT_accur	$overall\_accur$	$best\_accur$	$best\_n$
GNB	65.00	74.43	85.00	65
LR	87.50	89.51	96.25	117
SVM	82.50	88.55	96.25	68, 227

accuracies of all classifiers grow steeply within the range of $250 \leq n \leq 500$ and decrease after that. This suggests that the bottom half of ranked voxels are either noisy and/or non-relevant to the stimuli. Thus, not all voxels are equally important, and the *MI-descend* can reveal the range of informative voxels, which is crucial for classification performance.

We also compared the accuracy curves of all 3 classifiers using the *MI-descend* to rank the HRF features from voxels only in the VT cortex. As mentioned earlier, the VT cortex is selected because it appears to be involved in high-level visual processing of complex stimuli. The results are shown in Figure 3(b) and Table 2, whose second column from the left represents the accuracy (VT_accur) when using all the voxels within the VT cortex; and last column on the right represents the number of voxels ($best\_n$) that gives the best accuracy. In case of having multiple $best\_n$'s, only the first and the last are displayed. Both LR and SVM perform competitively; they tie at 96.25% for the best accuracy and their VT-accuracies are significantly lower when $100 \leq n \leq 250$. The observation suggests that even with the voxels selected according to the expert criteria, MI still plays a crucial role in helping the classifiers to achieve higher accuracies as seen by the accuracy curves dropping after a certain n in each classifier.

When considering the variation of the accuracy curves especially at the right end of the curve, it can be inferred that LR is less robust (to noise) among all three classifiers. That is because LR relies on a hyperplane whereas SVM takes margin into account and GNB models the class conditional directly. In fact, around the best voxel range $100 \leq n \leq 250$, which will be the range of interest in subsequent experiments, SVM is not only more robust but also performs slightly better than LR, which makes SVM the classifier of our choice in the next two experiments.

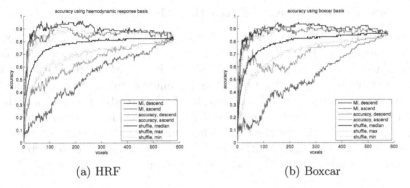

(a) HRF   (b) Boxcar

Fig. 4. Comparison of the accuracy from SVM when using HRF (a) and boxcar (b) as the basis to decompose the response and several measures to rank the voxels

Table 3. Comparison of percent of accuracy obtained from each ranking measure (using HRF and boxcar) when using SVM as the classifier

	HRF			Boxcar		
	overall_accur	best_accur	best_n	overall_accur	best_accur	best_n
MI-descend	88.55	96.25	68, 227	89.05	95.00	154, 234
acc-descend	85.40	95.00	126	87.02	92.50	277
Shuffle	77.27	83.75	568, 575	79.09	86.25	439
acc-ascend	64.39	83.75	562, 573	70.15	86.25	573, 577
MI-ascend	52.68	83.75	575	51.56	86.25	577

4.2   Comparison of Feature Ranking Measures

Linear SVM was used to evaluate the performances from different feature-ranking criteria listed in Section 3. The results illustrated in Figure 4(a) and Table 3 indicate that the *MI-descend* yielded the best overall accuracy and achieved the maximum accuracy. It is also interesting to see that the *acc-descend* did not perform as well as the *MI-descend*. A voxel having low score from ranking individual voxels independently according to their classification accuracies cannot be confidently claimed non-informative because the voxel can be found informative when used with other voxels to jointly classify certain stimuli. That is, the accuracy measure can unnecessarily remove jointly informative voxels. This finding is consistent with [1], which suggests that the information in the brain is distributed.

The shuffle accuracy curve is obtained by calculating the median of 100 accuracy curves, each from one realization of randomly shuffling the features. The curve is almost monotonically increasing with respect to n, suggesting that when the voxels are selected randomly for each time, using more feature tends to improve the performance. The fact that the *MI-ascend* yielded the worst performance indicates that small MI values are a good indicator that the voxel is non-informative with respect to the stimuli. Thus, these results suggest MI is a better criterion for feature ranking or filtering than an individual feature's accuracy.

4.3   Comparison of Feature Extraction Methods

We also investigated an alternative basis to extract the features using a boxcar function rather than HRF. The results shown in Figure 4(b) and Table 3 follow the same trend as in the previous results, that is, the *MI-descend* still yielded the best overall accuracy and achieved the maximum accuracy. It is worth noting that the *overall_accur* and *VT_accur* of the boxcar tends to outperform those of HRF in all the measures except the *MI-ascend*. Yet, its maximum accuracy is slightly inferior to that of the HRF. These findings suggest that the choice of feature extraction can significantly influence the accuracy curve characteristics, and more thorough investigations should be conducted in future work.

5   Conclusion and Future Work

In this paper, we proposed an information-theoretic based approach, specifically the use of mutual information (MI), for voxel ranking and selection to address the problem of low signal-to-noise and large feature-to-instance ratio of fMRI data, as used with pattern classification techniques. Using a benchmark fMRI data set [1], we demonstrated the utility of our approach by assessing the impact of feature (i.e. voxel) selection on classification accuracy with three linear classification algorithms. Our results demonstrated that inclusion of all brain voxels was counterproductive, resulting in classification accuracy comparable or below that obtained when using only the single highest-ranked MI voxel. Successive inclusion of voxels based on their MI ranking improved classification accuracy, with accuracy reaching an asymptote with roughly the 100 highest-ranked voxels. For SVM, these results outperformed several state-of-the-art machine learning approaches previously reported in the literature [17]. Degradation of classification accuracy was not observed until after the inclusion of roughly the top 1000 MI-ranked voxels, consistent with the idea of redundantly distributed information over voxels.

The use of MI ranking to select voxels also improved classification accuracy when limiting the set of voxels under consideration to a functional-anatomic predefined region (i.e., VT cortex). For a given number of voxels, classification accuracy varied depending on whether voxel inclusion was based on descending or ascending MI-ranked order. These results are consistent with object representation being to some extent distributed and redundantly encoded in the VT cortex. Classification accuracy also varied depending on the method of feature extraction and choice of classification algorithm. These findings underscore the ambiguity of MVPA results with respect to where and how cognitive representations are encoded in the brain. As such, one of the open challenges for MVPA approaches is the functional-anatomic interpretability of the results.

In ongoing work, the proposed approach is applied to multiple subjects under the same experiment, being studied in [1, 23, 24], and other relevant task-based data sets (e.g., semantic analysis in [25]). In future work, we plan to more extensively compare our MI-based feature selection approach with other such methods, for example, a 'stability score' as mentioned in [25] and the multivariate MI approach proposed in [6].

References

1. Haxby, J.V., Gobbini, M.I., Furey, M.L., Ishai, A., Schouten, J.L., Pietrini, P.: Distributed and overlapping representations of faces and objects in ventral temporal cortex. Science 293(5539), 2425–2430 (2001)
2. Poldrack, R.A., Mumford, J.A., Nichols, T.E.: Handbook of functional MRI data analysis. Cambridge University Press (2011)
3. Shannon, C.: A mathematical theory of communication. Bell System Technical Journal 27, 379–423, 623–656 (1948)
4. Guyon, I., Elisseeff, A.: An introduction to variable and feature selection. Journal of Machine Learning Research 3, 1157–1182 (2003)
5. Tsai, A., John, W., Fisher, I., Wible, C., William, M., Wells, I., Kim, J., Willsky, A.S.: Analysis of functional mri data using mutual information. In: Proceedings of the Second International Conference on Medical Image Computing and Computer-Assisted Intervention, pp. 473–480 (1999)
6. Michel, V., Damon, C., Thirion, B.: Mutual information-based feature selection enhances fmri brain activity classification. In: IEEE International Symposium on Biomedical Imaging, pp. 592–595 (2008)
7. Gómez-Verdejo, V., Martínez-Ramón, M., Florensa-Vila, J., Oliviero, A.: Analysis of fmri time series with mutual information. Medical Image Analysis 16(2), 451–458 (2012)
8. Pluim, J.P.W., Maintz, J.B.A., Viergever, M.A.: Mutual information based registration of medical images: a survey. IEEE Transactions on Medical Imaging 22, 986–1004 (2003)
9. Ding, C., Peng, H.: Minimum redundancy feature selection from microarray gene expression data. Journal of Bioinformatics and Computational Biology 3(2), 185–205 (2005)
10. Tourassia, G.D., Frederick, E.D., Markey, M.K., Carey, E., Floyd, J.: Application of the mutual information criterion for feature selection in computer-aided diagnosis. Medical Physics 28(12), 2394–2402 (2001)
11. Afshin-Pour, B., Soltanian-Zadeh, H., Hossein-Zadeh, G.A., Grady, C.L., Strother, S.C.: A mutual information-based metric for evaluation of fmri data-processing approaches. Human Brain Mapping 32(5), 699–715 (2011)
12. Mitchell, T.M., Hutchinson, R., Niculescu, R.S., Pereira, F., Wang, X.: Learning to decode cognitive states from brain images. Machine Learning 57, 145–175 (2004)
13. Haynes, J.D., Rees, G.: Decoding mental states from brain activity in humans. Neuroscience 7, 523–534 (2006)
14. Mourão-Miranda, J., Bokde, A.L., Born, C., Hampel, H., Stetter, M.: Classifying brain states and determining the discriminating activation patterns: support vector machine on functional mri data. Neuroimage 28(4), 980–995 (2005)
15. Mourão-Miranda, J., Reynaud, E., McGlone, F., Calvert, G., Brammer, M.: The impact of temporal compression and space selection on svm analysis of single-subject and multi-subject fmri data. Neuroimage 33(4), 1055–1065 (2006)
16. Martino, F.D., Valente, G., Staeren, N., Ashburner, J., Goebel, R., Formisano, E.: Combining multivariate voxel selection and support vector machines for mapping and classification of fmri spatial patterns. NeuroImage 43, 44–58 (2008)
17. Kuncheva, L.I., Rodréguez, J.J.: Classifier ensembles for fmri data analysis: An experiment. Magnetic Resonance Imaging 28, 583–593 (2010)
18. Norman, K.A., Polyn, S.M., Detre, G.J., Haxby, J.V.: Beyond mind-reading: multi-voxel pattern analysis of fmri data. RENDS in Cognitive Sciences 10(9), 424–430 (2006)

19. Friston, K.J., Fletcher, P., Josephs, O., Holmes, A., Rugg, M.D., Turner, R.: Event-related fmri: characterizing differential responses. NeuroImage 7, 30–40 (1998)
20. Pereira, F., Mitchell, T., Botvinick, M.: Machine learning classifiers and fmri: A tutorial overview. NeuroImage 45, 199–209 (2009)
21. Mitchell, T.M.: Machine learning. McGraw Hill (1997)
22. Jordan, A.: On discriminative vs. generative classifiers: A comparison of logistic regression and naive bayes. Advances in Neural Information Processing Systems 14, 841 (2002)
23. Hanson, S.J., Matsuka, T., Haxby, J.V.: Combinatorial codes in ventral temporal lobe for object recognition: Haxby (2001); revisited: is there a "face" area? NeuroImage 23, 156–166 (2004)
24. O'Toole, A.J., Jiang, F., Abdi, H., Haxby, J.V.: Partially distributed representations of objects and faces in ventral temporal cortex. Journal of Cognitive Neuroscience 17, 580–590 (2005)
25. Mitchell, T.M., Shinkareva, S.V., Carlson, A., Chang, K.M., Malave, V.L., Mason, R.A., Just, M.A.: Predicting human brain activity associated with the meanings of nouns. Science 320, 1191–1195 (2008)

Multiplication of EEG Samples through Replicating, Biasing, and Overlapping

Adham Atyabi[1], Sean P. Fitzgibbon[1], and David M.W. Powers[1,2]

[1] School of Computer Science, Engineering and Mathematics (CSEM),
Flinders University, Australia
[2] Beijing Municipal Lab for Multimedia & Intelligent Software,
Beijing University of Technology, Beijing, China
{Adham.Atyabi,Sean.Fitzgibbon,David.Powers}@flinders.edu.au

Abstract. EEG recording is a time consuming operation during which the subject is expected to stay still for a long time performing tasks. It is reasonable to expect some fluctuation in the level of focus toward the performed task during the task period. This study is focused on investigating various approaches for emphasizing regions of interest during the task period. Dividing the task period into three segments of beginning, middle and end, is expectable to improve the overall classification performance by changing the concentration of the training samples toward regions in which subject had better concentration toward the performed tasks. This issue is investigated through the use of techniques such as i) replication, ii) biasing, and iii) overlapping. A dataset with 4 motor imagery tasks (BCI Competition III dataset IIIa) is used. The results illustrate the existing variations within the potential of different segments of the task period and the feasibility of techniques that focus the training samples toward such regions.

Keywords: Brain Computer Interface, Replication, Segmentation, Biasing, Overlapping, Triangular Overlapping.

1 Introduction

EEG based Brain Computer Interface (BCI) is a communication device that transforms human scalp recordings to executable commands/tasks. EEG recording is a time consuming and tedious procedure during which the subject is expected to sit in a chair and repeatedly perform mental, computational (eg. motor imagery) tasks for some periods of time without being allowed to move. It is unlikely for a subject to consistently maintain a high level of concentration toward the tasks during the task period. That is, it is likely to have some variation in the degree of concentration and task engagement among different time segments of the task period.

Although it is common to assess the performed tasks by evaluating the entire task period as a block epoch, it might be better to only focus toward regions

F.M. Zanzotto et al. (Eds.): BI 2012, LNCS 7670, pp. 209–219, 2012.

of the task period during which the subject is expected to have better concentration toward the task. This issue is investigated in [1–3] by proposing various techniques such as segmentation, replication, biasing and overlapping.

In [3] segmentation and replication approaches are applied to a two class motor imagery dataset and it is concluded that the middle and end segments of the task period are more likely to represent higher concentration by subjects toward the task compared with the beginning segments.

In [2] this problem is further investigated through the use of biasing and overlapping techniques. Biasing is reported to be more advantageous compared with replicating since it maintains all sub-epochs originated from the same epoch and only provides higher number of samples within the epoch from regions of interest while in replication approach only samples originated from regions of interest are maintained and the rest are omitted. Similar to [3] the results indicate the potential of middle segments of the task period. In addition, the combination of biasing and overlapping showed better classification performance compared with either of biasing or overlapping. The study was conducted on a dataset with 2 motor imagery tasks.

The conducted studies in [3] and [2] lacked the generalization across datasets and number of classes. This study further evaluate these approaches using a new dataset containing EEG data of 3 subjects performing 4 motor imagery tasks. The out line of the study is as follows. Section 2 introduces the dataset and the applied preprocessing techniques. Section 3 discusses the employed techniques and represents 3 sets of designed experiments and their achieved results. Conclusion and future work are presented in section 4.

2   Dataset

EEG data from the dataset IIIa of BCI Competition III is used [4]. The dataset contains EEG data of 3 healthy subjects ($k3b$, $k6b$, $l1b$) performing a 4 motor imagery task (left hand, right hand, foot, tongue). The EEG dataset is sampled at 250Hz and is band pass filtered between 1Hz and 50Hz. 60 electrodes are used and the task period is set to 3s and 240 tasks are performed in a random order (except with $k3b$ that performed 360 trials) [4]. Common average referencing (CAR) and demeaning (D) are the applied preprocessing stages. This is denoted in the paper as CARD250Hz. Frequency features are used and a modified single layer perceptron that incorporates early stopping is employed for classification. All experiments implemented a 10×20 cross validation (CV) which results in 90%, 5%, and 5% ratio for training, validation and testing sets respectively.

Bookmaker informedness is used to assess the classification performance. Detailed discussion about bookmaker can be found in [5–7]. Significance tests (ANOVA if normal or Kruskal-Wallis if not) are performed to investigate the potential of null hypothesis that there is no significant difference among different segments of the epoch.

3   Experimental Design and Results

3.1   Exp. 1: The Impact of Different Sub-windowing

This experiment is designed to investigate the potential of different sub-segments of the task period (epoch) individually. This is implemented by dividing the epoch into non-overlapping sub-epochs with shorter window sizes and the potential of each sub-epoch is assessed individually by being passed to a classifier. Various window sizes are considered (0.8s, 0.6s, 0.5s, 0.4s, 0.3s). The results are demonstrated in Figs 1 and 2. In the figures, $CARD250HzxsRedy*240/360$ indicate that the sample rate is 250Hz and common average referencing and

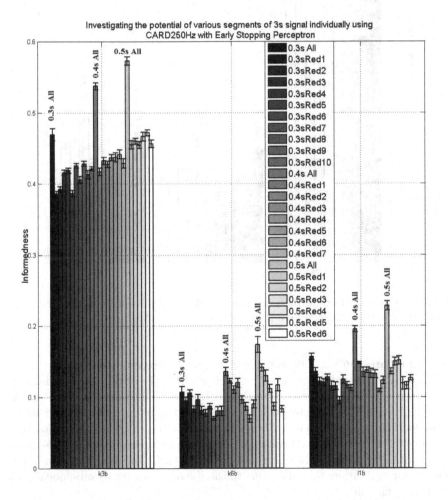

Fig. 1. An investigation on the potential of individual sub-epochs within the epoch using 0.3s, 0.4s, and 0.5s time windows (Exp. 1)

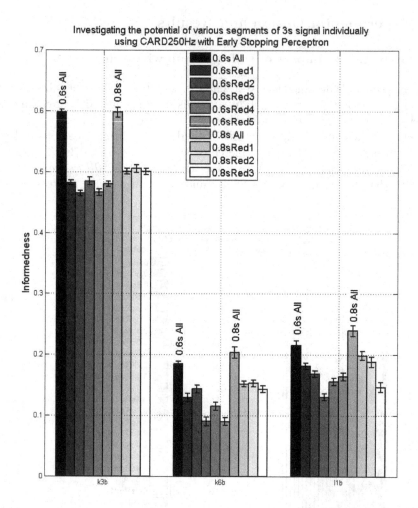

Fig. 2. An investigation on the potential of individual sub-epochs within the epoch using 0.6s and 0.8s time windows (Exp. 1)

demeaning are applied. The sub-epoch length is x second. *Redy* indicate that the illustrated bar represent the yth sub-epoch from the epoch. 240/360 indicate the number of performed tasks (samples). Due to replication in legend test the CRD250Hz and 240/360 are omitted and only the information related to the sub-epoch number is depicted. Therefor, *0.3sRed1* indicate that the epoch is divided to 0.3 s (10 times 0.3s) sub-epochs and among the resulting 10 sub-epochs (each with 0.3s length), the first sub-epoch in each trial is isolated in a new dataset for evaluation. *0.3s All* refers to the use of the entire 10 sub-epochs (0.3s each) in each trial.

The results illustrate variations on individual potential of different segments of the epoch. The use of longer window-sizes resulted in better overall classification performance. This is consistent with previous findings on a 2 motor imagery dataset in [1] and[3]. Using all sub-epochs resulted from dividing the epoch to shorter window sizes showed better classification performance compared to the use of individual sub-epochs. This might be due to the fact that the use of individual sub-epochs reduces the number of training sample compared to the use of all sub-epochs.

3.2   Exp. 2: Replication of Regions of Interest

The problem of having fewer number of training samples in experiment 1 is resolved in this experiment by replicating regions of interest. To do so, a replicating

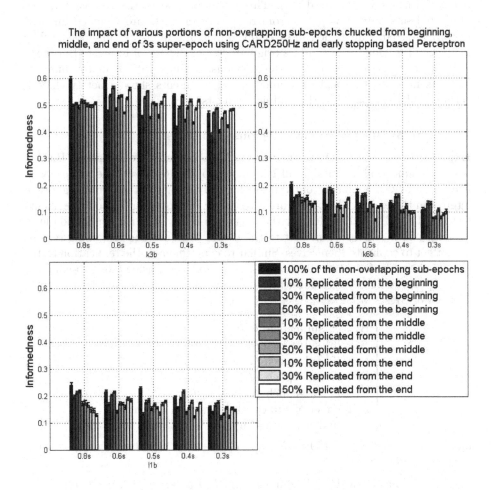

Fig. 3. Comparison of 10%, 30%, and 50% replication from beginning, middle and end segments of epoch and the use of the entire sub-epochs on various window sizes (0.8s, 0.6s, 0.5s, 0.4s, 0.3s) (Exp. 2)

factor denoted as R is considered (i.e., 10%, 30%, 50%). As the first step, based on the replicating factor, portions of sub-epochs originated from the same epoch are selected from the beginning, the middle, and the end of the epoch forming three new sets. At the next step these sets are replicated to provide new sets with approximately similar number of samples compared with the original set with sub-epochs. The outcome is three new sets that each isolate an specific region of the epoch with approximately equal number of training samples. This procedure is applied to various time windows and the results are illustrated in Fig. 3.

A comparison between Fig. 3 and Figs. 1 and 2 illustrate that the use of higher % as replication factor can improve the classification performance compared to the use of individual sub-epochs. However, in most cases using all sub-epochs out-performed the replicated sets. This might be due to the fact that in the replicated sets only sub-epochs from regions of interests are included and the rest are omitted. This issue can be resolved by maintaining all sub-epochs while increasing the number of samples originated from regions of interest (Biasing).

It is noteworthy that unlike the previous findings with 2 motor imagery datasets in [1–3], the beginning and the end segments showed better classification results compared to the middle segments.

3.3   Exp. 3: Biasing toward Regions of Interest

Exp. 3a: Biased Non-Overlapping vs. Non-biased Overlapping. Biasing is a technique that maintains all sub-epochs originated from the same epoch while it provides a higher contribution from those originating from regions of interest in the epoch. The procedure is to divide the epoch into 5 equal segments (B1,B2,M,E2,E1) and implement the biasing in a way that the replication level decreases from regions of interest to the nearby regions. The remaining regions do not get to replicate themselves. Similar to experiment 1, the replication factor is defined as a % (i.e., 10%, 30%, 50%). As an example, using 0.6s sub-windows in 3s epoch generates five sub-epochs within the epoch indexed from 1 to 5. Therefore, B1,B2,M,E2, and E1 are as follows:

$$
\begin{cases}
B1 = 1^{st} \text{ sub-epoch } (0.0s \ ... \ 0.6s) \\
B1 = 2^{nd} \text{ sub-epoch } (0.6s \ ... \ 1.2s) \\
M = 3^{rd} \text{ sub-epoch } (1.2s \ ... \ 1.8s) \\
E2 = 4^{th} \text{ sub-epoch } (1.8s \ ... \ 2.4s) \\
E1 = 5^{th} \text{ sub-epoch } (2.4s \ ... \ 3.0s) \\
\hline
n = \text{number of sub-epochs within an epoch} = 5 \\
p = \text{round(percentage*n)}
\end{cases}
\tag{1}
$$

for *percentage=50%*, $p = (50\% * 5) \approx 3$. The new set would be generated using following criterion:

$$
\begin{cases}
\text{Bias toward the beginning} = [2p(B1) \ p(B2) \ p(M) \ E2 \ E1] \\
\text{Bias toward the middle} = \ \ [B1 \ p(B2) \ 2p(M) \ p(E2) \ E1] \\
\text{Bias toward the end} = \ \ \ \ \ [B1 \ B2 \ p(M) \ p(E2) \ 2p(E1)]
\end{cases}
\tag{2}
$$

where $p(x)$ and $2p(x)$ represent p and $2*p$ times replicated versions of segment x respectively. In the $CARD250Hz0.6s5*240/360$ signal with 3s epoch, the resulting set within each epoch for 50% biasing would be as follow:

$$\left\{ \begin{array}{l} \text{Bias toward the beginning} = [B1\ B1\ B1\ B1\ B1\ B1\ B2\ B2\ B2\ M\ M\ M\ E2\ E1] \\ \text{Bias toward the middle} = \quad [B1\ B2\ B2\ B2\ M\ M\ M\ M\ M\ M\ E2\ E2\ E2\ E1] \\ \text{Bias toward the end} = \quad\ [B1\ B2\ M\ M\ M\ E2\ E2\ E2\ E1\ E1\ E1\ E1\ E1\ E1] \end{array} \right. \qquad (3)$$

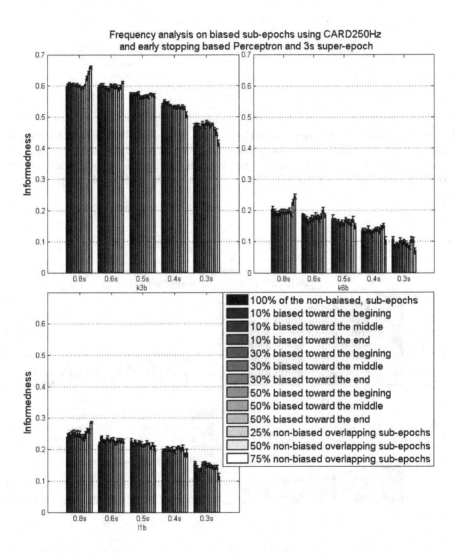

Fig. 4. 10%, 30%, and 50% biasing toward beginning, middle and end segments of epoch vs. 25%, 50%, and 75% standard overlapping using various window sizes (0.8s ,0.6s, 0.5s, 0.4s, 0.3s) (Exp. 3a)

Given that in biasing extra training samples are generated by replicating the regions of interest based on a replication factor while maintaining the remaining sub-epochs (unlike the replication approach), it is possible to assume that any improvement in overall classification performance might be due to having more training samples rather than focusing the training toward regions of interest. To

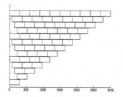

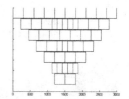

Fig. 5. Triangular Overlapping toward the beginning resulting in 67 sub-epochs using a 0.3s window size on 3s epoch with 1000Hz sample rate as an example (Exp. 3b).

Fig. 6. Triangular Overlapping toward the middle resulting in 48 sub-epochs using a 0.3s window size on 3s epoch with 1000Hz sample rate as an example (Exp. 3b).

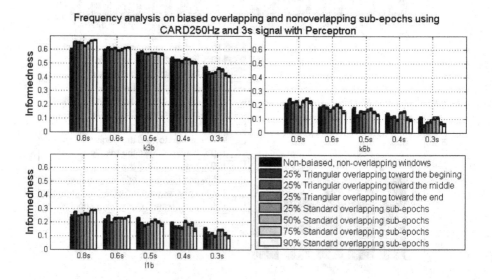

Fig. 7. A comparison of 25% triangular overlapping toward beginning, middle and end segments with various % of standard overlapping using various window sizes (0.8s ,0.6s, 0.5s, 0.4s, 0.3s) (Exp. 3b)

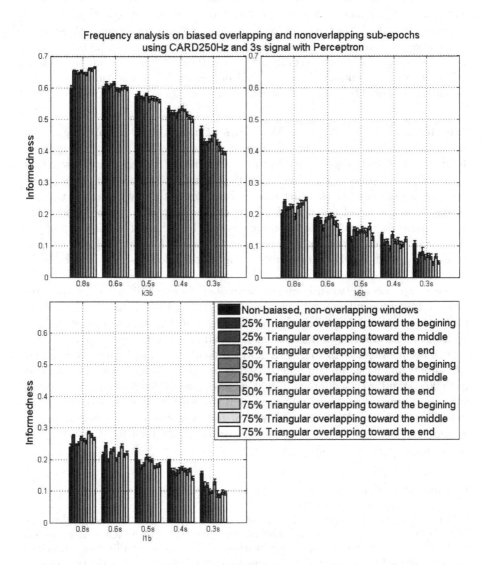

Fig. 8. A comparison of various % of triangular overlapping toward beginning, middle and end segments using various window sizes (0.8s ,0.6s, 0.5s, 0.4s, 0.3s) (Exp. 3b)

provide a better assessment, extra results indicating the impact of standard overlapping using various overlapping factors (25%, 50%, 75%, 90%) are included.
The results in Fig. 4 indicate that standard overlapping is only superior in higher
window sizes (0.8s and 0.6s) while biasing toward regions of interest performs
better in smaller window-sizes (0.5s-0.3s). A comparison between Figs. 4 and 3
illustrate the feasibility of biasing compared to replication in terms of achieving a
higher classification performance and out performing non-biased, non-replicated
sets. The results indicate a significant ($p = 0.0446 < 0.05$) within the potential of various segments of the epoch and biasing factor in addition to existing
significant within subjects and time windows ($p < 0.05$).

Exp. 3b: Biased Overlapping Windows (Triangular Overlapping). The
results achieved in experiment 3a illustrated the potential of both techniques
(biasing and overlapping) in terms of providing higher concentration toward regions of interest (biasing) and having higher number of training samples (overlapping). Triangular Overlapping takes advantage of this by biasing regions of
interest from the set of overlapped sub-epochs. Similar to previous experiments
the biasing is implemented on three regions (the beginning, the middle, and the
end). Examples of 25% triangular overlapping toward the beginning and the end
on 3s epoch with 1000Hz sample rate using 0.3s window size are illustrated in
Figs. 5 and 6.

The comparison between i) non-biased non-overlapped, ii) standard overlapping, and iii) triangular overlapping are provided in Figs. 7 and 8. The results
illustrate the potential of triangular overlapping in terms of achieving better classification performance compared to non-biased non-overlapped signal. A comparison between results in Figs. 7, 8, and 4 indicate the superiority of triangular
overlapping and no significant difference between 25% triangular overlapping and
up to 90% standard overlapping in high window sizes (0.8s) and a better classification performance in lower window sizes. The result of significant test indicate
a significant of $p = 0.0001 < 0.05$ within the potential of various percentage
of triangular overlapping in addition to existing significant within subjects and
time windows ($p = 0 < 0.05$).

4   Conclusion

This paper investigated the potential of several approaches to change the concentration of the training set toward regions of interest in which it is expected
from subjects to have higher concentration on the tasks. Replicating, Biasing,
and Triangular Overlapping are examined using a dataset of 3 subjects performing 4 motor imagery tasks. The conducted experiments illustrated variations
within different segments of the epoch (beginning, middle, and end). Among
the examined approaches triangular overlapping achieved better classification
performance. This is likely to be due to providing higher concentration toward
regions of interests in the epoch (caused by biasing) in addition to increasing the
number of training samples (caused by overlapping). The variation in achieved
performance by different segments of the epoch is inconsistent with the previous

findings with these approaches on a dataset of 5 subjects performing 2 motor imagery tasks in [1–3] and indicate the higher potential of the beginning and the end segments in most cases.

References

1. Atyabi, A., Fitzgibbon, S.P., Powers, D.M.W.: Multiplying the Mileage of Your Dataset with Subwindowing. In: Hu, B., Liu, J., Chen, L., Zhong, N. (eds.) BI 2011. LNCS, vol. 6889, pp. 173–184. Springer, Heidelberg (2011)
2. Atyabi, A., Fitzgibbon, S.P., Powers, D.M.W.: Biasing the Overlapping and Non-Overlapping Sub-Windows of EEG recording. In: IEEE International Joint Conference on Neural Networks (IJCNN 2012), The 2012 IEEE World Congress on Computational Intelligence (IEEE WCCI 2012), pp. 741–746 (2012)
3. Atyabi, A., Powers, D.M.W.: The impact of Segmentation and Replication on Non-Overlapping windows: An EEG study. In: The Second International Conference on Information Science and Technology (ICIST 2012), China, pp. 668–674 (2012)
4. Blankertz, B., Müller, K.-R., Krusienski, D.J., Schalk, G., Wolpaw, J.R., Schlögl, A., Pfurtscheller, G., del R. Millán, J., Schröder, M., Birbaumer, N.: The BCI competition III:Validating alternative approaches to actual BCI problems. Neural Syst. Rehabil. Eng. 14(2), 153–159 (2006)
5. Powers, D.M.W.: Recall and Precision versus the Bookmaker. In: International Conference on Cognitive Science (ICSC 2003), pp. 529–534 (2003)
6. Powers, D.M.W.: Evaluation: From Precision, Recall and F-Measure to ROC., Informedness, Markedness & Correlation. Journal of Machine Learning Technologies 2(1), 37–63 (2011)
7. Powers, D.M.W.: The Problem of Kappa. In: 13th Conference of the European Chapter of the Association for Computational Linguistics, Avignon, France (April 2012)

The Impact of PSO Based Dimension Reduction on EEG Classification

Adham Atyabi[1], Martin H. Luerssen[1], Sean P. Fitzgibbon[1], and David M.W. Powers[1,2]

[1] School of Computer Science, Engineering and Mathematics (CSEM), Flinders University, Australia
[2] Beijing Municipal Lab for Multimedia & Intelligent Software, Beijing University of Technology, Beijing, China
{Adham.Atyabi,Martin.Luerssen,
Sean.Fitzgibbon,David.Powers}@flinders.edu.au

Abstract. The high dimensional nature of EEG data due to large electrode numbers and long task periods is one of the main challenges of studying EEG. Evolutionary alternatives to conventional dimension reduction methods exhibit the advantage of not requiring the entire recording sessions for operation. Particle Swarm Optimization (PSO) is an Evolutionary method that achieves performance through evaluation of several generations of possible solutions. This study investigates the feasibility of a 2 layer PSO structure for synchronous reduction of both electrode and task period dimensions using 4 motor imagery EEG data. The results indicate the potential of the proposed PSO paradigm for dimension reduction with insignificant losses in classification and the practical uses in subject transfer applications.

Keywords: Particle Swarm Optimization, Electroencephalogram, Brain Computer Interface.

1   Introduction

Electroencephalography (EEG) is a non-invasive technique for signal acquisition that records variations of surface potential from the scalp using several electrodes. The dimensionality of the EEG data is measured as a factor of the number of used electrodes for signal acquisition and the number of extracted feature points during the task period (epoch). The high dimensional nature of EEG data caused by the use of a large number of electrodes (up to 256 electrodes) with long task periods (from few seconds to several hours) makes it unsuitable for being used with on-line systems, especially with EEG based Brain Computer Interfaces (BCI). Dimension Reduction (DR) is a preprocessing step that reduces the dimension of the EEG data. Conventional decomposition methods such as Principle Component Analysis (PCA), Singular Value Decomposition (SVD), and Common Spatial Pattern (CSP) reduces the dimensionality of the data by isolating a set of features or electrodes that comply with certain criteria

F.M. Zanzotto et al. (Eds.): BI 2012, LNCS 7670, pp. 220–231, 2012.

regardless of their impact on classification. In addition, these techniques require the entire trials of a recording session of subject for the reduction process.

Evolutionary based approaches are common alternatives for conventional methods due to their ability to address the shortcomings of such methods. This study investigates the potential of an Evolutionary based paradigm proposed in [1] to be used with a dataset containing EEG data of 3 healthy subjects performing 4 motor imagery tasks in multiple sessions. The outline of the study is as follows: Section 2 introduces the used Evolutionary based paradigm for synchronous feature and electrode reduction. Section 3 provides details about the used EEG data and the applied preprocessing techniques. Conducted experiments and the achieved results are presented in section 4. A conclusion is provided in section 5.

2   Evolutionary Based DR

Several studies employed evolutionary methods such as Genetic Algorithm (GA) [2–6], Particle Swarm Optimization (PSO) [7–10], and Ant Colony Optimization (ACO) [11] for either electrode or feature reduction in EEG data. The used paradigm in the majority of these studies is based on generating populations of possible solutions (subsets of indexes for either feature or electrode dimensions) and smoothly guide the optimization toward including features or electrodes that improve the overall classification performance. To do so, in most cases the EEG data is divided into two subsets of training and testing sets and the subset of indexes that results in the best discrimination of the performed task is chosen as the final solution. Despite the encouraging results achieved by such a paradigm it is reasonable to expect data contamination due to the fact that the final product is tuned to perform well on the testing set and therefore is likely to have low generalizability. Atyabi et al., in [1] and [12], suggested the addition of an extra evaluation step in the paradigm that allows the evaluation of the final product on an unseen set of data that is not being used within the previous selection/evaluation stages. The results indicate the lack of generalizability in the final product. This issue is resolved by introducing three new index sets representing the best performing indexes on the validation set, the testing set, and the most commonly used indexes. The results indicate the superiority of the set representing most commonly used indexes.

In [1], a new paradigm featuring a 2 layer PSO structure that allows over 90% DR through synchronous reduction of both feature and electrode dimensions is used. Although the study reports encouraging results through the use of most commonly used indexes, the fact that only one dataset containing 2 motor imagery tasks is used for assessment prevents any definitive conclusion from being made. The first objective of this study is to further analyze the proposed paradigm using a more complicated dataset featuring 4 motor imagery tasks.

In [13] the proposed paradigm in [1] is used in an inclusion with two frameworks to investigate *Subject Specificity* and *Task Specificity* in a subject transfer study. The results indicate the possibility of improving the classification performance through the use of a combination of commonly used indexes and a framework that provides *Task Specificity*. The second objective of this study is to further analyze this issue using a dataset of 4 motor imagery tasks. The proposed PSO paradigm and the used frameworks for *Subject* and *Task Specificity* are discussed in the following section.

2.1 PSO Paradigm

Particle Swarm Optimization (PSO) is a population-based method that achieves performance through local and global interactions among particles (members of population). PSO uses parameters such as velocity (v), position in the search/solution space (x), acceleration coefficients (c_1 and c_2), and inertia weight (w) in its formulation and has limited memory containing the best found solution with each particle (member of the population) and the swarm denoted as *Pbest*) and *Gbest* respectively. PSO achieves performance through updating the solutions in the population with respect to local and global found solutions iteratively using Eqs. 2 and 1 [14].

$$V_{i,j}(t) = w \times V_{i,j}(t-1) + C_{i,j} + S_{i,j}$$
$$C_{i,j} = c_1 r_{1,j} \times (p_{i,j}(t-1) - x_{i,j}(t-1)) \tag{1}$$
$$S_{i,j} = c_2 r_{2,j} \times (g_{i,j}(t-1) - x_{i,j}(t-1))$$

$$x_{i,j}(t) = x_{i,j}(t-1) + V_{i,j}(t) \tag{2}$$

The used PSO paradigm in this study follows a 2 layer swarm notation. The pseudo-code is illustrated in Algorithms. 1 and 2. In the pseudo-code, the subset of extracted indexes that represent the chosen electrode and feature indexes is referred to as a *Mask* and the swarm is a population of masks.

Algorithm 1. PSO based Feature & Electrode reduction

Initialization: creates two instance of the population (P_1 and *Gbest*). Each sub-swarm P_i represents a *mask* containing i) a set of $n \times k$ out of $N \times K$ possible features (in PSO notation, this can be considered as $x_{i,j}$ for $i \in [1...n]$ and $k \in [1...k]$), ii) a set of n out of N electrodes, iii) the best achieved mask denoted as *Pbest*, iv) a Velocity vector denoted as v_i for $i \in [1...n]$.

Gbest represents a *mask* containing i) a set of $n \times k$ out of $N \times K$ possible features, ii) a set of n out of N electrodes, and iii) the best achieved mask denoted as *Pbest*.

Evaluation

repeat

  Updating the population: Update the population using algorithm 2.

  Evaluation: Evaluate all members of the population (sub-swarms) using a classifier.

  Update Bests: Update Personal (*Pbest*) and Global (*Gbest*) Best.

until (*Termination:* the maximum iteration is achieved or the best member of the population (Global Best) has reached to the desired optimum)

Final Evaluation: Reevaluate the best mask of the swarm.

Algorithm 2. Pseudo-code for Updating the Population

Find the top 10 candidates: Sort particles based on their classification performance and only preserve the top 10.

for each particle P_i **do**

    1) Generate a child particle with new set of electrodes that are positioned in nearby areas.

    2) Generate a child particle with new set of electrodes that are positioned in the same areas.

    3) Generate a child particle with new set of $n \times k$ features using velocity vector v and position matrix x and update equations 1 and 2.

    4) Generate a child particle with new set of randomly chosen electrodes that are positioned in the same areas and a new set of $n \times k$ features using velocity vector v and position matrix x and update equations 1 and 2.

end for

In [1] and [13], the proposed paradigm is used in a 10×20 cross validation (CV) resulting in three sets of training, validation and testing with the ratio of 0.9, 0.05, and 0.05 among which the training and the validation are used for the production of the final solution in each fold and the testing set is used within the final evaluation step to assess the generalizability of the suggested masks. Given that in this paradigm the selected *Mask* as the best performing with the either the validation or testing set is referred to set of indexes that been trained and evaluated within the use of 95% of the data, re-appliance of such mask in a new 10×20 CV raise the possibility of contamination between training and testing sets. This issue can be extended to the most commonly used indexes too.

2.2 Subject and Task Specificity

The proposed PSO based DR paradigm in [1] is used to investigate its feasibility for subject transfer through two frameworks (Frame work 1 and 2) representing *Subject Specificity* and *Task Specificity* in [13]. These frameworks are demonstrated with diagrams in Figs. 1 and 2.

The achieved results in [13] indicate the feasibility of the combination of subsets of most commonly used indexes in the applied 10×20 CV (denoted as ComMask) and Framework 2 and the superiority of *Task Specificity* compared to *Subject Specificity* in a 2 motor imagery dataset.

3 Dataset

EEG data from the dataset IIIa of BCI Competition III is used [18]. The dataset contains EEG data of 3 healthy subjects (*k3b, k6b, l1b*) performing 4 motor imagery tasks (left hand, right hand, foot, tongue). The sample rate is 250Hz and band pass filter in the range of 1Hz and 50Hz is applied. 60 electrodes are used and the task period is set to 3s [18]. To be consistent with previous studies [1, 12, 12] the first and last 0.5s of each epoch are considered as pre and post transition

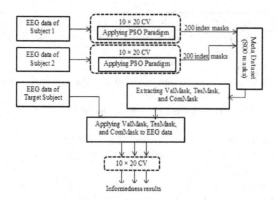

Fig. 1. Diagram representing the appliance of Framework 1 on a dataset with 3 subjects. Meta dataset represents a repository that contains the extracted masks for each fold of 10×20 CV and their informedness results. ValMask and TesMask represents the best performing masks on validation and testing sets respectively. ComMask represents a subset of most commonly used indexes in 10×20 CV.

periods and omitted and the signal is sub-windowed to 0.5s. Common Average Referencing (CAR) and Demeaning (D) are applied, and frequency features are extracted. An Extreme Learning Machine (ELM) with a sigmoid kernel and 80 nodes is used for internal evaluation of particles in the swarm and a polynomial SVM and a modified single layer perceptron that incorporates early stopping are used for final evaluation on the testing set. Polynomial SVM is used through LIBSVM library [22] with default parameter settings (gamma=1/3, coef0=0, and degree=3). All experiments follows 10×20 cross validation (CV) paradigm that creates sets with ratios of 90%, 5%, and 5% for training, validation and testing respectively. Bookmaker informedness is used to assess the classification performance. A detailed discussion about Bookmaker Informedness can be found in [19–21].

4   Experimental Design and Results

This section introduced the conducted experiments for investigating the objectives of the study presents the achieved results. In all experiments, the PSO paradigm is parameterized to generate masks that contain 30 feature and 10 electrode indexes. In the velocity equation of the PSO, EQ. 1, c_1 and c_2 are set to 0.5 and 2.5 respectively and r_1 and r_2 are random values in the range of 0 and 1. Linear Decreasing Inertia Weight (LDIW) is used to update the inertia weight (w_1=0.2 and w_2=1).

4.1   Experiment 1: The Impact of PSO

This experiment investigates the impact of the proposed PSO paradigm as a DR method. The results depicted in Figs. 3 and 4 illustrate the average achieved

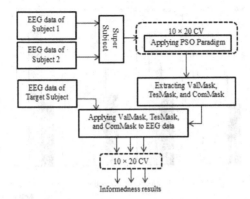

Fig. 2. Diagram representing the appliance of Framework 2 on a dataset with 3 subjects. Super Subject represents the EEG dataset resulting from the concatenation of preprocessed EEG signals of two other subjects that performed similar tasks. The preprocessing stage includes demeaning, common average referencing, and extraction of frequency features. ValMask and TesMask represents the best performing masks on validation and testing sets respectively. ComMask represents a subset of most commonly used indexes in 10 × 20 CV.

informedness with either of the used classifier (Polynomial SVM, Sigmoid ELM, and modified Perceptron) within each subject (k3b, k6b, l1b) with the masks that best represent the testing set, validation set and most commonly selected indexes. The procedure is based on, first, applying the PSO paradigm in a 10 × 20 CV to extract the masks and, later, reapplying the suggested masks to a second 10 × 20 CV to assess the performance. Given that the applied PSO paradigm reduces approximately 90% of the dimensions of the data, the loss of average 0.1 informedness within subjects is likely to be acceptable. Among the used masks and classifiers, the combination of common mask and polynomial SVM shows better performance across subjects. This is likely to be due to the fact that this mask provides better generalizability since it represents the indexes that appeared in most solutions while in each subject ValMask and Tesmask represents the masks that are fine tuned on validation and testing sets in the first 10 × 20 CV. The results achieved by each subject without any dimension reduction is included in figures to help understanding the impact. This is illustrated as FullSet in Figs. 3 and 4.

4.2   Experiment 2: Subject Specificity

This experiment is designed to investigate the feasibility of the extracted masks through PSO paradigm for *Subject Specificity* using Framework 1. The procedure is to use the masks generated by PSO on each subject on others. It is noteworthy that in experiment 1 the extracted masks through the first layer 10 × 20 CV where fine tuned on 95% of the data within different folds of CV, so contamination

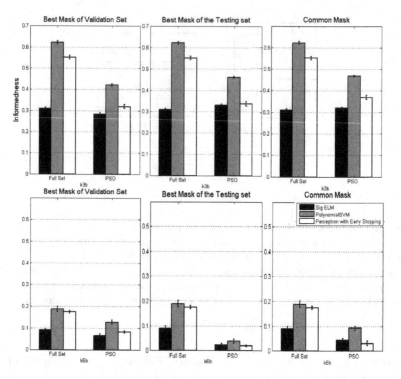

Fig. 3. The feasibility of the used masks on subject k3b and k6b (Exp. 1)

between training and testing samples is possible. This issue is resolved here because the used masks are generated from other subjects.

Subject Specificity is investigated with two experiments. Assuming three target subjects (k3b, k6b, l1b), in experiment 2(a) the masks generated on the EEG data of one subject is used to reduce the dimensions of another subject. For instance, assuming subject k3b as target subject, two experiments are conducted to investigate the impact of masks originated from subject k6b and subject l1b separately. In Fig. 5 this is denoted as $k6b->k3b$ and $l1b->k3b$ respectively.

In experiment 2b the masks extracted from two subjects (individually) are combined together in a meta dataset following the description of Framework 1 in Fig. 1. For example, assuming subject k3b as the target subject, this is illustrated as $k6bl1b->k3b$ in Fig. 6.

4.3   Experiment 3: Task Specificity

This experiment is designed to investigate the feasibility of the masks extracted by PSO for *Task Specificity* using Framework 2 (Fig. 2). Given that the used dataset only contains 3 subjects, a *Super Subject* is created based on the concatenation of EEG data of 2 subjects and the 3rd subject is considered as the target subject. The results are illustrated in Fig. 7.

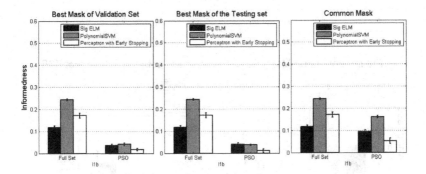

Fig. 4. The feasibility of the used masks on subject l1b (Exp. 1)

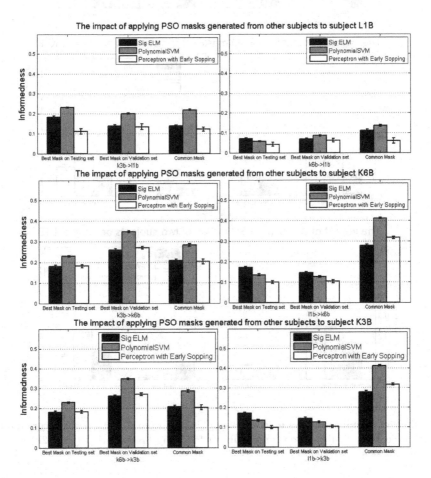

Fig. 5. The feasibility of the used masks of one subject on another using Framework 1 (Exp. 2a)

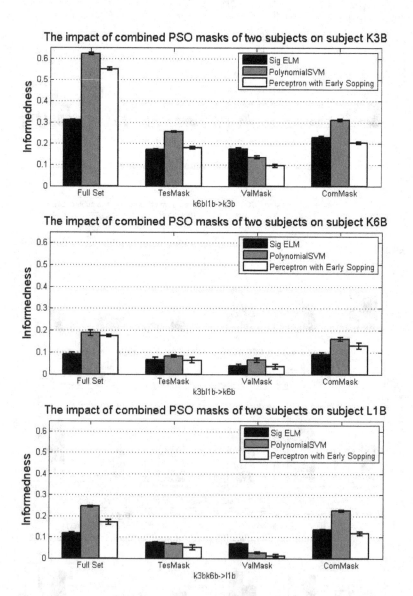

Fig. 6. The feasibility of the used masks originated from a meta dataset containing PSO masks of two subjects on target subject following Framework 1 (Exp. 2b)

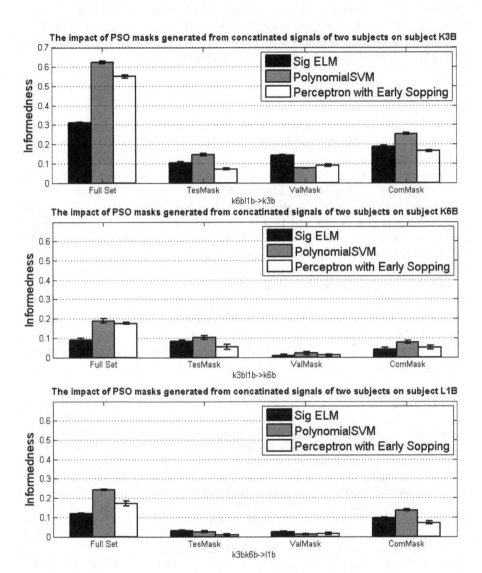

Fig. 7. The feasibility of the used PSO masks originated from a *Super Subject* generated as a result of concatenation of EEG signals of two subjects on target subject following Framework 2 (Exp. 3)

A comparison between the achieved performance with the conducted experiments indicate the potential of Framework 1 to be used for subject transfer. In addition, the results indicate the generalizability of the generated masks. Within the conducted experiments for subject transfer, the best average classification performance across subjects was achieved in experiment 2a with the combination of ComMask (commonly selected indexes) and polynomial SVM.

5 Conclusion

This study illustrates the potential of the proposed PSO paradigm for dimension reduction of EEG data in terms of providing generalizable solutions and demonstrating encouraging performance in the subject transfer problem.

The illustrated generalizability within the generated solutions is consistent with our previous findings in [1]. The results obtained from Frameworks 1 and 2 with respect to *Task Specificity* and *Subject Specificity* contradicts with our previous findings in [13]. In [13], the best overall performance was achieved through the use of a *Super Subject* representing EEG signal concatenation of 4 subjects within the Framework 2 paradigm (using 2 motor imagery dataset) while in this study the best overall performance across subjects was achieved through re-applying the ComMask (commonly selected indexes) within the Framework 1. The poor performance achieved with Framework 2 in this study is likely to be due to the lack of enough subjects with proper variation of expertise for creation of a *Super Subject*.

Further investigation with other datasets that contain larger numbers of subjects is required.

References

1. Atyabi, A., Luerssen, M., Fitzgibbon, S.P., Powers, D.M.W.: Dimension Reduction in EEG Data using Particle Swarm Optimization. In: IEEE Congress on computational Intelligence, CEC 2012 (2012)
2. Tov, E.Y., Inbar, G.F.: Feature selection for the classification of movements from single movement-related potentials. IEEE Transactions on Neural Systems and Rehabilitation Engineering 10(3), 170–177 (2002)
3. Dias, N.S., Jacinto, L.R., Mendes, P.M., Correia, J.H.: Feature Down Selection in Brain Computer Interface. In: Proceeding of the 4th International IEEE EMBS Conference on Neural Engineering, pp. 323–326 (2009)
4. Largo, R., Munteanu, C., Rosa, A.: CAP Event Detection by Wavelets and GA Tuning. In: WISP 2005, pp. 44–48 (2005)
5. Zhang, X., Wang, X.: A genetic algorithm based time-Frequency Approach to a Movement Prediction task. In: Proceeding of the 7th World Congress on Intelligent Control and Automation, pp. 1032–1036 (2008)
6. Palaniappan, R., Raveendran, P.: Genetic Algorithm to select features for Fuzzy ARTMAP classification of evoked EEG, pp. 53-56 (2002)
7. Jin, J., Wang, X., Zhang, J.: Optimal Selection of EEG Electrodes via DPSO Algorithm. In: Proceeding of the 7th World Congress on Intelligent Control and Automation, pp. 5095–5099 (2008)

8. Hasan, B.A.S., Gan, J.Q., Zhang, Q.: Multi-Objective Evolutionary Methods for channel selection in brain Computer interface: Some Preliminary Experimental Results. In: 2010 IEEE Congress on Evolutionary Computation (CEC), pp. 1–6 (2010)

9. Hasan, B.A.S., Gan, J.Q.: Multi-Objective Particle Swarm Optimization for Channel Selection in Brain Computer Interface. In: The UK Workshop on Computational Intelligence (UKCI 2009), Nottingham, UK (2009)

10. Moubayed, N.A., Hasan, B.A.S., Gan, J.Q., Petrovski, A., McCall, J.: Binary-SDMOPSO and its application in channel selection for brain computer interfaces. In: 2010 UK Workshop on Computational Intelligence (UKCI), pp. 1–6 (2010)

11. Khushaba, R.N., Al-Ani, A., Al-Jumaily, A., Nguyen, H.T.: A Hybrid Nonlinear-Discriminant Analysis Feature Projection Technique. In: Wobcke, W., Zhang, M. (eds.) AI 2008. LNCS (LNAI), vol. 5360, pp. 544–550. Springer, Heidelberg (2008)

12. Atyabi, A., Luerssen, M., Fitzgibbon, S.P., Powers, D.M.W.: Evolutionary feature selection and electrode reduction for EEG classification. In: IEEE Congress on Computational Intelligence, CEC 2012 (2012)

13. Atyabi, A., Luerssen, M., Fitzgibbon, S.P., Powers, D.M.W.: Adapting Subject-Independent Task-Specific EEG Feature Masks using PSO. In: IEEE Congress on computational Intelligence, CEC 2012 (2012)

14. Hwang, Y.K., Chen, P.C.: A Heuristic and Complete Planner for the Classical Mover's Problem. In: Proceedings of the 1995 IEEE International Conference on Robotics and Automation, pp. 729–736. IEEE (1995)

15. Atyabi, A., Fitzgibbon, S.P., Powers, D.M.W.: Multiplying the Mileage of Your Dataset with Subwindowing. In: Hu, B., Liu, J., Chen, L., Zhong, N. (eds.) BI 2011. LNCS, vol. 6889, pp. 173–184. Springer, Heidelberg (2011)

16. Atyabi, A., Fitzgibbon, S.P., Powers, D.M.W.: Biasing the Overlapping and Non-Overlapping Sub-Windows of EEG recording. In: IEEE International Joint Conference on Neural Networks, IJCNN 2012 (2012)

17. Atyabi, A., Powers, D.M.W.: The impact of Segmentation and Replication on Non-Overlapping windows: An EEG study. In: The Second International Conference on Information Science and Technology, ICIST 2012, China (2012)

18. Blankertz, B., Müller, K.-R., Krusienski, D.J., Schalk, G., Wolpaw, J.R., Schlögl, A., Pfurtscheller, G., del R. Millán, J., Schröder, M., Birbaumer, N.: The BCI competition III:Validating alternative approaches to actual BCI problems. Neural Syst. Rehabil. Eng. 14(2), 153–159 (2006)

19. Powers, D.M.W.: Recall and Precision versus the Bookmaker. In: International Conference on Cognitive Science (ICSC 2003), pp. 529–534 (2003)

20. Powers, D.M.W.: Evaluation: From Precision, Recall and F-Measure to ROC. Informedness, Markedness & Correlation. Journal of Machine Learning Technologies 2(1), 37–63 (2011)

21. Powers, D.M.W.: The Problem of Kappa. In: 13th Conference of the European Chapter of the Association for Computational Linguistics, Avignon France (April 2012)

22. Chih-Chung, C., Chih-Jen, L.: LIBSVM: A library for support vector machines. ACM Transactions on Intelligent Systems and Technology 2(3), 27:1–27:27 (2011)

Modified Shared Circuits Model for Manufacturing Processes Control:

From Psychology and Neuroscience to a Computational Solution

Rodolfo E. Haber Guerra[1,2], Alfonso Sánchez Boza[1],
Agustín Gajate[2], and Raúl M. del Toro[2]

[1] Escuela Politécnica Superior UAM, Madrid, Spain
{rodolfo.haber,alfonso.sanchez}@uam.es
[2] Center for Automation and Robotics UPM-CSIC, Arganda del Rey, Spain
{rodolfo.haber,agustin.gajate,raul.deltoro}@car.upm-csic.es

Abstract. There are many complex processes waiting for artificial cognitive solutions able to deal with new, complex, unknown, or arbitrary tasks efficiently. In this work, the modified shared circuits model (MSCM) for artificial cognitive control is presented. The main goal is to surpass the limitations of the shared circuits models and to formalize an integrated computational solution on the basis of a neuroscientific and psychological approach. Two novelties of the proposed systems are a commutation or switching mechanism between modules in order to reproduce efficiently the imitation, deliberation and mindreading characteristics of human sociocognitive skills. Another contribution is the introduction of a self-optimization strategy based on cross entropy in order to fulfil the control goals. The closed-loop behaviour of the drilling force demonstrates that the MSCM approach is an alternative and feasible option in the field of artificial cognitive control to deal with processes complexity and uncertainty.

Keywords: artificial cognitive control, embodied cognition, imitation, internal model control, bio-inspired control methods.

1 Introduction

Nowadays, artificial cognitive systems are widely studied to find reliable computational solutions by means of emulating the capacity of humans to develop new, complex, unknown, or arbitrary tasks efficiently [1]. There are a wide variety of strategies related to the partial or total learning of cognitive skills in the field of computer science [2, 3]. These strategies are producing basically new architectures in conjunction of Artificial Intelligence and Computer Science. In our previous work, we presented a novel approach inspired by a theoretical contribution in the field of psychology and neuroscience[4-8].

The Modified Shared Circuits Model (MSCM) is a connectionist framework, which is based on modules that perform a parallel-distributed processing. It is inspired in Shared Circuits Model (SCM)[5], that models the brain from a functional point of view rather than biological.

F.M. Zanzotto et al. (Eds.): BI 2012, LNCS 7670, pp. 232–242, 2012.

The conceptual framework of MSCM is integrated into a computational architecture with seven modules implementing and extending the function of the layers [9]. The interactions among modules make possible to artificially emulate the cognitive capacities of deliberation, imitation, and mindreading (see Fig. 1). There are similarities between this architecture and the internal model paradigm of Control Theory, in line with other proposals which argue that human reasoning is based on the use of internal models in its deliberative stage [6].

In this paper a realization of MSCM is presented to emulate sociocognitive skills, where mechanism for optimization and learning are introduced in the architecture. Moreover, an overall formalization of the modified shared circuit model (MSCM) is presented from the standpoint of Computer Science and Artificial Intelligence. The main novelties of this approach are twofold: the proposed artificial cognitive control system based on MSCM enables optimization and multi-objective management. Both capabilities are essential to surpass the intrinsic limitations of the shared circuit models and provide a new functionality to artificially emulate sociocognitive skills [10, 11].

The selected case study differs from the robotics applications where artificial cognitive strategies have been widely applied since the middle of 80's. The common issue is that manufacturing processes are also characterized by the presence of rapid, nonlinear dynamics which exponentially increase the functional and precision requirements of the sensors, actuators, and computational systems involved. As happens in human behaviour, production processes are mostly designed to achieve multiple objectives simultaneously.

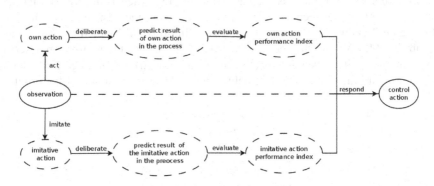

Fig. 1. Intermediate steps in the process of control by MSCM

The paper is organized as follows. Section 2 provides essentials on how MSCM provides an artificial cognitive control solution. Sec. 3 presents the formalization of this proposal from the standpoint of psychology to Computer Science and Artificial Intelligence. In Sec. 4 high-performance drilling process is described to present, in Sec. 5, the results of experimentation in a real process is presented, showing the reliability of MSCM artificial cognitive control system implementation. Finally, the conclusions are given in Sec. 6.

2   From MSCM Proposal to a Computational Solution

The relationship among modules of MSCM enables the artificial cognitive capacities, above-mentioned. Therefore from a computational viewpoint the system design follows the object-oriented programming paradigm since there is a direct module/class interpretation (i.e., each module forms a computational class of the architecture oriented to MSCM objects) [12].

One key issue in any layered or module-based approach is the implementation of a computationally efficient mechanism to manage module interactions. This is the main rationale for introducing an executive level in MSCM architecture to manage the switching between modules. Beyond a computational viewpoint, the brain of humans and some animals process in parallel information to choose the appropriate action according to the desired task. From the standpoint of control engineering, the objective of switching among modules is to achieve a performance index (e.g., error criterion) less than any module operating alone.

In order to carry out this commutation among modules, Makino concluded that inhibition of these capacities depends on failure monitoring: if the actual or own action is not successful, the imitation mechanism is triggered [11, 13, 14]. Similarities with control engineering are evident: a control system attempts that the process follows a desired behaviour.

In this work an alternative method on the basis of the foundations offered by computational sciences and Artificial Intelligence is proposed in order to deal with the theoretical framework of the shared circuit model. In order to evaluate the system's performance a figure of merit is used as estimator [15], whereas in MSCM a mechanism for switching between modules aims at achieving the best process behaviour [16]. Figure 2 shows a summary of the sets of information handled by the method described in MSCM with the necessary reasoning steps: (i) act to go from an observation to an own action given an objective to be attained, (ii) imitate to go from an observation to an imitative action, (iii) deliberate to obtain a prediction of the result of

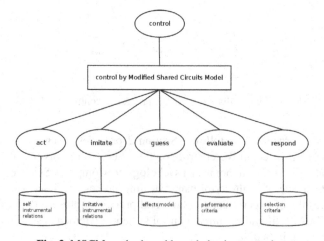

Fig. 2. MSCM methods and knowledge bases used

an action in the process, (iv) evaluate to go from the prediction of the result of the action to the performance index of the action given an objective to be attained, and (v) respond to go from performance indices to the control action that presents the better performance index.

2.1   Performing Own, Imitative and Deliberative Actions to Control

A simple feedback control is used to describe the phenomenon of the flow of information supplied by the effect of the actual output on the environment taking account of the actual state of the environment, i.e., the exogenous signal. It represents the performance of own actions.

Module 1 performs "own actions", while *Module 3* dictates "imitative actions". Indeed, there are two mechanisms to carry out the individual's action. One way is by using a control mechanism that estimates the necessary motor plan for accomplishing an objective in a given context, also called "own actions". The model-based control mechanism is in charge of mapping inputs to outputs by means of instrumental relationships. The information that feedback offers depends on the output and also on exogenous information, which is often considered a disturbances. Another mechanism to perform the individual's action is by imitating agent actions from observation of the "other's actions". It means that agent carries out an action that mirrors or copies behavior observed in others. Inverse models serve to produce imitative actions.

Indeed, the use of internal models in the mammalians brain has been one of the hypotheses to explain the development of control tasks by humans. Inverse models can be implemented in *Module 3* in order to estimate the necessary motor plan for accomplishing an objective in a given context and, a forward model enables the brain to anticipate the perceivable effects of its motor plan for improving efficiency of response. The link between the paradigm of internal model control and cerebrum-cerebellar connectivity as a basis of human intelligence has been already pointed out [6, 7].

On the other hand, forward models enable the brain to anticipate the perceivable effects of this motor plan, with the object of improving response efficiency. In this way, MSCM's *Module 2* handles a forward model or a set of forward models. These models contain a representation of the controlled process in order to simulate its behaviour. It performs deliberation or evaluation about own or imitative actions. It is important to remark that whatever be the role of forward and inverse models, an important issue is to select the most suitable technique or method for implementing the desired functionality. For the sake of analogy with biological systems, fuzzy artificial and neural systems are used in the results reported in this paper.

Cognitive systems acquire their intelligence, broaden their experience and adjust their behaviour through interaction with the environment. One way to consider this issue in artificial cognitive systems is by using modules optimized off line (i.e., before artificial cognitive control start up) according to a *performance index*. It implies the successful achievement of one or several user objectives.

The main goal is to incorporate to the artificial cognitive control system all the knowledge available. One way of reproducing this mechanism by a computational method is the optimal setting of modules' parameters represented by gains or scaling factors according to the MSCM approach.

For the sake of simplicity in this case study the module 1 and module 3 are represented by a fuzzy a neural-fuzzy controllers, respectively (see Fig. 3, 4)[17-19]. The
objective is to optimally set these parameters by minimizing a performance index (1).

$$K = [GAIN_{module1}, Kloop_{module1}, Kloop_{module3}, Kdir_{module3}] = \arg\min[performanceIndex] \qquad (1)$$

Where $Kloop_{module1}$ represents the open loop gain of the fuzzy module 1 controller,
$GAIN_{module1}$ and $Kloop_{module3}$ are scaling factors for the outputs of inverse models, and
$Kdir$ is a scaling factor for the output of direct model of the process. These gains are
detailed at figs. 3 and 4.

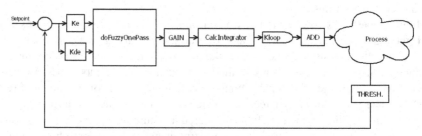

Fig. 3. Diagram of the fuzzy controller that uses module 1

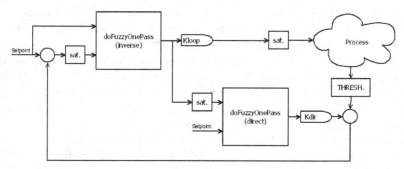

Fig. 4. Diagram of the neural-fuzzy controller of the module 3 (inverse model represented by
doFuzzyOnePass)

There are several deterministic and gradient-free optimization techniques. Cross-
entropy method is selected among different bio-inspired and physical-inspired
methods due to the computational simplicity, the excellent convergence, and the computational efficiency. The cross entropy method represents a general approach to
Monte Carlo for combinatorial optimization, continuous and multiplicity of ends [20,
21]. If x is a random variable in a space χ, with a probability density function p_x,
and if $\phi(x)$ is a real function defined in space, the objective of cross-entropy
method is to find the minimum of the function $\phi(x)$ and the related x^* statements
that meet this minimum:

$$\gamma^* = \phi(x^*) = \min_{x \in \chi} \phi(x) \qquad (2)$$

The CE method provides a methodology to create a sequence $x_0, x_1, ..., x_N$ and levels $\gamma_0, \gamma_1, ..., \gamma_N$, which γ converges to γ^* and x converges to x^*. This is achieved by an iterative calculation of μ and σ of a subset of samples with a lower cost, converging towards an optimum, or that set of parameters which has a lower performance index at simulation.

$$K_i \sim N\left(\mu'_t, \sigma'_t\right) \tag{3}$$

$$\mu'_t = \alpha \cdot \mu_t + (1-\alpha) \cdot \mu'_{t-1} \tag{4}$$

$$\sigma'_t = \beta_{MOD} \cdot \sigma_t + (1-\beta_{MOD}) \cdot \sigma'_{t-1} \tag{5}$$

$$\beta_{MOD} = \beta - \beta \cdot (1-1/t)^q \tag{6}$$

$$\mu = \overline{K_{NE}} \tag{7}$$

$$\sigma = s^2(K_{NE}) \tag{8}$$

Where K_{NE} is the subset of *NE* best samples (samples with lowest performance indices) of the **K** set, that is obtained using the normal distribution $N(\mu'_t, \sigma'_t)$.

2.2 Executive Level: Switching between Cognitive Modules for Adaptation

The cognitive skills of deliberation, imitation, and mindreading are emulated through the interactions and relations between modules. So it is necessary to establish mechanisms for activating the corresponding modules. Three modules are incorporated to the executive level of the architecture in order to manage the interaction between cognitive modules. These modules are *Module 0, Module A* and *Module 4*.

Module 0 uses objectives related to technical, production, and economic factors, among others defined by the user. *Module A* is in charge of calculated performance indices. Finally, *Module 4* defines the interaction between the other modules and manages the emulation of cognitive skills. On the basis on *Module 4*, MSCM can evaluate own and imitative actions. Cognitive cases are described at MSCM algorithm below.

MSCM Algorithm
Three scenarios have been identified in the MSCM architecture in order to switch among modules.

- Scenario 1: If the process is in the transient regime then, since the election between *act* and *imitate* can only be made when the process is in steady-state regime, there is no reason to assess the monitoring process, and the system can only *act* in the form of a simple loop (*Module 1*) until the steady-state regime is attained.

- Scenario 2: If the process is in the steady-state regime, then the system deliberates on which strategy is better to carry out (to *act* or to *imitate*) according to the value of the performance index that would correspond to these two options.
- Scenario 3: It is impossible to discern which strategy is better because both would lead to very similar results (in the evaluation, one prediction leads to a performance index similar to the other) then the task of *mindreading* is implemented.

In order to smooth out the switching between modules, a first order filter, low pass filter, is used to guarantee stability of the control process, attending to sharp changes in control output signal at switching.

$$action_t = action_{t-1} + \alpha \cdot (action_t - action_{t-1}) \qquad (9)$$

where $\alpha \in [0,1], \alpha \in \Re$ is the filter parameter.

At next section, an implementation of MSCM framework, adapted to the real case of high-performance drilling process will described to test the effectiveness of our proposal, and the commutations between modules to develop last algorithm.

3   MSCM Framework for High-Performance Drilling Processes

The drilling process is selected as case study because it is one of the most intensely used manufacturing processes for producing aircraft parts, automobile parts, and molds and dies in general. Moreover, it is a high complex process with nonlinear and time-variant dynamics of relevant variables such as torques, forces, temperatures, etc.

For the sake of simplicity only one controlled variable is considered: the drilling force. It is essential to keep constant the drilling force to obtain higher production rates for the entire useful life of the cutting tool. The drilling force can be kept constant by modifying the feed speed (feed rate) at which the cutting tool drills the work piece. For the sake of clarity, only two different work piece materials are considered. The typical behaviour of this process presents two regimes, one transient and one steady-state. There is a noise or perturbation in the drilling force whose value, according to the experiments varies between 5% to 10%.

The MSCM framework is implemented in two computers connected in a local area network, one PC runs the executive server and the other PC executes cognitive modules. The executive server receives drilling force data, manages cognitive modules, and it sends the corresponding control signal to the process. Executive server and cognitive modules are implemented in the object-oriented programming paradigm (*C++*, Linux operating system environment). The *Ice*[1] communications middleware was used for the communication between the executive and cognitive servers.

3.1   Implementation of Cognitive Modules

The implementation of modules requires the utilization of specific strategies or methods for modelling and control. The choice of modelling strategies and control laws is not straightforward. There are a lot modelling and control methods currently

---

[1] http://www.zeroc.com

available. Nevertheless, the goal is to demonstrate how soft-computing techniques such fuzzy and neural systems can also be applied in the framework given by MSCM.

A fuzzy system is selected for the controller C defined in the *Module* 1. The main rationale of this choice is the excellent characteristics for dealing with nonlinear process behaviour [22]. The internal model control paradigm is selected for *Modules* 2 and 3 [23]. This control paradigm theoretically ensures the stability and robustness of the control system in the presence of external disturbances, and it has some analogy with the performance of the MSCM *Modules* 2 and 3 (see Fig. 5). *Module* 3 is implemented using an ANFIS system [19, 24], since this is a computationally simple solution, and the best suited to real-time applications. Following the internal model control paradigm, an inverse model of the process is used to obtain the imitative actions. These modules as well as *Module* 1 are optimized using cross-entropy method using *ITAE* as performance index [21] .

Module 5 includes the roughly representation of the controlled process. Once again a simple approach (e.g., Z-transforms, Laplace transform) can be used. In this case study the following linear constant-coefficient difference equation is applied:

$$F_i = \frac{(a_1 \cdot u_i + a_2 \cdot u_{i-1} + a_3 \cdot u_{i-2} + a_4 \cdot u_{i-3}) - (b_1 \cdot F_{i-1} + b_2 \cdot F_{i-2} + b_3 \cdot F_{i-3})}{c} \qquad (10)$$

where F_i is the i-th output of the modelled, u_i is the i-th control signal and a_i and b_i are the linear coefficients, and c a constant.

Module 0 and *Module* A were developed. The *ExeServer* class is responsible for capturing the user's objectives from the command line at executive server machine. *Module* 0 will return a control reference and a performance index. In this version, it is only used to evaluate the *ITAE* cost function. *Module* 0 provides the objective or cost function to be calculated:

$$ITAE = \sum_0^T \left[(|e(t)| \cdot t) \cdot (t_i - t_{i-1}) \right] \qquad (11)$$

Using this performance index, parameters of *Module* 1 and *Module* 3 are optimized (see subsec 3.2). The values obtained were $GAIN_{module1} = 1.0084$, $Kloop_{module1} = 0.9$,

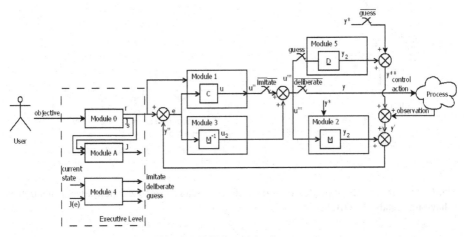

Fig. 5. MSCM module diagram

$Kloop_{module3}$ = 1.05, $Kdir_{module3}$ = 1. The result of *ITAE* at t time instant is used by *Module* 4 to switch between modules. This switching mechanism is implemented by a simple state machine depending on the process output and the current state of the system (see Fig. 6).

4   Experimental Results

The system was tested in the control of a real process, high-performance drilling, one of the most important processes in manufacturing industries. The objective is to keep the cutting force constant throughout the drilling operation as mentioned before. It is achieved by changing the feed rate in real time while the tool is drilling. In order to assess the effectiveness of the implemented MSCM system, it is tested conservative control in drilling GGG40 cast iron. The objective is to maintain a constant cutting force of 500 N.

MSCM deals with disturbances and noise to keep constant the process output. Fig. 6 shows the cutting force and *ITAE* obtained in different drilling *GGG40* trials: open loop, control only with Module 1 (own actions by a fuzzy control), only with Module 3 (ANFIS solution for imitative actions). The best performance index is achieved with the cognitive control (*ITAE*=0.451). The performance of the *Module* 1 (the most simple control mechanism) yields the worst results among them, according to the *ITAE* criterion and this specific case-study (0.62). By this way it is demonstrated the effectiveness of the switching mechanism.

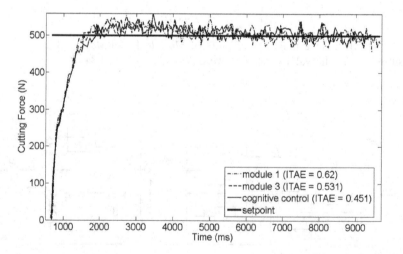

Fig. 6. Behavior of the cutting force for the different strategies analyzed (left), details about the behavior at steady state (right)

5   Conclusions

This paper describes a computational solution to perform an artificial cognitive control on the basis of the modified shared circuits model. A commutation mechanism and a self-optimization strategy are incorporated to effectively reproduce imitation, deliberation and mindreading of human sociocognitive skills. Both mechanisms are essential to surpass the theoretical and practical limitations of the shared circuits model. The shared circuits model is only a conceptual framework that describes how certain human capacities (i.e., imitation, deliberation, and mindreading) can be deployed thanks to sub-personal mechanisms of control, mirroring, and simulation. The shared circuits model does not sufficiently address the functional description of layers just between the level of neural structure and the level of conscious perceptions and deliberate actions. The modified shared circuits model with a self-optimization mechanism and commutation between modules represents a computational architecture that serve to carry out imitation, deliberation, and mindreading processes by means of efficient computational algorithms.

A simple case study of a single-input single-output system represented by a drilling force control is used to evaluate the performance of the proposed solution. The results on the basis of the integral time weighted absolute error demonstrate the enormous potential of this artificial cognitive control strategy. Future work will be focused on bio-inspired switching strategies between modules in order to improve the performance of the artificial cognitive control system.

Acknowledgement. This research is partially funded by the Spanish Ministry of Science and Innovation DPI2008-01978 COGNETCON and DPI2011-24447 C2MICRO projects.

References

1. Pylyshyn, Z.W.: Computation and cognition: Toward a foundation for cognitive science. MIT Press (1984)
2. Bar-Cohen, Y.: Biomimetics: biologically inspired technologies. CRC Press (2006)
3. Thelen, E.S.L.B.: A Dynamic Systems Approach to the Development of Cognition and Action. MIT Press, Cambridge (1994)
4. Boubertakh, H., et al.: Tuning fuzzy PD and PI controllers using reinforcement learning. ISA Transactions 49(4), 543–551 (2010)
5. Hurley, S.: The shared circuits model (SCM): How control, mirroring, and simulation can enable imitation, deliberation, and mindreading. Behavioral and Brain Sciences 31(1), 1–22 (2008)
6. Ito, M.: Control of mental activities by internal models in the cerebellum. Nature Reviews Neuroscience 9(4), 304–313 (2008)
7. Llinas, R.R., Roy, S.: The 'prediction imperative' as the basis for self-awareness. Philos. Trans. R. Soc. B Biol. Sci. 364(1561), 1301–1307 (2009)
8. Sánchez Boza, A., Haber Guerra, R.: Artificial Cognitive Control System Based on the Shared Circuits Model of Sociocognitive Capacities. A First Approach. Engineering Applications of Artificial Intelligence 24(2), 209–219 (2011)

9. Sánchez Boza, A., Haber Guerra, R.: A First Approach to an Artificial Networked Cognitive Control System Based on the Shared Circuits Model of Sociocognitive Capacities. In: Connectionist Models of Behavior and Cognition, pp. 259–276. World Scientific (2011)

10. Heyes, C.: Imitation as a conjunction. Behavioral and Brain Sciences 31(1), 28–29 (2008)

11. Makino, T.: Failure, instead of inhibition, should be monitored for the distinction of self/other and actual/possible actions. Behavioral and Brain Sciences 31(1), 32–33 (2008)

12. Heck, B.S., Wills, L.M., Vachtsevanos, G.: Software technology for implementing reusable, distributed control systems. IEEE Control Systems Magazine 23(1), 21–35 (2003)

13. Marinier, I., Laird, J.E., Lewis, R.L.: A computational unification of cognitive behavior and emotion. Cognitive Systems Research 10(1), 48–69 (2009)

14. Nattkemper, D., Ziessler, M.: Cognitive control of action: the role of action effects. Psychological research 68(2-3), 71–73 (2004)

15. Goodwin, G.C.: Control system design. Prentice Hall, Englewood Cliffs (2001)

16. Meiran, N.: Modeling cognitive control in task-switching. Psychological Research 63(3-4), 234–249 (2000)

17. Ying, H.: Fuzzy Control and Modeling: Analytical foundations and applications. Wiley-IEEE Press (2000)

18. Passino, K.M., Yurkovich, S.: Fuzzy control (1998)

19. Jang, J.-S.R.: ANFIS: adaptive-network-based fuzzy inference system. IEEE Transactions on Systems, Man and Cybernetics 23(3), 665–685 (1993)

20. Rubinstein, R.Y.: The cross-entropy method: a unified approach to combinatorial optimization. In: Monte-Carlo Simulation, and Machine Learning. Springer (2004)

21. Haber, R.E., Del Toro, R.M., Gajate, A.: Optimal fuzzy control system using the cross-entropy method. A case study of a drilling process. Information Sciences 180(14), 2777–2792 (2010)

22. Zadeh, L.A.: Toward human level machine intelligence - Is it achievable? the need for a paradigm shift. IEEE Computational Intelligence Magazine 3(3), 11–22 (2008)

23. Gajate, A.M., Haber, R.E.: Internal Model Control Based on a Neurofuzzy System for Network Applications. A Case Study on the High-Performance Drilling Process. IEEE Transactions on Automation Science and Engineering 6(2), 367–372 (2009)

24. Babuska, R., Verbruggen, H.: Neuro-fuzzy methods for nonlinear system identification. Annual Reviews in Control 27(1), 73–85 (2003)

A Brain-Inspired Computational Model of Emotion and Attention Interaction

Silviano Díaz Barriga[1], Luis-Felipe Rodríguez[1], Félix Ramos[1],
and Marco Ramos[2]

[1] Department of Computer Science, Cinvestav Guadalajara, México
{sdiaz,lrodrigue,framos}@gdl.cinvestav.mx
[2] Department of Computer Science,
Universidad Autónoma del Estado de México, Campus Toluca, México
mramos@univ-tlse1.fr

Abstract. Computational models of cognitive processes are usually developed as separate components. The importance of the interactions among these models has been widely disregarded. In recent years, research on the brain information processing has focused on the interrelationships among cognitive functions, providing a wealth of evidence capable of informing the development of more integrative computational models of cognition. In this paper, we present a brain-inspired computational model of emotion and attention interaction. This model addresses some aspects of the interplay between these two processes and is developed to be included in cognitive architectures of intelligent agents. Simulations based on the dot-probe paradigm are carried out to validate the proposed model.

1 Introduction

A great volume of theories and models have been proposed to explain the neural substrates of human cognition. These have inspired the development of computational models of specific cognitive functions such as perception, attention, and decision making. Particularly, in disciplines such as artificial intelligence (AI) and human-computer interaction (HCI), computational models of *emotion* and *attention* have been implemented in cognitive architectures for intelligent agents [2,15]. Attention mechanisms allow intelligent systems to focus on relevant elements in the environment, whereas emotion mechanisms allow them to evaluate their environment from an emotional perspective in order to develop consistent behavior. Nevertheless, although computational models of emotion and attention have contributed to increasing the believability of intelligent agents' behavior, these have been developed primarily as separate components.

Interactions between emotion and attention processes have been investigated from multidisciplinary perspectives. Behavioral experiments show that humans have a predisposition to attend to emotionally relevant elements in the environment, and that attended stimuli influence the emotional experience and behavioral response of individuals [13,18]. The neural substrates supporting these

F.M. Zanzotto et al. (Eds.): BI 2012, LNCS 7670, pp. 243–254, 2012.
© Springer-Verlag Berlin Heidelberg 2012

interactions have been also investigated. Studies from neuroscience have identified key brain structures and neural systems underlying the influences between attention and emotion processes [14,17]. Nevertheless, as noted above, evidence explaining these reciprocal interactions has been widely disregarded in the development of computational models of cognition (CMCs).

In this paper, we propose a *brain-inspired computational model of emotion and attention interaction*, which attempts to show that evidence from disciplines studying the brain information processing can properly inform the design of integrative computational models of cognition. This computational model is designed to serve as a component of cognitive architectures for intelligent agents. Its main purpose is to provide intelligent systems with mechanisms for attending and reacting to emotionally relevant visual stimuli in the environment. The paper is structured as follows. In the next section, we discuss the importance of biological findings as the theoretical foundations of CMCs. In section 3, we explore the neural substrates of emotion and attention processes and their interactions. The proposed computational model of emotion and attention interaction is described in section 4. In section 5, we present the results of simulations performed based on the dot-probe paradigm. Finally, concluding remarks are given in section 6.

2   Biological Findings as the Foundation of CMCs

The development process of CMCs is not only based on computational technologies, but also on findings contributed by multiple disciplines concerned with the study of human cognitive processes. Most developments of CMCs have been inspired by psychological theories, which explore human cognition from a functional perspective that focus on explaining the inputs, outputs, and behaviors of cognitive functions. Importantly, psychologically based CMCs have proven useful in various application domains and have been positively evaluated in different case studies. Thus, if psychological models have proven adequate to guide the development of CMCs, why would we need to consider additional theoretical approaches? In this section, we briefly discuss some reasons that support the idea of considering biological evidence in the development of CMCs.

Some issues in the development process of CMCs have to do with the theoretical basis of these computational models. For example, as psychological theories explain human cognition from a functional perspective and therefore lack the detail needed to fully implement a computational system, there are decision points in the development of CMCs in which psychological evidence is unable to provide adequate guidance. As a result, the inclusion of "working assumptions" in the design of CMCs becomes necessary in order to achieve functional systems. These working assumptions are usually software components that lack a theoretical basis and which are used to substitute missing or incompatible components in the theoretical models underlying the design of CMCs. These may also lead to the implementation of computational models whose design is far from being theoretically plausible, and prevent the creation of proper environments that facilitate the unification of CMCs in cognitive agent architectures.

This position is not suggesting that the development of CMCs must be completely based on well-grounded theoretical evidence, or that their computational plausibility depends on their theoretical basis, but that other theoretical approaches may provide further support to the development of CMCs. Particularly, biological evidence from fields that study the brain information processing may help understand the mechanisms underlying the psychological processes implemented in CMCs. Biological theories provide deep explanations about the inner workings of human cognition as these explore cognitive functions in terms of neural systems, brain structures, and neural pathways. From this perspective, a major assumption is that biological evidence can help devise well-defined and more theoretically plausible mechanisms for CMCs, thus reducing and validating the working assumptions included in their designs.

Biological evidence may also contribute to developing integrative CMCs that deal with the interaction between diverse cognitive functions. The study of the brain architecture have demonstrated that human behavior results from the joint operation of several cognitive systems [14, 17]. Also, multidisciplinary evidence suggests that all brain processes are interdependent, and that there is no single brain structure capable of generating cognitive behavior. Thus, evidence from disciplines such as neuroscience, neurophysiology, and neuropsychology become adequate to guide the development of integrative CMCs as these explain the neural mechanisms underlying the interactions between cognitive functions. Moreover, this type of evidence can help to design integrative frameworks for the consistent unification of CMCs in cognitive agent architectures.

3   Brain Evidence about Emotion and Attention Interaction

The proposed computational model of emotion and attention interaction is designed to model the mechanisms that allow humans to attend and react to emotionally relevant visual elements in the environment. In this section, we review multidisciplinary evidence that explains this crucial aspect of human behavior.

Results from behavioral experiments have shown that humans have a predisposition to attend to emotionally relevant elements in the environment [17, 18]. Öhman et al. [13] suggest that the ability to efficiently detect significant events in the environment is essential for survival purposes. Their studies indicate that certain types of stimuli such as threatening ones and unexpected and highly emotional events can automatically capture individuals' attention and interrupt their current cognitive and behavioral activities. Evidence also indicates that once a stimulus is attended to, it influences the subsequent emotional experience and behavior of individuals [14, 18]. Frijda [8] proposes that there are different states of action readiness that are elicited by objects appraised as emotionally relevant, which activate or deactivate mechanisms necessary to respond to emotional contingencies. Similarly, Fredrickson and Branigan [6] have identified important patterns of behavior induced by attended stimuli. Their experiments show that positive emotional experiences broaden individuals' thought-action repertoires and that negative ones narrow thought-action repertoires.

The neural substrates supporting these interactions have been also investigated. The ventral pathway (VP) has been recognized as a major neural system in which several attention processes take place. Key areas in the VP are the striate cortex (ST), extrastriate cortex (EST), and inferotemporal cortex (ITC). Evidence shows that environmental stimuli reach the ST from the retina through a thalamic pathway that includes the lateral geniculate nucleus (LGN) [1]. In the ST, neurons respond to simple visual attributes of perceived stimuli such as intensity, color, and orientation. The ST projects to the EST, where neurons respond to the shape and other complex geometric patterns of stimuli. According to Bisley et al. [4], the lateral intraparietal cortex (LIP), a brain structure located in the parietal lobe highly connected with components of the VP, maintains a representation of the relative stimulus saliency across the entire visual field [4], which is further shared with other brain areas such as the superior colliculus (SC) and frontal eye fields (FEF) [1]. The LIP activity is also correlated with the allocation of covert attention. This brain structure projects attentional modulations directly and through the pulvinar nucleus (PUL) to visual ventral areas such as the EST. Furthermore, the LIP has been associated with the FEF and SC, which provide support to the generation of eye movements for overt attention [1]. In the last phase of the VP, attention to a particular stimulus biases the competition for further processing, which occurs in the ITC.

Regarding the emotion process, the amygdala (Amy) has been identified as a key brain structure involved in the processing of emotional stimuli and organization of emotional reactions [7]. The Amy has been involved in a circuit that preattentively registers the emotional significance of environmental stimuli [17]. Evidence indicates that visual stimuli captured by humans are projected from the retina to the Amy through a tecto-pulvinar pathway (TP) [18]. This subcortical route is fast and conveys coarse visual data, which allows the Amy to perform rapid but inaccurate assessments of emotionally relevant stimuli in order to prepare the organism for emotional contingencies. The Amy plays a key role in the generation of emotional responses. For the Amy to perform such task, it has extensive connections with many brain structures that underlie cognitive and visceral functions [14]. The Amy maintains a dynamic data exchange with brain structures that convey, among other things, simple and complex sensory stimuli, contextual and social information, individuals' internal motivations and goals, and information about past experiences in which attended stimuli have been involved. The Amy integrates and evaluates these data and projects to several neural systems that control cognitive functions such as memory and attention, which ultimately control human behavior.

Evidence indicates that areas in the VP maintain reciprocal interactions with the Amy [18]. According to Freese and Amaral [7], the Amy projects to virtually all processing stages along the VP, but only receives projections from the latest phases. Particularly, the Amy projects to areas in the ST and EST, influencing neural systems that control the interpretation of environmental stimuli by directly enhancing the neural responses to the attended stimulus [18]. Similarly, the Amy receives inputs from the ITC, where a full recognition of attended stimuli takes place. This projection allows the Amy to organize consistent emotional responses based on fully interpreted environmental information.

4   Model of Emotion and Attention Interaction

In this section, we present a computational model of attention and emotion interaction (see Figure 1). This model is designed to provide intelligent virtual agents with mechanisms for attending and reacting to emotionally relevant elements in the environment. Its design is inspired by evidence from fields that study the brain information processing such as neuroscience, neuropsychology, and neurophysiology. The components of the model represent brain structures underlying the interactions between attention and emotion processes. The model comprises three phases: *saliency calculation, attentional deployment,* and *emotional response*. In the first phase, the most salient environmental stimulus is determined based on its physical characteristics and emotional relevance. In the second, this stimulus is attended to and fully interpreted. Finally, in the third phase, an emotional response is generated according to the significance of the attended stimulus. This model takes as input 2D images that represent the environment perceived by an intelligent agent. In the remainder of this section, we explain the proposed computational model based on these three phases.

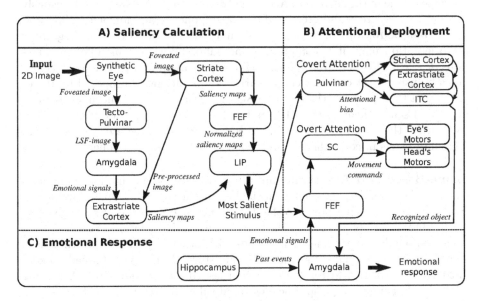

Fig. 1. A computational model of emotion and attention interaction (some components are used more than once to facilitate data flow understanding)

4.1   Saliency Calculation

Saliency calculation is carried out in three steps. 1) ICO-based saliency: for each location in the input image, a saliency value is computed based on intensity, color, and orientation attributes. 2) Shape-based and emotional saliency: pixels in the input image are grouped into objects so that a saliency value for each object is computed based on their emotional relevance and the contrast of their shapes. 3) Featured-based saliency: the two saliencies calculated in the previous phases are combined into a single feature-based saliency, which determines the most salient stimulus in the input image.

ICO-Based Saliency. In this phase, the synthetic Eye captures a 2D image representing the virtual agent's environment and establishes the foveal and peripheral areas. In the peripheral area, a blur is applied so that it maintains a lower resolution than the foveal area, as occurs in human vision. The Eye projects this foveated image to the ST and Amy components through LGN and TP thalamic relays, respectively.

In the ST, intensity, color, and orientation (ICO) conspicuity maps are calculated based on different scales of the input image. The intensity map is concerned with intensity contrast, which in humans is detected by neurons that are sensitive either to dark centers on bright surrounds or to the converse [10]. The color map is computed using a "color double-opponent" system. The center of neurons' receptive fields is excited by one color and inhibited by another, while the converse is true in the surround. Accordingly, maps are created to simultaneously account for red/green and green/red double opponency and for blue/yellow and yellow/blue double opponency that exists in human striate cortex [5]. Regarding the orientation map, it is computed using gabor filters in four different directions: $\theta \in \{0\,^\circ, 45\,^\circ, 90\,^\circ, 135\,^\circ\}$. The ST component computes ICO conspicuity maps by using a set of linear center-surround operations as proposed by Itti et al. [9] and then projects them to the SC and FEF. The FEF normalizes these maps and sends them to the LIP for further processing. In addition, in order to continue the visual processing in the VP, the ST pre-processes the 2D image (classifies pixels in color classes) and sends it to the EST component.

Shape-Based and Emotional Saliency. In this stage, the TP component converts the 2D image received form the Eye into a blurry low-spatial frequency (LSF) image and then sends it to the Amy, which segments the LSF image in order to obtain objects' shapes. In the Amy, a low-level evaluation of these objects is carried out by comparing their shapes with other objects' shapes that have associated an emotional value and which are stored in the Amy (already predefined and represented in terms of pleasantness and activation [16]). According to the level of similarity, a specific emotional value is given to each object in the agent's environment. The Amy projects these values to the EST component.

Following the hierarchy of visual processing in the ventral pathway, in the EST component, objects' shapes contained in the 2D image received from ST are extracted by grouping pixels into regions with similar properties. Then, the shapes

of the identified regions are defined and sent to the ITC component to continue
the visual object recognition process. In addition, by using the emotional valence
of each object received from the Amy, the EST assigns the corresponding emotional value to each basic shape and projects this data to the LIP component
for further processing.

In the LIP, before the calculation of shape-based saliency occurs, an ICO-
based saliency value is assigned to each basic shape received from the EST. This
saliency value is calculated based on the ICO-based saliency average of all the
pixels that are contained in a particular basic shape. Next, the LIP computes
shape-based saliency by considering how much the shape of an object stands
out from those of its neighboring objects (note that these shapes already have
associated an implicit emotional saliency value). The more the object's shape
differs (physically and/or emotionally) from its neighbors' shape, the greater
shape-based saliency value will have.

Feature-Based Saliency. The proposed model of attention considers the objects as units that compete for visual processing and attentional deployment.
Thus, a feature-based saliency is computed for each object that is extracted
from the input image. During this stage, this saliency is calculated and the object with the greatest saliency is selected for attentional deployment.

The LIP component is responsible for computing featured-based saliency.
Feature-based saliency calculation is based on the ICO- and shape-based saliencies of the objects in the visual scene and consists basically of a weighted average.
The LIP component assigns more weight to the (ICO- or shape-based) saliency
when the difference between this value and the average (ICO or shape-based)
saliency of the objects is greater than a certain threshold. Thus, once every object in the scene has a featured-based saliency value, the LIP determines the
most salient stimulus in the input image and sends this data to the PUL and
FEF components for attentional deployment.

4.2   Attentional Deployment

In the proposed model, both physical attributes and emotional significance of
stimuli are considered for attentional deployment. Since these two aspects are
embedded in the featured-based saliency of each stimulus, only featured-based
saliency is considered for the attentional deployment, which can be either overt
or covert depending on the location of the most salient stimulus in the input
image. Once the FEF component receives information about the most salient
stimulus from the LIP, it evaluates whether an eye movement (overt attention)
is required to attend to such stimulus and determines the direction and duration
of the eye fixation [11]. The direction of the eye movement is determined considering the stimulus and the foveal area locations. With respect to the fixation
duration, it is determined by considering that in humans the typical mean fixation duration is about 260-330 ms during scene perception and that emotionally
relevant stimuli (specially threatening ones) increase this duration. Thus, once
the Amy component determines the emotional significance of the most salient

stimulus, it sends this information to the FEF in order to influence fixation duration. It is important to note that during fixation period the attended stimulus (and the others around it) is fully recognized by the ITC component, which interprets object's characteristics and projects to the Amy to influence subsequent agent's emotional responses.

Covert Attention. If the stimulus to be attended to is located at the foveal area, the PUL component sends data about the most salient stimulus to the ST, EST, and ITC components so that the visual processing in the ventral pathway of such stimulus is favored. The processing of ICO and shape characteristics of such stimulus are favored in further competition for visual processing. This kind of attention does not involve eye movements. It is considered as a mental process that biases the competition for attentional deployment to certain stimulus whose physical attributes or emotional significance are salient or relevant. Thus, the FEF component will increase the average fixation duration when the most salient stimulus is a threatening one. This increment is computed according to the emotional valence that is associated to such stimulus.

Overt Attention. When the most salient stimulus is located outside the foveal area of the image, eye and head movements are required in order to attend to this stimulus. The FEF sends a signal that includes both direction and duration of the eye fixation to the SC to perform such movement. The SC component generates appropriate commands for eye movements based on information it maintains about stimulus location, contained in the saliency maps that were received from the ST component. Once the required eye movement has been carried out and the most salient object is located at the foveal area, then covert attention takes place.

4.3   Emotional Response

The Amy component carries out an evaluation of the attended stimulus to determine its emotional significance. In the proposed model, the Amy organizes emotional responses based on the evaluation of data projected from the ITC and the Hippocampus (HIP) components. Unlike the evaluations performed in the first phase (saliency calculation), which were fast and based on coarse data, during this phase the Amy evaluates the emotional significance of fully recognized objects. The Amy receives from the ITC the attended object and from the HIP information about its emotional significance (already predefined and represented in terms of pleasantness and activation [16]). The Amy implements a two-dimensional space consisting of pleasantness (pleasure/displeasure) and activation (arousal/non-arousal) to decide the emotional response. In this space, specific types of responses such as those induced by happiness and fear are associated with well-defined regions. The attended object is appropriately situated within this two-dimensional space and its particular position and proximity to a particular region is what defines the emotional response to be implemented by a virtual intelligent agent. In our model, the emotional responses are implemented as emotional facial expressions. For example, an object associated with high pleasure and moderate activation may fall in the region of happy responses, whereas an object associated with high displeasure and high activation in the region of fear responses. In this manner, the attention process influences the development of emotional responses as these are generated once detailed information about an attended object is available.

5   Simulations and Results

The proposed model of attention and emotion interaction was implemented as a component of cognitive architectures for intelligent agents. This component allows these intelligent systems to attend and react to emotionally significant stimuli in the environment. We used Alfred [3], a Facial Animation System designed to create facial expressions for animated agents, to implement a virtual agent whose underlying architecture includes the proposed model. Alfred enables virtual agents to control many individual facial muscles and head movements. Moreover, it allows the generation of a diversity of emotional facial expressions based on the Facial Action Coding System (FACS). Particularly, based on these Alfred's abilities, our virtual agent is capable of simulating gaze shifts when overt attention is required and of displaying emotional responses through facial expressions according to the attended stimulus.

We carried out simulations based on the dot-probe paradigm [12] to validate the proposed model. This task has been used by psychologists and neuroscientists to test human selective attention and particularly to determine the impact of threat-related stimuli on the distribution of visual attention. In this task, participants are situated in front of a computer screen and asked to look at a fixation cross on the center of the screen. Two stimuli, one threatening and one neutral, appear randomly on either side of the screen for a predetermined period of time. Once these stimuli disappear, a dot (target) is presented in one side of the screen and participants must indicate the location of the dot. In this task, response latency is measured. Another cycle of the task starts after the dot is detected.

We implemented two versions of the dot-probe paradigm to validate the proposed model: a) we randomly presented in one side of the screen a neutral stimulus and in the other an emotionally relevant stimulus (part A of Figure 2); b) we randomly presented only neutral stimuli with different physical attributes in both sides of the screen (part B of Figure 2). In both versions of the paradigm, we experimented with valid and invalid trials. Valid trials occurs when the dot appears at the location previously occupied by the emotional stimulus or the most salient stimuli, and invalid trials when the dot appears at the location that was previously occupied by the neutral stimulus or the stimulus with the lowest physical saliency. The emotional significance of the emotionally relevant stimulus in version 'a' and the saliency of the most salient stimulus in version 'b' varies in low, medium, and high values. As in the dot-probe task, we measure in both cases the time it takes to the virtual agent Alfred to attend to the presented dot.

Moreover, for the purpose of validating other aspects of the proposed model, we measure the following: 1) whether the virtual agent is capable of attending to emotionally relevant stimuli in the environment; 2) when all stimuli is neutral, whether the virtual agent is capable of attending to the stimulus with greater physical saliency; 3) whether the virtual agent is capable of developing consistent facial expressions based on the emotional significance of the attended stimulus.

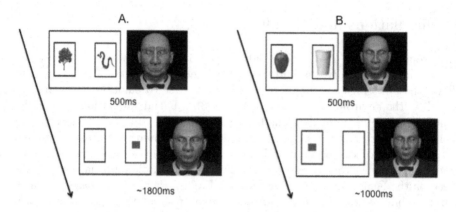

Fig. 2. Simulations based on the dot-probe paradigm

During the simulations, Alfred's response latency is mainly influenced by the emotional relevance of the attended stimulus. The particular emotional value assigned to each stimulus presented to Alfred determines eye fixation duration (the period of time the agent keeps looking at the attended stimulus and processing its physical and emotional characteristics). After the fixation period finishes, the virtual agent is capable of processing new stimuli.

Table 1 shows the results of the simulations. In version 'a' of the task, the latency for attending the dot during invalid trials is greater than that in valid trials. In both, valid and invalid trials, the latency is correlated with the level of emotional significance of the emotionally laden stimulus. When the emotional valence of the emotional stimulus is high, the fixation duration for attending such emotional stimulus is increased in order to get more information about such stimulus. Thus, the latency for attending the dot increases as a consequence of the previous condition. This latency is greater for invalid trials due to the additional movements are required (overt attention) to re-orient the focus of attention to the location where the target appears. With respect to the results of version 'b' of the paradigm, the latency for attending the dot is slightly greater in invalid trials than that in valid trials. This is due to the movements required to attend to the dot in the next step. In this version, the level of saliency of the most salient stimulus does not play an important role in the fixation duration of such salient stimulus. Thus, stimulus saliency does not affect the latency for attending the target in this version of the paradigm task.

Table 1. Results of the simulations based on the dot-probe paradigm

	Valid Trials			Invalid Trials		
Version *a*	Emotional Significance					
Average	High	Medium	Low	High	Medium	Low
Latency	1.83 seg	1.69 seg	1.36 seg	2.23 seg	1.97 seg	1.58 seg
Version *b*	Saliency Level					
Average	High	Medium	Low	High	Medium	Low
Latency	1.06 seg	1.04 seg	1.06 seg	1.24 seg	1.28 seg	1.25 seg

The results also showed that Alfred was capable of attending to the most emotionally relevant stimulus in case 'a' and to the one with the highest physical characteristics in case 'b'. In addition, Alfred's facial expressions were consistent with the emotional significance of perceived stimuli (see Figure 2).

From the computational perspective, all these results highlight the significance of the proposed model to areas such as AI, HCI, and virtual reality (VR). In HCI applications, for example, virtual entities are expected to exhibit very believable and natural behaviors that resemble those of humans. As a key aspect of human behavior is the predisposition to attend and react to emotionally relevant stimuli in the environment, virtual entities must be able to correspond to such behavior by directing their attentional resources toward the emotionally relevant objects attended to by humans when they share a virtual scenario, as well as by developing consistent reactions. Similarly, the proposed model allows the simulation of virtual environments in which a series of emotionally significant stimuli can compete among themselves and with other non-emotional stimuli to capture the agent's attention. Furthermore, in situations where it is difficult to determine the most relevant emotional stimulus, the proposed model provides appropriate mechanisms to decide the most relevant stimulus based on other objects' characteristics. These examples illustrate the extent to which the proposed model can improve the believability of agents' behavior in common scenarios of AI, HCI, and VR applications.

6   Conclusion

In this paper, evidence from disciplines that study the brain information processing was considered to develop a computational model of emotion and attention interaction. It was demonstrated that biological evidence is capable of informing the design of integrative models that address the interactions between two or more cognitive processes. The advantages of biologically based computational models were discussed. Virtual simulations based on the dot-probe paradigm were carried out to validate the proposed computational model. The results showed that the model provides intelligent agents with proper mechanisms to attend and react to emotionally relevant stimuli. The implementation of the model in the cognitive architecture of an intelligent system demonstrated its relevance to applications in areas of computer science such as HCI, AI, and VR.

References

1. Baluch, F., Itti, L.: Mechanisms of top-down attention. Trends in Neurosciences 34(4), 210–224 (2011)
2. Becker-Asano, C., Wachsmuth, I.: Affective computing with primary and secondary emotions in a virtual human. Autonomous Agents and Multi-Agent Systems 20(1), 32–49 (2010)
3. Bee, N., Falk, B., André, E.: Simplified facial animation control utilizing novel input devices: a comparative study. In: Proceedings of the 14th International Conference on Intelligent User Interfaces, pp. 197–206. ACM, New York (2009)
4. Bisley, J.W., Mirpour, K., Arcizet, F., Ong, W.S.: The role of the lateral intraparietal area in orienting attention and its implications for visual search. European Journal of Neuroscience 33(11), 1982–1990 (2011)
5. Engel, S., Zhang, X., Wandell, B.: Colour tuning in human visual cortex measured with functional magnetic resonance imaging. Nature 388(6637), 68–71 (1997)
6. Fredrickson, B.L., Branigan, C.: Positive emotions broaden the scope of attention and thought-action repertoires. Cognition & Emotion 19(3), 313–332 (2005)
7. Freese, J.L., Amaral, D.G.: Neuroanatomy of the primate amygdala. In: Whalen, P.J., Phelps, E.A. (eds.) The Human Amygdala, pp. 3–42. The Guilford Press (2009)
8. Frijda, N.: The Emotions. Cambridge University Press (1986)
9. Itti, L., Koch, C., Niebur, E.: A model of saliency-based visual attention for rapid scene analysis. IEEE Transactions on Pattern Analysis and Machine Intelligence 20(11), 1254–1259 (1998)
10. Leventhal, A.G.: The Neural Basis of Visual Function: Vision and Visual Dysfunction. CRC Press (1991)
11. Machado, H., Rafal, R.: Strategic control over saccadic eye movements: Studies of the fixation offset effect. Attention, Perception, & Psychophysics 62(6), 1236–1242 (2000)
12. MacLeod, C., Mathews, A., Tata, P.: Attentional bias in emotional disorders. Journal of Abnormal Psychology 95(1), 15–20 (1986)
13. Öhman, A., Flykt, A., Esteves, F.: Emotion drives attention: Detecting the snake in the grass. Journal of Experimental Psychology 130(3), 466–478 (2001)
14. Phelps, E.A.: Emotion and cognition: Insights from studies of the human amygdala. Annual Review of Psychology 57, 27–53 (2006)
15. Randall, W., Hill, J.: Modeling perceptual attention in virtual humans. In: Proceedings of the 8th Conference on Computer Generated Forces and Behavioral Representation (1999)
16. Russell, J.A.: Core affect and the psychological construction of emotion. Psychological Review 110(1), 145–172 (2003)
17. Taylor, J.G., Fragopanagos, N.F.: The interaction of attention and emotion. Neural Networks 18(4), 353–369 (2005)
18. Vuilleumier, P.: How brains beware: neural mechanisms of emotional attention. Trends in Cognitive Sciences 9(12), 585–594 (2005)

Chinese Medicine Formula Network Analysis for Core Herbal Discovery

Gao Yuan[1,2], Liu Zheng[1,2], Wang Chong-Jun[1,2,*],
Fan Xin-Sheng[3], and Xie Jun-Yuan[1,2]

[1] National Key Laboratory for Novel Software Technology (Nanjing University),
Nanjing 210093, China
[2] Department of Computer Science and Technology,
Nanjing University, Nanjing 210093, China
[3] Jiangsu Key Laboratory for Modern Traditional Chinese Medicine Formulae,
Nanjing University of Traditional Chinese Medicine, Nanjing, 210046, China

Abstract. Data mining is a hotspot in the traditional Chinese medical (TCM) field now. Because it glosses over the relation between herbals, the traditional Chinese medical formula (CMF) data organization method, in which different records are concerned different CMFs, cannot meet the need for deep data analysis. This paper proposes an effective approach for CMF networking according to the Jaccard similarity coefficient; then we carried out an analysis of the CMF network features which shows the CMF network has properties of complex network. Meanwhile, an algorithm for core herbal discovery is presented basing on key nodes discovery method and the MapReduce [1] parallel programming framework. The result indicates the feasibility of our ideas and the validity of the algorithm.

Keywords: core herbal discovery, complex network, data mining, traditional Chinese medicine, Chinese medical formula, MapReduce.

1 Introduction

Chinese medicinal herbal has always been an important part of traditional Chinese medicine (TCM). As its main form, Chinese medical formula (CMF) received a great deal of development during the past thousands years. Nowadays, the large-size CMF dataset makes knowledge discovery become an urgent issue.

The traditional Chinese medical data is organized as record, in which different records are concerned different CMFs. In this traditional way for data mining, CMF be seemed as a transaction which composed by herbals. Compared with the transaction model can't reflect the relationship between herbals clearly, which will cause a failure for deep mining task, network model offers a coherent view [2-3]. Thus, we construct a CMF network according to the Jaccard similarity coefficient. Further

---

* Corresponding author.

F.M. Zanzotto et al. (Eds.): BI 2012, LNCS 7670, pp. 255–264, 2012.
© Springer-Verlag Berlin Heidelberg 2012

research shows that CMF network has the properties of a complex network which allows an application of complex network analysis. Meanwhile, an algorithm for core herbal discovery is presented basing on key nodes discovery with complex network environment. Moreover, our algorithms are all based on the MapReduce [1] parallel programming framework for the large-size data.

The next of this paper is organized as the following: section 2 describes the procedure of networking; we have a representation of core herbal discovery in section 3; experiments showed in section 4; section 5 is a conclusion.

2   The Construction of CMF Network

2.1   Measurement Description

First, we need to give a definition of the relationship between vertexes for networking. One way to think about this intuitively, if two different herbals belong to the same CMF, we add an edge between them [3]. This simple and clear method seems one CMF as a complete graph and results in a large number of edges in the network. And it is unsuitable for complex network analysis with a dense network. Thus, we propose a similarity measurement for vertex linking, which helps for control the edges of the network by a threshold value α. If the degree of similarity between two different nodes is larger than α, we connecting them through an edge.

The Jaccard similarity coefficient is a statistic usually used for comparing the similarity of sample sets. Assuming there are two different sets called A and B, the Jaccard similarity coefficient J (A, B) between A and B is defined as follows:

$$J(A, B) = \frac{|A \cap B|}{|A \cup B|} \tag{1}$$

$|A \cap B|$ means the number of elements in their intersection. And $|A \cup B|$ stand for the number of elements in their union.

According to (1), we define the similarity of herbal A and herbal B, denoted as SC_{AB}:

$$SC_{AB} = \frac{|\phi(A) \cap \phi(B)|}{\min\{|\phi(A)|, |\phi(B)|\}} \tag{2}$$

Here, $\phi(x)$ corresponds to the set of CMFs which maps to herbal x. This set can be got by an inverted index, which storing a mapping from herbals to CMFs (Table 1 gives a description of the raw CMF data and table 2 is the result after store the raw data in inverted index).

Obviously, (2) is a modified version of (1). The denominator of (2) is the minimum element between $|\phi(A)|$ and $|\phi(B)|$ instead of the number of elements in $\phi(A) \cup \phi(B)$ in (1). We change it for comply with the TCM law better: in TCM there are some common herbal medicines which are an element of many CMFs and this kind of medicine can hardly build a connection with other herbals, especially with those rare ones, because of the low S_{AB} caused by a high denominator in (1).

Table 1. The standard format of CMF record

TCM	composition
Radix Platycodoni Powder	Radix Platycodonis, Radix Glycyrrhizae, Poria
Ju Fei soup	Radix Platycodonis, Radix Glycyrrhizae, Caulis Bambusae in Taenia, Radix Ophiopogonis, Radix Asparagei, Colla Corii Asini, Radix Adenophorae, Bulbus Lilii, Bulbus Fritillaria
Yi Shang Bu Xia pill	Radix Platycodonis, Fructus Aurantii, Radix Glycyrrhizae, Rhizonma Pinelliae
Red Poria Powder	Poria, Radix Glycyrrhizae, Radix Asteris, Rhizoma Cynanchi Stauntonii, Radix Peucedani, Flos Inulae
Radix Bupleuri Powder	Radix Bupleuri, Radix Ophiopogonis, Radix Scutellariae, Pericarrium Citri Reticulatae, Radix Ginseng, Radix Glycyrrhizae, Rhizonma Pinelliae, Radix Platycodonis, Poria

Table 2. The inverted index of table 1

Herbal	TCM
Radix Platycodonis	Radix Platycodoni Powder, Ju Fei soup, Yi Shang Bu Xia pill, Radix Bupleuri Powder
Radix Glycyrrhizae	Radix Platycodoni Powder, Ju Fei soup, Yi Shang Bu Xia pill, Red Poria Powder, Radix Bupleuri Powder
Poria	Radix Platycodoni Powder, Red Poria Powder, Radix Bupleuri Powder
Caulis Bambusae in Taenia	Ju Fei soup
Radix Ophiopogonis	Ju Fei soup, Radix Bupleuri Powder
… …	… …

2.2 Algorithms Description

It is easy to count the value of $|\varphi(A)|$ and $|\varphi(B)|$ based on an inverted index. In order to calculate the value of SC_{AB}, there are few preparations that need to be done. First, we create a composite key which looks like $x\%|\varphi(x)|$. Then, we get a new data set with inverted index, denoted as D_{new} (Fig 1).

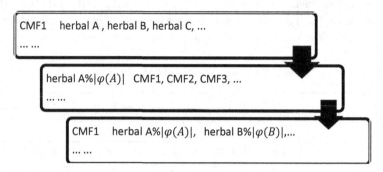

Fig. 1. Data process flow

Our algorithms are all based on the MapReduce [1] parallel programming framework for the large-size data. MapReduce is a data processing model who decomposing a data processing application into two phases named Map and Reduce [4]. In the Map phase, we generate key/value pairs pairwise which looks like $< A\%|\varphi(A)|, B\%|\varphi(B)|>$ for every record in D_{new}. Here, A and B are two different elements of one CMF. The value of $\min\{|\varphi(A)|, |\varphi(B)|\}$ can be directly obtained by separate its corresponding key/value pair during the reduce phase. Meanwhile, $|\phi(A) \cap \phi(B)|$ equals to the count of A&B key/value pairs, which can be obtained in the reduce phase too. The networking algorithm can be summarized as follows:

Table 3. The Map phase of networking algorithm

Mapper:mkGraph2Mapper
Input: D_{new} in text format, a line of text corresponds to a record, herbals and CMFs are all replace with a unique ID
Output: key/value pair, both K and V are a combination of x and $|\varphi(x)|$, x is a herbal ID and K<V

void map(object Key, Text Value, Context context)
   1.   Tmp[]←Value.spilt("\\s+")
   2.   Node[]←Tmp[1].split(",")
   3.   for i∈0→Node.Length do
   4.   for j∈i→Node.Length do
   5.   K←Node[i]
   6.   V←Node[j]
   7.   if K<V
   8.   context.write(K,V)
   9.   else if K!=V
  10.   context.write(V,K)

Table 4. The Reduce phase of networking algorithm

Reducer:mkGraph2Reducer
Input:<Key,[V]>, Key is a combination which looks like x%|φ(x)|, [v] is a list , <Key,[V]> correspond to Text Key and Iterable<Text> Values, respectively
Output:<K,SC$_{AB}$>, K is an edge in the CMF network

void reduce(Text Key, Iterable<Text> Values, Context context)
1. HashMap Node← ∅
2. for all n ∈ Values do
3.   if Node do not contains n
4.   Node.put(n,1)
5.   else
6.   Node.put(n,Node.get(n)+1)
7. for all M ∈ Node do
8.   K$_B$←M.getKey
9.   V$_B$←M.getValue
10.   min←Min{Key.Num,K$_B$.Num}
11.   SC$_{AB}$←$\frac{V_B}{min}$
12.   if SC$_{AB}$>C(C is a threshold value)
13.   K←Key.ID&&K$_B$.ID
14.   context.write(K,SC$_{AB}$)

The above algorithm avoids a large number of key-value pairs generated by pair off for all herbals. Assuming that the herbal number is n and each CMF be consisted of m herbals in average (m is certainly much less than n), the complexity of this algorithm is $O\left(n * \frac{m*(m-1)}{2}\right) = O(n * m^2)$. Because of m is usually close to a constant, the time complexity is close to linear in fact.

2.3   Feature Analysis of CMF Network

Complex network's degree distribution has the feature of power-law. It follows Zipf's [5] [6] law, too, which reveals a phenomenon in complex network that most of the nodes with a small number of degree and few with a large one. Zipf's law suggests that some nodes with an enormous impact of the net while a majority is insignificant.

Barabási and Albert try to answer the question why complex network's degree obeys a power-law. They proposed a BA model [7] for description the process of a network growing based on the degree distribution feature of complex network. Growth and preferential attachment are considered to be the reason in the model. Growth refers to the nodes increase which leads to a rise in size. And a preferential attachment process meaning a network growing process in which new node prefers to connect with those nodes with a large number of degree. These also happen to TCM, that is, new herbals discovery and those herbals prefer to form a CMF with some commonly used herbals.

Fig 2 shows the fitted curve of the node degree distribution and its approximate function plotted by the number of degree on the horizontal axis and the probability of X≥x on the vertical. It confirmed that the CMF network has the feature of a complex network.

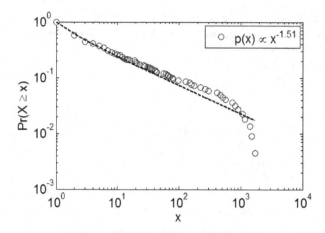

Fig. 2. The fitted curve of the node degree distribution

3   Core Herbal Discovery

The core herbal discovery helps CMF law study: research on CMF under certain conditions, such as asthma, shows those primary medicines used for treating the main symptom; when the study repeated with a different random sample, herbals used frequently in TCM are found. Here, PageRank [8] are used for node analysis. Node with a high PageRank is considered to be a core one.

PageRank is a link analysis algorithm that assigns a numerical weighting to each element of a hyperlinked set of documents with the purpose of "measuring" its relative importance with the set. The numerical weight that it assigns to any given element E is referred to as the PageRank of E , denoted as P:

$$P(n) = \alpha\left(\frac{1}{|G|}\right) + (1 - \alpha) \sum_{m \in L(n)} \frac{P(m)}{C(m)} \qquad (3)$$

Where |G| means the number of pages in the set, α is a constant, L(n) is the set of pages that link to n, and C(m) is the number of outbound links on page n.

In the CMF network, |G| is a total number of nodes, L(n) is neighbors of n, and C(m) is the number of m's neighbors (the CMF network is an undirected graph).

Table 5 and table 6 give the PageRank algorithm with undirected graph based on MapReduce.

Table 5. The Map phase of PageRank algorithm

Mapper: PageRIterMapper

Input: Text formatting, a line of text contains: herbal ID, adjacency list of the herbal and its PageRank in double type whose initial value is 1.0. A line of text looks like: ID adjacency(split with comma)#PageRank

Output: <K,V>,K refers to a neighbor node ID, V means $P' = \dfrac{P}{\text{AdjList.Length}}$

void map(Object Key, Text Value, Context context)
1.   Tmp[]←Value.split("\\s+")
2.   context write(Tmp[0],Tmp[1])   ▽ Send the node struct
3.   Tmp_[]←Tmp[1].split("#")
4.   AdjList←Tmp_[0].split(",")
5.   P←Tmp[1]
6.   L←AdjList.Length
7.   V←$\dfrac{P}{L}$
8.   for all node K∈AdjList do
9.   context.write(K,V)

Table 6. The Reduce phase of PageRank algorithm

Reducer: PageRIterReducer

Input:<K,V>, K refers to a herbal ID, [V] is a list of PageRank and node struct, <K,[V]> correspond to Text Key and Iterable<Text> Values, respectively

Output:<Key,apr>, Key is a herbal ID, apr means its node struct

void reduce(Text Key, Iterable<Text> Values, Context context)
1.   AdjpageRank apr ← ∅
2.   List ls ← ∅
3.   p←0.0
4.   for all V∈Values do
5.   if V is the struct of node
6.   apr←V
7.   else
8.   ls.add(V)
9.   for all C∈ls do
10.   P=P+C
11. P←$\alpha * \dfrac{1}{|G|} + (1 - \alpha) * P$
12. Set PageRankCentrality of apr with P
13. Context.write(Key,apr)

Computing PageRank is an iterative process where the determination of the number of iteration is important. It is ideal if our program to die naturally when the value of P does not change anyway. But that is very expensive and difficult to achieve. Here, we adopt an approximation solution where the maximum iterating times and the changing rate of the PageRank during iterating are used to control the terminating time. The set of maximum iterating time can avoid the cycle of death problem caused by shocks.

4   Experiments and Analysis

To discover the core herbals in CMF, We employ three subsets (Table 7) derived from the CMF dataset which collected by Nanjing University of Traditional Chinese Medicine.

Table 7. Data description

dataset	The number of records	description
data1	About 1000 records	CMFs for treatment of asthma
data2	40000 records	chosen at random
data3	80000 records	chosen at random

Table 8 shows the result on data1 with different SC_{AB} when $\alpha = 0.15$. Here, we set the maximum iterating time as 50 and a change rate lower than 10% is acceptable. And table 9 is the result on data2.

Table 8. The result on data1 with different SC_{AB}

SC_{AB}	Nodes	Edges	Herbals correspond to the top five PageRank	Iterations
1/4	850	13784	Radix Glycyrrhizae, Rhizoma Pinelliae, Amygdalus Communis Vas, Ramulus Cinnamomi, Radix Angelicae Sinensis	24
1/4	850	13004	Radix Glycyrrhizae, Amygdalus Communis Vas, Rhizoma Pinelliae,Radix Angelicae Sinensis, Ramulus Cinnamomi	24
1/2	822	6556	Radix Glycyrrhizae, Amygdalus Communis Vas, Rhizoma Pinelliae, Ramulus Cinnamomi, Herba Asari	24
2/3	821	6117	Radix Glycyrrhizae, Amygdalus Communis Vas, Rhizoma Pinelliae, Ramulus Cinnamomi, Ricinus communis	24
4/5	795	5324	Radix Glycyrrhizae, Amygdalus Communis Vas, Rhizoma Pinelliae, Mentha Piperita Officinalis, Fructus Citri	23

Table 9. The result on data2 with different SC_{AB}

SC_{AB}	Nodes	Edges	Herbals correspond to the top six PageRank	Iterations
1/4	11914	126509	Radix Glycyrrhizae, Radix Angelicae Sinensis, Radix Ginseng, Wine, Radix Saposhnikoviae, Rhizoma Chuanxiong	21
1/4	11913	121518	Radix Glycyrrhizae, Radix Angelicae Sinensis, Radix Ginseng, Wine, Radix Saposhnikoviae, Rhizoma Chuanxiong	21
1/2	11329	69216	Radix Glycyrrhizae, Radix Angelicae Sinensis, Radix Ginseng, Wine, Radix Saposhnikoviae, Moschus	21
2/3	11273	67875	Radix Glycyrrhizae, Radix Angelicae Sinensis, Wine, Radix Saposhnikoviae, Radix Ginseng, Moschus	21
4/5	11026	64853	Radix Glycyrrhizae, Radix Angelicae Sinensis, Wine, Radix Saposhnikoviae, Radix Ginseng, Moschus	21

Table 8 suggests Radix Glycyrrhizae, Amygdalus Communis Vas, Rhizoma Pinelliae, Ramulus Cinnamomi and Radix Angelicae Sinensis are core herbals in the CMFs for treatment of asthma. Meanwhile, Radix Glycyrrhizae, Radix Angelicae Sinensis, Radix Ginseng, Wine, Radix Saposhnikoviae, Rhizoma Chuanxiong and Moschus are herbals used frequently in TCM, according to table 9. All the results are confirmed by the TCM theory, which indicate the feasibility of our ideas and the validity of the algorithm.

The number of nodes and edges in the network tend to fail in response to the increasing of SC_{AB}, because a high SC_{AB} makes edge hard to build and the deletion of nodes with 0 degree. Furthermore, iterating time's inverse correlation with the data size is caused by the set of iteration termination conditions. Because the acceptable change rate is 10%, the program stops only when the change nodes lower than 10 on data1 who has about 1000 records. Thus, compared with data2 with 40000 records, data1 has a more stringent termination condition.

The experiment on data3 shows our algorithm can achieve better speedups ratio [9] (Fig 3). The average time consumption at iteration is seemed as the algorithm's time spent.

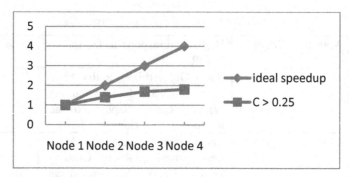

Fig. 3. The speedup ratio of core herbals discovery

5   Conclusion

It is an exploration and application of data mining on TCM for core herbal discovery. This paper proposed a new model different with the traditional data mining model based on transaction, that is, a CMF complex network. Then, we used the PageRank algorithm for the core herbal discovery on this CMF network.

For core herbals discovery, our algorithm is still plenty of room for improvement. First, it is debatable whether the measurement used for edge building is optimum. Secondly, there may exist a better MapReduce programming whose time complexity is lower. The parameters setting is another problem, a proper setting of parameters such as α and SC_{AB} need further experimentation.

Acknowledgement. This paper is funded by the Major State Basic Research Development Program of China (973 Program) (No.2011CB 505300).

References

1. Dean, J., Ghemawat, S.: MapReduce: Simplified Data Processing on Large Clusters. Google, Inc. (2004)
2. He, Y., Zhang, P.P., Tang, J.-Y.: A Collaboration Network Description on Tradition-al Chinese Medical Prescription Formulation System. Science & Technology Review 23(11), 36–39 (2005)
3. Zhou, X., Liu, B.: Network Analysis System for Traditional Chinese Medicine Clinical Data. Biomedical Engineering and Informatics (2009)
4. Lam, C.: Hadoop in Action, pp. 4–9. Manning Publications (2010)
5. Zipf, G.K.: Human behavior and the principle of least effort. Addison-Wesley Press, Oxford (1949)
6. Ferrer, R., Sole, R.V.: Least effort and the origins of scaling in human language. PNAS 100, 788–791 (2003)
7. Albert, R., Barabasi, A.-L.: Statistical mechanics of complex networks. University of Notre Dame, pp. 71–75 (2002)
8. Page, L.: The Page-Rank citation ranking: Bringing order to the Web. Stanford Digital Library Project (1998)
9. DeWitt, D.J., Gray, J.: Parallel database systems: The future of high performance database systems. Communications of the ACM 35(6), 85–98 (1992)

An EEG-Based Brain Informatics Application
for Enhancing Music Experience

Yike Guo[1], Chao Wu[1], and Diego Peteiro-Barral[2]

[1] Dept of Computing, Imperial College London, UK
{yg,chao.wu}@imperial.ac.uk
[2] Dept of Computer Science, University of A Coruña, Spain
diego.peteiro@udc.es

Abstract. Electroencephalography (EEG) technology has gained growing popularity in various applications. In this paper we propose a system based on affordable EEG devices to enhance music experience. Music is one of the major stimuli to which a brain responds. And the effect of music to our mood has long been recognized. Traditional music recommendation systems usually ignore the emotional effects of music on the users, but depend only on users' feedback through rating. With EEG device, it's possible to establish one's emotional profile while music listening, and thus design an emotion-based music recommendation engine. In this work, we present our effort on this research by exploiting how EEG could be applied to enhance the traditional music listening experience. Our research demonstrated that EEG applications should not be just limited in clinical field, but can be accessible to the public for broad use. In our system, we adopt an inexpensive EEG device (Emotiv EEG) to monitor brain activity in music listening to reflect emotional responses, and use mobile phone and Cloud based architecture to host the processing and recommendation algorithms to recognize, interpret and process EEG/music data. Such architecture is low cost, publicly accessible and generic to realize a wide class of brain informatics applications based on EEG.

1   Introduction

Electroencephalography (EEG) records differences of voltage on the scalp to monitor brain activity in the neocortex, through which neuroscientists could identify patterns of brain activity associated with cognitive functions. It provides an invasive way to measure brain activity and establishes a direct communication pathway between brain and computing system. Research in recent years has enabled a series of useful applications, especially those helping severely disabled users through sending commands, based on the measured EEG signals, to an external device, such as visual stimulation enabling to write [11] or a brain-actuated wheelchair [12]. With the advent of inexpensive EEG devices and Cloud computing paradigm, we believe the application scope of EEG can be widening dramatically. The key challenge, however, is how to transfer the EEG technology from clinical environment to be affordable and easily accessible for pervasive deployment as well as being fun to use to ensure popularity

F.M. Zanzotto et al. (Eds.): BI 2012, LNCS 7670, pp. 265–276, 2012.
© Springer-Verlag Berlin Heidelberg 2012

in general public. In this paper, we present an example of pervasive brain informatics application by adopting inexpensive EEG device, mobile computing, and Cloud computing to enhance the music experience for ordinary people.

Our brain is constantly processing information and reacting accordingly to all sorts of sensory inputs in our daily life. The impact of media (music, video, etc.) upon the brain is well known. And music is a type of media that people frequently interact with. It's helpful for enhancing music experience if we can understand how user perceive music, especially in real time, so that an adaptive music content provision service can be built.

Current rapid growth of the volume of media files on the Internet has already led to the emergence of music management and recommendation systems such as Last.fm and Pandora. Their algorithms analyze users' profiles of music listening and recommend new contents that might interest users based on the correlation between the music pieces established by the analysis. But these systems usually suffer several shortcomings:

- Many adopt supervised learning methods, in which users are encouraged to rate music files by hand. But it might not make users to do this. Such systems therefore often encounter with the "cold start" problem, with limited data for training the model at the beginning.
- The setting of recommendation engine is based on vague "like" or "dislike" approach and ratings approach, but ignores the real feelings from the users, which are complicated and hard to be captured with simple rating.
- The atom of information processing is a music file. It's not flexible for users to only rate songs, for example, what if they just like parts of a song?

With these considerations, in this paper, we propose a novel music system by applying EEG as a way of enhancing user's music experience in real-time. In brief, our system has following advantages:

- Users do not need to rate (and train) their music recommenders by hand, but implicitly build an emotional profile while they are listening via associating music with EEG patterns.
- The emotional profiles responding to music are stored and analyzed to form an emotional-based music recommendation engine.
- Given a list of music, the outcome of the system could be the music clips which have the positive emotional impact to the brain. Thus, the system provides a new experience of music listening.
- The system adopts low price EEG device and mobile phone as its hardware, so it's highly affordable and accessible for the public.
- The processing takes place on the Cloud to improve the performance with limited local resource, and the algorithm is open to research and development communities to keep evolution with the involvement of neuroscientists, services providers and user participation.
- The system doesn't need to change the way users interact with music player but wearing an EEG device while they doing.

The remainder of this paper is structured as follows. Section 2 reviews some related works in EEG-based music application. In Section 3, we outline the system's design and implementation. In Section 4, we briefly describe the experimental study we have done. Finally, we summarize our work in Section 5.

2   Related Work

In this part, we firstly review the existing research on detecting emotion through consumer EEG devices, and then the research on music recommendation systems and algorithms. Finally, the previous work on emotion-based approaches to music and video recommendation are discussed.

In order to detect different emotion status, it is - necessary to classify them. There are two main approaches. The first is to classify emotions into a set of categories, for example happiness, sadness, fear, etc. One study that followed such an approach is [5] based on the 'foundation emotions' model [4]. Six foundation emotions (happiness, surprise, fear, anger, disgust, and sadness) were elicited by playing audiovisual stimuli to the subjects, and their EEG responses were measured. A classifier was then trained with as a Bayesian classification method, based on frequency analysis by Fourier transform of the raw data. We mainly use such approach to detect emotions in this paper. A second approach is dimensional approach. [9] elicited emotion using the International Affective Picture System (IAPS), and emotions were classified along two dimensions - arousal and valence. Arousal represents a scale between calming / soothing to exciting / agitating, while valence represents a scale of positive emotion to negative emotion. For example fear would be high arousal and low valence.

Recommendation systems have become prevalent over the last few years with the expansion of online shopping, online delivery of music, films, etc. [1] and [7] gave good surveys on the algorithms of recommendation systems. There are broadly 3 approaches for recommendation systems, collaborative filtering, content based filtering, and hybrid systems. Collaborative filtering attempts to build a model using historical data from the user (ratings or purchase history) as well as similar decisions from other users, and then provide recommendations based on the established model. As noted by in [1], algorithms used for collaborative filtering approaches can be memory based, or model based. One obvious problem with collaborative filtering is the 'cold start', that the system needs a potentially quite large body of data on a user's past behavior in order to provide good recommendations. Also, as noted by Claypool et al [3] there is the 'sparsity problem' whereby the number of items can be very large and vastly exceed the capacity of any one user to rate. Content based filtering makes recommendations based on characteristics or properties of the items, essentially recommending similar items to those that the user has used or highly rated before. For instance, music recommendations could be based on band, genre, music key, instruments used and so on. In order to calculate item similarity various measures can be used, including the cosine distance measure above. Machine learning techniques can be used to induce those characteristics most valued by the user and find relevant similar items. Techniques used include Bayesian classifiers, clustering, decision trees, artificial neural networks, KNN, and regression.

We investigated several studies on using emotional information to recommend music: the method presented in [2] did not measure emotional responses directly, but inferred them for new pieces of music by analyzing features of the music like average intensity, forms of timbre, and so on. A feature selection algorithm called sequential floating forward selection was then used to find the most useful features from a selection of 21. The emotion classification model used was a two dimension model or arousal-valence. The study found seven music features relevant for arousal, and nine for valence. Two support vector machines (SVM) where then trained on the data, with one SVM for arousal and one for valence. The classifiers were then tested on previously untrained music files, recommending each as a specific emotion, achieving an accuracy rate of 68% as measured by human test subjects. [6] used an emotional response as part of an overall hybrid recommendation system. The content of music was analyzed by extracting features from the musical score, and was combined with collaborative data and emotional data on the music (obtained by user's explicitly rating music by emotion). This allows final recommendations to be made, which achieve accuracy as high as 90%. [9] used the same device we used in this paper (Emotiv EEG [14]) with the pre-trained emotion classifiers. The user selected an emotional state they wish to be in, and a Q-learning algorithm was used to guide the user into the desired state by playing music from a choice of genres. The results were combined to the Pandora music recommendation service, with results indicating users preferred the Q-learning based algorithm.

3   System Design

How do people perceive music? Key, loudness, time, signature, tempo, beats, sections, and harmony, are all attributes for a song. However these features do not tell the whole story. The impact of music in our emotions is undeniable, but yet largely inexplicable, which is affected by our memories, the environment, mood, and many other factors. So it's hard for user to specify these emotions or just give a rating while listening music with subjective descriptions. But with EEG approach, we can detect user's emotion responses while listening music; some of measurements are well defined and could be accurately extracted [13].

EEG is typically described in terms of rhythmic activity in which frequencies are divided into bands, which have certain biological significance, using spectral analysis methods. There are five different bands, ranging from the least activity to the most; delta, theta, alpha, beta, and gamma. In our music application, we mainly focus on the beta rhythm, frequency range between 14 and 30 Hz, which is associated with excitement and boredom level. Previous works [11] showed that these levels could be accurately measured from the EEG.

In our system, the users listen to the music while wearing EEG device. The beta wave is recorded and extracted to gain the emotional levels including long-term / short-term excitement, boredom, mediation, fractal feature, etc. Such emotional levels are used to index the music clips listened by the user to build up a user profile. Such a profiling mechanism forms the basis for a set of services to enhancing user's music experience. One service is for automatic music slicing and clipping, through which user create a favorite music clips after listening to a playlist. Another service is music recommendation, which find more music that would bring the users to the desired emotional stated according to their emotional profile.

The whole system contains three subsystems:

1. Emotion Indexing and Profile System

An emotion profile is a personal record that contains emotion data (emotion levels extracted from EEG records) responding to stimulus (music signals), these emotion levels and time index the music sequence user played, as shown in Figure 1. Before establishing the emotion profile, users' background profiles are firstly measured.

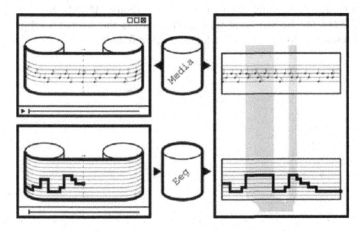

Fig. 1. Indexing music with emotional profile

The EEG data is acquired from the EPOC Emotiv headset, on 14 positions on the scalp: AF3, AF4, F7, F3, F4, F8, FC5, FC6, T7, T8, P7, P8, O1, O2 as Figure 2 shows.

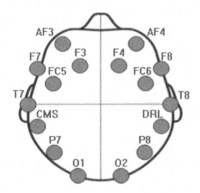

Fig. 2. Electrodes' positions of Emotiv EEG headset

Data were sampled at 128 Hz, and Hamming window is used to reduce spectrum leakage. EEG spectrum power was calculated per second, blink and facial power were calculated per 0.2 second. Although the data acquired by the headset appears quite noisy, its affordable price makes this device easily deployed at large scale. The device can monitor brain events very responsively in time but it suffers from high inter-trial variability and spatial mixing. These limitations have let to the assumption that one needs to average signal features across time to accurately discriminate mental states. Also, to increase the SNR of raw data as shown in Figure 3, bandpass filtering is used to blocks frequencies that are too high or too low (Figure 4).

Then the emotion levels including excitement (*EL*), boredom (*BL*) and mediation (*ML*) are extracted. We average these values in a time window (30 seconds, 1 minute, etc.) and gain a set of long-term levels (*L-EL*, *L-BL*, *L-ML*) for them. The short-time value is compared with long-term value to gain a more accurate indicator of emotional change, considering high noise of the device. So an emotion profile could be presented as a matrix O, in which each column O_i is a vector *[M_i, EL_i, BL_i, ML_i, L-EL_i, L-BL_i, L-ML_i, FD_i]* for the profile at time *i*, where *Mi* is the segments (clips) of music (instead of a song), and *FD_i* is the fractal dimension feature.

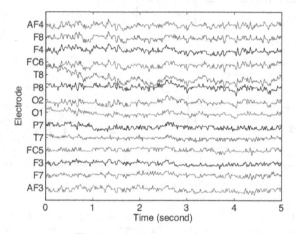

Fig. 3. Raw data from the headset

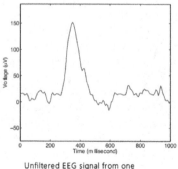

Unfiltered EEG signal from one electrode

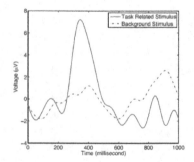

Bandpass filtered signal for both task related stimulus (music listening) and background stimulus

Fig. 4. Bandpass filtering

Other than power of EEG signals, fractal dimension feature is also computed, which is the measurement of complexity and irregularity of a signal. Higher fractal dimension values mean that the signal is more complex, while lower fractal dimension values mean that the signal is more regular, as shown in Figure 5. The complexity of EEG signals has strong relationship with the activity of the brain, and could be useful to determine the emotional status for emotion profile. We use Higuchi [15] algorithms to calculate fractal dimension. In Higuchi method, the samples are first clustered into several sub-sequences according to the poly-phase structure of signal:

$$X_k^m: x(m), x(m+k), x(m+2k), \dots, x(m + int\left[\frac{N-m}{k}\right]k)$$

where m donates the m-th subsequence, and N is the total number of samples of the original space. The length of the sequences $L(k)$ is calculated as below. The k denotes the number of the sub-sequence and $L_m(k)$ denotes the length of the m-th sub-sequence:

$$L_m(k) = 1/k[(\sum_{i=1}^{int((N-m)/k_{-}}|x(m+ik) - x(m+(i-i)k)|)\frac{N-1}{int\left[\frac{N-m}{k}\right]k}]$$

$$L(k) = \frac{1}{k}\sum_{m=1}^{k}L_k(m)$$

The total length $L(k)$ is proportional to k^{-fd}:

$$L(k) \sim K^{-FD}$$

Fractal dimension value can be calculated by the least-square linear best fitting line procedure over the graph $(\ln\left(\frac{1}{k}\right), \ln(l(k)))$. Calculated fractal dimension feature are then added to user's emotional profile.

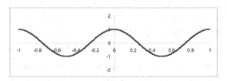
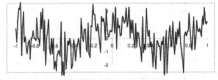

Signal with low fractal dimension value   Signal with high fractal dimension value

Fig. 5. Signals with low and high fractal dimension value

2.   Clipping Engine

Based on emotion profile, we can automatically tag those segments of music with im-print positive patterns as favorite and thus create a music clip, as shown in Figure 6.

The positive patterns could be recognized with many ways. Here we use an approach with the hypothesis that users give positive feedback to a segment of music, if the mediation level is high enough (higher than the threshold μ) and short time excitement is higher enough than long-term excitement (with threshold λ):

$$Clip(M_{i,j}): if\ EL_{i,j} > L\text{-}EL_{i,j} + \lambda\ \&\&\ ML_{i,j} > \mu$$

Parameters μ and λ are configurable and extensible, which in our application are optimized through a Bayesian based approach with users' training. With our Cloud based architecture, the clipping engine is open, so developers could adopt better clipping algorithm, and users could adopt their preferable algorithm or personalize it.

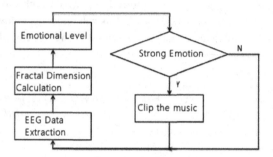

Fig. 6. Music clipping

In this manner, users could listen to their favorite clip collections derived from their emotion profile, instead of listening to the entire playlist. And all are done without extra editing work but automatically derived through our EEG analysis and indexing engine.

3. Cloud-Based Recommendation Engine

A recommendation engine would become much more powerful if data were tagged with emotions rather than just "like" and "dislike", or ratings. Based on the emotion profile, we used collaborative filtering algorithm as well as KNN to build the music recommendation engine. And the architecture is open to any recommendation algorithm. EEG headsets collect the EEG signals, and transmit the data via mobile phone. The mobile phone acts as a music player (Figure 7 shows its interface) as well as the local hub to collect data and communicate with music recommendation services on the Cloud. Data processing is taken place on the Cloud side, since the mobile device cannot handle the computation of EEG signal analysis like FFT, and fractal dimension feature calculation. Data compression is used for the transmission efficiency and the compression method is easily implemented on the low cost device.

Fig. 7. Mobile interface

On the Cloud side, methods and models are built as services based on the Software as a Service (SaaS) model as shown in Figure 8. With the involvement and contribution from developers, neuroscientists and the participation of users, services quality could be continuously improved. Users' data, including EEG-based emotional measurement, music listening history et.al are stored and accessed by mobile music application through the Internet. Users grant the services (such as various recommendation algorithms) to access their data (emotion profiles), and pay for the services quality and resource consumption. Such open architecture enables the users to enjoy the easy access of services and their continuous evolution. Using cloud-based architecture and low cost mobile devices and EEG headsets, the application could be accessed anywhere.

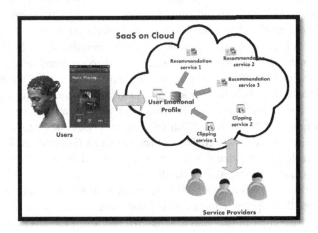

Fig. 8. EEG-based Music Cloud Architecture

4   Evaluation

To evaluate our system, 10 subjects, 5 men and 5 women (students from department of computing, Imperial College London) with 20-30 years of age were recruited. Playlists are created with the song database from Million Song Database[1]. For each subject, a session consisted of 10 songs were played, with 6 seconds of interval between two songs. Music Emotional profile for each subject was established and updated in every session. We collected multiple sessions from every subject. We found both clipping and recommendation performance were promising after a number of sessions (5 sessions by average). The accuracy of the system depends on the subjective appreciation of users, so we conduct a user survey, and asked them to rate the accuracy of the clipped music segment as well as the recommended content. As shown in Table 1, we got over 80% acceptance of music clip and approximately 70% user acceptance of recommendation through the evaluation.

Table 1. Evaluation result

Subjects	Average Session Number	Acceptance of clipping	Acceptance of recommendation	Length of playlist	Length of favorite clips
Men	5	81%	72%	30 mins	6 mins
Women	5	85%	70%	30 mins	4 mins
Total	5	83%	71%	30 mins	5 mins

5   Conclusions and Future Work

Until recently, the cost of EEG technology greatly limited its application. With the emergence of low cost solution, we believe EEG technology could be broadly applied to build up a wide class of brain informatics applications. For this purpose, an application for enhanced music experience has been proposed in this paper. Based on emotion profiles that reflect emotional responses to music recorded by an EEG device, we are able to automatically tag users' favorite clips and recommend new contents in a more accurate manner based on the brain activity measurement than a traditional rating approach. The system is built with a mobile device and Cloud computing architecture, which is open to users and service providers to facilitate the easy access and continuous evolution of the system. With the low price EEG device we adopted, the application provided a highly affordable and accessible EEG-based service for public. Experimental results showed that the system is appreciated by users, with high acceptance of clipping and recommendation result.

For future work, we plan to extend this research with new functionalities. Firstly, we plan to merge the clipping engine and recommendation engine to provide recommendation based on clips rather than a song. We are also planning to combine this application with other mechanisms. For example, we can integrate the music emotion

---

[1] http://labrosa.ee.columbia.edu/millionsong/

profiling system with music content management system; and users could utilize emotion measurements to index, organize, search and share their music. Also the music library indexed with our system could be a valuable reference for music composition. Secondly, we would adopt a set of different algorithms for clipping and recommendation services, and compare their performance in the application. For example, we are investigating how to avoid the problem of cold start with content filtering method, based on the pre-learned patterns about human's emotional reaction to music. Also, we plan to extend our system (practically with the cloud-based architecture) for application in music therapy. It is now believed that cognitive abilities can be improved by exercising the brain. Moreover, recent advances in clinical neuroscience and in psychiatry have demonstrated how brain signal patterns measured with EEG can be used effectively in guiding treatments of certain brain disorders as well as in improving the brain abilities. We would try to combine such research efforts with music system, and develop music therapy system for brain training services. Moreover, the infrastructure of the Cloud computing designed in our application, would be further designed to better fit the characteristics of EEG-based brain informatics applications.

Acknowledgment. This work is partially supported by the Guangdong Innovation Group Project from Guangdong government of China.

References

1. Adomavicius, G.: Toward the next generation of recommender systems: a survey of the state-of-the-art and possible extensions. IEEE Transactions on Knowledge and Data Engineering 17(6), 734–749 (2005)
2. Chang, C.-Y.: A music recommendation system with consideration of personal emotion (2010)
3. Claypool, M., Gokhale, A., Miranda, T., Murnikov, P., Netes, D., Sartin, M.: Combining content-based and collaborative filters in an online newspaper (1999)
4. Ekman, P.: Universals and cultural differences in facial expressions of emotion (1971)
5. Ko, K.-E.: Emotion recognition using EEG signals with relative power values and bayesian network. International Journal of Control, Automation, and Systems 7(5), 865–870 (2009)
6. Lu, C.-C.: A novel method for personalized music recommendation. Expert Systems with Applications 36(6), 10035–10044 (2009)
7. Park, D.: A literature review and classification of recommender systems research. Expert Systems with Applications 39(11), 10059–10072 (2012)
8. Petrantonakis, P.: Adaptive emotional information retrieval from EEG signals in the time-frequency domain. IEEE Transactions on Signal Processing 60(5), 2604–2616 (2012)
9. Radinsky, K., Kapoor, A., Oron, A., Master, K.: Brain-computer interfaces for music recommendation. In: Neural Information Processing Systems Foundations Workshop 2011 (2011); 5M.Sc. Individual Project Report (June 7, 2012)
10. Sourina, O.: Real-time EEG-based emotion recognition for music therapy. Journal on Multimodal User Interfaces 5(1), 27–35 (2012)
11. Krusienski, D.J.: A comparison of classification techniques for the p300 speller. Journal of Neural Engineering 3, 299 (2006)

12. Tanaka, K., Matsunaga, K., Wang, H.O.: Electroencephalogram-based control of an electric wheelchair. IEEE Transactions on Robotics 21(4), 762–766 (2005)
13. Hamadicharef, B., Zhang, H., Guan, C., Wang, C., Phua, K.S., Tee, K.P., Ang, K.K.: Learning EEG-based spectral-spatial patterns for attention level measurement. In: ISCAS 2009, pp. 1465–1468 (2009)
14. Emotiv. Emotiv - Brain Computer Interface Technology (2011), http://www.emotiv.com/
15. Higuchi, T.: Approach to an irregular time series on the basis of the fractal theory. Physica D: Nonlinear Phenomena 31(2), 277–283 (1988)

Decoding of EEG Activity from Object Views: Active Detection vs. Passive Visual Tasks

Sudhir Sasane and Lars Schwabe

Universität Rostock, Dept. of Computer Science and Electrical Engineering,
Adaptive and Regenerative Software Systems, 18051 Rostock, Germany
{sudhir.sasane,lars.schwabe}@uni-rostock.de

Abstract. Brain-computing interfaces (BCIs), which sense brain activity via electroencephalography (EEG), have principled limitations as they measure only the collective activity of many neurons. As a consequence, EEG-based BCIs need to employ carefully designed paradigms to circumvent these limitations. We were motivated by recent findings from the decoding of visual perception from functional magnetic resonance imaging (fMRI) to test if visual stimuli could also be decoded from EEG activity. We designed an experimental study, where subjects visually inspected computer-generated views of objects in two tasks: an active detection task and a passive viewing task. The first task triggers a robust P300 EEG response, which we use for single trial decoding as well as a "yardstick" for the decoding of visually evoked responses. We find that decoding in the detection task works reliable (approx. 72%), given that it is performed on single trials. We also find, however, that visually evoked responses in the passive task can be decoded clearly above chance level (approx. 60%). Our results suggest new directions for improving EEG-based BCIs, which rely on visual stimulation, such as as P300- or SSVEP-based BCIs, by carefully designing the visual stimuli and exploiting the contribution of decoding responses in the visual system as compared to relying only on, for example, P300 responses.

1 Introduction

Reliable decoding of brain activity from single trials, or only a few repetitions, is a necessary prerequisite for Brain-computing Interfaces (BCIs) [1]. These BCIs have their ultimate justification in controlling prostheses or other devices in cases when a physically handicapped user cannot operate them otherwise. This is the "classical" BCI setting (see Figure 1a). Most non-invasive BCIs still employ electroencephalography (EEG) in order to sense brain activity. Unfortunately, EEG signals are very noisy and measure only the collective activity of many neurons as compared to single unit activity, which is accessible to invasive BCIs. As a consequence, EEG-based BCIs need to employ carefully designed paradigms to circumvent these principled limitations. A few such paradigms have been established in the literature such as, for example, steady state visual evoked

F.M. Zanzotto et al. (Eds.): BI 2012, LNCS 7670, pp. 277–287, 2012.
© Springer-Verlag Berlin Heidelberg 2012

potentials (SSVEPs) [2], P300-based spelling [3], or sensorimotor rhythms (SM) [4]. The former two paradigms exploit the processing in a user's sensory system, most of the times this is the visual system.

Despite the principled limitations of EEG-based BCIs, much progress has been made in extending and refining the basic BCI paradigms. For example, P300-based BCIs are used in other modalities than vision, or SM-based BCIs were combined with the detection of error signals in a so-called shared control architecture. Another line of neuroscientific research recently made use of single trial decoding as a new analysis method. In functional magnetic resonance imaging (fMRI), for example, this is now known as multi-voxel pattern analysis (MVPA) [5]. One application of MVPA is certainly BCI, but from a neuroscientific point of view the single trial analyses are useful as a new analysis tool as well (see Figure 1b). Improving the decoding performance in such a setting will ultimately pave the way even to new paradigms for EEG-based BCIs (Figure 1c). It can be expected that including background knowledge about human neural information processing will improve decoding performance. The recent study [6] made such background knowledge explicit in the form of a forward model (from sensory stimuli to brain responses) in order to perform a model-based decoding of brain activity in the visual system by inverting this forward model using Bayes' rule (from brain responses to sensory stimuli).

We were motivated by this successful decoding of activity in the visual system and reasoned that visually induced responses could also be used to improve single trial decoding of EEG responses. Moreover, related research shows that this is possible using EEG, but in the context of language processing [7]. SSVEP-based BCIs already decode activity in the visual system, but they use simplistic stimuli, which flicker at different frequencies. The human visual system, however, has evolved and learned to process naturalistic stimuli. In addition, components in event-related potentials (ERPs) have been described as being selective to processing of more complex stimuli such as objects or faces. Therefore, here we designed a P300-based detection task (see Figure 2a,b for the typical P300 paradigms and their application in BCIs) using computer-generated object views (Figure 2c). We recorded the EEG activity of 12 subjects in this task and in an easier control task, where only passive visual perception was required. Then, we performed single trial decoding. The rational for this experiment was to determine – using the same visual stimuli in two tasks – if visually evoked EEG activity could be decoded beyond chance level, and to compare this decoding performance with the single trial decoding in an established P300 paradigm.

This paper is organized as follows: In Section 2 we describe the details of the task, the visual stimuli, our experimental setup, and the analysis procedure. In Section 3 we then present the results from the single trial decoding both for the whole group of subjects, and the individual subjects. Finally, in Section 4, we summarize our findings and discuss how future studies could build upon our results in order to improve P300- or SSVEP-based BCIs, which sense brain activity via EEG.

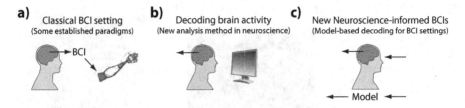

Fig. 1. Illustration of the different approaches to single trial decoding of brain activity. **a)** The classical BCI setting aims at controlling limbs or other devices via decoding brain signals. The focus is on applications. An understanding of the involved brain processes is not the main goal. **b)** The decoding of brain activity is a new analysis technique in neuroscience. By inspecting the informative features of successful decoding, neuroscientists can learn about brain functions. **c)** Recently a model-based approach has been proposed, which aims at using forward models (from stimuli to brain responses) in order to perform decoding by inverting these models. This approach makes explicit use of knowledge from neuroscience in order to investigate brain function, b), and ultimately improve BCI performance, a).

2   Methods

2.1   Tasks and Visual Stimuli

Visual stimuli were generated using freely available models on the internet using the software Blender. The experiment was divided into two sections: First, the visual task, then second the detection task. In each section stimulus images were appearing with the same 1 Hz frequency. Stimulus duration was 70ms.

The stimuli in the visual task were presented in 3 blocks of 3 mins duration each ($3 \times 3 \times 60$ stimuli $= 540$ presentations). In the detection task we used 10 blocks of 3 mins each ($10 \times 3 \times 60 = 1800$ presentations). The total number of presentations was selected such that there were at least 90 repetitions per target stimulus. A fixation cross at centre of the screen was always displayed for a second before a section starts. Data was recorded from 12 Subjects, which were students and/or volunteers working at the University of Rostock. Some of the subjects were remunerated for their contribution.

In the *visual task*, subjects were informed to look at the centre of the stimulus monitor, where each stimulus image out of the 6 was apearing with equal probability. In the *detection task* subjects were asked to count the infrequently appearing chairs. In this setup (see Figure 2c) the rare target was appearing on the screen with 10% probability in a series of standard stimuli which were appearing with 80% probability. Distractor stimuli appeared with 10%. In-house developed hardware was used to ensure timing accuracy of the appearance of stimuli on the screen, namely with a photo sensor mounted on the monitor. The time of appearance of each image was uniquely marked in EEG data via this hardware in terms of triggeres. The Matlab psychophysics toolbox was used as the presentation software.

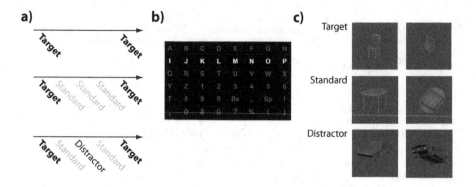

Fig. 2. Paradigms for P300-based EEG-BCIs and our stimuli. **a)** Shown are the variants of stimulus designs, which elicit P300 responses: rare targets elicit such responses in isolation (top), when embedded into a stream of frequent "standard" stimuli, and even when another rare stimulus is included ("distractor"). **b)** These P300 responses have been exploited in P300-based EEG-BCIs, where a user selects a letter within a matrix. Rows and columns flicker unpredictably. When the selected letter is part of a highlighted row or column, a P300 response is elicited, and hence the computer can intfer the selected letter. **c)** Visual stimuli in our study, which corresponds to a rare target (chair) embedded into a stream of frequent stimuli (table) with rare distractors (car). We show multiple object views (canonical and non-canonical) to ensure that subjects engage in object recognition as compared to a plain template-matching of the visual stimulus with a target template.

2.2   EEG Recording and Preprocessing

The EEG recording setup is shown in Fig. 3a. We used a 64 channel Biosemi system with active electrodes. Signals were recorded with 512 Hz sampling frequency. We used two different computers for data recording and stimulus presentation. The presented stimulus image was uniquely marked using 8-bit triggers controlled using Matlab. Also, a photo transistor was used on the stimulus presentation screen, which was generating logic signals when a stimulus image was actually appearing on the screen. Once data was recorded it was marked manually for eye or other artifacts. Then the EEG was seperated into epochs. Standard preprocessing techniques were applied, like common average reference (CAR), band-pass and notch filtering, and base line correction (Fig. 3b). ERPs were generated from these epochs via averaging. The epochs were then also used for classification.

2.3   Single Trial Classification with BDCA

We used the recently developed Bilinear Discriminant Analysis (BDCA) method [8,9], which takes spatial and temporal feature of the signal in to account. In other words, it is a linear classifier, which learned the weights for the classification of a whole multivariate time-series (an epoch) by assuming that it has the particular

a)

b)

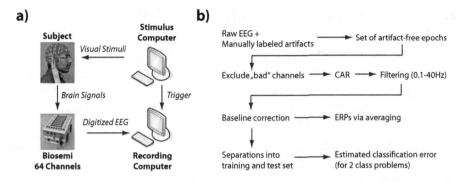

Fig. 3. Experimental setup and processing chain. **a)** We use a standard EEG setup (64 channel Biosemi system with active electrodes) with separate stimulus and recording computers. The stimulus computer sends triggers to the recording computer to inform the later analysis about the shown stimulus. In addition, a photo transistor mounted on the stimulus monitor detects the exact time of stimulus onset for each trial and sends these signals to the recording computer (not shown). **b)** Our processing chain: In the raw EEG data we manually label artifacts, exclude so-called bad channels, re-reference to common average reference (CAR), bandpass the signals, perform a baseline correction ($-125\,\text{ms}\ldots 0\,\text{ms}$), and then average the epochs for ERP analysis or use the signals from all electrodes ($0\,\text{ms}\ldots 1000\,\text{ms}$) as the input to the classifier.

space-time structure common to brain signals. We learned the classifier on 80% of the data, and tested it on 20%. The seperation into training and test set was repeated 20 times to estimate the classifciation error.

3   Results

3.1   Post-recognition and Visual Responses in the Detection Task

Here we first report on the EEG and ERP responses in the detction task. Recall that each subject was first exposed to the passive visual task, i. e. the object views were already familiar to each subject. The task was to mentally count the number of targets (chairs) in a sequence of rare targets, rare distractors (cars), and frequent standard stimuli (tables).

In order to give an impression of the nature of the single trial responses, we show a post-stimulus response for each stimulus (in the canonical view) in Figure 4a from the Pz electrode. The group-averaged responses (see Figure 4c) show that a P300 response should be expected for $350\ldots 600\,\text{ms}$, which in the single trial responses is clearly not as obvious as in the group-averaged responses. For comparison, Figure 4b shows the responses in the very same epoch (same subject, same stimuli) for the Oz electrode, which is expected to reveal visually evoked responses. These single-trial responses already suggest differences between these stimuli in the early phase of the response $\sim 100\,\text{ms}$ (see Section 4.2 for a discussion).

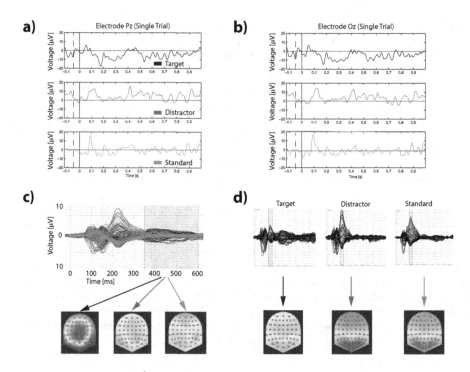

Fig. 4. Detection-related and perceptual components in the EEG activity. **a)** Shown are single trial responses from a subject for each of the three different stimuli for the Pz electrode, which may reflect post-recognition after the visual processing. **b)** Same as a), but for the Oz electrode, which may reflect more the visual processing. **c)** Superimposed signals for all 64 electrodes of the group-averaged ERPs. The red region (350...600 ms) highlights the P300 component, which is only present for the target stimulus and with a distinct topography on the scalp (plots below). **d)** Short window (200...250 ms) during an earlier phase of – presumably – mainly visual processing. All responses are from the detection task.

Of course, our classifiers take into account the responses recorded by all electrodes. The group-averaged ERPs in the detection task are shown in Figure 4c. The red region marks the typical P300 component with its distinct scalp topography (lower left scalp plot), which is absent for the distractor and standard stimuli. These ERPs also suggest differences between conditions for components earlier than 250 ms. In this paper we do not investigate such differences explicitly, but resort to the single trial analysis method as a first – and in fact much more challenging – approach. One difference in the presumably "visual" response phase is a difference in amplitude (200...250 ms, Figure 4d), which the classifier will automatically consider if it serves to improve classification performance.

3.2   Classification Results: Group-Averaged

We then learned the BDCA classifier on the individual EEG epochs for the whole time window $0 \ldots 1000$ ms. More specifically, we defined 12 classes of epochs: 2 tasks (detection task vs. visual task) x 3 stimuli (target, standard, distractor) x 2 views (canoncial vs. non-canoncial). Then, we trained the classifier for all 2-class problems seperately and estimated the classification error via cross-validation (see Section 2). The classification errors of each pair of classification between canoncial and non-canonical views were then averaged. The rational for averaging the classification error as compared to defining larger classes of epochs (with canonical and non-canonical views) is that we wanted to minimize the effects of inter-trial variability in the visual stimuli (see Section 4.2).

The outcomes of four classification problems (target vs. standard and target vs. distractor for each of the two tasks) is shown in Figure 5. As expected, the performance is better in the discrimination task compared to the visual task, due to the distinct P300 component present only for the target stimulus. Note that these results are based on the whole epoch $0 \ldots 1000$ ms, and they are for single trials. For comparison we also performed a classification based on the pre-stimulus time window $-125 \ldots 0$ ms, which yielded 50% chance level performance (not shown).

The classification results for the visual task, i. e. using the very same stimuli but only "view the stimuli" as a task instruction, also yielded clearly above chance level performance, but less correct classifications than in the detection task. In other words, single trial decoding of EEG activity from object views can be used to discriminate a target stimulus from *both* a much more frequently (in the detection task) and equally often (in the visual task) occuring standard stimulus. The same applies for discriminating the target from the also rarely (in the detection task) and equally often (in the visual task) occuring distractor stimulus.

3.3   Classification Results: Individual Subjects

Classification of brain activity is known to depend on the individual subjects. For example, most BCIs need to be trained before they can be used, and the problem of BCI illiteracy is adressed using various heuristics [10]. Therefore, we investigated the classification performance for the individual subjetcs. Figure 6a shows the performance for the individual subjects. Some subjects reach up to 80% correct classification (subjects 6 and 11) while others cause poor performance even in the detection task.

We then investiagted if the classification performance in the visual task is predictive for the performance in the detection task (Figure 6b). First, note that in all subjects the classification in the detection task is higher than in the visual task. Second, most interestingly, we find that performance in the visual task is predictive for performance in the detection task. Given that the visual task did not elicit a P300 response, this finding suggest that distinct visual components are either indeed a good predictor for distinct P300 responses (if

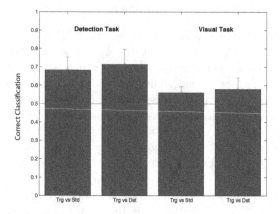

Fig. 5. Classification results. Shown are the classification results when averaged over subjects. Decoding performance is best in the detection task (two left bars), presumably due to the pronounced P300 component present only for the target stimulus. However, classification is above chance level even in the plain visual task (two right bars). Note that for decoding we used the same time windows in each task (0...1000 ms), and that decoding is a *single trial* decoding. With multiple repetition, as it is common practice for EEG-based BCIs, this performance is expected to increase.

the classification in the detection task is based mainly on the P300 response), or the classification in the detection task indeed makes use of visual components. A more detailed inspection of the classifiers' weights in future work (see Section 4.3) will distinguish between these alternatives.

4   Discussion

In summary, we have designed an experiment in order to determine if visually evoked responses in the EEG could be classified, where we did not do a any feature selection or selection of a time-window first but used the whole 1 sec response period for the BDCA classifier. The motivation for this experiment was to improve EEG-based BCIs by identifying – and then later exploiting – discriminative responses in the visual system. Improving EEG-based BCIs via well-chosen stimulus and task designs is necessary, because of the principled limitations of EEG-based BCIs. Our study was motivated by the successful model-based decoding of responses in the visual system [6] and other successful single-trial EEG decoding, e. g. [7]. Even though we did not use an explicitly model-based approach, the BDCA used in our study incorporates prior knowledge about the structure of brain signals and belongs – as a discriminative classifier – to the state-of-the- art for decoding brain responses. We find that visually evoked responses indeed carry information about the stimulus. This was shown in a plain "passive" visual task. The extend to which the classifier in the discrimination task makes use of visually evoked responses needs to be investigated further,

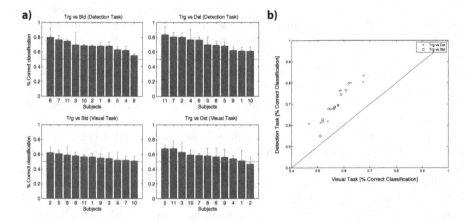

Fig. 6. Classification results for the individual subjects. **a)** Classification results for the detection task (upper row) and the visual task (lower row). The red horizontal line denotes chance level; error bars indicate the standard deviation over the cross-validation runs. **b)** Decoding performance in the visual task and in the detection task for each subject. All classifications are clearly above chance level. Moreover, decoding performance in the detection task correlated with decoding performance in the visual task.

but our results clearly suggest that carefully designing the visual stimuli is a promising new approach to sensory-driven BCIs, which go beyond the rather simple stimuli employed in SSVEP-based BCIs.

4.1   70% Classification Performance for EEG: Poor or Good Result?

In the detection task the classifier reached up to 80% correct classification for selected subjects, and approx. 72% when averaged over the whole group of subjects. Is this a poor or a good performance? Typical P300-based BCIs, such as those implemented in the BCI2000 system [11], usually require a training phase and, most importantly, need multiple presentations of target vs. standard stimuli in, for example, a speller application (see Figure 2b). Trained users may reach approx. 100% correct classification with such speller applications for less than 5 repetitions. However, we used only presentations of one stimulus at a time and performed decoding based on a single trial using the whole epoch $0 \ldots 1000\,\text{ms}$. Thus, a direct comparison to P300-based BCI is not straightforward. Applying the paradigm of rapid serial visual presentations [12] in a speller-like application with carefully designed visual stimuli as compared to letter, e. g., just letter sequences is an interesting next step.

4.2   Role of High-Level vs. Low-Level Visual Features

ERP components selective to visually presented objects (high-level features) have been traditionally reported at $\sim 140 \ldots 170\,\text{ms}$ after stimulus onset. Recently, it was suggested that such a selectivity might even be due to non-controlled confounding variables in a stimulus design such as the inter-trial variability of the stimuli. Could such inter-trial variability explain our findings? We don' think so, because for each of the 2-class classification problems we intentionally used only a single visual stimulus per class. Then, we averaged the classification performance for the different views afterwards. Thus, while the visual stimuli in our study are certainly different, inter-trial variability (low-level features) could not explain differences in ERPs.

In our study we presented fixation points before the stimulus onset, but we did not monitor eye movements throughout the experiment. Thus, inter-trial variability due to eye movements could in principle increase the variability of the EEG responses over trials. However, we excluded epochs with eye movement artifacts and, most importantly, variability over trials would be harmful for our single-trial analyses, because the classifier would have to take this variability into account. Thus, our reported classification results are conservative estimates.

Interestingly, a first non-quantitative inspection of single trial (Figures 4b) and ERP (Figures 4d) responses suggests that differences between conditions may even show up as early as 100 ms after stimulus onset. This is compatible with MEG studies showing such early selective responses [13], which may also be present in the EEG [14]. Thus, future studies (and future more detailed inspections of our data) may uncover that a careful design of visual stimuli could improve the performance of P300- and SSVEP-based BCIs as long as the decoding will also consider earlier visually evoked responses.

4.3   Future Work

Immediate future work need to inspect the weights of the learned BDCA classifiers in order to pinpoint the informative features underyling the correct classification results. Until now it is clear that visually evoked responses carry information about the visual targets (Figures 5 and 6), but the extent to which such response components are utilized by the classifier in the detection task remains to be determined. Restricting the classification on selected time windows is another approach to address this question. Future studies may then focus on explicitly designing visual stimuli, which can be easily discriminated based on visually evoked responses. This could result in improved P300- and SSVEP-based BCI paradigms.

References

1. Pfurtscheller, G., Flotzinger, D., Kalcher, J.: Brain-computer interface-a new communication device for handicapped persons. Journal of Microcomputer Applications 16(3), 293–299 (1993)
2. Muller-Putz, G.R., Pfurtscheller, G.: Control of an electrical prosthesis with an ssvep-based bci. IEEE Transactions on Biomedical Engineering 55(1), 361–364 (2008)

3. Sellers, E.W., Krusienski, D.J., McFarland, D.J., Vaughan, T.M., Wolpaw, J.R.: A p300 event-related potential brain-computer interface (bci): The effects of matrix size and inter stimulus interval on performance. Biological Psychology 73(3), 242–252 (2006)

4. Royer, A.S., McCullough, A., He, B.: A sensorimotor rhythm based goal selection brain-computer interface. In: Annual International Conference of the IEEE Engineering in Medicine and Biology Society, EMBC 2009, pp. 575–577 (September 2009)

5. Norman, K.A., Polyn, S.M., Detre, G.J., Haxby, J.V.: Beyond mind-reading: multivoxel pattern analysis of fMRI data. Trends in Cognitive Sciences 10(9), 424–430 (2006)

6. Kay, K.N., Naselaris, T., Prenger, R.J., Gallant, J.L.: Identifying natural images from human brain activity. Nature 452(7185), 352–355 (2008)

7. Murphy, B., Poesio, M., Bovolo, F., Bruzzone, L., Dalponte, M., Lakany, H.: EEG decoding of semantic category reveals distributed representations for single concepts. Brain and Language 117(1), 12–22 (2011)

8. Dyrholm, M., Parra, L.C.: Smooth bilinear classification of eeg. In: 28th Annual International Conference of the IEEE Engineering in Medicine and Biology Society, EMBS 2006, September 3, vol. 30, pp. 4249–4252 (2006)

9. Dyrholm, M., Christoforou, C., Parra, L.C.: Bilinear discriminant component analysis. J. Mach. Learn. Res. 8, 1097–1111 (2007)

10. V., Fau Blankertz, V.C., Benjamin, Blankertz, B.: Towards a cure for bci illiteracy

11. Schalk, G., McFarland, D.J., Hinterberger, T., Birbaumer, N., Wolpaw, J.R.: Bci 2000: a general-purpose brain-computer interface (bci) system. IEEE Transactions on Biomedical Engineering 51(6), 1034–1043 (2004)

12. Wang, J., Pohlmeyer, E., Hanna, B., Jiang, Y.-G., Sajda, P., Chang, S.-F.: Brain state decoding for rapid image retrieval. In: Proceedings of the 17th ACM International Conference on Multimedia, MM 2009, pp. 945–954. ACM, New York (2009)

13. Liu, J., Harris, A., Kanwisher, N.: Stages of processing in face perception: an MEG study. Nat. Neurosci. 5(9), 910–916 (2002)

14. Herrmann, M.J., Ehlis, A.C., Ellgring, H., Fallgatter, A.J.: Early stages (P100) of face perception in humans as measured with event-related potentials (ERPs). J. Neural Transm. 112(8), 1073–1081 (2005)

A Cognitive Architecture Based
on Cognitive/Neurological Dual-System Theories

Othalia Larue, Pierre Poirier, and Roger Nkambou

GDAC Research Laboratory, Université du Québec à Montréal
Montréal, QC, Canada
larue.othalia@courrier.uqam.ca, {poirier.pierre,nkambou.roger}@uqam.ca

Abstract. In previous work [11], we introduced a cognitive architecture
for the simulation of human behaviour based on Stanovich's tripartite
framework [1], which provides an explanation of how reflexive and adaptive human behaviour emerge from the interaction of three distinct cognitive levels (automatic/reactive, algorithmic and reflective) capable of
dynamically influencing each other in real time. Dynamic control between
the levels in the architecture was then enhanced with a diffuse control
system, based on the physiology of neuromodulations. In this paper, we
study the physiological, functional and gross (mesoscopic) anatomical
parallels between our architecture and the human brain, in order to understand how reactive yet sequential and planned behavior can emerge
from physical systems of interacting simple processors such as our agents
or low-level neural processors.

1 Introduction

Human behaviour is both reactive, manifesting dynamical sensitivity to multiple
parallel factors, and sequential, manifesting planned analytic concatenation of
basic or high-level actions. When uttering a sentence, for example, one respects
the order in which sounds must be produced while adapting the vocal apparatus
to many simultaneous constraints, both internal (need to breathe, to swallow,
and even chew if one is talking with gum in his mouth) and external (observed
response of interlocutor, unexpected events, etc.) The same is true of higher-
level behaviour. In making breakfast, one must toast bread before buttering
it but both toasting and buttering can only be achieved properly if they are
dynamically responsive to a number of simultaneous parallel factors. This fact,
which we will call the dynamical/sequential nature of behaviour, imposes a major
constraint both on cognitive theories of the mind and on the design of cognitive
architectures.

In this paper, after surveying previous attempts to account for the dynam-
ical/sequential nature of cognition both in cognitive science (theories of human cognition) and artificial intelligence (design of cognitive architectures),
we present our own proposal, based on a specific theory of human cognition,
Stanovich's Tripartite Framework [1]. We have presented concrete results else-
where [11][12] and, given the stated aims of the present conference, we shall focus

F.M. Zanzotto et al. (Eds.): BI 2012, LNCS 7670, pp. 288–299, 2012.
© Springer-Verlag Berlin Heidelberg 2012

here on a detailed account of how processing in our architecture parallels known cognitive and neurological processing and how this allows us to realize hybrid reactive/deliberative behaviour in a system.

2   Accounting for the Dynamical/Sequential Nature of Behaviour: Related Work

2.1   Dual-System Theories of Cognition and Stanovich's Tripartite Framework

Dual-system (or dual-process) theories are a major current trend in cognitive theories to account for the dynamical/sequential nature of behaviour. We shall not review the variety of dual-system theories here (for such a review, see [2]). Suffice to say that such theories posit a host of opposed (dual) traits. System 1 is said to be automatic, fast, implicit, heuristic, associative, domain-specific, unconscious and so on. It should be noted that although one speaks of "System 1," it is believed that System 1 is actually a number of system, that all possess System 1 traits (so a better name would be "Type 1 system"). System 2 by contrast is said to be under voluntary control, slow, explicit, logical, sequential, domain general, conscious, and so on. Dual process theories account for the dynamical/sequential nature of behaviour by claiming that the reactive and dynamical aspects of behaviour result from the action of System 1 while the sequential aspects of behavior reflect the involvement of System 2. There are a number of problems with this way of accounting for the dynamical/sequential nature of behaviour, but most researchers in the field believe that these problems ask for refinements of the theory rather than it outright rejection.

Stanovich's tripartite framework is one such refinement of a dual-process theory. Stanovich's System 1, which he calls the "Autonomous Mind," includes instinctive behaviours, over-learned process, domain-specific knowledge, emotional regulation and implicit learning. However, contrary to other dual process theories in Stanovich's tripartite framework, System 2 is divided in two classes of processes: the "Algorithmic Mind," (cognitive control), and the "Reflective Mind" (deliberative processes).

The Algorithmic Mind acts upon information provided by the Autonomous Mind by means of two sets of pre-attentive processes which supply content to Working Memory : perceptual processes and memory access and retrieval.Three processes initiated by the Reflective Mind are implemented by the Algorithmic Mind: (1) inhibition of Autonomous Mind processes, (2) cognitive simulation (decoupling), and (3) serial associative cognition. Performance of these processes leads to an activation of the anterior cingulate cortex (ACC) [3].

Decoupling , is the creation of temporary models of the world upon which different alternatives can be tested. It is not a mandatory step in the decision making process, and when decoupling occurs, it can be incomplete. Subjects may apply simple models that appear appropriate for the situation, and the simple model chosen is not necessarily the best solution for the given situation. In fact, through decoupling a better solution could have been found; however, since the cognitive load of decoupling is higher than that of serial associative cognition, subjects will often satisfy themselves with less optimal but cognitively easier solution provided by serial association. Serial associative cognition supports the implementation of the models. This operation is supported by the dorsolateral prefrontal cortex (DLPFC) [3].

Operations supported by the Reflective Mind define the subject's cognitive style. The Reflective Mind performs three processes: (1) initiation of inhibition of Autonomous Mind processes by the Algorithmic Mind (i.e., it tells the Algorithmic Mind: "Inhibit this Autonomous Mind process") and (2) initiation of decoupling in the Algorithmic Mind (i.e., it tells the Algorithmic Mind: "Start Decoupling") and (3) interruption of serial cognition, either by sending a new sequence to the Algorithmic Mind or by initiating a full simulation of the situation through decoupling. According to Stanovich, the division of human cognition into three sets of processes, instead of the traditional two of dual-process theories, provides a better account of individual cognitive differences. We chose the tripartite model Stanovich, precisely because it accounts of this diversity can help us to provide a good account of the hybrid nature of human behaviour.

2.2   Cognitive Architectures That Generate Dynamical/Sequential Behaviour

Many cognitive architectures have been designed over the years to explicitly exhibit behaviour that manifest a dynamical/sequential nature. We review two of the most influential here and one that theoreticallly resembles ours.

CLARION [4] reproduces the implicit/explicit duality. The architecture is divided into different subsystems: 1) oriented action subsystem (decision making level), 2) non action-oriented (general knowledge of the world), 3) motivational subsystem: ('why the action is performed'), and 4) the meta-cognitive subsystem (close to the 3) that monitors and regulates cognitive processes in the system). Each of these subsystems is split into two representational levels: implicit (distributed) and explicit (symbolic).

LIDA [14] is also a hybrid cognitive architecture approach, but unlike CLARION it models the duality that lies between conscious and unconscious processing. In LIDA's cognitive cycle, transition from conscious to unconscious processing is made through five steps: 1) Interpretation of sensory stimuli by perception units - unconscious stage; 2) Transmission of percepts to preconscious buffer (LIDA's working memory and emotions); 3) Local Associations between percepts and episodic, declarative memories (past emotions/situations); 4) Competition for attention (between coalitions of memories and perception; 5) Access of the winning coalition to the global workspace and broadcast of its content conscious; 6) Resource mobilization; 7) Production of a new hierarchy of objectives according to the context; 8) Action selection based on the new goal or the previously activated one; 9) Action execution.

HCogAff [5] was directly constructed in the context of dual-process theories. HCogAff is a tripartite architecture, with a reactive level (sensory and perceptual processes, constantly changing with environment), a deliberative level (motor processes, effectors action to modify the internal state of the system), and a thought processing level (meta-management units, planification, decision making). Higher levels exert control upon those below, but this control can be disrupted (alarm signals from the reactive level, environmental stimuli, and motivations).

This last architecture is probably the one architecture that is structurally closest to our own; however, as we will see, the design focus in our architecture is on the dynamics of interactions between three distinct levels for the production of a coherent behaviour. Various open issues that remain to be properly addressed have been identified [6]. One of them is a better combination of deliberative problem solving with reactive control, that is, the need for architectures that can combine deliberative problem solving with reactive control by changing their location on the deliberative vs. reactive behaviour spectrum dynamically-based on the situation in which they find themselves. Our proposal, we believe, clearly addresses this issue.

3 Accounting for the Dynamical/Sequential Nature of Behaviour: Our Proposal

We base our cognitive architecture on Stanovich's tripartite framework [1]. This allows us a complete model of the cognitive mind, from automatic and implicit processes to explicit processes involving control (attention and executive functions) to more abstract planning and reasoning. Our architecture is implemented in a multi-layer multi-agent simulation platform [16]. As shown in Fig. 1, each level presented is composed of groups of agents acting in parallel, each agent having one or more role (an abstract representation of their functionality). In the following sections, we present the three level of our architecture (inspired by Stanovich's tripartite framework) from the most deliberative to less deliberative (most reactive). Interaction between those three levels and inside each level is achieved thanks to the message passing activity between agents. We cannot claim fine-grained neurological plausibility for this system. Parallels can however be drawn at the higher level of gross neurological structure and mesoscopic dynamical activity, allowing us to claim that a measure of neurological plausibility for the architecture. The neurological plausibility of dual process theories has been extensively studied [8][9]. Stanovich's tripartite framework, individually, is also supported by neurological data [1]. Since the design of our architecture is based on this model, it naturally inherits its neural plausibility.

3.1 Reflective Level

Structure. The logical and analytical skills of the system will be implemented at this level. Each agent in this group has a shape (a distance matrix) which represents the state that the system must be in to achieve a simple goal. Goal agents (I) are organized in a direct graph. A path in this graph represents a

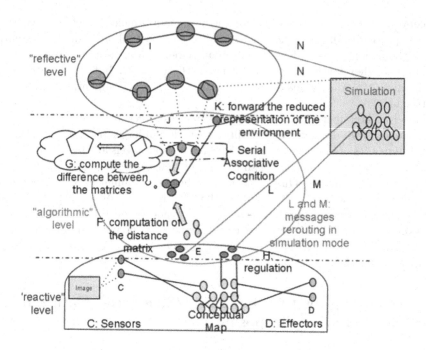

Fig. 1. Our architecture

plan that can be applied to achieve a complex behaviour A set of Goal agents represents a graph of several complex plans or strategies decomposed into a sequence of simple objectives. A succession of simple objectives (J) will be sent to the Algorithmic level, which will take care of its execution. Following Stanovich's Tripartite framework, agents in this group will have access to a reduced representation of the environment. This representation is provided by the Status agents of the Algorithmic Group to other status agents (K) that carry the reduced representation and announce themselves to the goal agents, which in turn compute their similarity to this representation. The activation of the Goal agents will be determined by the computed similarity between these two matrices. Activation propagates from the Goal agent most matching the reduced representation to those that follow in its path. The last agent in the path will send the parsed path to the Algorithmic level. Thus, the shortest path and the most active (with the most messages exchanged) will be sent first to the Algorithmic level. The shortest path (simplest model) or the one the most activated (model used more recently or more often) will prevail over the other paths. The limited serial associative cognition of the Algorithmic level will execute this path step by step. The path executed by serial associative cognition provides the system with the sequentiality necessary to achieve complex goals. However, the system is still a dynamical one. Indeed, a reduced representation of the environment is sent on a regular basis by the Status agents so that the Reflective organisation can interrupt serial cognitive association either by setting a new starting point in the path, or by taking a new branch in the path, based on the current state of the environment. Decision-making at the Reflective level is therefore dynamically influenced by the current strategy and the state of the environment. Gross structural and mesoscopic dynamical parallels. The DLPFC, which provides support for goal directed behaviour is implemented in our system thanks to the Goal Agents.

3.2 Algorithmic Level

Structure. Corresponding to Stanovich's Algorithmic Mind, the Algorithmic group is responsible for the control of the system. Control is achieved with the help of morphology [7]. RequestStatus agents (E) belong to both the Reactive and Algorithmic organisation. At regular intervals, they query Knowledge agents about their status (number of messages sent during that interval to each of the Agents to which they are connected). Status agents (F) represent the system's activity at a given time in the form of a distance matrix that describes the message passing activity of the system at that time. The distance between two concepts in the conceptual map is measured by the number of messages sent between the Knowledge agents bearing these two concepts as their role. Status agents also send the reduced representation of the activity in the Reactive organisation to the Reflective level as we described in the previous section. Globally, this matrix thus represents a form or shape, and it is this form that will be transformed to reach the shape describing the goal assigned to the system. At the Algorithmic level, we thus find the short-term goals of the system in the form of a graph of Goal agents sent by the Reflective level. Each Goal agent (I) contains a distance matrix that specifies the distance necessary between each Knowledge agents (that is, the number of messages that must be sent between Knowledge agents) if the system is to reach goal. Graphs of short-term goals in our architecture correspond to Stanovich's serial associative cognition. Delta agents (G) compute the difference between the matrix provided by the Status agents and the one provided by the Goal agents. The resulting difference (another matrix) is provided to Control agents (H), which in turn send regulation messages to agents in the Reactive organisation to modify (i.e., increase) their activation so that their global activity more closely matches the shape describing the current short-term goal. Attention and Working memory in the system are implemented thanks to agents of the Algorithmic organisation. Control agents regulate the activation of elements in the system's semantic memory in relation to its current goal. The system's long term memory is made up of the Knowledge agents in the Reactive organisation, and the system's working memory (WM) at a given time is made up of the Knowledge agents that are activated in the Reactive group at that time. Decoupling, an operation initiated by agents of the Reflective Group, is supported by agents of the Algorithmic Group. When multiple strategies (meaning two or more GoalSet Agents) are selected at the algorithmic level, the Goal Agent that belongs to the Algorithmic and Reflective Group triggers a simulation of the strategies. When the Algorithmic Group is in simulation mode, a possible world is created thanks to the reduced representation sent by the Delta agents. This secondary representation is realized with a limited number of agents (20). These agents are assigned dynamically the same roles and links as those agents from the Reactive Group they are replicating, as indicated by the reduced representation. Since this possible world is carried out thanks to distinct agents (SecondaryRepresentation Agents instead of Knowledge agents) and a distinct group (Algorithmic instead of Reactive), we can be sure that this secondary representation is totally independent from the current representation of the world (i.e., Knowledge Agents from the Reactive Group). To reproduce the cognitive cost of the simulation operation, the cognitive operations (goal inhibition and selection) are carried out by the Control Agents, Delta Agents, and agents from the Reflective Group. Messages from (L) and to these agents (M) are branched to the SecondaryRepresentation Agents of the Algorithmic Group instead of the Knowledge Agents of the Reactive Group. Once the simulation is completed, the activation of Goal Agents is regulated accordingly at the Reflective level (N), therefore potentially replacing the next action carried out by the Algorithmic level (by the first rule simulated).

Gross Structural and Mesoscopic Dynamical Parallels. Regulation of posterior brain regions is implemented by the regulating messages sent by the Control Agents to agents of the Reactive Group Cognitive tasks supported by the Algorithmic Mind lead to an activation of the Anterior Cingulate cortex (ACC) [1]. There is furthermore evidence that decoupling is achieved by the Dorsolateral PreFrontal Cortex (DLPFC) [1]. Furthermore, the different roles ascribed to the agents in the architecture correspond to functional roles that has been mapped to specific anatomical structures see Fig. 2 [15]. It must be noted that the ACC has been identified as the response conflicting monitoring system [15] in the human brain, regulating control's engagement. Conflict monitoring is achieved in our system by the collaboration between the Delta Agents and the Control Agents.

4   Reactive Level

Structure. The Reactive level in our model corresponds to Stanovich's Autonomous Mind. The main roles assigned to agents within this level are "sensor" (C), "effector" (D) and "knowledge" (A). The network of Knowledge agents (agents assigned with the "knowledge" role) is initialized with a knowledge base that makes up the system's declarative knowledge (semantic memory): a conceptual map made up of concepts and the semantic links between them. Knowledge agents therefore have two attributes: "knowledge" and a word from the knowledge base (e.g., "Red"); knowledge agents are also connected together according to the links in the conceptual map. Upon receiving a message from a Sensor agent or from another Knowledge agent, Knowledge agents send a message to those Knowledge agents they are connected to, therefore spreading activation in the network (a process similar to that of semantic memory, [13]). The number of messages exchanged between the agents, and therefore their activation, is at first determined by the distance between them in the conceptual map. The system's environment is similar to (portions of) human environments. Each Sensor agent is sensitive to some particular type of information in the environment (colors, sounds, texts, etc.). If the type of information to which they are sensitive to is present in the environment, Sensor agents will (at short intervals) extract it and send messages to Knowledge agents with a role associated with the sensor's function ("read" for Knowledge agents connected to Sensor agents reading characters, "recognizeColor" for Knowledge agents connected to Sensor agents recognizing colors). Activation in the network therefore depends on the number of messages sent by the Sensor agents and the activation of the Knowledge agents in the conceptual map. Taken together, the action of Sensor and Knowledge agents make up the system's sensory motor level. This means that the system's sensory abilities are always a function of the Sensor agents' information extracting capacities and of the system's knowledge about the environment: the system is fully situated. Effectors agents work similarly: a knowledge agent associated to the function of the effector ("sayRed", "sayBlue") sends messages to Effector agents with a similar role, which will then act on the environment.

Gross Structural and Mesoscopic Dynamical Parallels. Knowledge Agents are linked to Sensor Agents as the Medial Temporal Lobe (MTL in Fig. 2) is known to mediate sensory memory. The medial temporal lobe is also identified as the functional locus of semantic memory. "Effector" and "Sensor" agents are associated with distinct roles in the Reactive Group since their functional role is achieved by distinct anatomical structures (PreCentral Gyrus, PostCentral Gyrus and Visual Cortex in Fig. 2). Through nested sensorimotor and goal-directing loops, we are therefore able to implement the cognitive dynamics of a goal-sensitive sensory-motor architecture.

5 Neurological Parallels

Signals in dynamical systems are called diffuse if they rule secondary variables in large areas. In our system, neuromodulations are diffuse signals that control the overall state of our system. In the system, the processing occurs thanks to message passing. Messages are exchanged between group of agents inside the levels, and thanks to intermediary agents which belongs to both levels to pass information between levels. Messages are exchanged at regular intervals, those intervals varying from groups to groups (for example: Goal agents which send the future objective to the system at regular intervals, Control agents also send regulation messages at regular intervals to agents at the reactive level, this interval being inferior to the one used by Goal agents, and this interval (the one use by Control agents) is superior to the one used by Knowledge agents at the reactive level) Neuromodulations are messages sent by agents belonging to another group. Agents of the system (of the three levels) upon reception of those messages count the number of activation messages received, and , through a transfer function representing the sensitivity of the agents to this modulation (mirroring

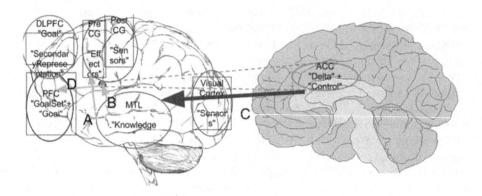

Fig. 2. Neurological parallels

the sensitivity of neurons to neuromodulations), compute the "modulated" interval that the agent will now be using. Neuromodulations help us modify the system's general dynamics (allowing us finer-grained control on the dynamics), giving specific profile to the system (reactive oriented, reflective oriented,). We intend on reproducing the four following neuromodulatory systems [10].

Dopamine is mainly present in two important brain pathways: the mesocortical pathway (frontal lobe and prefrontal cortex), involved in the update of working memory, and the nigrostriatal pathway (basal ganglia), involved in motor skills (A). In our system, the mesocortical pathway is implemented thanks to the messages sent by agents of the reactive group to the StatusUpdate agents of the algorithmic group (B). The nigrostriatal pathway, for its part, is implemented by the messages sent to the effector agents. The reward and motivation effect occur thanks to the reinforcement or inhibition of goal agents that have led to a success in the past (D).

For the *Serotonin* neuromodulation, we will replicate the pathway projecting from the raphea nuclei to the thalamus, subthalamus, limbic system and cerebral cortex, especially its role in long-term memory and executive control. The influence on long-term memory will be implemented through the modulation of the messages exchanged between agents with the "knowledge" role (D). The influence of executive control will be reproduced by modulating messages between control agents and agents belonging to the reactive group (E).

Norepinephrine (Noradrenergic system), acting on the pathway from the locus coreuleus to the the forebrain and brainstem, it can create arousal; in the system, this action will be represented by a global increase in the message passing activity at the Reactive level. The pathway from the locus coreulus to the posterior parietal lobe, responsible for the integration of sensory information will be represented in our system by the modulation of the sensitivity to sensory stimuli (E) (sensitivity of Sensor agents).

Concerning *Acetylcholine*, the cholinergic system also affects the regulation of specific sensory relay (by modulating activity in the basal forebrain). We will reproduce this by modulating the message passing activity from the sensor agents. The action of acetylcholine on the pathway from frontal cortex to nucleus basalis.impacts divided attention (attention to different tasks at the same time). In our system this would be represented by the message passing activity occurring with Decoupling agents.

6 Current Status and Future Directions

For now, we have validated the architecture for the first two levels (reactive and algorithmic) and part of the third levels, thanks to two psychological tasks (the Stroop task [11] and the Wisconsin card sorting task [12] for which we obtained results comparable to human results. The Stroop task is a task aimed at the evaluation of a subject's cognitive control: subject is confronted to two stimuli resulting in the competition of two responses, with the one required to fulfill the task not being the habitual response. With the Stroop task[11], we were able to evaluate the system perceptual's attention (achieved thanks to the regulation of knowledge agents and linked effector agents by the control agents) and cognitive control (tregulation of knowledge agents by control agents). With a variant of the Stroop task, Semantic Stroop task, we were able to evaluate its ability to process context and retrieve information in its long term memory (conceptual map formed by knowledge agents). In the Wisconsin Card Sorting Task[12], a subject has to discover and use different sorting rules on a set of cards. With this task, we were able to validate the system's cognitive flexibility, and the equilibrium between deliberative and reactive behaviours. Cognitive flexibility is made possible by the interaction between the three cognitive levels, that helps preserve this equilibrium in the architecture to make it efficiently adaptive : the rule discovery is made in conjunction by the reflective level (rules firing) and the algorithmic level (decoupling), the application of the rule is made thanks to a mechanism similar to the one involved in the Stroop task (regulation of the knowledge agents of the reactivel level by the Control agents of the algorithmic level). We have worked for now on the implementation of two neuromodulations : dopamine and serotonine. In the future, we plan on adding two other neuromodulations : acetylcholine (sensors and executive functions) and noradrenaline (arousal). In future work, we plan on addressing the physical embodiment and emotional modulation of cognitive processes. Neuromodulations that influence communications between organisations, and therefore modify the general dynamic of the system would be the basis of physiological dimension of emotions in the system (their conceptual/cognitive dimension is already present in the conceptual map). Neuromodulation agents could then be linked to emotional concepts/knowledge ("happy"), Allowing for an interaction between the physiological activation (neuromodulation) and conceptual interpretation of emotions.

7 Conclusion

We modeled our cognitive architecture on Stanovich's Tripartite Framework, which explains how cognition can be at once reactive and sequential by positing three levels of interacting cognitive processes. Brains are the physical systems we know that have best managed to dynamically integrate real-time reactivity with sequentiality; and human brains are perhaps the only system that has perfected this integration to allow such cognitive feats as sequential problem solving that is sensitive to the evolving problem space as actions are applied or long-term planning that can self-adapt as environments, knowledge and goals change. Our views on Artificial Intelligence thus recommend that we complement our functional-level model of cognition by neural-level knowledge of the implementation of the cognitive processes posited by such theories. To conclude, we therefore want to look at how processing may be organized in physical systems of interacting simple agents or processors to allow reactive and sequential processes to influence each other in order to fully take advantage of this interaction. The cognitive processes described here result from an interaction between the medial temporal lobe (MTL), the anterior cingulate cortex (ACC) and the dorsolateral prefrontal cortex (DLPFC). The MLT-based autonomous sensorimotor agent is sensitive to the meaning of inputs and outputs and to the semantic relations that make (declarative) knowledge into a spreading activation semantic memory. Because no perception or action is uninfluenced by knowledge, this sensorimotor agent always acts in an informed (or meaningful) way. However, in itself, it is not sensitive to internal goals or plans: it is condemned to live in the present. The ACC-based Goal agents provide internal motives to the reactive-level agents by slightly, but constantly, altering the activity of Knowledge agents (which in turn can affect the activity of Sensor agents). If this model is right, then goals merely influence the dynamics of a sensorimotor system already capable of meaningful action in the world. The emerging picture of MLTACC interaction at this point is one where the ACC forces MLT-processing into a preferred direction. This is not the extant of processing in our agent, however. We saw that DLPFC-based agents receive a reduced representation of the environment (through a reduced representation of the activity of Knowledge agents), which determines which path in the goal structure (the directed graph of Control agents) will be sent to the Algorithmic level for execution. Since these DLPFC agents can halt current execution of a goal-path (plan or strategy) or force a switch to a new goal-path, MLT-processing can influence, albeit indirectly, the pressures ACC imposes on its own processing. The resulting picture is one of two linked dynamical loops: the meaningful sensorimotor loop through the world and the goal-setting MLT-DLPFC-ATT-MLT loop. Our current agent has two additional control structures. The first is an ACC-based ability to simulate counterfactual situations, initiated by DLPFC-based agents, the result of which may determine which goal-path is sent to the ACC for execution. This first additional control structure is therefore part of the agents goal control loop, allowing the selection of goals that would be chosen in different yet related environments. The second is a lower-level modulatory influence (neuromodulations) diffusely controlling the activity of Knowledge agents (serotonin) and of Goal agents (dopamine). The effect of neuromodulation is either to make the agent more sensitive to the environment (serotonin) or more sensitive to its goals (dopamine). Serotonin neuromodulation is thus part of the sensorimotor loop, whereas dopamine neuromodulation is part of the goal control loop. At this point, however, neuromodulations are point quite crude in our system (we basically switch them on or off individually). We plan in future work to give neuromodulation its own dynamics, which would determine the modulatory state of the agent at any time. The neuromodulation dynamics would be influenced by low-level physiological parameters (drives, excitation, wakefulness) as well as by the system's other two loops that characterize, that is, by events in the environment (through the sensorimotor loop) and by current or coming goals (through the goal control loop).

References

1. Stanovich, K.E.: Rationality and the reflective mind. Oxford University Press (2010)
2. Evans, J.S.B.T.: Dual-Processing Accounts Of Reasoning, Judgment, and Social Cognition. Annual Review of Psychology 59, 255–278 (2008)
3. Frankish, K., Evans, J.S.B.T.: The duality of mind: a historical perspective. In: Frankish, K., Evans, J.S. (eds.) In Two Minds, pp. 1–29 (2009)
4. Sun, R., Lane, S., Matthews, R., et al.: The two systems of learning. In: Frankish, K., Evans, J.S. (eds.) In Two Minds. Oxford University Press (2009)
5. Sloman, A., Chrisley, R.L.: Virtual machines and consciousness. Journal of Consciousness Studies 10(4-5), 133–172 (2003)
6. Langley, P., Laird, J.E., Rogers, S.: Cognitive architectures: Research issues and challenges. Cognitive Systems Research 10(2), 141–160 (2009)
7. Cardon, A.: La complexit organise. Herms Science Publications, Paris (2005)
8. Goel, V.: Cognitive Neuroscience of Thinking. In: Berntson, G., Cacioppo, J. (eds.) Handbook of Neuroscience for the Behavioral Sciences. Wiley (2009)
9. Lieberman, M.: What zombies can't do: a social cognitive neuroscience approach to the irreducibility of reflective consciousness. In: Frankish, K., Evans, J.S. (eds.) In Two Minds: Dual Processes and Beyond, pp. 293–316. Oxford University Press (2009)
10. Bear, M.F., Connors, B.W., Nieoullon, A., Paradiso, M.A.: Neurosciences Additions Pradel (2007)
11. Larue, O., Poirier, P., Nkambou, R.: A Three level Cognitive architecture for the simulation of cognitive phenomena. In: CAI 2012 (2012)
12. Larue, O., Poirier, P., Nkambou, R.: Hybrid Reactive-Deliberative Behavior in a Symbolic Dynamical Cognitive Architecture. In: International Conference on Artificial Intelligence 2012 (2012)
13. Anderson, J.R.: The architecture of cognition. Harvard University Press, Cambridge (1983)
14. Franklin, S., Ramamurthy, U., D'Mello, S., McCauley, L., Negatu, A., Silva, R., Datla, V., et al.: LIDA: A computational model of global workspace theory and developmental learning. AAAI Fall Symposium on AI and Consciousness. Arlington (2007)
15. Botvinick, M.M., Braver, T.S., Barch, D.M., Carter, C.S., Cohen, J.D.: Conflict monitoring and cognitive control. Psychol. Rev. 108(3), 624–652 (2001)
16. Ferber, J., Gutknecht, O., Michel, F.: From Agents to Organizations: An Organizational View of Multi-agent Systems. In: Giorgini, P., Müller, J.P., Odell, J.J. (eds.) AOSE 2003. LNCS, vol. 2935, pp. 214–230. Springer, Heidelberg (2004)

A Preliminary Study Using Granular Computing for Remote Sensing Image Segmentation Involving Roughness

Ge Cui and Xin Wang

Department of Geomatics Engineering,
University of Calgary, Calgary, AB, Canada
{cuig,xcwang}@ucalgary.ca

Abstract. Granular computing partitions the universe into granules, allowing for their further analysis. For several years granular computing has been used to address problems in the field of machine learning, image analysis and data mining. In this paper, we discuss the application of granular computing to remote sensing image segmentation. A granule merging algorithm involving roughness is proposed.

Keywords: Granular computing, Image segmentation, Granule merging, Roughness.

1   Introduction

Image segmentation is an important research topic in computer vision and remote sensing. The goal of segmentation is the partitioning of images into homogeneous objects that do not overlap. The objects are generally superior to pixels as processing units in image analysis, due to affluent feature sets; therefore, segmentation is usually the first step in other higher level image processing tasks, including image interpretation, diagnosis, and analysis [4]. Many segmentation algorithms have been proposed, such as gray level thresholds, clustering methods and edge detection methods [9]. Most of these algorithms can achieve good results for regular color images; however, they do not handle remote sensing images very well, as they do not consider the uncertainty of these images. The uncertainty may come from sensors, data compression or data transmission and is mainly reflected in three aspects:

1) Several different ground surfaces exist in one pixel, resulting in roughness of the pixel;
2) The boundaries of regions in nature are not crisp;
3) The homogeneity degrees for objects are quite rough.

Most segmentation algorithms are unable to provide a multi-scale segmentation result for further image analysis. Multi-scale segmentation is significant in image analysis, as useful information can be extracted at different scales. For instance, global information

F.M. Zanzotto et al. (Eds.): BI 2012, LNCS 7670, pp. 300–308, 2012.

can be acquired at a large scale and specific information at a small one. These problems could be addressed effectively by granular computing.

Zadeh (1997) proposed that there are three concepts underlying human recognition: granulation, organization, and causation. Granulation involves decomposition of the whole into parts; organization involves integration of parts into the whole; and, causation relates to the association of causes with effects [18]. The mind uses granular computing to partition an object into similar, indistinguishable granules in which we are interested. For instance, a laptop is composed of various parts, such as a CPU, memory, a monitor, a keyboard and so on.

Many studies have been conducted in the field of granular computing. Bargiela presented granular computing as a computing paradigm of information processing with multiple levels [2]. Yao proposed a unified framework for granular computing based on three perspectives: the philosophical perspective on structured thinking, the methodological perspective on structured problem solving and the computational perspective on structured information processing [17]. The unified framework provides a holistic understanding of a granular system and a direction for further development. Zhou and Yao introduced an adaptive learning method to further classify deferred cases by searching for effective granularity based on the decision-theoretical rough set model [20]. Yao presented trends and development in the field of granular computing, concluding that granular computing is receiving increased attention and needs more interaction with other research communities [15].

There are some unique advantages of granular computing. One advantage lies in its hierarchical structure with levels in the structure at different scales. The scale here is different from the map scale, which is the ratio of a distance on the map to the corresponding distance on the ground. For example, we could study a whole province at a large scale and a specific city at a smaller scale. The fact that a year is at a much larger scale as that of a second is another example. Therefore, province, city, year and second are granules at different scale. An object can be taken as a hierarchy structure of arbitrary levels, with each level consisting of granules at the same scale. A close connection exists among levels. Another advantage of granular computing is that its uncertainty theory provides a convenient conceptual framework for dealing with information granulation [19].

Granular computing has been applied in many fields including machine learning [16], data mining [8], and Rough set theory [10].

This paper is organized as follows: Section 2 introduces the application of granular computing to image segmentation. Section 3 discusses an algorithm based on rough region merging, and Section 4 gives the conclusions and recommendations for future work.

2 Granular Computing and Image Segmentation

A complete granulation system contains the following features: homogeneity, multi-scales, a hierarchical network and uncertainty. For image segmentation, we formulate the problem as described in the following paragraph.

An image is represented as a universe, $\mathcal{G}$; and, the subsets of $\mathcal{G}$ are $\{G_1, G_2, ..., G_i,...\}$, where G_i is the i-th level subset of specific granulation. G_i reflects granules at a larger scale than G_{i-1} and a smaller scale than G_{i+1}. G_1 has the smallest scale, with every pixel a granule. In each level, $G_i = \{g_{i,1}, g_{i,2}, ..., g_{i,k},...\}$, where $g_{i,k}$ is the k-th granule in the i-th level in image $\mathcal{G}$. At the same level, granules have strong topologi-cal relationship with their neighbor granules, where the neighbors of granule $g_{i,j}$ are $N(g_{i,j}) = \{g_{i,m}, ..., g_{i,n}\}$. For adjacent levels, a parent-child relationship exists for the granules, namely $Chd(g_{i,j}) = \{g_{i-1,s}, ..., g_{i-1,t}\}$. In the system, there is a set of features $F = \{f_1, f_2, ..., f_i,...\}$ that measure the degree of granules, which could reflect the cha-racteristics of a granule at a certain level.

The granulation hierarchical structure of an image can be represented as shown in Fig. 1.

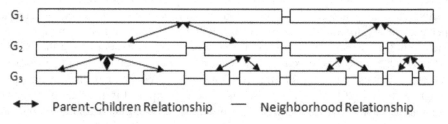

Fig. 1. Three-level granulation hierarchical structure of an image

Granular computing can be applied to the segmentation of remote sensing images. First, granulation of a universe (image) involves dividing the universe into subsets or grouping individual objects into clusters [7], so that an image can be seen as a group of meaningful, homogeneous regions or information granules that possess similar features. Second, granular computing can provide a hierarchical framework for the multi-scale segmentation of images. Observation of objects in multiple scales is quite important in the field of remote sensing, since the information of objects is distinct at different scales. Global information is extracted at a large scale and detailed informa-tion at a small scale. For example, we could study a whole forest as a granule in a large scale, and we can also take the information of conifers and broad-leaved plants in the forest as two granules at a smaller scale.

The hierarchical network of granular computing organizes multi-scale segmenta-tion into individual levels. Each level corresponds to the segmentation result at a spe-cific scale. This network can provide a precise relationship between individual levels of multi-scale segmentation, with segmentation of a new level between lower and upper levels [3].

Granular computing is applicable for dealing with the uncertainty problem in re-mote sensing image segmentation. The uncertainty in the image can be described and considered by rough set theory in the process of segmentation. In the following sec-tion, we propose an algorithm of using rough set theory for the segmentation of a remote sensing image.

3   Segmentation Algorithm Involving Roughness

3.1   Review of Segmentation Algorithm

Image segmentation is aimed at partitioning a scene (image) into individual non-intersecting, homogeneous regions or objects. Thus, segmentation is a critical step for further image analysis.

Requirements of a good image segmentation algorithm include [1]:

1) The primitive regions from the segmentation algorithm should be applicable for high-level image analysis;
2) The algorithm should be a multi-scale segmentation so that interesting objects can be studied at different scales;
3) The size of all resulting objects should be comparable;
4) The segmentation results should be reproducible;
5) The algorithm should be applicable to any type of data; and,
6) The algorithm should have reasonable performance with complicated data.

Schiewe concluded that segmentation techniques could be categorized as: point-based, edge-based, region-based and combined methods [13]. Point-based methods, such as gray value thresholds and K-means clustering, search for homogeneous pixels in the whole image and assign them into groups. Edge-based approaches describe segments by their outlines according to the fact that the pixel values at the boundary of objects are not continuous. The most common edge-based algorithms are edge detection methods based on the Canny operator and the Prewitt operator. Region-based algorithms start from a set of available elements, like points or regions, and then merge or split the elements until the given segmentation criteria can no longer be satisfied.

3.2   Rough Set Theory and Roughness

Rough set theory was first introduced by Pawlak in 1982. It is a mathematical tool to address uncertainty by an approximation of a crisp set by providing lower and upper approximations of the original set [11]. One of the main advantages of rough set theory is that it does not need any preliminary or additional information about the data [12]. It handles vagueness through the boundary region of the set.

The universe is presented by U, R is the indiscernibility relationship and the objects located inside the lower approximation boundary of set X are definitely parts of the set. The lower approximation can, therefore, be defined as:

$$\underline{R}(X) = \bigcup_{x \in U} \{R(x): R(x) \subseteq X\}; \tag{1}$$

The objects located inside the upper approximation boundary of set X are possible parts of the set. The upper approximation is defined as:

$$\overline{R}(X) = \bigcup_{x \in U} \{R(x): R(x) \cap X \neq \emptyset\}; \tag{2}$$

If the boundary region of the set X is empty, then the set is crisp; otherwise, it is considered to be a rough set. The boundary region is defined as:

$$BN_R(X) = \overline{R}(X) - \underline{R}(X). \tag{3}$$

The classic rough set theory can be displayed as presented in Fig. 2.

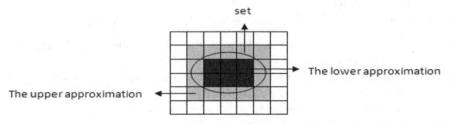

Fig. 2. Classic rough set

The rough degree of set X could be reflected by a ratio of the number of objects in its lower approximation to that in its upper approximation. The roughness is defined as:

$$\rho_X = 1 - \frac{|\underline{R}(X)|}{|\overline{R}(X)|} \tag{4}$$

where $|\underline{R}(X)|$ and $|\overline{R}(X)|$ are the cardinalities of the lower and upper approximations, respectively. The greater the value of the ratio, the lower the value of the roughness.

3.3   Rough Granule Merging

Given that various ambiguities inherently exist in real remote sensing images [14], a granule merging algorithm involving roughness is proposed in this paper. In region merging techniques, the input image is first tessellated into a set of homogeneous primitive regions [6]. In the algorithm, the initial primitive regions are all pixels of the image.

The target of the segmentation is minimum heterogeneity of the image granules. *eCognition* software (www.ecognition.com) [5] selects spectral and shape feature as segmentation parameters. An introduction of the related method has been presented in [3], but the uncertainty of the image was not considered. Roughness is a very important feature in the measurement of the ambiguous condition of objects in rough set theory. Therefore, in this paper, the spectral information, shape and roughness, as features of granules, are all accounted for as heterogeneity. After merging, the total heterogeneity, H, should be less than a given threshold, T. If the heterogeneity exceeds the threshold, merging will not occur.

The increase of heterogeneity is defined as:

$$H = w_{color} \cdot \Delta h_{color} + w_{shape} \cdot \Delta h_{shape} + w_{rough} \cdot \Delta h_{rough} \tag{5}$$

$$w_{color} \in [0,1], w_{rough} \in [0,1], w_{rough} \in [0,1], w_{color} + w_{shape} + w_{rough} = 1 \tag{6}$$

Spectral heterogeneity is defined as,

$$\Delta h_{color} = \Sigma_c w_c \left(n_{merges} \cdot \sigma_{c,merge} - (n_{g\_1} \cdot \sigma_{c,g\_1} + n_{g\_2} \cdot \sigma_{c,g\_2}) \right) \tag{7}$$

where n_{merges} is the number of pixels within a merged object, n_{g_1} is the number of pixels in granule 1, n_{g_2} is the number of pixels in granule 2, σ_c is the standard deviation within a granule of channel c, and 'merge' subscripts refer to the merged granule and granule 1 and granule 2 are prior to merge, respectively.

Shape heterogeneity is defined as:

$$\Delta h_{shape} = w_{compt} \cdot \Delta h_{compt} + w_{smooth} \cdot \Delta h_{smooth} \tag{8}$$

$$\Delta h_{smooth} = n_{merge} \cdot \frac{l_{merge}}{b_{merge}} - \left(n_{g\_1} \cdot \frac{l_{g\_1}}{b_{g\_1}} + n_{g\_2} \cdot \frac{l_{g\_2}}{b_{g\_2}} \right) \tag{9}$$

$$\Delta h_{compt} = n_{merge} \cdot \frac{l_{merge}}{\sqrt{n_{merge}}} - \left(n_{g\_1} \cdot \frac{l_{g\_1}}{\sqrt{n_{g\_1}}} + n_{g\_2} \cdot \frac{l_{g\_2}}{\sqrt{n_{g\_2}}} \right) \tag{10}$$

where l is the perimeter of a granule and b is the perimeter of a granule's bounding box.

Rough heterogeneity is defined as:

$$\Delta h_{rough} = \Sigma_c w_c \left(n_{merges} \cdot \rho_{c,merge} - (n_{g_1} \cdot \rho_{c,g_1} + n_{g_2} \cdot \rho_{c,g_2}) \right) \tag{11}$$

where ρ_c is the roughness within the granule of channel c.

The flow chat of the image processing is displayed in Fig. 3.

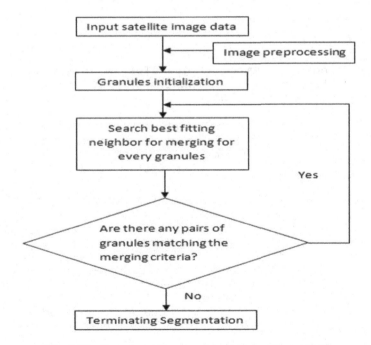

Fig. 3. The flow chart of image segmentation with roughness

Before segmentation, the remote sensing image is preprocessed, which may include geometric and radioactive corrections. After corrections, the threshold and various weight parameters in the algorithm are assigned values by the user. The original granules are then initialized by pixels, so that the granules get features, such as spectral information (mean, standard deviation), shape information (perimeter, bounding box), roughness, topological information and size. The following iterative process is undertaken:

1) Traversing each granule in the image, search for its best fitting granule (the minimum increase of heterogeneity after merging) in the neighbors.
2) If the increased heterogeneity is less than the threshold, record the pairs of granules in the collection, M.
3) When the traversing ends, sort the pairs of granules according to the hetero-geneity.
4) If M is not empty, merge the pairs of granules in the order. The fresh gra-nules and its neighbors will need to update topological information. Then, go to step 1). If M is empty, there are not any pairs of granules meeting the cri-teria, and the segmentation is terminated.

The pseudocode of the segmentation algorithm is as follows:

```
//initialization of parameters
Initializing threshold T;
Initializing weight parameters;

//initialization of original granules from pixels
Initializing all pixels into granules g(i);


While(merging happens){

            //ng: the number of granules in the image
            //traversing the granules
              While(i++ < ng){

                        //Search neighbors
                        //get the most similar one with
                        //minimum  H
                            Find best fitting granule g(j);

                        //H: obtained from equation 5 to 11
                            if (H(i, j) < T) {
                                        GetNeigbors(g(i), g(j));
                                        Merge(g(i), g(j));

                        //create topologic relationship
                        //for the fresh granule and its
                        //neighbors
                                        UpdateNeigborhood();
                            }

              }
}
```

4   Conclusions and Future Work

In this paper, we discuss the use of granular computing for remote sensing image segmentation. The uncertainty embedded in images can be addressed by using granular computing. Every region in the images can be interpreted as a granule. A rough granule merging algorithm is presented. The granules that are merged by their children are derived with criteria involving spectral, shape information and roughness, which guarantees maximum homogeneity and minimum roughness of the granule.

In the future, we will carry out experiments to investigate the performance of the algorithm in this paper and compare the results with existing segmentation algorithms to verify the effectiveness of the method. Rough set theory will be further studied for addressing the uncertainty problems in remote sensing image segmentation.

References

1. Baatz, M., Schape, A.: Multiresolution Segmentation—An Optimization Approach for High Quality Multi-Scale Image Segmentation. In: Strobl, J., Blaschke, T., Griesebner, G. (eds.) Angewandte Geographische Informations-Verarbeitung XII, pp. 12–23. Wichmann Verlag, Karlsruhe (2000)
2. Bargiela, A., Pedrycz, W.: Granular Computing: An Introduction. Kluwer Acadamic Publishers, Boston (2002)
3. Benz, U.C., Hofmann, P., Willhauck, G., Lingenfelder, I., Heynen, M.: Multi-Resolution, Object-Oriented Fuzzy Analysis of Remote Sensing Data for GIS-Ready Information. ISPRS Journal of Photogrammetry & Remote Sensing 58, 239–258 (2004)
4. Ciesielski, K.C., Udupa, J.K.: A Framework for Comparing Different Image Segmentation Methods and Its Use in Studying Equivalences between Level Set and Fuzzy Connectedness Frameworks. Computer Vision and Image Understanding 115, 721–734 (2011)
5. Definiens Imaging: User Guide 4. eCognition (2004)
6. Haris, K., Efstratiadis, S.N., Maglaveras, N., Katsaggelos, A.K.: Hybrid Image Segmentation Using Watersheds and Fast Region Merging. IEEE Transactions on Image Processing 7(12) (1998)
7. Herbert, J.P., Yao, J.T.: A Granular Computing Framework for Self-Organizing Maps. Neurocomputing 72, 2865–2872 (2009)
8. Lin, T.Y., Yao, Y.Y., Zadeh, L.A. (eds.): Data Mining, Rough Sets and Granular Computing. Physica-Verlag, Heidelberg (2002)
9. Pal, N.R., Pal, S.K.: A Review on Image Segmentation Techniques. Pattern Recognition 26(9), 1277–1294 (1993)
10. Pawlak, Z.: Granularity of Knowledge, Indiscernibility and Rough Sets. In: Proc IEEE International Conference on Fuzzy Systems, vol. 1, pp. 106–110 (1998)
11. Pawlak, Z.: Rough Sets. International Journal of Computer and Information Sciences 11(5), 341–356 (1982)
12. Pawlak, Z.: Some Issues on Rough Sets. In: Peters, J.F., Skowron, A., Grzymała-Busse, J.W., Kostek, B.z., Świniarski, R.W., Szczuka, M.S. (eds.) Transactions on Rough Sets I. LNCS, vol. 3100, pp. 1–58. Springer, Heidelberg (2004)
13. Schiewe, J.: Segmentation of High-Resolution Remotely Sensed Data: Concepts, Applications and Problems. International Archives of Photogrammetry and Remote Sensing 34, 380–385 (2002)

14. Sen, D., Pal, S.K.: Generalized Rough Sets, Entropy, and Image Ambiguity Measures. IEEE Transactions on Systems, Man, and Cybernetics—Part B: Cybernetics 39(1) (2009)

15. Yao, J.T.: A Ten-Year Review of Granular Computing. In: Proceedings of 2007 IEEE International Conference on Granular Computing, pp. 734–739 (2007)

16. Yao, J.T., Yao, Y.Y.: A Granular Computing Approach to Machine Learning. In: Proceedings of the 1st International Conference on Fuzzy Systems and Knowledge Discovery, Singapore, pp. 732–736 (2002)

17. Yao, Y.Y.: A Unified Framework of Granular Computing. In: Pedrycz, W., Skowron, A., Kreinovich, V. (eds.) Handbook of Granular Computing, pp. 401–410. Wiley (2008)

18. Zadeh, L.A.: Towards A Theory of Fuzzy Information Granulation and Its Centrality in Human Reasoning and Fuzzy Logic. Fuzzy Sets and Systems 90, 111–127 (1997)

19. Zadeh, L.A.: Fuzzy Sets and Information Granularity, Advances in Fuzzy Set Theory and Applications. In: Gupta, M., Ragade, R.K., Yager, R.R. (eds.), pp. 3–18. North-Holland Publishing Company (1979)

20. Zhou, B., Yao, Y.Y.: In Search for Effective Granularity with DTRS for Ternary Classification. The International Journal of Cognitive Informatics & Natural Intelligence 5(3), 47–60 (2011)

Semi-supervised Clustering via Constrained Symmetric Non-negative Matrix Factorization

Liping Jing[1], Jian Yu[1], Tieyong Zeng[2], and Yan Zhu[1]

[1] School of Computer and Information Technology, Beijing Jiaotong University,
Beijing, China
{lpjing,jianyu}@bjtu.edu.cn
[2] Department of Mathematics, Hong Kong Baptist University,
Kowloon Toog, Hong Kong

Abstract. Semi-supervised clustering based on pairwise constraints has been very active in recent years. The pairwise constraints consist of must-link and cannot-link. Since different types of constraints provide different information, they should be utilized with different strategies in the learning process. In this paper, we investigate the effect of must-link and cannot-link constraints on non-negative matrix factorization (NMF) and show that they play different roles when guiding the factorization procedure. A new semi-supervised NMF model is then proposed with pairwise constraints penalties. Among them, must-link constraints are used to control the distance of the data in the compressed form, and cannot-link constraints are used to control the encoding factor. Meanwhile, the same penalty strategies are applied on symmetric NMF model to handle the similarity matrix. The proposed two models are implemented by an alternating nonnegative least squares algorithm. We examine the performance of our models on series of real similarity data, and compare them with state-of-the-art, illustrating that the new models provide superior clustering performance.

Keywords: Semi-supervised Clustering, Pairwise Constraints, NMF, Symmetric NMF.

1 Introduction

The classical machine learning is supervised learning for classification with large amounts of labeled training data. However, it is often hard to obtain the training data. In order to reduce the burden of collecting the labeled data, two solutions have been proposed in literature: active learning methods [1] and semi-supervised learning methods [2]. Active learning methods reduce the number of required labels by intelligently choosing which instances to label firstly. Semi-supervised learning methods make use of both labeled and unlabeled data to improve clustering performance which can efficiently provide a foundation for granular computing [3–5].

In semi-supervised learning, a small amount knowledge is available concerning either partial data labels or pairwise constraints between data. Such knowledge

F.M. Zanzotto et al. (Eds.): BI 2012, LNCS 7670, pp. 309–319, 2012.
© Springer-Verlag Berlin Heidelberg 2012

is used to guide or adjust the clustering process to obtain better clustering performance. Since labeled data can always be translated into pairwise constraints while the converse does not hold in general, and the pairwise constraints are often faster or cheaper to obtain than labels and can sometimes be automatically collected, the constrained clustering becomes popular in semi-supervised clustering and has been extensively studied in many fields such as text mining, network analysis, image processing, and etc. To date, the pairwise constraints have been added into many popular clustering algorithms such as k-means [6–8], complete-link hierarchical clustering [9], mixture modeling [10, 11], spectral clustering [12–14], affinity propagation [15], NMF [16–21], and etc.

In this paper, we consider the NMF-based method for semi-supervised learning with the aid of pairwise constraints. The NMF [22] attempts to recover hidden structures or bases from the original data and then compute the linear projection of the original data onto the new basis. The clustering capability of the linear projection method is strongly dependent on how well the new basis describes the cluster structure of the data in the original data space. Such simple and interpretable part-based representations make the NMF especially useful in text mining [23, 24, 19, 25], community discovery [26], heterogeneous data coclustering [20] and etc. The NMF under certain conditions is proven to be equal to the traditional clustering methods such as k-means and spectral clustering [27, 17].

Besides clustering, researches also studied and extended the standard NMF formulation to different semi-supervised models by considering the pairwise constraints (including must-link and cannot-link) in order to improve the final clustering performance. A pair of must-link indicates the the corresponding two data points must belong to the same class, while the cannot-link indicates that the two points should belong to different classes. These two kinds of constraints play different roles when dealing with data. For example, the must-link constraints are transitive, i.e., a group of must-link constraints can be merged using a transitive closure, while the cannot-link constraints are not transitive. Since different types of pairwise constraints provide different information, they should be treated with different strategies in the learning process. For instance, Klein et al. [9] modified the distance between must-link constrained data points using the all-pairs-shortest-paths, and set a large value for the data points with cannot-link constraints. Shental et al. [10] used must-link constraints to construct the transitive closure and incorporated cannot-link to a inference procedure with hidden MRF. However, most existing constrained NMF methods [16–21] do not distinguish the must-link and cannot-link when embedding them into the traditional NMF model.

In this paper, we present different strategies for must-link and cannot-link constraints respectively and propose new semi-supervised clustering methods based on symmetric NMF models with the aid of pairwise constraints. Indeed, our goal here is to improve the quality of clustering by guiding the matrix factorization process with these constraints. Using an alternating nonnegative least squares algorithm, we perform the constrained matrix factorization to infer the central data clusters while simultaneously grouping the data points.

The rest of the paper is organized as follows. In Section 2, some preliminaries and related works are addressed. In Section 3, the novel semi-supervised symmetric NMF (SSCsNMF) model is proposed and implemented. Experiments on similarity data and UCI data are conducted in Section 4 to show the effectiveness of SSCsNMF by comparing with the existing popular constrained clustering methods. Finally, the conclusions are drawn in Section 5.

2   Background and Preliminaries

The non-negative factorization (NMF) is a matrix factorization algorithm that finds the non-negative factorization of a given non-negative matrix [22]. In real applications, the original data is pre-transformed to a non-negative matrix X before the NMF is adopted. The NMF can be formulated as the following minimizing problem:

$$\min_{W \geq 0, H \geq 0} F_1(W, H) \equiv ||X - WH||_F^2 \qquad (1)$$

By (1), the NMF decomposes each data point $(X._j)$ into a nonnegative linear combination (with weight H_{pj}) of nonnegative basis elements $(W._p)$.

In real applications, many data matrices are symmetric. This is the case for the adjacency matrix of an undirected graph, the matrix of geometric distances between points, correlation matrices, etc. Intuitively, since the NMF is to find the WH^T approximation of a nonnegative matrix, its symmetric version should try to find approximations where $W = H$. However, the given symmetric data matrix X is indefinite sometimes, i.e., X has negative eigenvalues, in this case, HH^T will not approximate X well because HH^T can not obtain the subspace associated with negative eigenvalues. Ding et al. [27] proposed a symmetric NMF model (sNMF) which is formulated as follows:

$$\min_{G \geq 0, S \geq 0} F_2(G, S) \equiv ||X - GSG^T||_F^2 \qquad (2)$$

where X is a $n \times n$ symmetric matrix, G is $n \times k$ and S is $k \times k$. This symmetric model is derived based on the linear algebra where if the matrix is s.p.d, the matrix factorizations have Choresky factorization $A = LL^T$, otherwise, $A = LDL^T$ here D takes care of the negative eigenvalues.

Chen et al. [17] used the pairwise constraints to alter the similarities between data points and then implemented semi-supervised NMF (called SSNMF) with symmetric factorization model as follows:

$$\min_{G \geq 0, S \geq 0} F_3(G, S) \equiv ||\tilde{X} - GSG^T||_F^2, \qquad (3)$$

where $\tilde{X} = X - A_{reward} + A_{penalty} \in \mathbb{R}^{n \times n}$ is the similarity matrix of the data X with constraints $A_{reward} = \{a_{ij}|(x_i, x_j) \in C_{ML}$ subject to $y_i = y_j\}$ and $A_{penalty} = \{a_{ij}|(x_i, x_j) \in C_{CL}$ subject to $y_i = y_j\}$. The quantity a_{ij} is the penalty cost for violating a constraint between x_i and x_j, and y_i is the cluster label of x_i. Moreover, $S \in R^{k \times k}$ is the cluster centroid, and $G \in R^{n \times k}$ is the cluster indicator. Later, Chen et al. [19, 20] extended SS-NMF to deal with heterogeneous data.

According to the existing pairwise constrained NMF models, the same strategy was used to evaluate the penalties for both cannot-link and must-link. However, these two kinds of constraints play different roles in the NMF factorization, an illustration example about this point will be given in the next section. Thus we will propose novel constrained penalties for semi-supervised NMF models (including symmetric model), leading to improved learning performance.

3   Constrained Semi-supervised Symmetric NMF

Even though the NMF received much attention in the data analyzing community, esp., its clustering capabilities, it has some disadvantages that all the other unsupervised clustering methods have, e.g., it cannot deal with the boundary points well. Thus, we will present a new penalty strategy to do the following things.

- Superior to the traditional NMF model and existing pairwise constrained NMF model, it can not deal with boundary points well.
- In the new method, Must-link and Cannot-link constraints are treated in different ways because they play different roles in semi-supervised learning.

3.1   The Proposed Constraint Penalty

In order to deal with well the boundary points, it is necessary to do the following two procedures for data points in must-link constraint:

- increase the similarity of their corresponding cluster indicator,
- make them far away from the incorrect cluster center in the transformed form WH.

Thus, a new penalty strategy for must-link constraints is proposed in this section which considers the distance between the constrained data in the compressed form.

Recall that in the NMF, W is the bases factor and H is the encoding factor (or cluster indicator in NMF-based clustering). Moreover, their production WH can be regarded as the transformed form of the original data X, e.g., $(WH)_{.i}$ is the transformed form of data $X_{.i}$. In [28], we presented a new penalty strategy for must-link constraints to guarantee that the distance between the projected expression of two points constrained by must-link is as small as possible. Meanwhile, the penalty strategy in PNMF method is a useful method for the cannot-link constraints. In the next section, we will integrate these two strategies into the symmetric NMF model to do semi-supervised clustering.

3.2   Model Formulation

Based on the above analysis, we can see that different types of pairwise constraints should be treated in different ways. Thus, in this section, we propose a new constrained symmetric NMF model (Eq.(2)) with the effective strategy to combine the must-link and cannot-link constraints. We wish to endow the proposed model with the ability to make full use of the different types of pairwise constraints, and then improve the semi-supervised clustering performance. In Eq.(2), the similarity matrix X is factorized into two parts G and S. Among them, GSG^T is an approximation or transformed form of the data X, G is the cluster indicator matrix indicating the cluster membership of all data points. S provides a good characterization of the quality of the clustering because it represents properly normalized within-cluster sum of weights (the diagonal values) and between-cluster sum of weights (the off-diagonal values) [27].

As mentioned above, the must-link constraints are useful when the data transformed form is expected to preserve the property of the original data X. It is a good idea to add $\sum_{(i,j)\in C_{ML}}\|(GSG^T)._i - (GSG^T)._j\|_F^2$ in Eq.(2) for introducing the must-link constraints. Similarly, adding the term $tr(G^T\Theta G)$ is to combine the cannot-link constraints. Finally, the semi-supervised clustering via symmetric NMF can be formulated as:

$$\min_{G\geq0,S\geq0} F_4(G,S) \equiv \frac{1}{2}\left(\|X - GSG^T\|_F^2 + tr((GSG^T)L(GSG^T)^T) + tr(G^T\Theta G)\right),$$
(4)

where
$$\Theta_{ij} = \begin{cases} \tilde{\theta} & \text{if } (i,j) \text{ or } (j,i) \in C_{CL} \\ 0 & \text{otherwise,} \end{cases}$$

with $L = D - R$ and
$$R_{ij} = \begin{cases} \lambda & \text{if } (i,j) \text{ or } (j,i) \in C_{ML} \\ 0 & \text{otherwise,} \end{cases}$$

and D is a diagonal matrix with
$$D_{ii} = \sum_j R_{ij}.$$

It can be seen that L and Θ are symmetric $n \times n$ matrices. The coefficient $\frac{1}{2}$ is used here to express the solution of the model in a simple form. The model is denoted as SSCsNMF.

3.3   Implementation

Eq.(4) is in general nonconvex programming and hence there might exist many local minimizers. For nonconvex programming we often design algorithms seeking stationary point. A stationary point is a point that satisfies the first-order necessary condition for a minimizer. The first-order necessary condition is based on the gradient of the objective function. By direct computation, we know that the gradient of the function $F_7(G, S)$ consists of two parts:

$$\nabla_G F_7(G, S) = 2GS^T G^T GS - 2X^T GS + GS^T G^T L^T GS^T$$
$$+ LGSG^T GS + \Theta G,$$
$$\nabla_S F_7(G, S) = 2G^T GSG^T G - 2G^T XG + G^T GS^T G^T L^T G$$
$$+ G^T L^T GS^T G^T G. \tag{5}$$

From the Karush-Kuhn-Tucker (KKT) optimality condition, (G, S) is a stationary point of Eq.(4) if and only if:

$$\begin{cases} G \geq 0, \\ \nabla_G F_7(G, S) \geq 0, \\ \langle G, \nabla_G F_7(G, S) \rangle = 0; \end{cases} \qquad \begin{cases} S \geq 0, \\ \nabla_S F_7(G, S) \geq 0, \\ \langle S, \nabla_S F_7(G, S) \rangle = 0. \end{cases} \tag{6}$$

Here $\langle \cdot, \cdot \rangle$ means the sum of dot product of two given matrices with same dimension. By solving the model in Eq.(4), two nonnegative matrices G and S can be obtained and hence the k clusters can be identified. In particular, G_{pi} in G gives the degree of association of objects X_i with cluster p. The cluster membership of an object is given by finding the cluster with the maximum association value.

For the traditional NMF, 2-block ANLS method [29] is effective and widely employed, by fixing one block and improve the other with respect to the objective function value. The convergence of the algorithm is guaranteed. For the proposed semi-supervised NMF models, SSCsNMF, 2-block ANLS is also suitable to find the optimal results. The detail steps can be illustrated in Algorithm 1.

---

1 **Step 0:** *initialize $G^0 \geq 0$ and $S^0 \geq 0$ for SSCsNMF. (S should be symmetric.)*
2 **Step 1:** *For $k = 0, 1, 2, \cdots, k_{\max}$, do the iteration*
3

$$G^{k+1} = \arg\min_{G \geq 0}\{F_7(G, S^k) \tag{7}$$

$$S^{k+1} = \arg\min_{S \geq 0}\{F_7(G^{k+1}, S) \tag{8}$$

Algorithm 1. 2-block ANLS for SSCsNMF

The k-means method is usually used to initialize matrices G and S is initialized with a diagonal matrix with $S_{ii} = 1$, see for instance [30]. While each subproblem among (3)-(8), is a strictly convex quadratic programming and its objective function has zero as its lower bound. By using Frank-Wolfe theorem, there is a minimizer of each subproblem. Together with the strict convexity of the objective function, we can deduce that each subproblem has a unique minimizer.

For each subproblem, the matrix-based projected gradient (PG) method [31] is adopted to find its optimal point. The idea is that in each iteration, it determines an improved iterate point by either tracing along the opposite direction of the gradient if no bound is encountered, or along the "bent" search direction by projecting on the nonnegative orthant to guarantee both feasibility and sufficient decrease in the objective function value.

4   Experimental Results and Discussion

In this section, a series of experiments on real-world datasets are conducted to evaluate the clustering performance of the proposed method by comparing with the state-of-the-art semi-supervised clustering methods. Since the proposed SSCsNMF are based on the pairwise constrained and the traditional sNMF, we take the following methods as the baselines: sNMF [27], SS-NMF [17], SSAP [15], CCSR [13].

In order to investigate the effect of the number of pairwise constraints on the clustering performance, we sample 4 pairs of constraints to 200 pairwise constraints for every data set. For any desired number of pairwise constraints, half of them belong to the must-link constraints, half of them belong to the cannot-link constraints. And such split can ensure that the effect of must-link or cannot-link constraints will not be ignored due to bias sampling. When conducting experiments, for any desired number pairwise constraints, pairwise constraints are randomly sampled for 10 times. For each NMF factorization, we randomly initialized two factors 10 times. Thus, all NMF-based semi-supervised methods will be run for 100 times, and the average results over these 100 times are recorded. For unsupervised NMF, the average result over 10 initializations is recorded,

All experimental data sets are benchmark data, i.e., the category information of each document is known, thus the external cluster validation methods *FScore* [32] is adopted here to evaluate the clustering results.

$$FScore = \sum_{j=1}^{k} \frac{n_j}{n} \cdot \max_{1 \leq l \leq k} \left\{ \frac{2 \cdot n_{jl}/n_h \cdot n_{jl}/n_l}{n_{jl}/n_j + n_{jl}/n_l} \right\}$$

where n_j , n_l are the numbers of objects in class L_j and in cluster C_l respectively, n_{jl} is the number of objects occurring in both class L_j and cluster C_l, n is the total number of objects in the data set, and k is the number of classes. The larger the *FScore*, the better the clustering performance.

4.1   On Real Similarity Data

We compared the semi-supervised clustering methods on five real similarity datasets[1] as shown in Table 1.

The AuralSonar dataset is about the human ability to distinguish different types of sonar signals by ear. There are 100 signals, 50 target-of-interest and

---

[1] http://idl.ee.washington.edu/similaritylearning/

Table 1. Real Similarity Data Summary

Data	♯ Points	♯ Classes
AuralSonar	100	2
Yeast-pfam-7-12	200	2
Yeast-sw-5-7	200	2
Protein	213	4
Voting	435	2

50 clutter signals. The Yeast-pfam-7-12 and Yeast-SW-5-7 data sets contain 200 samples from 2 classes where each class has 100 samples. The similarity is pfam kernel and Smith-Waterman E-value respectively. These datasets are provided as a pairwise matrix and the similarity definitions include human judgement, Smith-Waterman distance and purchasing trends. The Protein data set has sequence-alignment similarities for 213 proteins from 4 classes with different number of samples 72, 72, 39 and 30 respectively. The Voting data set is a two class classification problem with 435 samples, where each sample is a categorical feature vector with 16 components and 3 possibilities for each component, see [33] for more detail. The datasets all have class labels which were used as the ground truth to compute the clustering accuracy shown in Fig.1.

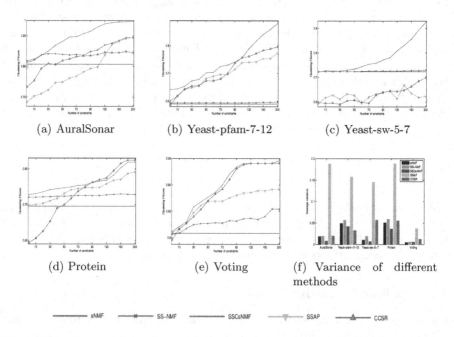

    (a) AuralSonar   (b) Yeast-pfam-7-12   (c) Yeast-sw-5-7

    (d) Protein   (e) Voting   (f) Variance of different methods

sNMF   SS–NMF   SSCsNMF   SSAP   CCSR

Fig. 1. Comparison of clustering results under varying number of pairwise constraints on real similarity data. a)-e) for clustering FScore on a) AuralSonar, b) Yeast-pfam-7-12, c) Yeast-sw-5-7, d) Protein and e) Voting respectively. f) for clustering variance of each method on each dataset under varying constraints.

As shown in Fig.1, the final clustering performances of all semi-supervised methods become better as the number of constraints increases. The proposed SSCsNMF always outperforms other methods on AuralSonar, Yeast-pfam-7-12, Yeast-SW-5-7 and Voting data sets. On Protein, SSCsNMF is the best one given limited constraints, meanwhile, SSCsNMF is competitive with CCSR when the supervision information (pairwise constraints) is enough. In real application, it is more expensive if more supervision information is given, thus, SSCsNMF is more practical than CCSR.

Fig.1(f) presents the average variance of each method on each data set. Again, the proposed SSCsNMF is the stablest method with the changing of constraints and initializations. And SSAP is the worse one and the other three methods (NMF, SS-NMF and CCSR) are nearly the same.

5 Conclusions

In this paper, a new semi-supervised symmetric NMF models via pairwise constraints are proposed. Based on the principle of cannot-link and must-link constraints, different penalty strategies are designed to semi-supervise matrix factorization procedure. Among them, must-link constraints are used to control the distance of the data in the compressed form, and cannot-link constraints are used to control the encoding factor. The proposed semi-supervised symmetric NMF model was tested on real similarity data. The experimental results have shown that the proposed method outperform the existing semi-supervised methods based on pairwise constraints such as sNMFm, SS-NMF, CCSR and SSAP.

Acknowledgement. This work was supported by the Fundamental Research Funds for the Central Universities (2011JBM030), the National Natural Science Foundation of China (60905028, 90820013), and the Project-sponsored by SRF for ROCS, SEM.

References

1. Zhu, X., Lafferty, J., Ghahramani, Z.: Combining active learning and semi-supervised learning using gaussian fields and harmonic functions. In: Proc. of ICML (2003)
2. Chapelle, O., Scholkopf, B., Zien, A.: Semi-Supervised Learning. MIT Press (2006)
3. Pedrycz, W.: Knowledge-Based Clustering: From Data to Information Granules. John Wiley & Sons, Inc. (2005)
4. Yao, J.: A ten-year review of granular computing. In: Proc. of IEEE ICGC (2007)
5. Jing, L., Yu, J.: Text clustering based on granular computing and wikipedia. In: Proc. of WI-IAT (2010)
6. Wagstaff, K., Cardie, C., Rogers, S., Schroedl, S.: Constrained k-means clustering with background knowledge. In: Proc. of ICML, pp. 798–803 (2001)
7. Basu, S., Bilenko, M., Mooney, R.: A probabilistic framework for semi-supervised clustering. In: Proc. of ACM SIGKDD, pp. 59–68 (2004)

8. Hong, Y., Kwong, S.: Learning assignment order of instances for the constrained k-means clustering algorithm. IEEE Trans. Syst. Man Cybern. Part B 39, 568–574 (2009)
9. Klein, D., Kamvar, S., Manning, C.: From instance-level constraints to space-level constraints: making the most of prior knowledge in data clustering. In: Proc. of ICML (2002)
10. Shental, N., Bar-Hillel, A., Hertz, T., Weinshall, D.: Computing gaussian mixture models with em using equivalence constraints. In: Proc. of NIPS (2003)
11. Lu, Z., Leen, T.: Semi-supervised learning with penalized probabilistic clustering. In: Proc. of NIPS, vol. 17, pp. 849–856 (2005)
12. Coleman, T., Saunderson, J., Wirth, A.: Spectral clustering with inconsistent advice. In: Proc. of ICML, pp. 152–159 (2008)
13. Li, Z., Liu, J., Tang, X.: Constrained clustering via spectral regularization. In: Proc. of CVPR (2009)
14. Wang, X., Davidson, I.: Flexible constrained spectral clustering. In: Proc. of ACM SIGKDD, pp. 563–571 (2010)
15. Givoni, I., Frey, B.: Semi-supervised affinity propagation with instance-level constraints. In: Proc. of AISTATS (2009)
16. Li, T., Ding, C., Jordan, M.: Solving consensus and semi-supervised clustering problems using nonnegative matrix factorization. In: Proceedings of ICDM, pp. 577–582 (2007)
17. Chen, Y., Rege, M., Dong, M., Hua, J.: Non-negative matrix factorization for semi-supervised data clustering. Knowledge and Information Systems 17, 355–379 (2008)
18. Wang, F., Li, T., Zhang, C.: Semi-supervised clustering via matrix factorization. In: Proceedings of SIAM DM (2008)
19. Chen, Y., Wang, L., Dong, M.: Semi-supervised Document Clustering with Simultaneous Text Representation and Categorization. In: Buntine, W., Grobelnik, M., Mladenić, D., Shawe-Taylor, J. (eds.) ECML PKDD 2009, Part I. LNCS, vol. 5781, pp. 211–226. Springer, Heidelberg (2009)
20. Chen, Y., Wang, L., Dong, M.: Non-negative matrix factorization for semisupervised heterogeneous data coclustering. IEEE Trans. on Knowledge and Data Engineering 22, 1459–1474 (2010)
21. Liu, H., Wu, Z.: Non-negative matrix factorization with constraints. In: Proceedings of AAAI, pp. 506–511 (2010)
22. Lee, D., Seung, H.: Learning the parts of objects by nonnegative matrix factorization. Nature 401, 788–791 (1999)
23. Xu, W., Liu, X., Gong, Y.: Document clustering based on non-negative matrix factorization. In: Proc. of ACM SIGIR, pp. 267–273 (2003)
24. Shahnaz, F., Berry, M., Pauca, V., Plemmons, R.: Document clustering using non-negative matrix factorization. Information Processing and Management 42, 373–386 (2006)
25. Berry, M., Gillis, N., Gilineur, F.: Document classification using nonnegative matrix factorization and underapproximation. In: Proc. of IEEE Intl. Symp. on Circuits and Systems, pp. 2782–2785 (2009)
26. Wang, F., Li, T., Wang, X., Zhu, S., Ding, C.: Community discovery using nonnegative matrix factorization. Data Mining Knowledge Discovery 22, 493–521 (2011)
27. Ding, C., He, X., Simon, H.: On the equivalence of nonnegative matrix factorization and spectral clustering. In: Proceedings of SIAM DM (2005)
28. Zhu, Y., Jing, L., Yu, J.: Text clustering with constrained non-negative matrix factorization. In: Proc. of ICDM, pp. 1278–1283 (2011)

29. Paatero, P.: The multilinear engine: A table-driven, least squares program for solving multilinear problems, including the n-way parallel factor analysis model. Journal of Computational and Graphical Statistics 8, 854–888 (1999)
30. Ding, C., Li, T., Peng, W., Park, H.: Orthogonal nonnegative matrix trifactorizations for clustering. In: Proceedings of ACM SIGKDD (2006)
31. Lin, C.: Projected gradient methods for nonnegative matrix factorization. Neural Computation 19, 2756–2779 (2007)
32. Zhao, Y., Karypis, G.: Comparison of agglomerative and partitional document clustering algorithms. University of Minnesota. Tech. Rep. 02-014 (2002)
33. Chen, Y., Garcia, E., Gupta, M., Rahimi, A., Cazzanti, L.: Similarity-based classification: concepts and algorithms. J. of Machine Learning Research 10, 747–776 (2009)

Granular Association Rule Mining through Parametric Rough Sets

Fan Min and William Zhu

Lab of Granular Computing,
Zhangzhou Normal University, Zhangzhou 363000, China
minfanphd@163.com, williamfengzhu@gmail.com

Abstract. Granular association rules reveal patterns hide in many-to-many relationships which are common in databases. An example of such rules might be "40% men like at least 30% kinds of alcohol; 45% customers are men and 6% products are alcohol." Mining all rules satisfying four thresholds is a challenging problem due to pattern explosion. In this paper, we propose a new type of parametric rough sets on two universes to study this problem. The model is deliberately defined such that the parameter corresponds to one threshold of rules. With the lower approximation operator in the new parametric rough sets, a backward algorithm is designed to deal with the rule mining problem. Experiments on a real world dataset show that the new algorithm is significantly faster than the existing sandwich algorithm. This study builds connections among granular computing, association rule mining and rough sets.

Keywords: Granular association rule, parametric rough sets, recommendation, lower approximation, measure.

1 Introduction

The many-to-many relationship is fundamental in relational databases. Suppose there are two entities `customer` and `product` connected by a relation `buys`. We are often interested in the following problem: what kind of customers likes what kind of products? With the answer, we can recommend products to customers, especially to new customers of E-commerce systems. In fact, collaborative recommendation [1] and collaborative filtering [2] are devoted to this issue. However, they often require purchasing history of the current customer. In case of new customers or new products, there is a cold start problem [3].

Recently, the concept of granular association rule [4,5] was proposed to reveal patterns hide in many-to-many relationships. With this type of rules, we undertake product recommendation without the purchasing history of the current customer or the current product. Examples of granular association rules include "men like alcohol," "young men like France alcohol," and "Chinese men like blue stuff." Both people and products can be described by different granules [6,7,8,9,10], hence these rules are called granular association rules.

There are four measures to evaluate the quality of a granular association rule. A complete example of granular association rules might be "40% men like at least

F.M. Zanzotto et al. (Eds.): BI 2012, LNCS 7670, pp. 320–331, 2012.

30% kinds of alcohol; 45% customers are men and 6% products are alcohol." Here 45%, 6%, 40%, and 30% are the *source coverage*, the *target coverage*, the *source confidence*, and the *target confidence*, respectively. With these four measures, the strongness of the rule is well defined. Therefore granular association rules are semantically richer than most relational association rules (see, e.g., [11,12,13,14]).

In this paper, we propose a new type of parametric rough sets to study the granular association rule mining problem. The problem is defined as finding all granular association rules given thresholds on four measures [5]. It is challenging due to pattern explosion, and the performance of a sandwich algorithm [5] is not satisfactory. We deliberately define the model such that the parameter, being 30% for the example, is semantic and specified by the user directly. The monotonicity of the lower approximation for the model is studied.

With the lower approximation of the proposed parametric rough sets, we design a backward algorithm. This algorithm starts from the second universe and proceeds to the first one, hence it is called a *backward* algorithm. Compared with the existing sandwich algorithm [5], the new algorithm avoids some redundant computation. Experiments are undertaken on the course selection data from Zhangzhou Normal University. Results show that the new algorithm is more than 3 times faster than the existing one.

Section 2 reviews granular association rules through some examples. Section 3 presents a new model of parametric rough sets on two universes for granular association rules. Then Section 4 presents a backward algorithm for the problem. Experiments on the course selection data are discussed in Section 5. Finally, Section 6 presents some concluding remarks and further research directions.

2   Granular Association Rules

In this section, we revisit granular association rules [4]. We will discuss the data model, the definition, and four measures of such rules. A rule mining problem will also be presented.

2.1   The Data Model

The data model is based on information systems and binary relations.

Definition 1. $S = (U, A)$ *is an information system, where* $U = \{x_1, x_2, \ldots, x_n\}$ *is the set of all objects,* $A = \{a_1, a_2, \ldots, a_m\}$ *is the set of all attributes, and* $a_j(x_i)$ *is the value of* x_i *on attribute* a_j *for* $i \in [1..n]$ *and* $j \in [1..m]$.

An example of information system is given by Table 1, where $U = \{$c1, c2, c3, c4, c5$\}$, and $A = \{$Age, Gender, Married, Country, Income, NumCars$\}$. Another example is given by Table 2.

In an information system, any $A' \subseteq A$ induces an equivalence relation [15,16]

$$E_{A'} = \{(x, y) \in U \times U | \forall a \in A', a(x) = a(y)\}, \qquad (1)$$

Table 1. Customer

CID	Name	Age	Gender	Married	Country	Income	NumCars
c1	Ron	20..29	Male	No	USA	60k..69k	0..1
c2	Michelle	20..29	Female	Yes	USA	80k..89k	0..1
c3	Shun	20..29	Male	No	China	40k..49k	0..1
c4	Yamago	30..39	Female	Yes	Japan	80k..89k	2
c5	Wang	30..39	Male	Yes	China	90k..99k	2

Table 2. Product

PID	Name	Country	Category	Color	Price
p1	Bread	Australia	Staple	Black	1..9
p2	Diaper	China	Daily	White	1..9
p3	Pork	China	Meat	Red	1..9
p4	Beef	Australia	Meat	Red	10..19
p5	Beer	France	Alcohol	Black	10..19
p6	Wine	France	Alcohol	White	10..19

and partitions U into a number of disjoint subsets called *blocks*. The block containing $x \in U$ is

$$E_{A'}(x) = \{y \in U | \forall a \in A', a(y) = a(x)\}. \tag{2}$$

According to Yao and Deng [17], many views of concepts have been proposed and studied. Here we employ a viewpoint which is very close to the classical one. A pair $C = (A', x)$ where $x \in U$ and $A' \subseteq A$ is called a *concept* in $S = (U, A)$. The *extension* of the concept is

$$ET(C) = ET(A', x) = E_{A'}(x); \tag{3}$$

while the *intension* of the concept is the conjunction of respective attribute-value pairs, i.e.,

$$IT(C) = IT(A', x) = \bigwedge_{a \in A'} \langle a : a(x) \rangle. \tag{4}$$

The *support* of the concept is the size of its extension divided by the size of the universe, namely,

$$
\begin{aligned}
support(C) = support(A', x) &= support(\textstyle\bigwedge_{a \in A'} \langle a : a(x) \rangle) \\
&= support(E_{A'}(x)) = \frac{|ET(A', x)|}{|U|} \\
&= \frac{|E_{A'}(x)|}{|U|}.
\end{aligned} \tag{5}
$$

Definition 2. *Let $U = \{x_1, x_2, \ldots, x_n\}$ and $V = \{y_1, y_2, \ldots, y_k\}$ be two sets of objects. Any $R \subseteq U \times V$ is a binary relation from U to V. The neighborhood of $x \in U$ is*

$$R(x) = \{y \in V | (x, y) \in R\}. \tag{6}$$

Table 3. Buys

CID\ PID	p1	p2	p3	p4	p5	p6
c1	1	1	0	1	1	0
c2	1	0	0	1	0	1
c3	0	1	1	0	1	1
c4	0	1	0	1	1	0
c5	1	0	1	1	1	1

When $U = V$ and R is an equivalence relation, $R(x)$ is the equivalence class containing x. From Definition 2 we know immediately that for $y \in V$,

$$R^{-1}(y) = \{x \in U | (x, y) \in R\}. \tag{7}$$

A binary relation is more often stored in the database as a table with two foreign keys. In this way the storage is saved. For the convenience of illustration, here we represented it with an $n \times k$ boolean matrix. An example is given by Table 3, where U is the set of customers as indicated by Table 1, and V is the set of products as indicated by Table 2.

With Definitions 1 and 2, we propose the following definition.

Definition 3. *A many-to-many entity-relationship system (MMER) is a 5-tuple $ES = (U, A, V, B, R)$, where (U, A) and (V, B) are two information systems, and $R \subseteq U \times V$ is a binary relation from U to V.*

An example of MMER is given by Tables 1, 2 and 3.

2.2 Granular Association Rules with Four Measures

Now we come to the central definition of granular association rules.

Definition 4. *A granular association rule is an implication of the form*

$$(GR) : \bigwedge_{a \in A'} \langle a : a(x) \rangle \Rightarrow \bigwedge_{b \in B'} \langle b : b(y) \rangle, \tag{8}$$

where $A' \subseteq A$ and $B' \subseteq B$.

According to Equation (5), the set of objects meeting the left-hand side of the granular association rule is

$$LH(GR) = E_{A'}(x); \tag{9}$$

while the set of objects meeting the right-hand side of the granular association rule is

$$RH(GR) = E_{B'}(y). \tag{10}$$

From the MMER given by Tables 1, 2 and 3 we may obtain a number of rules, e.g.,

(Rule 1) $\langle$Gender: Male$\rangle \Rightarrow \langle$Category: Alcohol$\rangle$.

It can be read as "men like alcohol." There are some issues concerning the strongness of a rule. For example, we may ask the following questions:

1. How many customers are men?
2. How many products are alcohol?
3. Do all men like alcohol?
4. Do all kinds of alcohol favor men?

A detailed explanation of Rule 1 with might be "40% men like at least 30% kinds of alcohol; 45% customers are men and 6% products are alcohol." Here 45%, 6%, 40%, and 30% are the *source coverage*, the *target coverage*, the *source confidence*, and the *target confidence*, respectively. These four measures answer these four questions. These measures are defined as follows.

The *source coverage* of a granular association rule is

$$scoverage(GR) = |LH(GR)|/|U|. \tag{11}$$

The *target coverage* of GR is

$$tcoverage(GR) = |RH(GR)|/|V|. \tag{12}$$

There is a tradeoff between the source confidence and the target confidence of a rule. Consequently, neither value can be obtained directly from the rule. To compute any one of them, we should specify the threshold of the other. Let tc be the target confidence threshold. The *source confidence* of the rule is

$$sconfidence(GR, tc) = \frac{|\{x \in LH(GR) | \frac{|R(x) \cap RH(GR)|}{|RH(GR)|} \geq tc\}|}{|LH(GR)|}. \tag{13}$$

Let mc be the source confidence threshold, and

$$\begin{aligned}
&|\{x \in LH(GR) || R(x) \cap RH(GR)| \geq K+1\}| \\
&< mc \times |LH(GR)| \\
&\leq |\{x \in LH(GR) || R(x) \cap RH(GR)| \geq K\}|.
\end{aligned} \tag{14}$$

The *target confidence* of the rule is

$$tconfidence(GR, mc) = K/|RH(GR)|. \tag{15}$$

In fact, the computation of K is non-trivial. First, for any $x \in LH(GR)$, we need to compute $tc(x) = |R(x) \cap RH(GR)|$ and obtain an array of integers. Second, we sort the array in a descending order. Third, let $k = \lfloor mc \times |LH(GR)| \rfloor$, K is the k-th element in the array.

2.3   The Granular Association Rule Mining Problem

A straightforward rule mining problem is as follow.

Problem 1. The granular association rule mining problem.

Input: An $ES = (U, A, V, B, R)$, a minimal source coverage threshold ms, a minimal target coverage threshold mt, a minimal source confidence threshold mc, and a minimal target confidence threshold tc.

Output: All granular association rules satisfying $scoverage(GR) \geq ms$, $tcoverage(GR) \geq mt$, $sconfidence(GR) \geq mc$, and $tconfidence(GR) \geq tc$.

Since both mc and tc are specified, we can choose either Equation (13) or Equation (15) to decide whether or not a rule satisfies these thresholds. Equation (13) is a better choice.

3   Parametric Rough Sets on Two Universes

In this section, we first review rough approximations [15] on one universe. Then we present rough approximations on two universes. Finally we present parametric rough approximations on two universes.

Lower and upper approximations are fundamental concepts in rough sets.

Definition 5. *Let U be a universe and $R \subseteq U \times U$ be an indiscernibility relation. The lower and upper approximations of $X \subseteq U$ with respect to R are*

$$\underline{R}(X) = \{x \in X | R(x) \subseteq X\} \tag{16}$$

and

$$\overline{R}(X) = \{x \in X | R(x) \cap X \neq \emptyset\}, \tag{17}$$

respectively.

People extended the indiscernibility relation to other kinds of relations (see, e.g., [6,9,18,19]). We can simply remove "indiscernibility" from Definition 5 for arbitrary binary relations [20]. To cope with granular association rules, we propose the following definition which is different from [20].

Definition 6. *Let U and V be two universes, $R \subseteq U \times V$ be a binary relation. The lower and upper approximations of $X \subseteq U$ with respect to R are*

$$\underline{R}(X) = \{y \in V | R^{-1}(y) \supseteq X\} \tag{18}$$

and

$$\overline{R}(X) = \{y \in V | R^{-1}(y) \cap X \neq \emptyset\}, \tag{19}$$

respectively.

From Definition 6 we know immediately that for $Y \subseteq V$,

$$\underline{R^{-1}}(Y) = \{x \in U | R(x) \supseteq Y\}, \tag{20}$$

$$\overline{R^{-1}}(Y) = \{x \in U | R(x) \cap Y \neq \emptyset\}. \tag{21}$$

Now we explain these notions through our example. $\underline{R}(X)$ contains products that favor all people in X, $\underline{R}^{-1}(Y)$ contains people who like all products in Y, $\overline{R}(X)$ contains products that favor at least one person in X, and $\overline{R}^{-1}(Y)$ contains people who like at least one product in Y.

We have the following property concerning the monotonicity of these approximations.

Property 1. Let $X_1 \subset X_2$.

$$\underline{R}(X_1) \supseteq \underline{R}(X_2). \tag{22}$$

$$\overline{R}(X_1) \subseteq \overline{R}(X_2). \tag{23}$$

That is, with the increase of the object subset, the lower approximation decreases while the upper approximation increases. One may argue that Equation (18) should be rewritten as

$$\underline{R}(X) = \{y \in V | R^{-1}(y) \subseteq X\}. \tag{24}$$

In this way, $\underline{R}(X_1) \subseteq \underline{R}(X_2)$. Moreover, it would coincide with Equation (17) when $U = V$. However, with Equation (24) we are looking for products that favor people only in X. This type of restriction is not interesting in our context.

Given a group of people, the number of products that favor all of them is often quite small. On the other hand, the number of products that favor at least one of them is not quite meaningful. Therefore Definition 5 is inappropriate for granular association rules. According to the source confidence measure introduced in the Section 2.2, we propose the following definition.

Definition 7. *Let U and V be two universes, $R \subseteq U \times V$ be a binary relation, and $0 < \beta \leq 1$ be a user-specified threshold. The lower approximation of $X \subseteq U$ with respect to R for threshold β is*

$$\underline{R}_\beta(X) = \{y \in V | \frac{|R^{-1}(y) \cap X|}{|X|} \geq \beta\}. \tag{25}$$

From Definition 7 we know immediately that the lower approximation of $Y \subseteq V$ with respect to R is

$$\underline{R^{-1}}_\beta(Y) = \{x \in U | \frac{|R(x) \cap Y|}{|Y|} \geq \beta\}. \tag{26}$$

Here β corresponds with the target confidence instead. In our example, $\underline{R}_\beta(X)$ are products that favor at least $\beta \times 100\%$ people in X, and $\underline{R}^{-1}(Y)$ are people who like at least $\beta \times 100\%$ products in Y. It is unnecessary to discuss the upper approximation in the new context.

The following property shows the monotonicity of $\underline{R}_\beta(X)$.

Property 2. Let $0 < \beta_1 < \beta_2 \leq 1$.

$$\underline{R}_{\beta_2}(X) \subseteq \underline{R}_{\beta_1}(X). \tag{27}$$

Algorithm 1. The backward algorithm

Input: $ES = (U, A, V, B, R)$, ms, mt, mc, tc.
Output: All granular association rules satisfying given thresholds.
Method: backward

1: $SC(ms) = \{(A', x) \in 2^A \times U | \frac{|E_{A'}(x)|}{|U|} \geq ms\}$; //Candidate source concepts
2: $TC(mt) = \{(B', y) \in 2^B \times V | \frac{|E_{B'}(y)|}{|V|} \geq mt\}$; //Candidate target concepts
3: **for each** $C' \in TC(mt)$ **do**
4:     $Y = ET(C')$;
5:     $X = \underline{R^{-1}}_{tc}(Y)$;
6:     **for each** $C \in SC(ms)$ **do**
7:         **if** $(|ET(C) \cap X|/|ET(C)| \geq mc)$ **then**
8:             output rule $IT(C) \Rightarrow IT(C')$;
9:         **end if**
10:     **end for**
11: **end for**

However, given $X_1 \subset X_2$, we obtain neither $\underline{R}_\beta(X_1) \subseteq \underline{R}_\beta(X_2)$ nor $\underline{R}_\beta(X_1) \supseteq \underline{R}_\beta(X_2)$. The relationships between $\underline{R}_\beta(X_1)$ and $\underline{R}_\beta(X_2)$ depend on β. Generally, if β is big, $\underline{R}_\beta(X_1)$ tends to be bigger, otherwise $\underline{R}_\beta(X_1)$ tends to be smaller. Equation (22) indicates the extreme case for $\beta \approx 0$, and Equation (23) indicates the other extreme case for $\beta = 1$.

β is the coverage of $R(x)$ (or $R^{-1}(y)$) to Y (or X). It does not mean *precision* of an approximation. This is why we call this model *parametric rough sets* instead of *variable precision rough sets*.

4   A Backward Algorithm to Granular Association Rule Mining

In our previous work [5], we have proposed an algorithm according to Equation (13). The algorithm starts from both sides and checks the validity of all possible rules. Therefore it was named a *sandwich* algorithm.

To make use of the concept proposed in the Section 3, we should rewrite Equation (13) as follows.

$$
\begin{aligned}
sconfidence(GR, tc) &= \frac{|\{x \in LH(GR)| \frac{|R(x) \cap RH(GR)|}{|RH(GR)|} \geq tc\}|}{|LH(GR)|} \\
&= \frac{|\{x \in U| \frac{|R(x) \cap RH(GR)|}{|RH(GR)|} \geq tc\} \cap LH(GR)|}{|LH(GR)|} \\
&= \frac{|\underline{R^{-1}}_{tc}(RH(GR)) \cap LH(GR)|}{|LH(GR)|}.
\end{aligned}
\tag{28}
$$

With this equation, we propose an algorithm to deal with Problem 1. The algorithm is listed in Algorithm 1. It essentially has four steps.

Step 1. Build all concepts meeting the minimal source coverage threshold ms from (U, A). These concepts are candidates for $LH(GR)$. This step corresponds to Line 1 of the algorithm, where SC stands for source concept.

Step 2. Build all concepts meeting the minimal target coverage threshold mt from (V, B). These concepts are candidates for $RH(GR)$. This step corresponds to Line 2 of the algorithm, where TC stands for target concept.

Step 3. Pick up a concept from $TC(ms)$ and compute its lower approximation with parameter tc. This step corresponds to Lines 3 through 5 of the algorithm.

Step 4. Pick up a concept from $SC(mt)$ and build a candidate rule. At the same time, check the validity the rule with threshold mc. This step corresponds to Lines 6 through 10 of the algorithm.

Because the algorithm starts from the right-hand side of the rule and proceeds to the left-hand side, it is called a backward algorithm. It avoids computing $R(x) \cap RH(GR)$ for different rules with the same right hand side. Hence it should be less time consuming than the sandwich algorithm [5]. We will analyze this issue through experiments in the next section.

5   Experiments on a Real World Dataset

In this section, we try to answer the following question: does the backward algorithm outperform the sandwich algorithm? If the answer is yes, then the new type of parametric rough sets is useful in dealing with the granular association rule mining problem.

5.1   Dataset

We obtained a real-world dataset from Zhangzhou Normal University. The database schema is as follows.

- Student (<u>studentID</u>, name, gender, birth-year, politics-status, grade, department, nationality, length-of-schooling)
- Course (<u>courseID</u>, credit, class-hours, availability, department)
- Selects (<u>studentID, courseID</u>)

We collected data during the semester between 2011 and 2012. There are 145 general education courses in the university, and 9,654 students took part in course selection.

5.2   Results

When $ms = mt = 0.06$, $mc = 0.18$, $tc = 0.11$, we only obtain 40 rules. For higher thresholds, we obtain no rule at all. Therefore we use the following settings. $mc = 0.18$, $tc = 0.11$, $ms = mt$, and $ms \in \{0.02, 0.03, 0.04, 0.05, 0.06\}$. We only study the run time of Lines 3 through 11, since these codes are the difference between the backward and the sandwich algorithms.

Figure 1 shows the actual run time in mini-seconds. Figure 2 shows the number of basic operations, including addition, comparison, etc. of numbers. Here we observe that the backward algorithm is more than 3 times faster than the

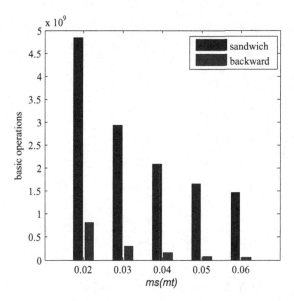

Fig. 1. The run time of two algorithms

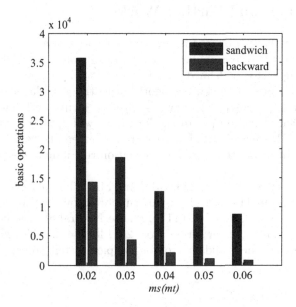

Fig. 2. Basic operations of two algorithms

sandwich algorithm. The reason is that it avoids computing the lower approximation for the same object in U more than once. Finally, Figure 3 shows the change of the number rules with respect to ms and mt. Naturally, more rules are obtained with smaller thresholds.

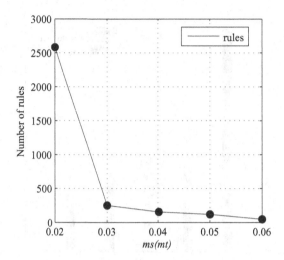

Fig. 3. Number of granular association rules

6   Conclusions and Further Works

In this paper, we have proposed a new type of parametric rough sets on two universes to deal with the granular association rule mining problem. The lower approximation operator is defined, and its monotonicity is analyzed. With the help of the new model, a backward algorithm to the granular association rule mining problem is proposed. The new algorithm is significantly faster than the existing sandwich algorithm [5]. In the future we will apply the new model to other problems [21] where approximations are fundamental. We will also develop even faster algorithm for the granular association rule mining problem.

Acknowledgements. We would like to thank Mrs. Chunmei Zhou for her help in the data collection. This work is in part supported by National Science Foundation of China under Grant No. 61170128, the Natural Science Foundation of Fujian Province, China under Grant Nos. 2011J01374, 2012J01294, State key laboratory of management and control for complex systems open project under Grant No. 20110106.

References

1. Balabanović, M., Shoham, Y.: Fab: content-based, collaborative recommendation. Communication of ACM 40(3), 66–72 (1997)
2. Goldberg, D., Nichols, D., Oki, B.M., Terry, D.: Using collaborative filtering to weave an information tapestry. Communications of the ACM 35, 61–70 (1992)
3. Schein, A.I., Popescul, A., Ungar, L.H., Pennock, D.M.: Methods and metrics for cold-start recommendations. In: SIGIR 2002, pp. 253–260 (2002)

4. Min, F., Hu, Q.H., Zhu, W.: Granular association rules with four subtypes. In: Proceedings of the 2011 IEEE International Conference on Granular Computing, pp. 432–437 (2012)
5. Min, F., Hu, Q., Zhu, W.: Granular association rules on two universes with four measures. submitted to Information Sciences (2012)
6. Lin, T.Y.: Granular computing on binary relations i: Data mining and neighborhood systems. In: Rough Sets in Knowledge Discovery, pp. 107–121 (1998)
7. Yao, J.T.: Recent developments in granular computing: A bibliometrics study. In: IEEE International Conference on Granular Computing, pp. 74–79 (2008)
8. Yao, Y.Y.: Granular computing: basic issues and possible solutions. In: Proceedings of the 5th Joint Conference on Information Sciences, vol. 1, pp. 186–189 (2000)
9. Zhu, W., Wang, F.: Reduction and axiomization of covering generalized rough sets. Information Sciences 152(1), 217–230 (2003)
10. Zhu, W.: Generalized rough sets based on relations. Information Sciences 177(22), 4997–5011 (2007)
11. Dehaspe, L., Toivonen, H., King, R.D.: Finding frequent substructures in chemical compounds. In: 4th International Conference on Knowledge Discovery and Data Mining, pp. 30–36 (1998)
12. Jensen, V.C., Soparkar, N.: Frequent Itemset Counting Across Multiple Tables. In: Terano, T., Chen, A.L.P. (eds.) PAKDD 2000. LNCS, vol. 1805, pp. 49–61. Springer, Heidelberg (2000)
13. Goethals, B., Page, W.L., Mampaey, M.: Mining interesting sets and rules in relational databases. In: Proceedings of the 2010 ACM Symposium on Applied Computing, pp. 997–1001 (2010)
14. Goethals, B., Page, W.L., Mannila, H.: Mining association rules of simple conjunctive queries. In: Proceedings of the SIAM International Conference on Data Mining (SDM), pp. 96–107 (2008)
15. Pawlak, Z.: Rough sets. International Journal of Computer and Information Sciences 11, 341–356 (1982)
16. Skowron, A., Stepaniuk, J.: Approximation of relations. In: Ziarko, W. (ed.) Proceedings of Rough Sets, Fuzzy Sets and Knowledge Discovery, pp. 161–166 (1994)
17. Yao, Y., Deng, X.: A Granular Computing Paradigm for Concept Learning. In: Ramanna, S., Howlett, R.J. (eds.) Emerging Paradigms in ML and Applications. SIST, vol. 13, pp. 307–326. Springer, Heidelberg (2013)
18. Qin, K., Yang, J., Pei, Z.: Generalized rough sets based on reflexive and transitive relations. Information Sciences 178(21), 4138–4141 (2008)
19. Skowron, A., Stepaniuk, J.: Tolerance approximation spaces. Fundamenta Informaticae 27, 245–253 (1996)
20. Wong, S., Wang, L., Yao, Y.Y.: Interval structure: a framework for representing uncertain information. In: Uncertainty in Artificial Intelligence, pp. 336–343 (1993)
21. Min, F., He, H.P., Qian, Y.H., Zhu, W.: Test-cost-sensitive attribute reduction. Information Sciences 181, 4928–4942 (2011)

Comparison of Granular Computing Models in a Set-Theoretic Framework

Ying Wang and Duoqian Miao

Department of Computer Science and Technology,
Tongji University, Shanghai 201804, P.R. China
wangy@tongji.edu.cn, miaoduoqian@163.com

Abstract. Many granular computing models have been proposed. A set-theoretic framework for constructing granules is easy to understand. A granule is a subset of a universal set, and a granular structure is a family of subsets of the universal set. By comparing set-based granular structures, the relationships and differences among rough set modal, hierarchical multi-dimensional data model and multi-granulation rough set model are discussed in this paper.

Keywords: Rough sets, Granular computing, Granule construction, Multi-granulation, Problem solving.

1 Introduction

Granular computing (GrC) is originated to mimic human's ability to perceive the world and to solve the problem under multiple levels of granularity for reasons for example, imprecise data, simplicity, cost, and so on [1-7]. It is a general computation theory that effectively uses granules, such as classes, clusters, subsets, groups, and intervals, to build an efficient computational model for complex applications with huge amounts of data, information and knowledge. The most apparent characteristics of GrC are representation and reasoning using granules at different levels of abstraction, and switching between them in problem solving [8,9].

The two principle issues of GrC are construction of granules to represent a problem and inference with granules in problem solving [10,11,3]. The granulation of a problem concerns granules construction and a hierarchical granular structure formation by a family of granules. Inference with granules relates to choosing an appropriate level or levels of granularity and reasoning in a granular space.

Rough sets (RS) provide one of the useful computing models of GrC. A partition model in GrC can be easily derived from it [17]. In constructing set-based granular structures, we assume that a granule is a subset of a universal set, and a granular structure is constructed based on the standard set-inclusion relation on a family of subsets of the universal set [12,13]. Many GrC models have been proposed. In this paper, we compare three set-based models, namely, rough sets

F.M. Zanzotto et al. (Eds.): BI 2012, LNCS 7670, pp. 332–337, 2012.

model proposed by Pawlak [19], hierarchical multi-dimensional data model proposed by Feng and Miao [14,15], and multi-granulation rough sets by Qian and Liang [16]. The relations and differences of these models are investigated.

2   Set-Based Granular Structure in Rough Sets

In rough set theory, a universe is divided into indiscernible classes by an equivalence relation. The granules and granular structure can be defined as the equivalence classes [13].

2.1   Set-Based Definition of Granules

Definition 1. *Let U a finite nonempty universal set. A subset $g \in 2^U$ is defined as a granule, where 2^U is the power set of U.*

Definition 2. *For $g, g' \in 2^U$, if $g \subseteq g'$, g is a sub-granule of g' and g' a super-granule of g.*

Under the partial order $\subseteq$, the empty set ϕ is the smallest granule and the universe U is the largest granule. When constructing a granular structure, we may consider a family G of subsets of U and an order relation on G.

Definition 3. *Suppose $G \subseteq 2^U$ is a nonempty family of subsets of U. The poset $(G, \subseteq)$ is a granular structure, where $\subseteq$ is the set-inclusion relation.*

2.2   Set-Based Granule Construction and Granular Structure

Rough set theory gives a partition-based model of GrC [17]. The theory concerns the analysis of data given in a tabular form. Formally, an information system or information table is represented by:

$$IS = (U, A, V, f) = (U, A, \{V_a | a \in A\}, \{f_a | U \times a \longrightarrow V_a\})$$

where

   U : is a finite nonempty set of objects;
   A : is a finite nonempty set of attributes;
   V_a : is a nonempty set of values for an attribute $a \in A$,ie. $V = Va$;
   f_a: is an information function.

A basic notion of rough sets is a granulation of the sets of objects based on their descriptions. For an attribute subset $P \subseteq A$, one can define an equivalence relation E_P on U as:

$$xE_Py \Leftrightarrow \forall a \in P, f_a(x) = f_a(y)$$

The equivalence class containing x is denoted by $[x]_{Ep} = \{y | xE_Py\}$, and is a granule. The granular partition level constructed by equivalence relation E_P is consist of equivalence classes $\{[x]_{E_p}\}$. It can be denoted by $GLP(E_P)$ or

$GLP\{[x]_{E_p}\}$. Both $GLP(E_P)$ and $GLP\{[x]_{E_p}\}$ mean the granule level governed by equivalence relation E_P, but the later indicates it by equivalence classes.

In order to understand the RS from a view of GrC, more concepts are emphasized as follows.

Original granule level is the granular partition level $GLP(E_A)$, where A is a set including all attributes , is the finest nonzero granule level in the information table $IS = (U, A, V, f)$.

A granular space is the granule levels which a problem is resolved. Single-granulation granular space and multi-granulation granular space is distinguished by its numbers of granule level.

Basic granules and definable granules are related to granule levels. The granules $[x]_{E_p} = \{y|xE_Py\}$, constructed by equivalence relation E_P, are basic granules of $GLP(E_P)$. A set $X = \cup\{[x]_{E_p}|x \in U\}$, a union of basic granules of $GLP(E_P)$, is a single-granulation definable granule in the level $GLP(E_P)$. A multi-granulation definable granule is a union of basic granules from multiple granule levels.

Basic granules are different from definable granules. The basic ones can act as primary units to compose definable granules. A basic granule is the finest granule and cannot be decomposed in its granule level, but may be decomposed into basic granules of finer granule levels. A basic granule in the coarser granule level may be a definable granule in the finer level. A basic granule in the coarser granule level is a super-granule of some basic granules in the finer level, and a basic granule in the finer level is a sub-granule of a basic granule in the coarser granule level.

In information system $IS = (U, A, V, f)$, let attribute sets $P_i \subseteq A$, $i = \{1, 2, ..., N\}$. If $P_1 \subset P_2 \subset ... \subset P_N \subseteq A$, then $GLP(E_{P_N}) \prec ... \prec GLP(E_{P_2}) \prec GLP(E_{P_1})$. The basic granules of $GLP(E_{P_i})$ are nested.

The above step-finer levels of granule make up a granular structure. This provides an effective method to obtain a granular structure. In rough sets, the attribute sets which satisfy set inclusion relation $P_1 \subset P_2 \subset ... \subset P_N \subseteq A$, can be derived by adding attributes gradually.

From the above statement, the following conclusions can be drawn: (1) A granular space is consist of basic granules. Basic granules are different from definable granules. (2) A granular structure can be derived according to increasing or decreasing data description number, i.e. attribute number. (3) Processing data in different attribute description means in different granulation level. (4) The concepts of single-granulation and multi-granulation are proposed definitely.

2.3   Reduction from View of GrC

The knowledge reduction is a primary concept in rough sets. Reducing of knowledge consists of removing of superfluous partitions (equivalence relations) or /and superfluous basic categories in the knowledge base in such a way that the set of elementary categories in the knowledge base is preserved [19]. This procedure enables us to eliminate all unnecessary knowledge from the knowledge base, preserving only the part of the knowledge which is really useful.

From the view of GrC, the reduction in RS is the process to change the granular space from the original granule level to the coarsest level of problem solving.

Choosing a granular space from all possible granular structures is a huge work. Suppose a information table $IS = (U, A, V, f)$ have N attributes, attribute sets P_i containing M attributes is the subset of A, total possible number of granule levels $GLP(P_i)$ is C_N^M. The reduction of an IS is a NP-hard problem, a heuristic method is needed to find a reduction.

Let an attribute set $R \subset A$. If R is a reduction of A, after reducing, the actual problem-solving granule level jumps from $GLP(E_A)$ to $GLP(E_R)$, namely a granular space jumps. The problem can be resolved in this level, such as rules minning. In this sense, rough sets are considered as a single-granulation tool.

3   Granules in Hierarchical Multi-dimensional Data Model

The data in rough sets are given in a tabular form. If the attribute in the table is capable of generalizing to more abstracting levels, then one table should be changed to more tables. Every table provides one single-granulation granular space, so hierarchical multi-dimensional data model [14] contributes a multi-granulation granular space. The problem solving can be proceeded in multi-granulation, for example, hierarchical decision rules mining [15].

The discussions in section 2 are suitable for hierarchical multi-dimensional data model. With reference to that, the following definitions are obvious.

Given a information table $IS = (U, A, V, f)$ and concept hierarchical tree of all attributes. The original granule level of IS becomes the $(0, 0, \ldots, 0)$th information table, with all attribute values at leaves level of their concept hierarchies respectively. The $(0, 0, \ldots, 0)$th information table can be denoted as follows:

$$IS_{00\ldots0} = (U_{00\ldots0}, A, V^{00\ldots0}, f_{00\ldots0})$$

When the attribute A_i is generalized to k_i concept hierarchy, the $(k_1, k_2, ..., k_m)$th information table is referred to as:

$$IS_{k_1k_2\ldots k_m} = (U_{k_1k_2\ldots k_m}, A, V^{k_1k_2\ldots k_m}, f_{k_1k_2\ldots k_m})$$

For more detail, see the papers [14,15].

In $IS_{k_1k_2\ldots k_m}$, let an attribute set $P \subset A$, R is a reduction of A.

Definition 4. *The basic granules in* $GLP(E_P^{k_1k_2\ldots k_m})$ *of* $IS_{k_1k_2\ldots k_m}$ *are denoted as:*

$$[x]_{E_P}^{k_1k_2\ldots k_m} = \{y | x E_P^{k_1k_2\ldots k_m} y\} \Leftrightarrow \forall a_i \in P, f_{k_i}(x) = f_{k_i}(y)$$

Definition 5. *The original granule level of* $IS_{k_1k_2\ldots k_m}$ *is denoted as* $GLP(E_A^{k_1k_2\ldots k_m})$. *The problem-solving granule level of it is denoted as* $GLP(E_R^{k_1k_2\ldots k_m})$

When the attribute A_i is generalizes from k_i -1 to k_i concept hierarchy, the basic granules get coarser. Some definable granules in granulation level k_i -1 are also changed to basic granules in granulation level k_i. The original granule level of the according information table is also changed, and gets coarser. A lattice is formatted by all the original granule levels of $IS_{k_1 k_2 \ldots k_m}$. This is proved in the literature [14].

In this section, the hierarchical multi-dimensional data model produces a multi-granulation granular space by generalizing the attributes. So the problem can be resolved in multi-granulation granular space and the results derived may be more flexible and efficiency than that in rough sets.

4   Granule Construction in Multi-granulation Rough Sets

Rough sets are mainly concerned with the approximation of sets described by a single binary relation on the universe. Qian et al. extend Pawlak's rough sets to a multi-granulation rough set model (MGRS), where the set approximations are defined by using multi-equivalence relation on the universe [16].

Definition 6. Let P, Q be two partitions on the universe U, and $X \subseteq U$. The lower approximation and upper approximation of X in U are defined as:

$$\underline{X}_{P+Q} = \{x : P(x) \subseteq X, \text{ or } Q(x) \subseteq X\} \text{ and } \overline{X}^{P+Q} = \sim \underline{(\sim X)}_{P+Q}$$

In the view of granular computing, the granules in MGRS are as follows: $[x]_{E_{P+Q}} = [x]_{E_P}$ or $[x]_{E_Q}$. Acorrding to statement in section 2, the granules in MGRS constitute a granular covering level, is denoted as $GLC(E_{P+Q})$. The granular space in MGRS is a multi-granulation granular covering level.

In the view of GrC, the relationships and differences among rough set model, hierarchical multi-dimensional data model and multi-granulation model can be discovered from their granular spaces. The granular space in rough sets is a single-granulation partition level, in hierarchical multi-dimensional data model is multi-granulation partition levels, and in MGRS is a two-granulation cover level.

A two-granulation cover level in MGRS is consisit of two single-granulation partition level in rough sets. The former has more granules and can produce more precise result[16] than any of its partition level in rough sets.

5   Conclusions

From the set-based granules construction, the hierarchical RS on multi-dimensional data model and MGRS model provide new granule levels according to rough sets by different methods. Many concepts are proposed in this paper definitely. The relations and differences of these models are investigated.

The more GrC models proposed the more granule levels occured. In actual applications, how to choose the most appropriate one becomes a challenge problem and is greatly problem-oriented. This will be the most important problem in the future.

Acknowledgments. This work was supported by National Natural Science Fund of China (Nos. 60970061, 61075056, 61103067).

References

1. Zedah, L.A.: Towards a theory of fuzzy information granulation and its centrality in human reasoning and fuzzy logic. Fuzzy Sets and Systems 90, 111–127 (1997)
2. Bargiela, A., Pedryz, W.: Granular Computing: An Introduction. Kluwer Academic Publishers, Boston (2002)
3. Bargiela, A., Pedryz, W.: The roots of Granular Computing. In: IEEE International Conference on Granular Computing, pp. 806–809 (2006)
4. Yao, Y.: Human-inspired granular computing. In: Yao, J.T. (ed.) Novel Developments in Granular Computing: Applications for Advanced Human Reasoning and Soft Computation, pp. 1–15. Information Science Reference, Herskey (2010)
5. Bargiela, A., Pedrycz, W.: Toward a theory of granular computing for human-centered information processing. IEEE Transactions on Fuzzy Systems 16(2), 320–330 (2008)
6. Pedrycz, W.: Granular computing and human-centricity in computational intelligence. In: IEEE International Conference on Cognitive Informatics (ICCI), p. 2 (2010)
7. Skowron, A., Wasilewski, P.: An Introduction to Perception Based Computing. In: Kim, T.-h., Lee, Y.-h., Kang, B.-H., Ślęzak, D. (eds.) FGIT 2010. LNCS, vol. 6485, pp. 12–25. Springer, Heidelberg (2010)
8. Hobbs, J.R.: Granularity. In: Proceedings of the 9th International Joint Conference on Artificial Intelligence, pp. 432–435 (1985)
9. Zhang, L., Zhang, B.: The Theory and Application for problem solving, 2nd edn. TsingHua University Publisher, Beijing (2007) (in Chinese)
10. Yao, Y.: Granular computing. Computer Science (Ji Suan Ji Ke Xue) 31, 1–5 (2004)
11. Yao, Y.: Perspectives of granular computing. In: Proceedings of 2005 IEEE International Conference on Granular Computing, vol. 1, pp. 85–90 (2005)
12. Yao, Y., Miao, D., Zhang, N., Xu, F.: Set-Theoretic Models of Granular Structures. In: Yu, J., Greco, S., Lingras, P., Wang, G., Skowron, A. (eds.) RSKT 2010. LNCS, vol. 6401, pp. 94–101. Springer, Heidelberg (2010)
13. Yao, Y., Miao, D.Q., Zhan, N., Xu, F.F.: Set-theoretic Approaches to Granular Computing. J. Fundamenta Informaticae 115, 247–264 (2012)
14. Feng, Q.: Research on Methods of Granular Computing based on Multidimensional Data Model, Shanghai, Tongji University (2009) (dissertation in Chinese)
15. Feng, Q., Miao, D., Cheng, Y.: Hierarchical decision rules mining. Expert Systems with Applications 37(3), 2081–2091 (2010)
16. Qian, Y.H., Liang, J.Y., Yao, Y., et al.: MGRS: A multi-granulation rough set. J. Information Sciences. 180, 949–970 (2010)
17. Yao, Y.: A Partition Model of Granular Computing. In: Peters, J.F., Skowron, A., Grzymała-Busse, J.W., Kostek, B.z., Świniarski, R.W., Szczuka, M.S. (eds.) Transactions on Rough Sets I. LNCS, vol. 3100, pp. 232–253. Springer, Heidelberg (2004)
18. Feng, Q., Miao, D.: Structured Prior Knowledge and Granular Structures. In: Zhong, N., Li, K., Lu, S., Chen, L. (eds.) BI 2009. LNCS, vol. 5819, pp. 115–126. Springer, Heidelberg (2009)
19. Pawlak, Z.: Rough Sets, Theoretical Aspects of Reasoning about Data. Kluwer Academic Publishers, Dordrecht (1991)

Multiple Representations of Web Content for Effective Knowledge Utilization

Yiyu Yao[1] and Sheila Petty[2]

[1] Department of Computer Science, University of Regina
Regina, Saskatchewan, Canada S4S 0A2
`yyao@cs.uregina.ca`
[2] Faculty of Fine Arts, University of Regina
Regina, Saskatchewan, Canada S4S 0A2
`Sheila.Petty@uregina.ca`

Abstract. The web, as a new medium for information and knowledge creation, storage, communication, and sharing, offers both opportunities and challenges. By applying the principles of granular computing, we argue that multiple representations and presentations of web content are essential to effective knowledge utilization through the web. The same web content should be represented in many versions and in multiple levels in each version to facilitate informative communication, personalized searches, web exploration, and tailored presentation of retrieval results.

1 Introduction

With the fast growth of web content, it becomes more difficult to organize and represent web content for different users and for different purposes. While many search engines have proven to be very effective, there is still room for improvement. In this paper, we propose a framework of multiple representations of web content as a means to meet the challenges of the diversity of users, the wide spectrum of user needs, and user information overload. The underlying mechanism is the multilevel and multiview granular structure.

The concept of multiple representations has been extensively studied in a number of fields, including for example databases [3, 19], geographic information systems [22], video retrieval [8], and web-based learning [21]. However, multiple representations of web content are not as widely utilized as they should be.

One can easily observe effective uses of multiple versions of text documents prior to the web age. For example, the same novel may be adapted into several versions, including, for example, condensed versions or movies. A look of any scientific paper easily reveals a multilevel granular structure, including title, section headings, and subsection headings, etc. [25]. A reader can read a paper differently by focusing on different levels to avoid information overloading. For future web based information systems, it is also useful to explore multiple representations of web content.

Challenges posed by computer-based narratives and the way in which digital technology is challenging existing aesthetic frameworks is important. As Lunenfeld argues, "the study of aesthetics" focused on "the study of stable forms" prior

F.M. Zanzotto et al. (Eds.): BI 2012, LNCS 7670, pp. 338–347, 2012.
© Springer-Verlag Berlin Heidelberg 2012

to the emergence of new media as a cultural phenomenon [13]. In other words, prior to the computer, various disciplines such as literature, film and video, photography and so on, stood as more or less discrete strands or fields, each with specific textual approaches associated with the discipline: literary studies, for example, focused on the written word, and film and video studies focused on primarily visually-driven texts. But digital technology changes all of this. Visit any type of website and you could be faced with a convergence of many different media approaches including still images, video streaming, text panels, including those specific to the computer such as interactivity or digital composition.

All of these convergences work together to create meaning in a digital text, and because they are so recombinant and changeable, the text, as a concept, is no longer stable. Thus, computer-based digital artworks undermine previously discrete categories of aesthetic disciplines. When text, visual images, sound collage, compositing, and a myriad of other media devices merge into a seamless whole, the analytical challenge becomes not one of determining a stable means of describing the form of a narrative, but rather emerges as a need to address the fundamental hybridity of digital texts.

Based on principles of granular computing, this paper advocates the use of multiple representations of web content for effective knowledge utilization.

2   Multiple Representations Using Granular Structures

An important notion of granular computing is granular structures characterized by multilevel and multiview [33, 35], which leads naturally to multiple representations and descriptions.

2.1   Granular Computing and Granular Structures

Granular computing concerns a particular human-centric paradigm of problem solving by means of multiple levels of granularity and their applications in intelligent machines and systems [2, 20, 35]. Among many theories and frameworks, the triarchic theory [30–32] promotes granular computing as a new field of study, pictorially depicted by the granular computing triangle. The three nodes of the triangle correspond to a philosophy of structured thinking, a methodology of structured problem solving, and a computational paradigm of structured information processing. It is the emphasis on useful granular structures that make granular computing a promising field of investigation.

Granules are a primitive notion of granular computing. Descriptions and representations of granules provide the basic vocabularies of granular computing. A granular structure is a set of (partially) ordered levels with each level consisting of a family of granules [34]. Using the terminology of systems theory, a granule represents a part of a whole. Granular computing studies the whole through an integration of its parts in terms of their interrelations and their connections to the whole. A family of smaller granules may be combined into a larger granule and, conversely, a larger granule may be decomposed into smaller granules. The concept of granularity reflects naturally orderings of granules and levels, interpreted as the degree of abstraction, generalization, complexity or details [34].

A granular structure may be more formally described as a multilevel hierarchy. Multiple representations and descriptions in granular computing arise in two ways, namely, multilevel and multiview [32, 34, 35]. The former concerns representations at different levels in a single hierarchy, and the latter concerns presentations provided by many hierarchies. Their needs and benefits are discussed next.

2.2 Multilevel

Human memory, thinking and intelligence depend crucially on categorization, conceptualization, and organization of knowledge and experiences [26]. One of the effective ways is to make abstractions at multiple levels of granularity. From a cognitive point of view, this is necessary due to our limited capacity for information processing. A study by Miller [17] shows that humans can normally process about seven plus or minus two units of information. Other studies suggest that the actual number of units is in fact smaller and is around four [6]. To accommodate such a limitation and to decrease cognitive overload, a technique of chunking is used to format information into a manageable number of units. A chunk is in fact a granule. A sequence of multi-stage chunking leads to a multilevel granular structure. Concept formation, categorization, and languages are inherently associated with many levels of granularity. As nicely summarized by Hobbs [11], humans consider a problem at multiple levels of granularity so that we focus on solving a problem at the most appropriate level of granularity by ignoring unimportant and irrelevant details. In addition, we can readily switch between levels of granularity at different stages of problem solving.

Each level in a hierarchy provides a specific description or representation. Different levels may use different vocabularies for description. Multilevels lead naturally to multiple representations. There are two-way connections between two adjacent levels in a hierarchy. A higher level may control or constrain its immediate lower level on the one hand, but is also determined and explained by the latter on the other hand. With a hierarchy, we can also easily switch from one description to another.

The concept of multilevel representation and understanding has been promoted by researchers across many disciplines. Gilbert and Treagust [9] consider three levels of representation, consisting of macro, submicro and symbolic representations, in chemical education. Marr [14] promotes understanding an information processing system at three levels, consisting of "computational theory," "representation and algorithm," and "hardware implementation." He convincingly argues that a full understanding of an information processing system requires understanding at different levels. With different levels of descriptions, one explores different kinds of explanations. Hawkins [10] suggests that the human brain can be interpreted as a multilevel hierarchical structure that stores a model of the hierarchical structure of the real world. Our recent paper [34] provides a more detailed discussion on integrative multiple levels.

2.3   Multiview

A fundamental issue in interpreting a multilevel hierarchy centers on objectivity and subjectivity [34]. Simply stated, levels and hierarchical structures are used to represent either the reality (i.e., an objective interpretation) or our perception and conceptualization of the reality (i.e., a subjective interpretation). It seems reasonable to adopt the subjective interpretation by considering a hierarchy as a specific conceptualization of the reality from a certain angle. As such, a hierarchy may not truthfully reflect the reality and a family of hierarchies is needed to have a complete comprehensive description. The use of many hierarchies gives rise to multiview.

The needs and benefits of multiview have been considered by many authors across many disciplines. Bateson [1] demonstrates "bonus or increment of knowing" from combining "multiple versions of the world." Minsky [18] explains the versatility of human minds based on multiview, namely, a) "we can see things from many points of view," b) "we have ways to rapidly switch among these" points of views, c) "we have many different ways to represent things," and d) "we develop good ways to organize these representations." A demonstration of effectiveness of multiview data analysis is given by Chen and Yao [5].

There are many benefits from multiview representations. A family of many views would remedy the limitation and correct the bias of a single view in representing and explaining the reality. A combination of many views generally would lead to "bonus or increment of knowing." A family of views may reveal some emerged properties that cannot be observed from any single view. Many views also offer a possiblity for switching when one finds that a specific view does not work. In addition, different views may better serve the needs of a diversity of users.

2.4   Modes of Processing

Multilevel and multiview granular structures can be used as a basis of information representation and processing. While multilevel offers level-wise processing, multiview offers compare and contrast analysis.

With multilevel representations of a hierarchy, we can derive at least three modes of processing, namely, top-down, bottom-up, and middle-out from a particular level [36]. Top-down approaches move from a higher more abstract level (i.e., coarser granulation) to a lower more concrete (i.e., finer granulation) level, and in the process more detailed information is added. More specifically, large granules are broken into smaller granules and are explained by these smaller granules. Bottom-up approaches work the other direction and in the process some information is ignored. Finally, middle-out approaches start from a particular level and move either up or down, depending which way is more fruitful. In general, one may use a mixture of the three modes.

With a family of views, we can take a compare and contrast approach to study relationships among different views. The combined and emerged properties from many views can also be studied. Through these studies, it may be possible to select a most suitable view for a specific group of users.

3   Multiple Representations of Web Content

Given that multiple representations are essential to human intelligence and human ways of problem solving, it follows that they will also play an indispensable role in management of web content for effective utilization and deployment of knowledge.

3.1   Multiple Representations on the Web

In developing a cognitive flexibility theory for advanced learning, Spiro et al. [23, 24] emphasize the importance of multiple representations of knowledge: "Knowledge that will have to be used in many ways has to be learned, represented, and tried out (in application) in many different ways." They suggest a close connection between cognitive flexibility theory and hypertext systems. Hypertext systems facilitate flexible restructuring, multiple knowledge representations, multiple linkages among different knowledge components, which makes non-linear, multidimensional and interactive exploration possible. Thus, hypertext systems are an appropriate technology for promoting cognitive flexibility. Conversely, cognitive flexibility theory provides a sound basis for designing hypertext systems for the purpose of effective learning and knowledge utilization. The web is based essentially on the same conceptual principles of hypertext, but offers many more useful features, functionalities and connectivities. It provides a new media of communication, collaboration, interaction, and intercreation [4]. The findings of Spiro et al. are equally applicable to context of the web.

There are two sides to the issue of multiple representations on the web. On the one hand, in contrast to conventional media such as books, films, etc., the web provides an infrastructure and platform that readily and easily supports multiple representations. Although web content may exist in a wide range of formats, including texts, tables, databases, images, audios, and videos, multiple representations are universally applicable. On the other hand, in order to more effectively utilize knowledge on the web, it is essential to have multiple representations on the web. A user can navigate and explore multiple representations in non-linear, multidimensional and interactive ways to gain deeper knowledge. Furthermore, various modes of processing based on granular structures can be used to assist users. In summary, it is both feasible and necessary to implement and exploit multiple representations on the web.

3.2   Multiple Representations of Web Documents

As a concrete example, consider a text-based web document. We can observe at least the following levels of granularity: title, subtitles, sections, paragraphs, sentences, and words. Consider in more detail the sentence level. A sentence granule consists of a set of word granules. While each word has its own meaning, their combination provides an emerging meaning that each of the words may not have. Similarly, a sequence of sentences forming a paragraph leads to a particular topic. In a bottom-up way, the meaning of a sentence emerges from the meaning of words; the meaning of a paragraph emerges from the meaning of sentences; the meaning of a section emerges from the meaning of paragraphs; and the meaning of a document emerges from the meaning of sections. An understanding of a web document depends crucially on understanding all these differing levels of granularity.

The same document may also have many representations, each of them providing either a different level of detail or a different angle. For example, one may have a brief summary of the document, an excerpt of the document, or a review of the document. With multiple representations, different users may view the same document differently from their unique perspectives, based on culture, race, gender, etc. To meet this challenge, we need to represent the same content in multiple versions, with each version emphasizing a particular aspect or serving a specific purpose. By so doing, it is possible to meet the needs of different groups of readers.

Multiple representations of a document may be useful in designing websites including such aspects as low content, medium content and high content as suggested by Eccher [7]. The concept of multiview suggests an effective tool in website design. For example, McNeil [15] classifies websites with reference to design into several views, consisting of sites by type, sites by design style, sites by theme, sites by color, sites by element, and sites by structure. This classification well serves the purpose of guiding a website designer, but fails to serve the purpose of a content-based searcher. On the other hand, a representation of a web document as a list of words serves the purpose of a searcher, but fails to serve a web designer. With multiview of the web, one may serve a wide range of users.

Multiple representations based on granular computing are also related to design in general. For example, in their study of universal principles of design, Lidwell et al. [12] consider a few such principles. In order to help people in recalling and retaining information, chunking is a commonly used technique for combining many units of information into a limited number of units. Layering is a process that organizes information into related groups to reduce complexity and to reinforce relationships in the information. Hierarchical organization provides a simple structure for visualization and understanding complexity. Progressive disclosure is a strategy that displays only necessary or requested information at any given time. According to our earlier discussion, notions of chunking, layering, hierarchical organizing, and progressive disclosure are closely related to granular structures and the induced multiple representations.

3.3   Multiple Representations in Geographic Information Systems

One of the most commonly encountered examples of multiple representations of web content is the multi-resolution maps. There usually coexist several versions of maps that allow a user to zoom-in and zoom-out in the process of exploration and information seeking. The benefits of using multiple maps are obvious. It is easy to imagine difficulties that may arise from using a single map with either a too low resolution or a too high resolution.

Maps are the most natural way to represent and convey geographical information. The ideas of multiple representations of maps can be applied to handle other types of entities in geographic information systems [3, 16, 22]. A few such studies on multiple representations are reviewed.

Medeiros et al. [16] give a framework for managing multiple representations of georeferenced elements. Their motivation for multiple representations stems from the fact that users must model and store georeferenced data for different types of applications. Multiple representations can be explained and modeled by considering granularity from perspectives, for example, of resolution, time, model, user point of view, and others. Their solution to handling multiple representations is based on the database version approach.

Spaccapietra et al. [22] consider different facets of geographic data that require and support multiple representations, including multiple geometry, many abstract levels of object classification, many abstract levels of object description, and multiple thematic information. They argue that geographic information systems need to support multiple resolutions, multiple viewpoints, and multiple classifications, where multiple representations are at the center of consideration.

Bédard and Bernier [3] introduce the concept of VUEL (View Element) as the basic construct of a spatial database view. The VUEL model enables them to represent and process geometric multiplicity, semantic multiplicity, and graphical multiplicity. Different VUELs may describe a same real world element from different points of view or at different abstraction levels. Multiple representations are a main characteristics of the VUEL model.

Multiple representations of geographical data depend on temporal granularity, spatial granularity, or levels of abstraction. They are closely related to granular structures introduced earlier. As multiple resolution maps have demonstrated, web-based geographic information systems with multiple representations provide a more effective means for exploring geographical data on the web.

3.4   Multiple Representations in Information Retrieval Support Systems

The framework of information retrieval support systems (IRSS) shows a move beyond the search and browsing centered philosophy of the conventional retrieval systems and search engines [28, 29]. It can be viewed as the next generation of systems in the evolution of retrieval systems, from data retrieval to information retrieval, and from information retrieval to information retrieval/seeking support. An objective of an IRSS is to support many different types of users in finding and utilizing information and knowledge on the web, in a similar way that a decision support system assists users in making management decisions.

Granular computing serves as a basis for designing and implementing IRSS. A key issue of IRSS is the construction and use of granular structures. Information on the web can be classified into web content, web structure, web usage and user profiles. From such information and the relationships between different types of information, one can obtain many kinds of granular structures, including, for example, index term space granulation, document space granulation, user space granulation, and retrieval results granulation [29]. Once granular structures are obtained, they can be used to derive multiple representations and to choose the best representation for a particular user or a group of users. Users can also explore granular structures according to various modes of processing offered by granular structures.

Web-based geographic information systems and Web-based IRSS may be viewed as special classes of web-based support systems [27]. The advantages and value of using multiple representations in those systems suggest that the same principle is applicable to other types of systems. To make effective use of knowledge on the web, it may be necessary to rely on the integration, interaction and interworking of many different types of web-based support systems that explore multiple representations of web content.

4   Conclusion

We argue that multiple representations of web content hold the key to effective knowledge utilization on the web. While some efforts have been made from the viewpoint of website design so that a user is not overloaded with the huge amount of information, there is still much more that can be done. Multilevel and multiview granular structures offer a promising model for organizing, representing and presenting web content. Several modes of processing may be used to explore granular structures.

The discussion of the paper mainly focuses on a conceptual level. One must realize that there is a big gap between the conceptual formulation and practical implementation. As future work, it may be fruitful to investigate actual implementations of multiple representations of web content on a grand scale.

References

1. Bateson, G.: Mind and Nature: A Necessary Unity. E.P. Button, New York (1979)
2. Bargiela, A., Pedrycz, W. (eds.): Human-Centric Information Processing Through Granular Modelling. Springer, Berlin (2009)
3. Bédard, Y., Bernier, E.: Supporting multiple representations with spatial view management and the concept of "VUEL". In: The Joint Workshop on Multi-Scale Representations of Spatial Data (2002)
4. Berners-Lee, T., Fischetti, M.: Weaving the Web. Harper, San Francisco (1999)
5. Chen, Y.H., Yao, Y.Y.: A multiview approach for intelligent data analysis based on data operators. Information Sciences 178, 1–20 (2008)
6. Cowan, N.: The magical number 4 in short-term memory: A reconsideration of mental storage capacity. Behavioral and Brain Sciences 24, 87–114 (2001)
7. Eccher, C.: Professional Web Design, Techniques and Templates. Course Technology, Boston (2011)
8. Fan, J.P., Aref, W.G., Elmagarmid, A.K., Hacid, M.S., Marzouk, M.S., Zhu, X.Q.: MultiView: Multilevel video content representation and retrieval. Journal of Electronic Imaging 10, 895–908 (2001)

9. Gilbert, J.K., Treagust, D.: Introduction: Macro, submicro and symbolic representations and the relationship between them: Key models in chemical education. In: Gilbert, J.K., Treagust, D. (eds.) Multiple Representations in Chemical Education, pp. 1–8. Springer, Berlin (2009)

10. Hawkins, J., Blakeslee, S.: On Intelligence. Henry Holt and Company, New York (2004)

11. Hobbs, J.R.: Granularity. In: Proceedings of the Ninth International Joint Conference on Artificial Intelligence, pp. 432–435 (1985)

12. Lidwell, W.: Holden. K., Butler, J.: Universal Principles of Design. Rockport Publishers, Gloucester (2003)

13. Lunenfeld, P.: Snap to Grid: A User's Guide to Digital Arts, Media, and Cultures. The MIT Press, Cambridge (2000)

14. Marr, D.: Vision, A Computational Investigation into Human Representation and Processing of Visual Information. W.H. Freeman and Company, San Francisco (1982)

15. McNeil, P.: The Web Designer's Idea Book, the Ultimate Guide to Themes, Trends and Styles in Website Design. How Books, Cincinnati (2008)

16. Medeiros, C.B., Bellosta, M.J., Jomier, G.: Managing multiple representations of georeferenced elements. In: Proceedings of the Seventh International Workshop on Database and Expert Systems Applications, pp. 364–370 (1996)

17. Miller, G.A.: The magical number seven, plus or minus two: Some limits on our capacity for processing information. Psychological Review 63, 81–97 (1956)

18. Minsky, M.: The Emotion Machine: Commonsense Thinking, Artificial Intelligence, and the Future of the Human Mind. Simon & Schuster Paperbacks, New York (2006)

19. Parent, C., Spaccapietra, S., Zimányi, E.: MurMur: Database management of multiple representations. AAAI Technical Report WS-00-08, pp. 83–86 (2000)

20. Pedrycz, W., Chen, S.-M. (eds.): Granular Computing and Intelligent Systems: Design with Information Granules of Higher Order and Higher Type. ISRL, vol. 13. Springer, Heidelberg (2011)

21. Salter, G., Stratti, H.: Multiple representations of content in web-based learning. In: Proceedings of the IASTED International Conference on Web-Based Education, pp. 143–147 (2004)

22. Spaccapietra, S., Parent, C., Vangenot, C.: GIS Databases: From Multiscale to MultiRepresentation. In: Choueiry, B.Y., Walsh, T. (eds.) SARA 2000. LNCS (LNAI), vol. 1864, pp. 57–70. Springer, Heidelberg (2000)

23. Spiro, R.J., Coulson, R.L., Feltovich, P.J., Anderson, D.: Cognitive flexibility theory: Advanced knowledge acquisition in ill-structured domains. In: Proceedings of the 10th Annual Conference of the Cognitive Science Society (1988)

24. Spiro, R.J., Feltovich, P.J., Jacobson, M.J., Coulson, R.L.: Cognitive flexibility, constructivism and hypertext: Random access instruction for advanced knowledge acquisition in ill-structured domains. In: Duffy, T., Jonassen, D. (eds.) Constructivism and the Technology of Instruction, pp. 57–74. Erlbaum, Hillsdale (1992)

25. Sword, H.: Stylish Academic Writing. Harvard University Press, Cambridge (2012)

26. van Mechelen, I., Hampton, J., Michalski, R.S., Theuns, P. (eds.): Categories and Concepts, Theoretical Views and Inductive Data Analysis. Academic Press, New York (1993)

27. Yao, J.T. (ed.): Web-based Support Systems. Springer, London (2010)

28. Yao, Y. Y.: Information retrieval support systems. In: Proceedings of The 2002 IEEE World Congress on Computational Intelligence, pp. 1092-1097 (2002)

29. Yao, Y. Y.: Granular computing for the design of information retrieval support systems. In: Wu, W., Xiong, H. and Shekhar, S. (eds.), Clustering and Information Retrieval, pp. 299-329. Kluwer Academic Publishers, Boston (2003)
30. Yao, Y. Y.: Perspectives of granular computing. In: Proceedings of 2005 IEEE International Conference on Granular Computing, pp. 85–90 (2005)
31. Yao, Y. Y.: Three perspectives of granular computing. Journal of Nanchang Institute of Technology 25, 16–21 (2006)
32. Yao, Y. Y.: Granular computing: Past, present and future. In: Proceedings of 2008 IEEE International Conference on Granular Computing, pp. 80–85 (2008)
33. Yao, Y. Y.: A unified framework of granular computing. In: Pedrycz, W., Skowron, A., Kreinovich, V. (eds.) Handbook of Granular Computing, pp. 401–410. John Wiley and Sons, Chichester (2008)
34. Yao, Y. Y.: Integrative levels of granularity. In: Bargiela, A., Pedrycz, W. (eds.) Human-Centric Information Processing Through Granular Modelling, pp. 31–47. Springer, Berlin (2009)
35. Yao, Y.Y.: Human-inspired granular computing. In: Yao, J.T. (ed.) Novel Developments in Granular Computing: Applications for Advanced Human Reasoning and Soft Computation, pp. 1–15. Information Science Reference, Herskey (2010)
36. Yao, Y. Y.: Artificial Intelligence Perspectives on Granular Computing. In: Pedrycz, W., Chen, S.-M. (eds.) Granular Computing and Intelligent Systems. ISRL, vol. 13, pp. 17–34. Springer, Heidelberg (2011)

Rule Measures Tradeoff
Using Game-Theoretic Rough Sets

Yan Zhang and JingTao Yao

Department of Computer Science, University of Regina
Regina, Saskatchewan, Canada S4S 0A2
{zhang83y,jtyao}@cs.uregina.ca

Abstract. The game-theoretic rough sets (GTRS) is a recent proposal
to determine optimal thresholds in probabilistic rough sets by setting up
a game for trading-off between different criteria. Different competitions
or cooperations can be formulated depending on objectives of users. In
this article, five approaches for applying GTRS are reviewed. The GTRS
for formulating competition or cooperation among measures is described.
We investigate potential players of GTRS, in the form of measures for
evaluating a set of immediate decision rules. The definition and properties of these measures are discussed. We demonstrate that GTRS meet
the challenge for determining a balanced and optimal threshold pair that
leads to a moderate, cost effective or efficient level of acceptance, rejection or deferment decision by providing a game mechanism.

Keywords: Rough sets, immediate decision rules, measures, game-
theoretic rough sets (GTRS).

1 Introduction

Classification rules can be induced from equivalence classes in rough sets [11].
The decision rules induced from positive and negative regions versus those induced from boundary region are referred as certain rules and uncertain rules [10],
positive rules and boundary rules [19], immediate decision rules and deferred decision rules [7] respectively in the literature. We adopt the terms of immediate
decision rules and deferred decision rules in this paper. Traditional Pawlak rough
sets define the positive and negative regions with strict conditions. This leads
to less positive and negative regions and larger boundary regions, which in turn
limits the practical applicability of rough sets [16].

The probabilistic rough set approach aims to decrease the boundary region by
introducing a pair of thresholds (α, β) to weaken the strict conditions in order
to classify more objects in positive and negative regions [14]. More immediate
decision rules may be induced and the applicability of rough sets is increased at
a cost of classification errors [16]. How to determine and interpret the thresholds is one of the fundamental semantics-related questions in probabilistic rough
sets [17]. The decision-theoretic rough sets (DTRS) proposed by Yao calculated
the required parameters based on notions of costs through Bayesian decision

F.M. Zanzotto et al. (Eds.): BI 2012, LNCS 7670, pp. 348–359, 2012.
© Springer-Verlag Berlin Heidelberg 2012

procedure [15] [18]. Deng and Yao proposed an information theoretic approach to interpret and determine probabilistic thresholds, in which the problem of searching for optimal thresholds was formulated as minimization of uncertainty of three regions [4].

Game-theoretic rough sets (GTRS) was recently introduced for determining the thresholds by formulating competition or cooperation among multiple criteria [8]. Herbert and Yao constructed two types of games in which the region parameters and classification approximation measures were defined as game players respectively [8]. Azam and Yao extended GTRS by treating the problem of determining thresholds as a decision making problem and constructed games to formulate and analyze multiple criteria [2]. GTRS can also be applied in rules mining [2], feature selection [1], classification [8], uncertainty analysis [3]. How to formulate games depends on the objectives of the users in GTRS. Generally, a game is formulated as a set of players, a set of actions or strategies for each player, and the respective payoff functions for each action. Each player chooses actions to be performed according to expected payoff, usually some actions maximizing payoff while minimizing other players payoff [8]. When applying GTRS for rules mining, there are four fundamental issues should be considered: selecting suitable players, setting available strategies, defining payoff functions, and finding equilibria. Selecting players is basic for the whole process. Players decide how to set strategies and payoff functions. Measures for evaluating decision rules may be set as game players when we aim to extract effective classification rules from a decision table employing probabilistic rough sets. Different measures may compete against each other to reach equilibria which correspond to optimal probabilistic threshold (α, β) pairs. In this article, we present GTRS for formulating competition between measures. We discuss possible measures for evaluating a set of immediate decision rules and analyze their properties. More games can be formulated by using these measures, and the result in this study may enhance our understanding and the applicability of GTRS.

2   Rules Mining with Game-Theoretic Rough Sets

The GTRS exploit the relationship between multiple criteria and probabilistic thresholds of probabilistic rough sets by formulating a solution for effective decision making [2]. The GTRS enable simultaneous consideration of multiple criteria when improving the performance of rough sets from different aspects, such as effective rule mining, reducing uncertainties of regions, classification ability.

2.1   A Framework of Game-Theoretic Rough Sets

When using game theory to help determine suitable thresholds of probabilistic rough sets, players compete against or cooperation each other in order to gain the maximum payoff. In a game, three factors need to be formulated, i.e. a set of players, sets of strategies for players, and sets of payoff functions resulting from players performing actions [8]. A game can be defined as:

$$G = \{O, S, F\}, \tag{1}$$

Table 1. Payoff table for general GTRS

		o_2		
		a_{21}	a_{22}	.....
	a_{11}	$\langle u_1(a_{11}, a_{21}), u_2(a_{11}, a_{21}) \rangle$	$\langle u_1(a_{11}, a_{22}), u_2(a_{11}, a_{22}) \rangle$	......
o_1	a_{12}	$\langle u_1(a_{12}, a_{21}), u_2(a_{12}, a_{21}) \rangle$	$\langle u_1(a_{12}, a_{22}), u_2(a_{12}, a_{22}) \rangle$	......
	......	......	......	......

where O denotes a set of players $O = \{o_1, o_2, ..., o_n\}$, S a set of strategies $S = \{S_1, S_2, ..., S_n\}$ and F the payoff functions. S_i denotes a set of possible actions for player o_i, i.e. $S_i = \{a_{i1}, a_{i2}, ..., a_{im_i}\}$, where $a_{ij}(j = 1...m_i)$ means m_i actions can be performed by player o_i. These strategies are executed by players in order to better their position in the future. A payoff table can be formed according to strategies of each player and its corresponding payoffs. The number of payoff elements in the payoff table depends on the number of actions each player can access. In order to find optimal solutions for competition or cooperation between players, we need to determine whether or not there exists an equilibrium within the payoff table [8]. This intuitively means that both players attempt to maximize their payoffs given the other player's chosen action, once found, cannot rationally increase this payoff [8].

Table 1 shows a payoff table of GTRS with two players, i.e. $O = \{o_1, o_2\}$. The payoff element $u_1(a_{1i}, a_{2j})$ denotes the payoff of player o_1 performing an action a_{1i} when player o_2 performs the action a_{2j}. In Table 1, a cell $\langle u_1(a_{1k}, a_{2l}), u_2(a_{1k}, a_{2l}) \rangle$ is an equilibrium if there exist actions a_{1k} and a_{2l}, where

$$u_1(a_{1k}, a_{2j}) > u_1(a_{1i}, a_{2j}), \text{for all } i \neq k, \text{for all } j,$$
$$u_2(a_{1i}, a_{2l}) > u_2(a_{1i}, a_{2j}), \text{for all } j \neq l, \text{for all } i. \qquad (2)$$

2.2 Immediate Decision Rules and Related Measures

In classification problems, an information system can be denoted by a decision table $S = (U, C \cup D)$, where U is a finite non-empty set of objects, C is a set of condition attributes, D is a set of decision attributes, and C and D are disjoint [9] [10]. A decision rule induced from S can be expressed in the form of $des([x]) \rightarrow des(D_i)$, read as if $des([x])$ then $des(D_i)$. Here $des([x])$ is the description of equivalence class $[x]$ derived from condition attributes. $des(D_i)$ is the description of decision class D_i derived from decision attributes and the value of decision attributes are D_i. In fact, $des([x])$ and $des(D_i)$ can be described as formulas built up from attribute-value pairs (a, v) where $a \in (C \cup D)$ by means of logical connectives $\{\wedge, \vee, \sim\}$, $a \in C$ for $des([x])$ and $a \in D$ for $des(D_i)$ [10] [21]. The equivalence class $[x]$ and D_i denote the set of objects with the description of $des([x])$ and $des(D_i)$ respectively. In this paper, X and $des(X)$ can be understood as the intension and extension of the concept X [13]. We adopt immediate decision rules for the rules induced from the positive regions of $D_i(i = 1...k)$. The immediate decision rule $des([x]) \rightarrow des(D_i)$ satisfies

$\frac{|[x] \cap (D_i)|}{|[x]|} = 1$ in Pawlak rough sets. In probabilistic rough sets, they satisfy $\frac{|[x] \cap (D_i)|}{|[x]|} \geq \alpha$.

Binary values of decision attributes, i.e. $D = \{D_+, D_-\}$, are the simplest but fundamental scenario. Multiple values of decision attributes can be converted to multiple binary values. In probabilistic rough sets, with thresholds (α, β) value $1 \geq \alpha > 0.5 > \beta \geq 0$, the immediate decision rules can be induced from the positive regions of D_+ and D_-:

$$\{des([x]) \to des(D_+)\}_{[x] \subseteq POS_{(\alpha,\beta)}(D_+)} \bigcup \{des([x]) \to des(D_-)\}_{[x] \subseteq POS_{(\alpha,\beta)}(D_-)}. \tag{3}$$

Measures for evaluating decision rules have attracted researchers' attentions recently [5] [6] [20] [19]. They can be classified into two groups according to the number of rules they evaluate. For single decision rule, Düntsch introduced some uncertainty measures and presented three model selection criteria using information theoretic entropy in the spirit of the minimum description length principle [5]. Greco et al. applied some confirmation measures to the rough set approach to discover relationships in data sets by means of decision rules [6]. Moreover, certain measure of a decision rule is defined as $\mu(des([x]) \to des(D_i)) = \frac{|[x] \cap (D_i)|}{|[x]|}$, support measure is defined as $s(des([x]) \to des(D_i)) = \frac{|[x] \cap (D_i)|}{|U|}$ in [21]. For evaluating a set of decision rules, Yao and Zhong analyzed quantitative measures associated with if-then type rules, representing the confidence, uncertainty, applicability, quality, accuracy and interestingness of rule [20]. three measures were introduced for evaluating all decision rules induced from a decision table, namely certainty, consistency and support [12]. Yao and Zhao defined measures that can be used to evaluate a single decision rule and positive rules set, including confidence, coverage, generality and cost [19]. Pawlak defined approximation accuracy for classification and consistency for a decision table [11].

2.3 Different Formulating Approaches with GTRS

Different competitions or cooperations can be formulated with GTRS. This section describes five possible approaches of applying GTRS to find optimal probabilistic thresholds, including formulating the competition between two thresholds, the competition between two classification approximation measures, the competition between two properties of rough sets, the competition between regions and the competition between two measures for evaluating positive rules.

The Competition between Two Probabilistic Thresholds: Herbert and Yao proposed a GTRS with two probabilistic thresholds (α, β) competing against each other to reach the goal directly by reducing the boundary region [8]. In the competition, the players are α and β, and changing the values of α and β can directly manipulate the regions' sizes, i.e. players were formulated as $O = \{\alpha, \beta\}$. The competition between thresholds exposed possible strategies for decreasing the boundary region. α and β can access three actions differentiated by values of a scalar $c_i(i = 1, 2, 3)$ [8]:

$$S_\alpha = \{\alpha \times (1 - c_1), \alpha \times (1 - c_2), \alpha \times (1 - c_3)\}$$
$$S_\beta = \{\beta \times (1 + c_1), \beta \times (1 + c_2), \beta \times (1 + c_3)\} \tag{4}$$

The payoff functions were defined as [8]:

$$u(\alpha_i) = \frac{|POS|^{'} - |POS|}{\alpha \times (1 - c_i)}, u(\beta_i) = \frac{|NEG|^{'} - |NEG|}{\beta \times (c_i - 1)} \tag{5}$$

The Competition between Classification Measures: The competition between two classification approximation measures, such as accuracy(ϕ) and precision(ψ), was formulated in order to improve the classification ability of rough sets [8]. In the game, each player represented a measure, i.e. $O = \{\phi, \psi\}$. The players ϕ and ψ have the same strategies $S_\phi = S_\psi = \{\downarrow R_P, \uparrow R_N, \uparrow R_B\}$, where $R_\Diamond(\Diamond = P, N$ or $B)$ denotes the conditional risk defined in DTRS [15]. In this competition, payoff functions $F = \{u_\phi, u_\psi\}$ measured the increase in accuracy and precision respectively [8].

The Competition between Two Properties of Rough Sets: Azam and Yao calculated the probabilistic thresholds with GTRS by considering the properties of accuracy and generality of the rough sets [3]. The players were $O = \{a, g\}$; each player had four possible strategies, i can be a or g:

$$S_i = \{(\alpha, \beta), (\alpha(1 - c\%), \beta), (\alpha, \beta(1 + c\%)), (\alpha(1 - c\%), \beta(1 + c\%))\} \tag{6}$$

For S_a, $c = 20\%$, and for S_g, $c = 30\%$. The change of thresholds equals to the sum of two changes [3]. The payoffs were calculated as the values of measures with the probabilistic thresholds. The payoff table was a matrix with 4 rows and 4 columns. The Nash equilibrium in the payoff table was a strategy profile such that no player would want to change his strategy if he has the knowledge of other players strategies [3].

The Competition between Regions for Analyzing Uncertainties: Azam and Yao proposed the game as a competition between the regions to improve the overall uncertainty level of the rough set classification [3]. In the game, the positive and negative regions as a single player competed against the boundary region, i.e. $O = \{I, D\}$ [3]. The change of probabilistic thresholds were formulated as strategies, i.e. $S_I = S_D = \{s_1, s_2, s_3\} = \{\alpha \downarrow, \beta \uparrow, \alpha \downarrow \beta \uparrow\}$. The payoff of the players were represented as [3]:

$$u_I(s_i, s_j) = \frac{(1 - \triangle_P(\alpha, \beta)) + (1 - \triangle_N(\alpha, \beta))}{2}, u_D(s_i, s_j) = 1 - \triangle_B(\alpha, \beta) \tag{7}$$

where $\triangle_P(\alpha, \beta)$, $\triangle_N(\alpha, \beta)$ and $\triangle_N(\alpha, \beta)$ denoted the entropy with respect to positive region, negative region and boundary region respectively. Learning optimal thresholds process would be repeated until stop conditions were satisfied [3].

The Competition between Two Measures for Evaluating Positive Rules: Azam and Yao analyzed multiple criteria decision making problems

Table 2. Payoff table

		m_2		
		$a_{21} = f_{21}(\alpha, \beta)$	$a_{22} = f_{22}(\alpha, \beta)$	.....
	$a_{11} = f_{11}(\alpha, \beta)$	$\langle u_1(\alpha_{11}, \beta_{11}), u_2(\alpha_{11}, \beta_{11})\rangle$	$\langle u_1(\alpha_{12}, \beta_{12}), u_2(\alpha_{12}, \beta_{12})\rangle$	......
m_1	$a_{12} = f_{12}(\alpha, \beta)$	$\langle u_1(\alpha_{21}, \beta_{21}), u_2(\alpha_{21}, \beta_{21})\rangle$	$\langle u_1(\alpha_{21}, \beta_{22}), u_2(\alpha_{22}, \beta_{22})\rangle$	......
	......		......	......	......

in rough set employing GTRS [2]. The competition between two measures for evaluating positive rules was formulated. As an example to show the feasibility of the proposed approach [2], the players were represented as confidence and coverage which were two measures for evaluating positive rules set, $O = \{con, cov\}$; the strategies were the possible decrease to threshold α, $S_{con} = S_{cov} = \{s_1, s_2, s_3\} = \{\alpha, \alpha \times (1 - 5\%), \alpha \times (1 - 10\%)\}$; the payoffs of players performing actions were the values of measures with the corresponding probabilistic thresholds [2]. The updated value of α was the average value of (α_i, α_j) if the pair $< u_{con}((\alpha_i, \alpha_j), u_{cov}((\alpha_i, \alpha_j)) >$ was the equilibrium [2]. The game would be repeated several times until stop condition was satisfied.

3 Formulating Competition between Measures with GTRS

We aim to extract immediate decision rules employing probabilistic rough sets with thresholds (α, β). The measures for evaluating these rules can be used as players to formulate competitions to find optimal thresholds. In order to reach equilibria, two measures which have the opposite change trend (increase or decrease) with the change of (α, β) can compete against each other. We formulate game $G = \{O, S, P\}$ as follows: the players $O = \{m_1, m_2\}$; each player has a set of actions or strategies which can be the change of (α, β), i.e. for player i, $S_i = \{a_{i1}, ..., a_{ik}\}$ and the action $a_{ij} = f_{ij}(\alpha, \beta)$ which is a function of (α, β); payoffs or utilities $P = \{u_1, u_2\}$ result from players performing actions, i.e. $u_1(a_{1i}, a_{2j})$ or $u_1(\alpha_{ij}, \beta_{ij})$ means the payoff of player m_1 performing action i and $u_2(a_{1i}, a_{2j})$ or $u_2(\alpha_{ij}, \beta_{ij})$ means the payoff of player m_2 performing action j, where $(\alpha_{ij}, \beta_{ij}) = F(f_{1i}(\alpha, \beta), f_{2j}(\alpha, \beta))$.

Table 2 shows the payoff table for a two-measure competition. The actions of player m_1 are shown row-wise and the actions of player m_2 are column-wise. Each cell in the table has a payoff pair $\langle u_1(\alpha_{ij}, \beta_{ij}), u_2(\alpha_{ij}, \beta_{ij})\rangle$. The cell $\langle u_1(\alpha_{kl}, \beta_{kl}), u_2(\alpha_{kl}, \beta_{kl})\rangle$ is an equilibrium if actions a_{1k} and a_{2l} satisfy:

$$u_1(a_{1k}, a_{2j}) > u_1(a_{1i}, a_{2j}), \text{for all } i \neq k, \text{for all } j,$$
$$u_2(a_{1i}, a_{2l}) > u_2(a_{1i}, a_{2j}), \text{for all } j \neq l, \text{for all } i. \qquad (8)$$

Selecting suitable players, strategies and payoffs depends on the objectives of users when formulating competitions. When we employ GTRS to formulate competitions between measures to determine thresholds, measures for evaluating a set of immediate decision rules can be selected as game players. We discuss six measures in this section, and they can be set as players and compete against each other in GTRS to reach equilibria to get optimal thresholds. We denote a set of immediate decision rules as IDRS.

3.1 Accuracy

The accuracy of approximation of classification was introduced in [11]. Let $X = \{X_1, X_2, ..., X_n\}$ be a classification of U and C be a condition attribute set, then $\underline{C} = \{\underline{C}(X_1), ..., \underline{C}(X_n)\}$ and $\overline{C} = \{\overline{C}(X_1), ..., \overline{C}(X_n)\}$ are called the C-lower and the C-upper approximation of X [11]. The accuracy of approximation of X by C was defined as [11]:

$$\alpha_C(X) = \frac{\sum_{X_i \in X} |\underline{C}(X_i)|}{\sum_{X_i \in X} |\overline{C}(X_i)|} \tag{9}$$

According to the values of decision attributes, we can get a classification on U, $U_D = \{D_1, D_2, ..., D_k\}$. The lower and upper approximation of classification vary with the probabilistic thresholds (α, β), so the accuracy of approximation classification can evaluate the rules induced from the positive regions, we call it the accuracy of immediate decision rules set.

Definition 1. *Let $S = (U, C \cup D)$ be a decision table and $D = \{D_+, D_-\}$, from which immediate decision rules can be induced employing probabilistic rough sets with thresholds (α, β), the accuracy of IDRS is defined as the ratio of the number of objects in positive region of each decision class and the number of objects in non-negative region of each decision class:*

$$\alpha_{(\alpha,\beta)}(IDRS) = \frac{|POS_{(\alpha,\beta)}(D_+)| + |POS_{(\alpha,\beta)}(D_-)|}{|(NEG_{(\alpha,\beta)}(D_+))^c| + |(NEG_{(\alpha,\beta)}(D_-))^c|} \tag{10}$$

Properties: (1) the value range of $\rho_{(\alpha,\beta)}(IDRS)$ is $0 \leq \rho_{(\alpha,\beta)}(IDRS) \leq 1$, when the decision table S is consistent, the value of $\rho_{(\alpha,\beta)}(IDRS)$ equals 1; (2) the value of $\rho_{(\alpha,\beta)}(IDRS)$ increases with the decrease of ρ, also increases as the value of β increases.

3.2 Confidence

The confidence of the set of positive rules was proposed by Yao and Zhao [19]:

$$confidence(IDRS) = \frac{\# \text{ of correctly classified objects by PRS}}{\# \text{ of classified objects by PRS}} \tag{11}$$

PRS denoted a set of positive rules. The definition of immediate decision rules is same to that of positive rules set defined in [19], so the above confidence measure can evaluate a set of immediate decision rules as well. The difference is that the values of decision attributes discussed in this paper are binary.

Definition 2. *Let* $S = (U, C \cup D)$ *be a decision table and* $D = \{D_+, D_-\}$, *from which immediate decision rules can be induced employing probabilistic rough sets with thresholds* (α, β), *the confidence of IDRS is defined as the ratio of the number of correctly classified objects and the number of classified objects covered by all immediate decision rules:*

$$\gamma_{(\alpha,\beta)}(IDRS) = \frac{\sum_{[x] \in POS_{(\alpha,\beta)}(D_+)} |[x] \cap (D_+)| + \sum_{[x] \in POS_{(\alpha,\beta)}(D_-)} |[x] \cap (D_-)|}{\sum_{[x] \in POS_{(\alpha,\beta)}(D_+)} |[x]| + \sum_{[x] \in POS_{(\alpha,\beta)}(D_-)} |[x]|}$$

(12)

Properties: (1) the value range of $\gamma_{(\alpha,\beta)}(IDRS)$ is $0 \leq \gamma_{(\alpha,\beta)}(IDRS) \leq 1$, when the rules induced from the positive regions are absolutely correct, i.e. $(\alpha, \beta) = (1, 0)$, it gets the maximum value 1; (2) the value of $\gamma_{(\alpha,\beta)}(IDRS)$ decreases with the decrease of α, and it also decreases with the increase of β.

3.3   Coverage

The coverage of positive rules set was defined by Yao and Zhao as [19]:

$$coverage(IDRS) = \frac{\# \text{ of correctly classified objects by PRS}}{\# \text{ of objects in U}}$$

(13)

So we can define the coverage of a set of immediate decision rules according to the above definition since immediate decision rules are induced from the positive regions.

Definition 3. *Let* $S = (U, C \cup D)$ *be a decision table and* $D = \{D_+, D_-\}$, *from which immediate decision rules can be induced employing probabilistic rough sets with thresholds* (α, β), *the coverage of IDRS is defined as the ratio of the number of correctly classified objects and the number of all objects in the universe:*

$$\eta_{(\alpha,\beta)}(IDRS) = \frac{\sum_{[x] \in POS_{(\alpha,\beta)}(D_+)} |[x] \cap (D_+)| + \sum_{[x] \in POS_{(\alpha,\beta)}(D_-)} |[x] \cap (D_-)|}{|U|}$$

(14)

Properties: (1) the value range of $\eta_{(\alpha,\beta)}(IDRS)$ is $0 \leq \eta_{(\alpha,\beta)}(IDRS) \leq 1$, when the decision table is consistent, the value of $\eta_{(\alpha,\beta)}(IDRS)$ equals 1; (2) the value of $\eta_{(\alpha,\beta)}(IDRS)$ increases with the decrease of α, also increases with the increase of β.

3.4   Generality

The generality measure of positive rules set was defined as [19]:

$$generality(IDRS) = \frac{\# \text{ of classified objects by IDRS}}{\# \text{ of objects in U}}$$

(15)

The measure can evaluate the generality of a set of immediate decision rules.

Definition 4. *Let $S = (U, C \cup D)$ be a decision table and $D = \{D_+, D_-\}$, from which immediate decision rules can be induced employing probabilistic rough sets with thresholds (α, β), the generality of IDRS is defined as the ratio of the number of classified objects covered by all immediate decision rules and the number of all objects in the universe:*

$$\tau_{(\alpha,\beta)}(IDRS) = \frac{\sum_{[x] \in POS_{(\alpha,\beta)}(D_+)} |[x]| + \sum_{[x] \in POS_{(\alpha,\beta)}(D_-)} |[x]|}{|U|} \qquad (16)$$

Properties: (1) the value range of $\tau_{(\alpha,\beta)}(IDRS)$ is $0 \leq \tau_{(\alpha,\beta)}(IDRS) \leq 1$, when the decision table is consistent, the value of $\tau_{(\alpha,\beta)}(IDRS)$ equals 1; (2) the value of $\tau_{(\alpha,\beta)}(IDRS)$ increases with the decrease of α, also increases with the increase of β.

3.5   Certainty

The certainty measure of decision table was proposed by Qian et al [12]. For a decision table $S = (U, C \cup D)$ and $RULE = \{Z_{ij} - Z_{ij} : des(X_i) \rightarrow des(Y_j), X_i \in U/C, Y_j \in U/D\}$, the certainty measure of S was defined as [12]:

$$\delta(S) = \sum_{i=1}^{m} \sum_{j=1}^{n} \frac{|X_i \cap Y_j|^2}{|U||X_i|} \qquad (17)$$

The certainty measure defined in [12] aimed to evaluate the certainty of all decision rules induced from a decision table. If deferred decision rules are excluded from the rules, the measure can evaluate the certainty of a set of immediate decision rules.

Definition 5. *Let $S = (U, C \cup D)$ be a decision table and $D = \{D_+, D_-\}$, from which immediate decision rules can be induced employing probabilistic rough sets with thresholds (α, β), the certainty of IDRS is defined as the sum of the product of the certainty and support of each immediate decision rule:*

$$\delta_{(\alpha,\beta)}(IDRS) = \sum_{[x] \in POS_{(\alpha,\beta)}(D_+)} \frac{|[x] \cap (D_+)|^2}{|[x]| \times |U|} + \sum_{[x] \in POS_{(\alpha,\beta)}(D_-)} \frac{|[x] \cap (D_-)|^2}{|[x]| \times |U|} \qquad (18)$$

Properties: (1) the value range of $\delta_{(\alpha,\beta)}(IDRS)$ is $\frac{1}{|U|} \leq \delta_{(\alpha,\beta)}(IDRS) \leq 1$ [12], when the certainty measure of every immediate decision rule equals 1, $\delta_{(\alpha,\beta)}(IDRS)$ gets the maximum value; (2) the value of $\delta_{(\alpha,\beta)}(IDRS)$ increases with the decrease of α, and also increases as β rises.

3.6   Support

The support measure of decision rules set was proposed in [12]. For decision table $S = (U, C \cup D)$ and $RULE = \{Z_{ij} - Z_{ij} : des(X_i) \rightarrow des(Y_j), X_i \in U/C, Y_j \in U/D\}$, the certainty measure of S was defined as: [12]

$$\xi(S) = \sum_{i=1}^{m} \sum_{j=1}^{n} \frac{|X_i \cap Y_j|^2}{|U|^2} \tag{19}$$

The support measure defined in [12] aimed to evaluate the certainty of all decision rules induced from a decision table. According to Equation (20), we can define the support of a set of immediate decision rules.

Definition 6. *Let $S = (U, C \cup D)$ be a decision table and $D = \{D_+, D_-\}$, from which immediate decision rules can be induced employing probabilistic rough sets with thresholds (α, β), the support of IDRS is defined as the sum of the square of the support of each immediate decision rule:*

$$\xi_{(\alpha,\beta)}(IDRS) = \sum_{[x] \in POS_{(\alpha,\beta)}(D_+)} \frac{|[x] \cap (D_+)|^2}{|U|^2} + \sum_{[x] \in POS_{(\alpha,\beta)}(D_-)} \frac{|[x] \cap (D_-)|^2}{|U|^2} \tag{20}$$

Properties: (1) the value range of $\xi_{(\alpha,\beta)}(IDRS)$ is $\frac{1}{|U|} \leq \xi_{(\alpha,\beta)}(IDRS) \leq 1$ (2) the value of $\xi_{(\alpha,\beta)}(IDRS)$ increases with the decrease of α, and also increases as β rises.

4   Example of Using Measures in GTRS

In this section, we present a demonstrative example to formulate competitions between measures that can be used as players in GTRS. In this example, the players are represented as confidence (γ) and generality (τ) which are defined in Definition (2) and (4) respectively. The set of immediate decision rules which have greater confidence tend to be less general, a general decision rules set may not have higher confidence. Therefore, changing the probabilistic thresholds to increase the value of generality may decrease the value of confidence.

If we stay with probabilistic rough sets and allow maximum 50% of decrease of α, the player γ may access to six actions with decreasing step 10% decrease of α. The strategies of γ are formulated as $S_\gamma = \{a_{11}, a_{12}, a_{13}, a_{14}, a_{15}, a_{16}\}$:

$$a_{11} = (\alpha, \beta) = (1, 0), \ a_{1i} = (\alpha \times (1 - 10 \times (i-1) \times 100\%), \beta), \ i = 2, 3, 4, 5, 6 \tag{21}$$

The set of strategies will be: $S_\gamma = \{(1, 0), (0.9, 0), (0.8, 0), (0.7, 0), (0.6, 0), (0.5, 0)\}$. The player τ can access the similiar actions with the player γ, the strategies of τ are $S_\tau = S_\gamma$.

With a function $F = \frac{f_{1i} + f_{2j}}{2}$, the payoff function is defined as:

$$\langle u_1(\alpha_{ij}, \beta_{ij}), u_2(\alpha_{ij}, \beta_{ij}) \rangle = \langle \gamma(\frac{f_{1i}(\alpha, \beta) + f_{2j}(\alpha, \beta)}{2}), \tau(\frac{f_{1i}(\alpha, \beta) + f_{2j}(\alpha, \beta)}{2}) \rangle. \tag{22}$$

The payoff table contains 36 cells, as shown in Table 3. We aim to find equilibria of the payoff table. Based on Equation (8), the probabilistic thresholds (α, β) corresponding to the equilibrium can be calculated. If the values of α, β do not

Table 3. Payoff table of competition between confidence and generality

		generality(τ)		
		$a_{21} = (\alpha, \beta)$	$a_{22} = (0.9\alpha, \beta)$	......
confidence(γ)	$a_{11} = (\alpha, \beta)$	$\langle\gamma(\alpha, \beta),$ $\tau(\alpha, \beta)\rangle$	$\langle\gamma(0.95\alpha, \beta),$ $\tau(0.95\alpha, \beta)\rangle$	....
	$a_{12} = (0.9\alpha, \beta)$	$\langle\gamma(0.95\alpha, \beta),$ $\tau(0.95\alpha, \beta)\rangle$	$\langle\gamma(0.90\alpha, \beta),$ $\tau(0.90\alpha, \beta)\rangle$	....
	......	......	......	......

satisfied stop conditions, the process of finding a new pair of thresholds can be repeated until the stop conditions are satisfied. In the iterations, the players still are γ and τ, new thresholds pair will be set as (α, β), each player can access to six actions and the decrease step depends on the difference value of new α and 0.5. The stop conditions can be formulated according to the objectives of users or the requirement of probabilistic rough sets, such as α should be greater than β, the values of measures are both greater than a specific value, etc.

5   Conclusion

Game-theoretic rough sets is a recent proposal to determine the optimal probabilistic thresholds by setting up a game for trading-off between different criteria. In this article, we review five approaches for applying GTRS, which show different competitions can be formulated according to the objectives of users. When we aim to extract effective decision rules using probabilistic rough sets, we can formulate competitions between two measures of decision rules to find the optimal thresholds. The GTRS for formulating competition between two measures is described in detail; measures for evaluating a set of immediate decision rules are investigated, including accuracy, confidence, coverage, generality, certainty and support. The discussed measures can be set as players in GTRS to formulate competitions or cooperation to determine the optimal probabilistic thresholds, which shows the extendibility and suitability of GTRS.

GTRS can be used to formulate competitions or cooperations of other measures for evaluating other aspects of rough sets, so more measures can be analyzed or defined in order to be used in GTRS.

References

1. Azam, N., Yao, J.T.: Classifying Attributes with Game-Theoretic Rough Sets. In: Watada, J., Watanabe, T., Phillips-Wren, G., Howlett, R.J., Jain, L.C. (eds.) Intelligent Decision Technologies. SIST, vol. 15, pp. 175–184. Springer, Heidelberg (2012)
2. Azam, N., Yao, J.T.: Multiple Criteria Decision Analysis with Game-Theoretic Rough Sets. In: Li, T. (ed.) RSKT 2012. LNCS, vol. 7414, pp. 399–408. Springer, Heidelberg (2012)

3. Azam, N., Yao, J.T.: Analyzing uncertainties of probabilistic rough set regions with game-theoretic rough sets. International Journal of Approximate Reasoning (manuscript)
4. Deng, X.F., Yao, Y.Y.: An Information-Theoretic Interpretation of Thresholds in Probabilistic Rough Sets. In: Li, T. (ed.) RSKT 2012. LNCS, vol. 7414, pp. 369–378. Springer, Heidelberg (2012)
5. Düntsch, I., Gediga, G.: Uncertainty measures of rough set prediction. Artificial Intelligence 106(1), 109–137 (1998)
6. Greco, S., Pawlak, Z., Słowiński, R.: Can Bayesian confirmation measures be useful for rough set decision rules? Engineering Applications of Artificial Intelligence 17(4), 345–361 (2004)
7. Herbert, J.P., Yao, J.T.: Criteria for choosing a rough set model. Computers & Mathematics with Applications 57(6), 908–918 (2009)
8. Herbert, J.P., Yao, J.T.: Game-theoretic rough sets. Fundamenta Informaticae 108(3-4), 267–286 (2011)
9. Pawlak, Z.: Decision rules, Bayes' rule and rough sets. In: New Directions in Rough Sets, Data Mining, and Granular-Soft Computing, pp. 1–9 (1999)
10. Pawlak, Z.: Rough sets, decision algorithms and Bayes' theorem. European Journal of Operational Research 136(1), 181–189 (2002)
11. Pawlak, Z.: Rough Sets: Theoretical Aspects of Reasoning About Data. Kluwer Academic Publishers, Boston (1991)
12. Qian, Y.H., Liang, J.Y., Li, D.Y., Zhang, H.Y., Dang, C.Y.: Measures for evaluating the decision performance of a decision table in rough set theory. Information Sciences 178(1), 181–202 (2008)
13. Yao, J.T., Yao, Y.Y.: Induction of Classification Rules by Granular Computing. In: Alpigini, J.J., Peters, J.F., Skowron, A., Zhong, N. (eds.) RSCTC 2002. LNCS (LNAI), vol. 2475, pp. 331–338. Springer, Heidelberg (2002)
14. Yao, J.T., Yao, Y.Y., Ziarko, W.: Probabilistic rough sets: Approximations, decision-makings, and applications. International Journal of Approximate Reasoning 49(2), 253–254 (2008)
15. Yao, Y.Y.: Decision-Theoretic Rough Set Models. In: Yao, J., Lingras, P., Wu, W.-Z., Szczuka, M.S., Cercone, N.J., Ślęzak, D. (eds.) RSKT 2007. LNCS (LNAI), vol. 4481, pp. 1–12. Springer, Heidelberg (2007)
16. Yao, Y.Y.: Probabilistic rough set approximations. International Journal of Approximate Reasoning 49(2), 255–271 (2008)
17. Yao, Y.Y.: Two semantic issues in a probabilistic rough set model. Fundamenta Informaticae 108(3), 249–265 (2011)
18. Yao, Y.Y., Wong, S.K.M.: A decision theoretic framework for approximating concepts. International Journal of Man-Machine Studies 37(6), 793–809 (1992)
19. Yao, Y.Y., Zhao, Y.: Attribute reduction in decision-theoretic rough set models. Information Sciences 178(17), 3356–3373 (2008)
20. Yao, Y.Y., Zhong, N.: An Analysis of Quantitative Measures Associated with Rules. In: Zhong, N., Zhou, L. (eds.) PAKDD 1999. LNCS (LNAI), vol. 1574, pp. 479–488. Springer, Heidelberg (1999)
21. Zhang, W.J., Wu, W.Z., Liang, J.Y., Li, D.Y.: Theory and method of Rough Sets. Science Press, Beijing (2001)

A Comparison Study of Cost-Sensitive Classifier Evaluations

Bing Zhou and Qingzhong Liu

Department of Computer Science, Sam Houston State University
Huntsville, Texas, USA 77340
{bxz003,qxl005}@shsu.edu

Abstract. Performance evaluation plays an important role in the rule induction and classification process. Classic evaluation measures have been extensively studied in the past. In recent years, cost-sensitive classification has received much attention. In a typical classification task, all types of classification errors are treated equally. In many practical cases, not all errors are equal. Therefore, it is critical to build a cost-sensitive classifier to minimize the expected cost. This also brings us to another important issue, namely, cost-sensitive classifier evaluations. The main objective is to investigate different aspects of this problem. We review five existing cost-sensitive evaluation measures and compare their similarities and differences. We find that the cost-sensitive measures provide consistent evaluation results comparing to classic evaluation measures in most cases. However, when applying different cost values to the evaluation, the differences between the performances of each algorithm change. It is reasonable to conclude that the evaluation results could change dramatically when certain cost values applied. Moreover, by using cost curves to visualize the classification results, performance and performance differences of different classifiers can be easily seen.

Keywords: cost-sensitive classification, rule evaluation, evaluation measures.

1 Introduction

Performance evaluation plays an important role in the rule induction and classification process. In the traditional classification task, minimizing misclassification rate is used as the guideline of designing a good classifier. The misclassification rate is also called the error rate or 0/1 loss function, which assigns no loss to a correct classification, and assigns a unit loss to any error. Thus, all errors are equally costly. In real-world applications, each error has an associated cost. For instance, the cost of false positive errors (i.e., giving treatment to a patient who does not have cancer) is different from the cost of false negative errors (i.e., failing to treat a patient who has cancer). Therefore, it is important to build a cost-sensitive classifier to incorporate different types of costs into the classification process. Cost-sensitive learning is one of the challenging problems in the

F.M. Zanzotto et al. (Eds.): BI 2012, LNCS 7670, pp. 360–371, 2012.
© Springer-Verlag Berlin Heidelberg 2012

current stage of data mining and machine learning research [1–3, 5, 13, 12, 11]. As an example of different kinds of classification errors having different costs, in credit card fraud detection, failure to detect fraud could be very expensive. On the other hand, resources will be wasted for investigating non-fraud. Therefore, the goal of cost-sensitive learning is to minimize the expected cost of misclassification instead of misclassification errors [6, 9, 14, 15].

Classification performance evaluation is an essential part in the data mining process, and is the primary way to identify the optimal learning algorithm from many existing ones. With cost-sensitive learning, the classic evaluation measures, such as precision and recall, are no longer appropriate. This calls for the effective measures that are able to handle the cost-sensitive settings. The main objective of this paper is to investigate the existing cost-sensitive evaluation methods. Five cost-sensitive measures are selected for comparison including one measure that can visualize the classifier performance. We compare these measures through theoretical and numerical examinations. We hope that this work can bridge the gap between the classifier evaluations with or without the consideration of cost-sensitive aspect, and provide evidences for choosing appropriate cost-sensitive evaluation methods for different applications.

The rest of the paper is organized as follows. In Section 2, we briefly review the traditional evaluation measures. In Section 3, the basic ideas of cost-sensitive evaluations and five existing measures are analyzed. Experimental comparison results are shown in Section 4. We conclude the paper and explain future work in Section 5.

2   Traditional Classifier Evaluation Measures

In traditional classification tasks, classifiers' performances are measured in terms of precision, recall, accuracy (Acc) and error rate (Err = 1 - Acc). Precision and recall are used for measuring the classification performance for certain classes, while Acc and Err are used to measure the overall system performance. The details of these measures are explained as follows. Let $n_{C \to C}$ denote the number of objects classified as class C which truly are, $n_{C^c \to C}$ denote the number of objects incorrectly classified as class C, and $n_{C \to C^c}$ denote the number of objects incorrectly classified as Not C. The classification results can be represented by a confusion matrix as shown in Table 1. Precision is defined as the proportion of testing examples classified as class C that actually are, which can be expressed as:

$$Precision(C) = \frac{n_{C \to C}}{n_{C \to C} + n_{C^c \to C}}. \tag{1}$$

And recall is defined as the proportion of testing examples belonging to class C that are correctly classified.

$$Recall(C) = \frac{n_{C \to C}}{n_{C \to C} + n_{C \to C^c}}. \tag{2}$$

In classification problems, accuracy is the most common measure used to evaluate the overall quality of a classifier, which is defined as the ratio of total number of testing examples that are correctly classified.

Table 1. A confusion matrix

Count	$C(i \mid j)$	Predicted class		
		Class=yes	Class=no	Total
Actual	Class=yes	$n_{C \to C}$	$n_{C \to C^c}$	N_C
	Class=no	$n_{C^c \to C}$	$n_{C^c \to C^c}$	N_{C^c}

$$Acc = \frac{n_{C \to C} + n_{C^c \to C^c}}{N_C + N_{C^c}}, \tag{3}$$

where N_C is the total number of testing examples that are in class C and N_{C^c} is the total number of examples that are not in class C. The error rate is defined as the the ratio of total number of testing examples that are incorrectly classified.

$$Err = \frac{n_{C \to C^c} + n_{C^c \to C}}{N_C + N_{C^c}}, \tag{4}$$

ROC curves is a graphical performance evaluation measure which has been widely used to visualize classifier performances. For binary classifications, a ROC space is a two-dimensional plot with false positive rate (FP) on the x-axis and true positive rate (TP) on the y-axis. A single confusion matrix produces a single point in the ROC space. A ROC curve is produced by varying the threshold values in certain classifiers. One point in ROC space dominates another if it has a higher true positive rate and a lower false positive rate. Figure 1 shows the ROC points for two classifiers 1R and C4.5 [5].

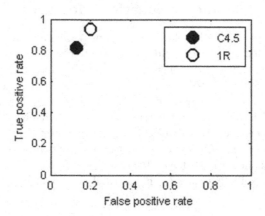

Fig. 1. Two ROC points

The traditional evaluation measures play an important role in the classification and learning process. Each of these measures captures some important but distinct aspects of classifier performance, and they are complementary to each other. However, all of these measures are based on a 0/1 loss function, the costs associated with each error are not considered.

Table 2. A cost matrix

	$C(i \mid j)$	Predicted class	
		Class=yes	Class=no
Actual	Class=yes	$C(yes \mid yes)$	$C(no \mid yes)$
	Class=no	$C(yes \mid no)$	$C(no \mid no)$

3   Cost-Sensitive Classifier Evaluations

More recently, researchers start to realize that certain classification tasks must be evaluated using measures that incorporate the notion of cost; and a cost-sensitive evaluation reveals that additional safety nets are necessary for those classifiers to be viable in practice. In order to perform a cost-sensitive evaluation, in addition to the confusion matrix containing the classification results of the testing examples, we also need a cost matrix either give by the user, or by some adaptive learning algorithms [4]. Suppose we have a binary classification task with two classification results marked as yes/no, Table 1 shows the basic form of this cost matrix, in which $C(i \mid j)$ represents the cost of misclassifying class j examples as class i. For example, $C(no \mid yes)$ represents the cost of misclassifying examples are actually in the *yes* class as *no*. Given a confusion matrix (Table 1) and a cost matrix (Table 2) for a specific classification task, the cost measure is defined as follows,

$$Cost = C(yes|yes)*n_{C \to C} + C(yes|no)*n_{C \to C^c} + C(no|yes)*n_{C^c \to C} + C(no|no)*n_{C^c \to C^c}, \quad (5)$$

that is, the overall cost of a classifier is the sum of numbers of examples classified for each category times their corresponding costs. In the following subsections, we will discuss the cost measures modified based on the traditional evaluation measures by adding cost as a weight factor.

3.1   Weighted Accuracy and Weighted Error

In 2000, Androutsopoulos et al. [1] suggested to use weighted accuracy for measuring spam filter performance. Spam filtering is a typical cost-sensitive learning task, misclassifying a legitimate email into spam is usually considered more costly than misclassifying a spam email into legitimate. A cost factor λ is added to accuracy measure. Misclassifying a legitimate email as spam is λ times more costly than misclassifying a spam email as legitimate. Let class C represent Legitimate emails and class C^c represent spam emails, the definitions of weighted accuracy (WAcc):

$$WAcc = \frac{\lambda \cdot n_{C \to C} + n_{C^c \to C^c}}{\lambda \cdot N_C + N_{C^c}}. \quad (6)$$

Similarly, the weighted error rate (WErr = 1 - WAcc) is defined as:

$$WErr = \frac{\lambda \cdot n_{C \to C^c} + n_{C^c \to C}}{\lambda \cdot N_C + N_{C^c}}. \quad (7)$$

3.2 Total Cost Ratio

As the values of accuracy and error rate (or their weighted versions) are often misleadingly high, another measure is defined to get a clear picture of a classifiers' performance, the ratio of its error rate and that of a simplistic baseline approach [1]. The baseline approach is the classifier that never blocks legitimate emails and always passes spam emails. The weighted error rate of the baseline is:

$$WErr^b = \frac{N_{C^c}}{\lambda \cdot N_C + N_{C^c}}.$$ (8)

The total cost ratio(TCR) is:

$$TCR = \frac{WErr^b}{WErr}.$$ (9)

Greater TCR indicates better performance.If cost is proportional to wasted time, TCR measures how much time is wasted to delete manually all spam emails when no filter is used, compared to the time wasted to delete manually any spam emails that pass the filter plus the time needed to recover from mistakenly blocked legitimate emails. This measure can also be applied to general classification problems.

3.3 Cost Curves

Cost curve is an alternative to ROC curve in which the expected cost of a classifier is represented explicitly [2, 3]. The x-axis in a cost curve is the probability-cost function for positive examples, which is defined as:

$$PCF(+) = \frac{p(+)C(- \mid +)}{p(+)C(- \mid +) + p(-)C(+ \mid -)},$$ (10)

where $C(- \mid +)$ is the cost of misclassifying a positive example as negative, $C(+ \mid -)$ is the cost of misclassifying a negative example as positive, $p(+)$ is the probability of positive examples, and $p(-) = 1 - p(+)$. The y-axis is the expected cost normalized with respect to the cost incurred when every example is incorrectly classified, which is defined as:

$$NE(\lambda) = (1 - TP - FP) * PCF(C) + FP,$$

where TP is the true positive rate, and FP is the false positive rate. If one classifier is lower in expected cost across the whole range of the probability-cost function, it dominates the other. The normalized expected cost is defined as:

$$NE(C) = (1 - TP) * PCF(+) + FP.$$ (11)

The corresponding cost curves of algorithms in Figure 1 are shown in Figure 2, each point in the ROC space became a line in the cost space.

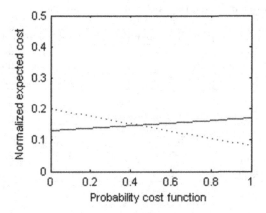

Fig. 2. Two cost curves

Other than adding the cost factor, cost curves have the following advantages over ROC curves [2, 3]:

- Performance and performance differences of different classifiers can be easily seen in cost curves.
- Cost curves can be average up and there exists a cost curve that represents the average of the performances represented by the given curves. But there is no agreed upon way to average ROC curves.
- Cost curves allow confidence intervals to be estimated for a classifier's performance, and allow the statistical significance of performance differences to be assessed. Whereas we can not achieve these two goals in the ROC curves.

4   Experimental Results

The goal of this experimental study is to use the cost-sensitive evaluation measures discussed in this paper to evaluate the performance of different classification algorithms on chosen datasets. We compare the evaluation results between these measures and check whether they give consistent evaluation results on different algorithms and datasets, especially when the cost values change.

The experiments were performed based on two benchmark datasets. The first one is the spam dataset from UCI Machine Learning Repository [7]. The second one is the diabetes dataset included in WEKA data mining software [10]. The spam dataset consists of 4601 instances, with 1813 instances as *spam*, and 2788 instances as *legitimate*, each instance is described by 58 attributes. The diabetes dataset consists of 768 instances and 9 attributes including a binary class attribute. An instance is either tested-positive of having diabetes or tested-negative without diabetes. We choose three algorithms as representatives of different classification methods to perform on the above two datasets. That is, naive Bayes classifier from Bayes classifiers, Prism from rule-based classifiers, and ID3 from decision tree-based classifiers.

Table 3. Naive Bayes classifier on spam dataset

	Classified spam	Classified legitimate	Total
Actual spam	516	90	606
Actual legitimate	36	922	958
Total	552	1012	1564

Table 4. Prism on spam dataset

	Classified spam	Classified legitimate	Total
Actual spam	587	10	597
Actual legitimate	285	661	946
Total	872	671	1564

Table 5. ID3 on spam dataset

	Classified spam	Classified legitimate	Total
Actual spam	532	63	595
Actual legitimate	35	915	950
Total	567	978	1564

Table 3, 4 and 5 contain classification results by applying naive Bayes classifier, Prism and ID3 to spam dataset, respectively. Data preprocessing includes feature selection of 16 out of 58 attributes, discretizing continuous-valued attributes, and re-sampling the instances. 66% percent of the instances of the dataset are selected as the training set and the rest are testing set. The above preprocessing steps are done using WEKA data mining software [10]. Suppose Table 6 is the cost matrix given by the user. The evaluation results of three chosen algorithms are shown in Table 7. We can see that for this particular dataset, the evaluation results of the traditional measures (i.e., precision and recall) and the cost-sensitive measures (i.e., weighted accuracy and total cost ratio) are consistent. They all agree that ID3 provides the best classification results among the three chosen algorithms, and ID3 and naive Bayes both perform better than the Prism. Figure 3 is the ROC curves produced from the classification results of three chosen algorithms, and Figure 4 is the corresponding cost curves. In the ROC space, we can see that ID3 dominates naive Bayes since it has lower false positive rate and higher true positive rate. On the other hand, it is difficult to tell the performance between ID3, naive Bayes and Prism since Prism has a higher false positive rate and higher true positive rate. But in cost space, it is easy to see that ID3 has the lowest expected cost among three algorithms. The expected cost of Prism became smaller when the probability cost function is close to 1.

Table 8, 9 and 10 are confusion matrices generated by applying naive Bayes classifier, Prism and ID3 to diabetes dataset, respectively. The continuous-valued attributes are discretized, and 10-fold cross validation are used. Suppose Table 11 is the cost matrix given by the user. The evaluation results of the

Table 6. The cost matrix for spam dataset

	Classified spam	Classified legitimate
Actual spam	0	1
Actual legitimate	99	0

Table 7. The evaluation results for spam dataset

Classifier	Precision	Recall	Cost	WAcc	WErr	TCR
Naive Bayes	0.920	0.919	3654	0.962	0.038	0.158
Prism	0.864	0.809	28225	0.700	0.299	0.020
ID3	0.937	0.937	3528	0.962	0.037	0.162

performances of three chosen algorithms are shown in Table 12. We can see that for this particular dataset, the evaluation results given by the traditional measures and the cost-sensitive measures are consistent. However, different to the experimental results on spam dataset, all the evaluation measures agree that naive Bayes provides the best classification results among the three algorithms; both naive Bayes and ID3 perform better than the Prism. Figure 5 is the ROC curves generated from the classification results and Figure 6 is the corresponding cost curves. In cost space, it is easy to see that naive Bayes has the lowest expected cost, and Prism has the highest expected cost, but the results are not clear in ROC space. Overall, we can conclude that:

1. The selected cost-sensitive measures give consistent evaluation results compare to traditional evaluation measures. However, when apply different cost values to the evaluation, the differences between the performance of each algorithm change:
- In spam dataset evaluation, the cost of misclassifying a legitimate email to spam is 99 times more than the cost of misclassifying a spam to legitimate. Using the traditional evaluation measures (i.e., precision), the differences between the performances of three algorithms are less than 0.1. With the consideration of cost, the performances of naive Bayes and ID3 remain the same, but the differences between these two algorithms and Prism become larger.
- In diabetes dataset evaluation, the cost of misclassifying a tested-positive patient into tested-negative is 800 times more than the cost of misclassifying a tested-negative patient to tested-positive. Using the traditional evaluation measures, the differences between the performances of three algorithms are less than 0.05. With the consideration cost, the differences between these three algorithms are more than 0.3. It is reasonable to conclude that the evaluation results could change dramatically when certain cost values applied.

2. By using cost curves to visualize the classification results, performance and performance differences of different classifiers can be easily seen.

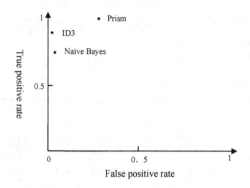

Fig. 3. Comparing three ROC curves

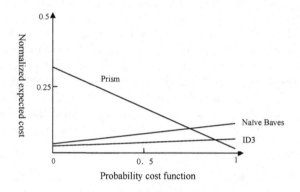

Fig. 4. Comparing three cost curves

Table 8. Naive Bayes classifier on diabetes dataset

	Classified as tested-negative	Classified as tested-positive	Total
Tested-negative	415	85	500
Testted-positive	85	183	268
Total	500	268	768

Table 9. Prism on diabetes dataset

	Classified as tested-negative	Classified as tested-positive	Total
Tested-negative	486	13	493
Testted-positive	206	59	265
Total	686	72	768

Table 10. ID3 on diabetes dataset

	Classified as tested-negative	Classified as tested-positive	Total
Tested-negative	442	58	500
Testted-positive	117	150	267
Total	559	208	768

Table 11. The cost matrix for diabetes dataset

	Classified as tested-negative	Classified as tested-positive
Tested-negative	0	1
Tested-positive	800	0

Table 12. The evaluation results for diabetes dataset

Classifier	Precision	Recall	Cost	WAcc	WErr	TCR
Naive Bayes	0.779	0.779	68085	0.683	0.317	0.006
Prism	0.742	0.711	164813	0.224	0.776	0.003
ID3	0.766	0.772	93658	0.563	0.437	0.005

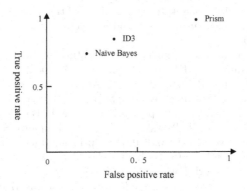

Fig. 5. Comparing three ROC curves

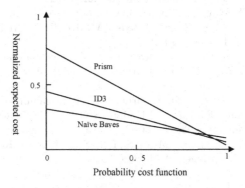

Fig. 6. Comparing three cost curves

5   Conclusions and Future Work

In this paper, we have reviewed and compared five existing cost-sensitive evaluation measures. Some interesting findings were obtained through theoretical and empirical comparisons. The cost-sensitive measures provide consistent evaluation results comparing to classic evaluation measures in most cases. However, when apply different cost values to the evaluation, the differences between the performances of each algorithm change. It is reasonable to conclude that the evaluation results could change dramatically when certain cost values applied. Moreover, by using cost curves to visualize the classification results, performance and performance differences of different classifiers can be easily seen.

The empirical comparison is based on two benchmark datasets and only two settings of the cost values are applied. Empirical comparisons based on large test collections under various cost values may derive more interesting results.

References

1. Androutsopoulos, I., Koutsias, J., Chandrinos, K.V., Spyropoulos, C.D.: An experimental comparison of naive Bayesian and keyword-based anti-spam filtering with personal e-mail messages. In: Proceedings of the 23rd Annual International ACM SIGIR Conference on Research and Development in Information Retrieval, pp. 160–167 (2000)
2. Drummond, C., Holte, R.C.: Explicitly representing expected cost: an alternative to ROC representation. In: KDD 2000, pp. 198–207 (2000)
3. Drummond, C., Holte, R.C.: Cost curves: An improved method for visualizing classifier performance. Machine Learning 65(1), 95–130 (2006)
4. Herbert, J.P., Yao, J.: Learning Optimal Parameters in Decision-Theoretic Rough Sets. In: Wen, P., Li, Y., Polkowski, L., Yao, Y., Tsumoto, S., Wang, G. (eds.) RSKT 2009. LNCS, vol. 5589, pp. 610–617. Springer, Heidelberg (2009)
5. Holte, R.C., Drummond, C.: Cost-sensitive classifier evaluation. In: Proceedings of the 1st International Workshop on Utility-Based Data Mining (2005)
6. Min, F., Liu, H.Q.: A hierarchical model for test-cost-sensitive decision systems. Information Sciences 179(14), 2442–2452 (2009)
7. http://www.ics.uci.edu/mlearn/MLRepository.html
8. Qin, Z., Zhang, C., Wang, T., Zhang, S.: Cost Sensitive Classification in Data Mining. In: Cao, L., Feng, Y., Zhong, J. (eds.) ADMA 2010, Part I. LNCS, vol. 6440, pp. 1–11. Springer, Heidelberg (2010)
9. Turney, P.D.: Cost-sensitive classification: Empirical evaluation of a hybrid genetic decision tree induction algorithm. Journal of Artificial Intelligence Research 2, 369–409 (1995)
10. Hall, M., Frank, E., Holmes, G., Pfahringer, B., Reutemann, B., Witten, I.H.: The WEKA Data Mining Software: An Update. SIGKDD Explorations 11(1) (2009)
11. Yao, Y.: An Outline of a Theory of Three-Way Decisions. In: Yao, J., Yang, Y., Słowiński, R., Greco, S., Li, H., Mitra, S., Polkowski, L. (eds.) RSCTC 2012. LNCS, vol. 7413, pp. 1–17. Springer, Heidelberg (2012)

12. Yao, Y.: The superiority of three-way decisions in probabilistic rough set models. Information Science 181(6), 1080–1096 (2011)
13. Yao, Y.: Three-way decisions with probabilistic rough sets. Information Science 180(3), 341–353 (2010)
14. Zhou, Z.H., Liu, X.Y.: Training cost-sensitive neural networks with methods addressing the class imbalance problem. IEEE Transactions on Knowledge and Data Engineering 18(1), 63–77 (2006)
15. Zhou, B., Yao, Y., Luo, J.: A Three-Way Decision Approach to Email Spam Filtering. In: Farzindar, A., Kešelj, V. (eds.) Canadian AI 2010. LNCS, vol. 6085, pp. 28–39. Springer, Heidelberg (2010)

Author Index